About Island Press

Island Press is the only nonprofit organization in the United States whose principal purpose is the publication of books on environmental issues and natural resource management. We provide solutions-oriented information to professionals, public officials, business and community leaders, and concerned citizens who are shaping responses to environmental problems.

In 2002, Island Press celebrates its eighteenth anniversary as the leading provider of timely and practical books that take a multidisciplinary approach to critical environmental concerns. Our growing list of titles reflects our commitment to bringing the best of an expanding body of literature to the environmental community throughout North America and the world.

Support for Island Press is provided by The Bullitt Foundation, The Mary Flagler Cary Charitable Trust, The Nathan Cummings Foundation, Geraldine R. Dodge Foundation, Doris Duke Charitable Foundation, The Charles Engelhard Foundation, The Ford Foundation, The George Gund Foundation, The Vira I. Heinz Endowment, The William and Flora Hewlett Foundation, W. Alton Jones Foundation, The Henry Luce Foundation, The John D. and Catherine T. MacArthur Foundation, The Andrew W. Mellon Foundation, The Charles Stewart Mott Foundation, The Curtis and Edith Munson Foundation, National Fish and Wildlife Foundation, The New-Land Foundation, Oak Foundation, The Overbrook Foundation, The David and Lucile Packard Foundation, The Pew Charitable Trusts, Rockefeller Brothers Fund, The Winslow Foundation, and other generous donors.

FIRE,
NATIVE PEOPLES,
and
THE NATURAL
LANDSCAPE

FIRE,
NATIVE PEOPLES,
and
THE NATURAL
LANDSCAPE

Edited by

Thomas R. Vale

ISLAND PRESS

Washington • Covelo • London

ISBN 1-55963-888-5 (cloth) — ISBN 1-55963-889-3 (paper)

Printed on recycled, acid-free paper ⊛

Library of Congress and British Cataloging-in-Publication Data available.

Manufactured in the United States of America
09 08 07 06 05 04 03 02   8 7 6 5 4 3 2 1

Contents

List of Figures, Boxes, and Tables   ix

Preface   xiii

Chapter 1   The Pre-European Landscape of the United
States: Pristine or Humanized?   1
THOMAS R. VALE

Chapter 2   Indians and Fire in the Rocky Mountains:
The Wilderness Hypothesis Renewed   41
WILLIAM L. BAKER

Chapter 3   Prehistoric Human Impacts on Fire Regimes
and Vegetation in the Northern Intermountain
West   77
DUANE GRIFFIN

Chapter 4   Fire in the Pre-European Lowlands of the
American Southwest   101
KATHLEEN C. PARKER

Chapter 5   Lots of Lightning and Plenty of People:
An Ecological History of Fire in the Upland
Southwest   143
CRAIG D. ALLEN

Chapter 6 Prehistoric Burning in the Pacific Northwest:
           Human versus Climatic Influences   195
           CATHY WHITLOCK AND MARGARET A. KNOX

Chapter 7 Fire in Sierra Nevada Forests: Evaluating
           the Ecological Impact of Burning by Native
           Americans   233
           ALBERT J. PARKER

Chapter 8 Pre-European Fire in California Chaparral   269
           JACOB BENDIX

Chapter 9 Reflections   295
           THOMAS R. VALE

List of Contributors   303
Index   305

Figures, Boxes, and Tables

Figures

1.1. Three gradients along which landscapes may vary from unambiguously humanized to unarguably pristine   3

1.2. People vary in their perception of the degree of overlap in the natural and human worlds   9

1.3. Human numbers in the cultural regions of North America at the time of European contact (1492)   11

1.4. Tribal villages and camps of the Yurok of northwestern California   13

1.5. The agricultural landscape of the southwestern cultural region   16

1.6. Two examples of mapped agricultural landscapes   18

1.7. Rockpiles for agave cultivation and associated features in central Arizona   20

1.8. Generalized pre-European fire regimes for various parts of North America   29

1.9. National forests and average number of lightning fires per state per year on national forest land in the eleven western states   30

2.1. Trends in fires in the Rocky Mountains   46

3.1. The floristic Great Basin and the Great Basin Cultural Area   79

3.2. Locales where human populations are known to have been concentrated in prehistoric times   81

3.3. Fire return intervals for regional Küchler vegetation types arrayed along a generalized moisture gradient   87

3.4. Locations of all fires on federal lands from 1986 through 1996 listed in the National Fire Occurrence Database   90

3.5. Temporal distribution of fires and ignition sources in the study area, 1986–1996   91

3.6. Areas where human activities ignited more than half of all fires on federal lands from 1986 through 1996   92

4.1. Map of the study area showing place-names mentioned and climate diagrams for selected locations within the southern intermontane region   103

4.2. Map of the different types of lowland vegetation in the southern intermontane region   105

4.3. Representative vegetation   106

4.4. The incidence of cloud-to-ground lightning strikes over the Southwest   108

4.5. Native cultures of the southwestern lowlands   112

4.6. Estimated population shifts in the southwestern lowlands   117

4.7. Shifts in settlement pattern along the Santa Cruz River   118

4.8. Zones of land use around riverine Hohokam communities   120

4.9. Changes in the distribution of agricultural peoples in the southern intermontane region   123

5.1. Location of the Jemez Mountains in New Mexico   144

5.2. Lightning strikes in the Jemez Mountains, 1986   147

5.3. Monthly patterns of lightning strikes, insolation, and precipitation in the Jemez Mountains area   148

5.4. Point locations of historic fires in the Jemez Mountains, 1909–1996   151

5.5. Jemez Mountains, extent of fires in 1748   155

5.6. Fire-scar chronology, Monument Canyon Research Natural Area   156

5.7. Composite fire-scar chronologies from four sites, Jemez Mountains   156

6.1. Map of geographic regions referred to in text   198

6.2. Inferred fire frequency and pollen percentages of selected taxa from Little Lake in the Oregon Coast Range   205

6.3. The location of David Douglas's camps as he traveled through the Willamette Valley in the fall of 1826   209

6.4. Prehistoric and historic juniper expansion   217

7.1. Map of California and surrounding region, emphasizing the Sierra Nevada and locating places mentioned in the text   234

7.2. Map of the Sierra Nevada, locating places mentioned in the text   235

7.3. A generalized mosaic diagram of vegetation patterns in California uplands   238
7.4. Principal groups of Native American cultures inhabiting the Sierra Nevada   242
7.5. Charcoal accumulation/influx curves from Lake Moran sediments and a composite of eight meadow stratigraphies   248
8.1. Cultural boundaries, vegetation distribution, and core sites   271
8.2. Change in flammability of a chaparral stand with time since previous fire   284
9.1. Landscape characteristics on a continuum between the extreme conditions of universally humanized and universally pristine   298

Boxes

1.1. Characteristics that may tend to encourage individual observers to see the pre-European North American landscape as "pristine" or "humanized"   6
1.2. The continuum of plant-people interactions   19
2.1. Indian tribes of the Rocky Mountains in the middle 1800s   47
2.2. Some reasons cited for burning by Indians in the Rocky Mountains   52
2.3. Some themes in quotes from Rocky Mountain fire history studies that address Indian fires   61
5.1. Varied perspectives on the cause of early fires in the Southwest   161
5.2. John Wesley Powell provides a confessional description of a Colorado crown fire   171
5.3. Selected historical references on fire causation in the western United States   172
5.4. Historic views of fire in the Southwest by the U.S. Bureau of Biological Survey   175
8.1. Breakdown of chaparral burning patterns ascribed to native Californians   277

Tables

2.1. Number of fires attributed to Indians, Whites, and lightning   54
3.1. Great Basin food plants   84
6.1. Fire return intervals for the Pacific Northwest   197
6.2. Location and distance traveled, vegetation, and fire observations made by David Douglas during the 1826 journey through the Willamette Valley   208

7.1. Timeline of climatic change and aboriginal human occupancy in the Sierra Nevada   239
7.2. Summary of fire return intervals in montane forests of California uplands   245
8.1. Occurrence of lightning fire in brush within California Department of Forestry jurisdictions   283

Preface

For nearly two centuries, the creation myth for the United States envisioned an initial condition of wild nature, of wilderness. Although challenged by some, this view until recently remained the dominant view, uncritically and naively accepted by layperson and scholar alike. Over the last two decades, however, a contrary vision has emerged. Driven by heightened appreciation for the activities of Native Americans as landscape modifiers, the conventional wisdom now sees the country's roots not in a state of nature, not a "pristine landscape," but in a human-modified world, a "humanized landscape." As a reaction against the hyperbole of the older view, the modern perspective has merit, but the spokespersons for a human-altered continent in pre-European North America may carry their critique to excess: the older monolithic "myth of the pristine landscape" has been replaced by a new and equally monolithic "myth of the humanized landscape."

This book attempts to demythologize the newer paradigm by assessing the role of Native Americans as modifiers of the landscapes in a major portion of the North American continent—the western states—in hopes of establishing a middle ground between the polar positions represented by categorical beliefs in either "pristine" or "humanized" landscapes. Several factors prompt a focus on the American West for this assessment: (1) fires—always potentially linked to humans—were, and remain today, widespread in western ecosystems; (2) the likelihood of finding evidence for a state of nature is greater in the West (to assess the eastern states and conclude that the region, or at least large parts of it, were modified by Native Americans [a likely conclusion] would not move the dialogue toward a middle ground); (3) the presence of wild vegetation over large areas of the West makes the assessment more immediately relevant to the present-day landscape; and (4) the importance of "wilderness" protection in the West enhances the potential for policy contributions. Moreover, the western states provide an arena wherein certain assumptions about Native American activity serve to simplify the issue: formal agriculture was restricted to the extreme Southwest; population sizes were small, except in lowland California and in the agricultural Southwest; and construction of landforms such as mounds—so conspicuous in parts of the Midwest—seems less common in the West. The preeminent human impact—one that was *potentially* important in almost any part of the West and that could have altered the environment at the broad, landscape scale—is that of burning, of fires set by Native Americans. It is this impact in the American West that is the focus of this volume.

Most specifically, then, this book asks the question: "For the American West, were the fire regimes existent at the time of European contact basically the product of natural factors—conditions of vegetation, attributes of climatic episode, characteristics of short-term weather—or did ignitions by Native Americans fundamentally change those regimes and thus the vegetations associated with them?" The book addresses this question for major subregions of the West, each evaluated by a different author: the Rocky Mountains, the forests of the Southwest, the southern deserts, the northern deserts, the Sierra Nevada, the California chaparral, and the forests of the Cascades and Pacific Northwest. By focusing on one particular human impact, these regional evaluations will help move to a more centrist position the dialogue over the "naturalness" of the pre-European continent.

An introductory essay precedes the regional chapters, which make up the heart of the book. This essay presents the ideals of the pristine versus humanized landscapes, justifies the focus on the American West, assesses broadly the types of impacts by native peoples in the pre-European West, establishes the centrality of fires as the most likely Indian impact on the landscape, and poses the question (whether or not the pre-European fire regime was "natural") subsequently addressed by each author.

In the regional chapters that follow the introductory essay, the authors attempt to answer the central question in the context of particular parts of the West. The ability to provide such answers varies by region and by the type of ecosystem within a region, and ambiguities involving data and meanings of data render definitive conclusions uneven. The authors have been encouraged to make their assessments as completely and honestly as possible, taking their respective arguments in whatever direction their data and judgments lead.

After the regional treatments, the book concludes with a summarizing statement that compares results from the various chapters and high-lights patterns both common to the West as a whole and distinctive to various parts of the western states. This summary relates the research findings to questions of policy involving the management of natural areas (particularly on federal lands) and to questions of the "naturalness" of the pre-European western landscape.

The most general goal of this book is to change the character of the debate over whether North America at the time of European contact was pristine or humanized. I yearn for the emergence of a middle ground that recognizes the validity of both possibilities, of a landscape vision that allows a state of nature as plausibly as a cultural artifact. Whether or not we end up with such a rapprochement, of course, depends on what the various authors conclude. It is their judgment and their wisdom that guide the final words.

FIRE,
NATIVE PEOPLES,
and
THE NATURAL
LANDSCAPE

CHAPTER I

THE PRE-EUROPEAN LANDSCAPE OF THE UNITED STATES: PRISTINE OR HUMANIZED?

Thomas R. Vale

All peoples embrace creation myths—stories that tell whence they came. Commonly considered unique to premodern societies, such narratives of origins are also told in contemporary nations. More specifically, the United States—for most of its existence—has envisioned its beginnings as wilderness, a state of nature, a natural landscape. American society expanded across the continent, extending its frontiers through a wild and primeval environment. Over the last couple of decades, however, a contrary creation myth has emerged, rising like a crescendo until it has become conventional wisdom: the nation's roots extend back not into wilderness but into a landscape inhabited by the First Americans, a place both psychologically a home and hearth, and physically an artifact of human activities. According to the extreme version of this vision, the pre-European North American landscape—from the Atlantic to the Pacific, from the Gulf of Mexico to the Arctic Ocean—unfolded as sprawling villages and fields of corn, terraced agricultural plots and diverted streams, meticulously tended trees and clear-cut forests, over-hunted elk and burned-over woodlands. The pristine landscape of an old creation myth has been replaced by the humanized landscape of a newer national narrative.

But the conflicting stories remain a source of contention. The debate

1

over the character of pre-Columbian America typically focuses on the polar assertions that the continent was either a "natural landscape" or a "human-modified landscape." The strongest characterizations of the former, a pristine America, come from romantics of an earlier day or from popular writers of contemporary times: "All the Western mountains are still rich in wildness" (Muir 1901:2); "Until 1881 the valley of the Little Missouri . . . was absolutely unchanged in any respect from its original condition of primeval wildness" (Roosevelt 1897, quoted in Callicott and Nelson 1998:74); "The parks . . . are . . . America primeval, preserved miraculously" (Anonymous 1991:11); the Americas were "ancient, primeval, undisturbed wilderness" (Bakeless 1961:201).

By contrast, the champions of an omnipresent humanized landscape include both scholars and popular writers: "The Indian impact was neither benign nor localized and ephemeral. . . . What they did was to change their landscape nearly everywhere" (Denevan 1992:370); "the forest primeval had already been widely cleared, converted, and otherwise managed" (Pyne 1982:83); "the Indians . . . created that 'wilderness' we call the Great Plains" (Pollan 1991:221); "most of this continent was owned, used, and modified by native peoples" (Kay 1994:381); "human influence is woven through even what to our eyes are the most pristine landscapes" (Budiansky 1995:5); "the land that the early settlers found in the West . . . was not made that way by God alone but partly by man" (Chase 1987:97); "Wilderness is certainly the wrong word for what early America was. . . . it was a managed landscape" (Flores 1997:6); "In the Western hemisphere, pre-Columbian people changed the landscape nearly everywhere from the Arctic to Patagonia" (Stevens 1993). In spite of the logic of an intermediate position—some areas were humanized, some were not (Vale 1998, 2000)—the rhetoric often reverts to the polar positions.

Explaining the Extremes

Several considerations explain and help mediate the stances at the extremes. These factors, characterized as ambiguities, can be portrayed along gradients that separate the polar opposites.

Intensity Ambiguity

The meanings of key concepts defy clarity: what do the words "humanized" and "pristine" actually mean? Given a series of landscapes that vary continuously between unambiguously "humanized" and unarguably "pristine," such intermediate landscapes might be classified as belonging to one polar condition or the other (the human tendency to classify phenomena into dichotomies encourages such polarization of intermediate conditions), depending upon the criteria of "modification" and "naturalness" employed. An example of five landscapes from the Yosemite region of California illustrates the point (Figure 1.1). A Miwok village site in upper Yosemite Valley—dwellings walled with tree bark, acorns stored in elevated granaries, nearby stands of hazelnut (*Corylus cornuta*) pruned, bracken (*Pteridium*) on a river terrace dug for roots, broadea (*Brodiaea*) bulbs harvested, killed mule deer (*Odocoileus hemionus*) hanging for butchering, campfires burning collected dead tree limbs—presents a humanized landscape. But nonhuman processes play a role as well: the regional and local climate; the nearby Merced River's hydrology; the granitic bedrock; the landforms of glacier, river, and slope erosion; the soil development beneath the trees; and even the presence of those biological species whose abundance may be influenced by Miwok activities. Away from the village, at the lower end of the valley, a green meadow—perhaps maintained by Indian burning—feels the footsteps of

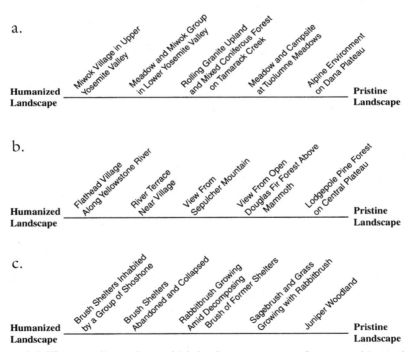

Figure 1.1. Three gradients along which landscapes may vary from unambiguously humanized to unarguably pristine. a. Intensity scale: Intensity of landscape modification by humans and their activities, as exemplified by examples from the Yosemite region of California. b. Spatial scale: Degree to which a local humanizing effect extends spatially, as illustrated by examples from the Yellowstone region of Montana and Wyoming. c. Temporal scale: Degree to which a one-time human influence continues to be perceived in the landscape, as represented by a settlement in eastern Nevada.

a group of Miwok gatherers who search for raspberries (*Rubus*) in thickets along the forest edge. High above the valley floor, on an expanse of rolling granite that falls away into Tamarack Creek, a cluster of smooth and rounded bedrock holes indicates that the Miwok grind acorns here, although no person is visible at the moment. Surrounding the granite surface, the mixed-conifer forest may or may not be influenced by Indian burning (lightning fires are common here). Up in the high country, in Tuolumne Meadows, a group of Miwok walk beside the river as they travel from the eastern side of the Sierra Nevada back toward Yosemite Valley, but their activities may involve only an overnight campsite (perhaps not unlike that of a modern backpacker), charcoal from a nighttime warming fire amid gathered rocks, or debris made up of obsidian or pine nuts (*Pinus monophylla*) left scattered about. On Dana Plateau, well above tree line and empty of people, nothing would suggest a humanized landscape—the sky, the rock, the canyon, the trickle of water from receding snow banks, the alpine plants hugging cobbles and soil, the occasional summering deer alert for mountain lion (*Felis concolor*)—all create a scene completely the product of natural processes. Taken together, then, these landscapes form a gradient that reveals both an array of major and minor human alternations of nature and a categorical presence or absence of people. Where to draw a line along the gradient to separate landscapes that are "humanized" from those that are "pristine" could be argued endlessly.

Space Ambiguity

Questions of spatial scale confound the issue: how far away from an unquestioned human impact should the landscape be considered "humanized"? An illustration of five landscapes from the Yellowstone region exemplifies the point (Figure 1.1). Along the Yellowstone River near present-day Gardiner, a cluster of conical lodges, home to a group of Flathead people, rests beside the rushing water of the Yellowstone River. Beyond the immediate living space of the settlement, a vegetation of brush and grass extends over the upland terrace from which the lodges and campfire smoke remain prominently conspicuous. From the eastern flank of Sepulcher Mountain, south of the village, the human artifacts remain visible from many vantage points, although from others the swells of hills and ravines block the view. Still farther south, in the open forest of Douglas fir (*Pseudotsuga menziesii*) that drapes over the steep slopes above present-day Mammoth, only wisps of campfire smoke tell of the village, and even those may be partially hidden behind individual trees. Much farther away, amid a forest of lodgepole pine (*Pinus contorta*) on Yellowstone's Central Plateau—little visited and appearing untouched by humans—the image of the Flathead lodges can be only mental. Taken together, these sites form a gradient, from the middle of a human settlement to a distant forest. The adjective "humanized" might be applied to only the intensely modified environment where the Flathead cook and sleep or to the entirety of the broader landscape—including the Central Plateau—of which the village is only a tiny spot. Or the point separating the "humanized" from the "natural" could be anywhere between these extremes.

Time Ambiguity

Similarly, a temporal scale of human disturbance that includes a gradient of recovery away from the disturbed condition identifies no universally recognized and categorical demarcation between "humanized" and "pristine." How long after abandonment, for example, might a hypothetical Shoshone settlement (Figure 1.1), in what is today eastern Nevada, maintain its human imprint? Circular structures of brush serve for shelter when the site is occupied, but after abandonment (as might have happened following a season of hunting and gathering in the surrounding area), the forces of nature would gradually mute, even erase, the effects of people. The dead brush walls would collapse and decompose; rabbitbrush (*Chrysothamnus*) would establish on the former living site; sagebrush (*Artemisia*) and perennial grasses might subsequently increase amid the rabbitbrush; and small juniper trees (*Juniperus*) could germinate, then mature into a woodland cover. Evidence of the former village might persist either in the vegetation (plant covers may long maintain characteristics of major disturbance events) or in the soils altered by campfires or wastes. We can only arbitrarily decide, invoking differing criteria, if and when the humanized characteristics have been replaced by those of nature, thereby rendering the landscape "natural."

Beyond the Ambiguities

The three gradients suggest no single way of defining the critical adjectives of "humanized" and "pristine." For purposes of landscape protection and management, however, a working definition emerges from a simple (albeit difficult-to-answer) question: For any particular area of America (and anywhere else, for that matter), did (and do) the fundamental characteristics of vegetation, wildlife, landform, soil, hydrology, and climate result from natural, nonhuman processes, and would these characteristics exist whether or not humans were (and are) present? (See Vale 1998.) In attempting responses to the query, different people might quarrel over the meaning of "fundamental" or choose to emphasize one part of the natural world over others. Nonetheless, such a question invites empirical study and assessment that leads toward appreciation of the presence or absence of human impacts, including those that are local and immediate as well as those that begin at specific loci and propagate through landscapes, à la the effects of keystone species (Power et al. 1996). Most generally, attempts to answer the question, in detail and for particular places, should elevate the dialogue from its current domination by arm-waving, careless generalizations.

Even this sort of empirical enlightenment, however, will not erase differing interpretations. Disciplinary training, specialized interests, and individual predilections: each contributes to the myths and metaphors with which we interpret the world (Botkin 1990) and each influences where different people see the boundary between the two categories of humanity and nature (Box 1.1). Anthropologically minded observers with biases toward human institutions and cultural behaviors may want to push the point of demarcation that separates

---

BOX 1.1. Characteristics that may tend to encourage individual observers to see the pre-European North American landscape as "pristine" or "humanized."

The two-part classification of characteristics is tentative and speculative: the array of characteristics in each group may lack internal consistency, and individuals who identify themselves as strong believers in either the "pristine" or the "humanized" viewpoint may find appealing particular characteristics in the opposing group. One pairing—equilibrium models linked to "natural" nature and nonequilibrium models linked to "humanized" nature—should not be seen in isolation from other pairings in the table. The equilibrium view encourages a belief in pristine landscapes because the two are so intertwined in historical thought (Bodkin 1990) and remain linked in much popular imagery of "the balance of nature"; for example, Interior Secretary Bruce Babbitt extolled restoration projects as efforts to reestablish landscapes with "a presettlement equilibrium" (quoted by Kloor 2000). By contrast, the nonequilibrium view is commonly invoked by those who wish to incorporate humans into nature (Pickett and McDonnell 1993), even to the point of dismissing attempts to protect natural landscapes (Zimmerer 2000). Nonetheless, modern physical geographical, ecological, and nature protectionist sentiment is dominated by nonequilibrium views, testimony to some of the other pairings in this table.

Advocates of the reality of pristine landscapes—their position is facilitated by . . .	Advocates for the ubiquity of humanized landscapes—their position is facilitated by . . .
Certain schooling in, or intellectual sympathy for, . . .	
(1) Biology, physical geography, and the natural sciences (particularly natural history), which stress the world of nature; the "old" history of the American past	(1) Anthropology and the social sciences generally, which stress the human world; the "new" or "revisionist" history of the American past
Certain ecosystem characteristics, such as . . .	
(1) Generalized definitions of ecosystems, in which human impacts are seen as minor modifications	(1) Specific details of ecosystems as critical to ecosystem definition, a procedure that emphasizes human impacts
(2) Broad landscape scale, in which local-scale human impacts are swamped by natural processes	(2) Local spatial scale, in which human modifications of nature are more likely to be emphasized
(3) Ecosystems reflect interactions of contemporary processes and situations, and past events damp out with time	(3) Ecosystems reflect historical events—which persist into the present—a perspective that stresses past human modifications
(4) Equilibrium models of ecosystems and landscapes, in which the present can be understood by seeking knowledge of contemporary processes and situations	(4) Nonequilibrium models of ecosystems and landscapes, in which historical events—including human impacts—structure contemporary situations
Certain characterizations of native peoples, such as . . .	
(1) Their fundamental difference, prior to European contact, from contemporary Americans, either culturally or technologically or both	(1) Their fundamental similarity, prior to European contact, to contemporary Americans, either culturally or technologically or both
(2) Their fundamental similarity, today, to contemporary Americans, in terms of environmental sensitivity	(2) Their fundamental difference, today, from contemporary Americans, which prompts traditional modifications of nature as a means for cultural survival
Certain characteristics of the people-nature dichotomy, such as . . .	
(1) The reality and utility of the dichotomy, even while recognizing a broad overlap (processes and effects in the two realms can be distinguished from one another)	(1) The falsity and destructiveness of the dichotomy, which divides people from nature (human impacts cannot be separated from natural processes)

continues

BOX 1.1. *Continued*

(2) Nature and wilderness are categories of reality independent of the human mind, and thus either can be identified in the world	(2) Nature and wilderness are socially constructed categories, which distort the real world of an intertwining of nature and people

A certain perspective on the need to
manipulate nature, particularly . . .

(1) The legitimacy of hands-off protection as a policy, although appreciating situations when active management may be desirable	(1) The need for manipulating nature as a universal policy for the management of nature preserves

"humanized" from "pristine" toward the right side of the gradients on the box (i.e., much or most of the pre-European continent was "humanized"). This view is encouraged by stressing certain biases or interpretations associated with ecosystems (local spatial scale; detailed features; historical persistence of impacts; nonequilibrium models that stress constant and endless change in nature), with pre-European Americans (as part of a universal humanity; as politically "dis-empowered"), with the human-nature dichotomy (the dichotomy as false and destructive; nature as socially constructed), and with the need to manipulate the natural world, even within protected landscape reserves (active management of nature is necessary).

By contrast, biologically inclined persons, particularly those concerned with protecting ecosystems against commodity resource development, might argue that the dividing point lies toward the left side of the continua (i.e., at least some of the pre-European landscape was basically "natural" and "pristine"). This perspective is prompted by contrary interpretations associated with ecosystems (broad landscape scale; generalized ecosystem features; damping out of impacts with time; equilibrium models that see systems adjusting to forcing functions, even if those functions themselves change through time), with pre-European Americans (as distinct from contemporary Americans; as lacking a position deserving political privilege), with the human-nature dichotomy (dichotomy as real; nature as physical reality), and with the need to manipulate nature (hands-off protection of nature is a legitimate policy). At the most fundamental level, the two positions vary in underlying assumptions about the degree to which the natural and human worlds

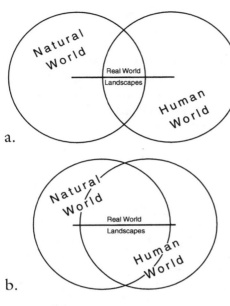

a.

b.

Figure 1.2. People vary in their perception of the degree of overlap in the natural and human worlds. In part a, with a strong dichotomy between the realms of nature and people, real-world landscapes include a strong representation of those that can be described as pristine or natural. In part b, most real-world landscapes represent blends of the natural and the human worlds, and thus most are humanized.

overlap and even the extent to which an external, nonhuman reality described as "natural" ever exists (Figure 1.2).

Regional Differences and Pristine Landscapes in the American West

Individual or group tendencies may help explain differences between those who defend the "humanized" versus "pristine" landscape perspectives, but, in addition, variations in the appropriateness of the two viewpoints probably existed in the pre-European North American landscape. On a local scale, such variability likely occurred throughout the continent: in the Northeast, for example, where areas were transformed into agricultural fields, human settlements, and burned forest (Cronon 1983). Nonetheless, "large segments of the interior, i.e., northern New England, the Allegheny Plateau region of Pennsylvania and New York, and the High Plains region of Michigan, were almost devoid of Indian activity" (Whitney 1994:120). By contrast, in parts of southern California, "the Spanish saw—but failed to recognize—a system of planting, harvesting, and managing the environment . . . [by] the native peoples" (Shipek in Blackburn and Anderson 1993:388), but large areas of desert must have been little modified by humans (Vankat 1979:201; Barbour et al. 1993:157–158). In spite of the mosaic of "natural" and "humanized" landscapes that probably spanned the continent—and regardless of the focus on either local, nonkeystone versus broad, keystone human impacts—most generally, at the regional scale, the subcontinental area of the eastern forests and tallgrass prairies may be a likely candidate for a strongly "humanized" environment. On the other hand, the American West, including the short-grass plains and extending through the arid and semiarid brushlands to the forested mountains, may be a region where, if anywhere, "pristine" landscapes likely occurred. Several lines of evidence support this regional characterization.

Population Size

The number of native people living in different parts of the West varied greatly, but much of the interior West supported small human populations. The numbers of people living in the Americas at the time of European contact has long been a question for scholarly debate. The most recent and thorough treatment is provided by Denevan (1992), who updates his earlier effort (Denevan 1976) and remains convinced that a large human population, some 53,904,000, lived in the hemisphere in the year 1492. (Such a large population supports Denevan's view of a landscape modified "nearly everywhere" [Denevan 1992:370], although Snow [1995] argues for smaller numbers.) One-third of that total inhabited present-day Mexico (more than 17 million) and another 20 percent (almost 12 million) called the Andes home. North America, by comparison, was lightly populated, with only 7 percent of the total, or 3,790,000. Denevan derived this North American figure from a simple doubling of Ubelaker's (1988) estimate of 1,894,350, which Denevan considers "very conservative" (Denevan 1992:xx). (Estimating the size of pre-European populations is difficult: Indian populations were decimated by introduced European diseases that spread ahead of even the earliest record-keeping explorers.) By extension, a twofold increase in each of Ubelaker's regional estimates for ten areas of North America allows a portrait of human numbers in different parts of the continent (Figure 1.3): 355,000 in the far North; 1,124,000 in the eastern forests; 378,000 in the prairies and plains (into the northern Rockies); 231,000 in the intermountain West; 793,000 along the Pacific Coast; and 908,000 in the Southwest (the cultural region of which extends into northern Mexico). Expressed by densities, human numbers were sparse in the Arctic, Subarctic, Plains/Prairies, and Great Basin, much higher in the eastern forests and Southwest, but highest of all along the northwest coast and, especially, lowland California. Although large numbers of native people lived in the West as a whole, then, much of the area of the West was only lighted inhabited.

Figure 1.3. Human numbers in the cultural regions of North America at the time of European contact (1492). The figures represent doublings of the population estimates of Ubelaker (1988:291), consistent with the judgment of Denevan (1992:xx, 291). The geographic areas of the cultural regions, as reported by Ubelaker (1988:291) and expressed in thousands of square kilometers, include Arctic, 2,378; Subarctic, 5,626; Northwest Coast, 326; California, 296; Southwest, 1,612; Great Basin, 900; Plateau, 509; Plains, 3,006; Northeast, 1,894; and Southeast, 910. The total of 17.5 million square kilometers (6,739,839 square miles) is about 5 percent lower than the figures reported for land area in the United States and Canada in the *Statistical Abstract of the United States.*

Settlements

The areal extent of human-constructed forms, such as settlement dwellings, would have echoed population densities and thus occupied larger parts of the eastern landscape than of much of the West. Living dwellings in the pre-European West varied from simple shelters of brush to elaborate houses walled with wooden planks (Thomas, Pendleton, and Cappannari 1986:268; Suttles and Lane 1990:491), from tiny lodges to buffalo-robed tepees to tule-matted dwellings to adobe and rock-cemented buildings (Spier 1978b:430; Wilson and Towne 1978:388; Malinowski 1998a:253–254; Malinowski 1998b:215). Sometimes sheltering communal assemblies but more often single family groups, the houses were usually clustered in villages, although occasionally were scattered in loose and open settlements (Pilling 1978:139; Hackenberg 1983:165; Stewart 1983:57; Fowler and Liljeblad 1986:443; deLaguna 1990:207).

Despite this diversity, the dwelling patterns shared a common characteristic: they provided crowded, even cramped, living spaces. For example, on the Rio Mimbres of New Mexico, Minnis (1985:52–53) identified a house space of 5 to 10 square meters per person; in northern California, Shastan peoples built dwellings with 5 to 7 square meters per person (Silver 1978:214); on the Great Plains, the Osage lived in houses that enclosed 3 to 18 square meters per person (Malinowski 1998b:322). Even less space per individual characterized many peoples: 3 to 5 square meters for the Salish of Washington, the Pomo of northern California, the Yokut of south-central California, the Washoe of western Nevada, the Ute of eastern Utah, and the Kalispel of northern Idaho (Bean and Theodoratus 1978:292; Spier 1978a:476; Callaway, Janetski, and Stewart 1986:348; D'Azevedo 1986:479–481; Hajda 1990:509; Lahren 1998:288).

These numbers allow estimates of the percentage of pre-European landscape devoted to human living space. At the rate of 10 square meters per person (on the high end of most of the sources consulted above), the 2.3 million people in cultural regions of the West (which extend north along the Pacific Coast into Alaska and south into northern Mexico) would account for 23.1 million square meters or 23.1 square kilometers of dwellings, only 0.00034 percent of the total landscape area. In the sparsely inhabited Great Basin, the percentage shrinks to 0.00008 percent; in more populated California, it climbs to 0.0015. The regional percentage for the less populated West is smaller, although only marginally, than the 0.0004 percent attributed to the cultural regions in the more densely populated eastern forests.

Villages included more than everyday living space—sweat lodges, ceremonial centers, assembly shelters, storage facilities, specialized dwellings, and enclosing palisades. Moreover, all such structures rested within larger, more generalized settlement areas. Still, this land use accounted for only a tiny fraction of the total landscape (Figure 1.4), probably concentrated in small areas and surrounded by a series of circular bands of decreasing human impact (Hammett 1992). Even the use

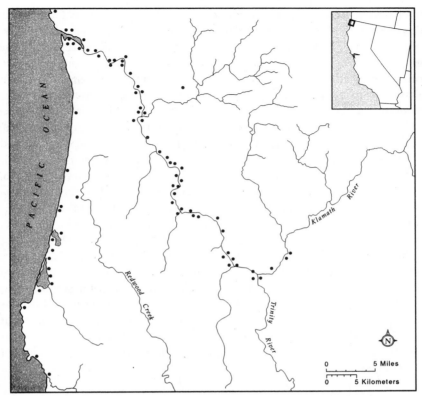

Figure 1.4. Tribal villages and camps of the Yurok of northwestern California (Pilling 1978:139). Settlements were concentrated along the Klamath River and the immediate Pacific coast, leaving most of the landscape without such communities. The size of the villages was modest—most had no more than seven or eight houses (Pilling 1978:145)—which makes their spatial extent much smaller than depicted by the cartographic circles on the map.

of statistics for contemporary Western cities—which include not only houses but also retail stores, manufacturing space, public buildings, roads, parking lots, sidewalks, parks, playgrounds, yards, landscaped property, and idle land—cannot change the picture. Western cities today commonly enclose 780 to 1,000 square meters (0.0003 to 0.0004 square mile) per person: examples include Spokane, Washington; Portland and Eugene, Oregon; Sacramento, Santa Rosa, and Concord, California; Tucson, Arizona; Albuquerque, New Mexico; Denver, Colorado; and Boise, Idaho (data from *Statistical Abstract of the United States* 1997:45–47). Older and more mature cities, such as San Francisco, California (180 square meters or 0.00007 square mile), and Seattle, Washington (520 square meters or 0.0002 square mile), provide much less space per person, whereas newer, sprawling cities have more: Mesa, Arizona (1,800 square meters or 0.0007 square mile) and Scottsdale, Arizona (5,180 square meters or 0.002 square mile), represent the other extreme. Using the figure of 780 to 1,000 square meters per person—a value that can only greatly exaggerate the true expanse of Indian villages—the 2.31 million people in pre-European times would have generated a settlement area of 1,802 million to 2,310 million square meters (696 to 892 square miles), or only 0.03 to 0.04 percent of the total landscape in the western cultural regions.

Other types of construction—omitting for the moment those associated with agriculture—must have been similarly restricted in spatial extent. Burial grounds, roads (even the celebrated road system radiating from New Mexico's Chaco Canyon [Trombold 1991] or those of Arizona's Hohokam [Motsinger 1998]), locales for human wastes, refuse dumps, water reservoirs (Wilshusen, Churchill, and Potter 1997)—even in the aggregate, these occupied only small areas of landscape. Moreover, the high mobility of certain peoples, which would increase the area of settlement considerably, would nonetheless alter the total landscape in only a minor way. The upshot is simple: the modest numbers of humans in pre-European times, living with much simpler technologies and lifestyles (compared with today's) and demanding much less of the natural world (relative to modern people), modified only a tiny fraction of the total landscape for their everyday living needs.

Agriculture

Agriculture, widespread in the East, was restricted in the West to the Southwest and parts of the Great Plains. The American Southwest supported agricultural societies that were among the most sophisticated in pre-European North America (north of the Aztec cities of central Mexico), and crop plants appear long ago in archaeological sites. Corn (*Zea mays*) may have been first cultivated between 3,000 and 3,500 years ago, to be joined by squashes (*Cucurbita*), gourds (*Lagenaria*), and various beans (*Phaseolus*), among other plants (Cordell 1997:129, 135). By about 2,000 years ago, agriculture had spread through the Southwest, although not all peoples cultivated crop plants (Cordell 1997:148).

Recent reviews identify several patterns of landscape modification associated with pre-European southwestern agriculture (Doolittle 1992, 2000; Fish and Fish 1994; Cordell 1997). First, uplands cleared of their forest cover supported dry farming in areas where rainfall was sufficient for crop plants; the mesas in southwestern Colorado serve as examples (Wyckoff 1977; Stiger 1979). Second, water control devices such as terraces enhanced the agricultural utility of both intermittent stream beds and mountain slopes in some environments; the Point of Pines area in eastern Arizona serves as a classic study of such agriculture (Woodbury 1961). Third, desert lowlands required more elaborate water manipulations, including stream diversions and canals; the Hohokam society of central Arizona is an often-cited illustration (Masse 1981; Crown 1987).

A number of studies suggest the area of cropped field per person in pre-European societies of the Southwest. For systems without irrigation or only minimal water manipulation, Woodbury (1961), Matson, Lipe, and Haase (1988), and Williams (1993) use 1 hectare per person as the standard, a value consistent with other studies (Vivian 1974; Tuggle and Reid 1984; Orcutt 1986), including Hopi agriculturalists in historic times (Bradfield 1971). By contrast, the greater productivity of irrigated systems reduces the field size per person: Minnis (1985)—working in the Rio Mimbres region of New Mexico—increases the values reported for contemporary pueblos by 50 percent (to allow for increased production needed in dry years) and derives 0.6 hectare per person. This number exceeds the 0.17 to 0.43 hectare per person calculated by Fish and Fish (1992) for prehistoric Hohokam and historic Pima communities in the desert of central Arizona.

These values may be applied to the estimated number of people living within the Southwest at the time of initial European contact to derive the maximum possible acreage in agricultural fields (Figure 1.5); such a calculation assumes that all pre-European people were engaged in agriculture, an assumption that will overestimate the magnitude of the agricultural landscape. Given a human population of 908,000 (a doubling of Ubelaker's number for the region, as derived above), the area of agricultural fields would be 908,000 hectares, assuming dryland farming (at 1 hectare per person), or 545,000 hectares for irrigated agriculture (at 0.6 hectare per person). The total seems large, but when compared with the 161,160,000 hectares within the cultural region (Ubelaker 1988), the extent of the agricultural landscape shrinks considerably: of the total land area, only 0.56 percent (by the dryland farming calculation) or 0.34 percent (by the irrigated farming estimation) might have lain in agricultural fields (and keep in mind the generous assumptions about the extent of agricultural activity among pre-European peoples). By comparison, the planted cropland in contemporary Arizona (1.1 percent of the state area) and New Mexico (1.6 percent) suggests slightly larger but surprisingly similar magnitudes (data from *Statistical Abstract of the United States* 1997).

The sum of agricultural fields in use at one instant in time, however, probably underestimates the total landscape modified by agricultural activity. Dryland farming systems, unencumbered by constructed—and thus spatially anchored—water control devices, seem the most likely can-

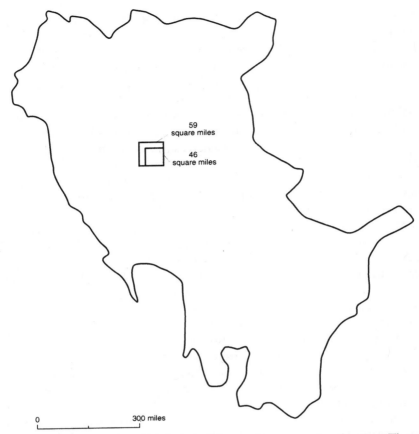

Figure 1.5. The agricultural landscape of the southwestern cultural region. The two squares represent the maximum total cropland within the region, given 1.0 hectare per person (the larger square, 59 miles on a side) and given 0.6 hectare per person (the smaller square, 46 miles on a side). Both calculated cropland areas are based on generous assumptions, as discussed in the text.

didates for such expanded impacts. At Mesa Verde, for example, Stiger (1979) suggested that native people shifted their agricultural fields in a sort of swidden agriculture, an interpretation deemed "plausible but as yet unconfirmed" by Fish and Fish (1994). Matson, Lipe, and Hasse (1998), in a study at Cedar Mesa, Utah, calculate an acreage twenty times the field area used at any one time to be necessary to support a shifting cultivation system. A similar order of magnitude is suggested by Kohler and Matthews (1988) on Grass Mesa in southwestern Colorado, where their numbers indicate that about 19 hectares of land was "deforested" per person. Applying these figures to the total population in the Southwest—a most reckless procedure because not all peoples were agriculturalists, nor were all of those who did engage in agriculture dryland farmers, nor were those who were dryland farmers necessarily shifting cultivators—yields 11.2 percent of the total landscape area as modified by agriculture, ten times the area of contemporary cropland and, even though a most unlikely figure, still a relatively modest percentage.

In regions other than the Southwest, this type of calculation generates a similar portrayal of small areas in agricultural fields. On the Great Plains, Malinowski (1998b) suggests individual Hidatsa families farmed 3–5 acres (p. 258)—1–2 hectares—whereas the Osage farmed about 1.5 acres per person (p. 299)—about 0.6 hectare. If the entire human population of 378,000 in the Plains cultural region farmed 0.6 hectare per individual (an extravagant assumption, because most Native Americans in the region did not depend upon agriculture), the aggregated sum would be 226,800 hectares, only 7.5 percent of the region's total area. Even in the eastern forested region of North America the area in fields and fallow was small: Williams (1993:30–31) suggested as many as 28 million acres was so modified in the thirty-one easternmost states—a number that impressed him as large—but it represents less than 4 percent of the total area of those states.

Agricultural activity marks the landscape not only by cropland but also, sometimes, by constructed landforms—the canals of the Hohokam serve as an obvious example. Low rock check dams across ravines that collect sediment and thus form small surfaces for planting, short rock walls running along the contour on slopes that similarly create low terraces ("linear borders" or "contour terraces"), rectangular fields on level ground that are edged by earth or rock borders ("bordered gardens"), fields with veneers of gravel mulch—all result in landforms that persist long after agriculture has ended (Cordell 1997). But, as with agricultural fields more generally, these forms occupy only tiny parts of the landscape.

The manner of portraying archaeological sites in the anthropological literature may contribute to an exaggerated sense of the spatial scale of Indian agricultural impact. Typically in such studies, the maps of sites focus on the immediate environment in which artifacts and modifications are located—a logical and appropriate custom for purposes of presenting the data (Figure 1.6). This local scale, however, cannot reveal the landscape context for the impacts, which account for only small areas of the total environment.

The upshot of these various estimates and calculations is that not much of the pre-European landscape of the American Southwest or the Great Plains was—in cropland or otherwise—modified by agricultural activity. Certain areas were deforested, modified, and even utterly transformed by human cultivators. The bulk of the region, however, was not.

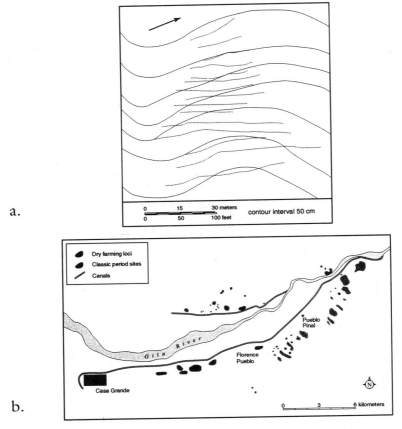

Figure 1.6. Two examples of mapped agricultural landscapes. a. Low rock walls that form short terraces for nonirrigated cropland at Point of Pines in east-central Arizona (Woodbury 1961:19). b. Irrigation canals, other agricultural features, and dwelling sites at Casa Grande (Hohokam) in central Arizona (Crown 1987:149). In both examples, the local scale emphasizes the agricultural forms; a larger, landscape scale would de-emphasize them.

Vegetation Modification

Vegetation modifications other than formal agriculture may have been more prevalent in the East, but evidence of such activities is common in the West. Doolittle (2000) compiles a comprehensive compendium of specific Indian manipulations of plants throughout North America, and the results are dizzily rich in both number of instances and diversity of activities. Documented from firsthand accounts, ethnographies, and archaeological evidence, Doolittle's detailed listing is organized into categories arrayed along a continuum between the poles of formal *agriculture* (in which crop plants require human action to reproduce) and sim-

BOX 1.2. The continuum of plant-people interactions. (Modified from Doolittle 2000.)

Agriculture	Crop plants require human action for successful reproduction
Cultivation	Humans propagate wild plant species that reproduce in the wild
Encouragement	Humans manipulate individual plants that occur naturally in the wild
Protection	Humans enhance some characteristics of individual plants that occur naturally in the wild
Gathering	Humans gather products from wild, naturally occurring plants, but the plants are unaltered by the gathering activity

ple *gathering* (in which wild plants yield products for people but are unaffected by them) (Box 1.2). Most closely resembling agriculture, the category of *cultivation* describes human planting of species that readily and commonly reproduce in the wild. Activities labeled as *encouragement* include manipulations of naturally occurring plants (e.g., diverting water from streams to wild stands of sedge), whereas, closer to gathering, those activities classified as *protection* involve management to enhance the persistence of particular natural plants (e.g., removing potentially damaging dead branches from shrubs).

Within Doolittle's work, instances of cultivation, encouragement, and protection span the continent, although the larger number from the West, compared to the East, may reflect more the character of the data sources than the degree of proliferation of pre-European societies. Within the West, more than two-thirds of the documented examples occur in more densely populated California and the Southwest, again perhaps a consequence of the history of anthropological and archaeological study (and preservation of certain types of evidence in dry environments) and not a result of regional differences in human activities. These instances from the American West contribute to the question of the degree to which the pre-European landscape was humanized.

Cultivation

The category of cultivation includes such activities as the spreading of seeds of herbaceous species (e.g., Winter and Hogan 1986), but the transplanting of woody plants constitutes perhaps the most obvious illustration. A celebrated example involves the prehistoric Hohokam of central Arizona, who constructed piles of cobbles (which increased the infil-

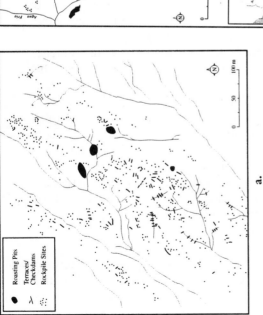

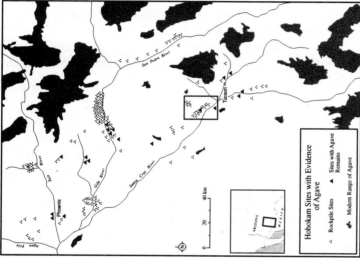

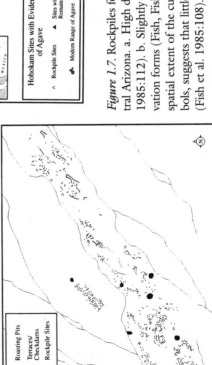

a.

c.

Roasting Pits
Terraces/Checkdams
Rockpile Sites

Roasting Pits
Terraces/Checkdams
Rockpile Sites

Hohokam Sites with Evidence
of Agave

Rockpile Sites   Sites with Agave
                   Remains

Modern Range of Agave

Figure 1.7. Rockpiles for agave cultivation and associated features (Hohokam) in central Arizona. a. High density of forms suggests total landscape modification (Fish et al. 1985:112). b. Slightly broader view reveals much landscape unmodified by the cultivation forms (Fish, Fish, and Madsen 1990:202). c. Still broader view, in which the spatial extent of the cultivation forms are greatly exaggerated by the cartographic symbols, suggests that little of the landscape was modified by the rockpile cultivation (Fish et al. 1985:108).

tration of rainwater and/or runoff and thus enhanced available soil moisture) in which they planted agave (*Agave* spp.), prized for their edible fruits. The rockpiles, modest in size (1.5 meters in diameter and no more than 75 centimeters high) but numerous (about 42,000 in a study area of 350 square kilometers north of Tucson), represent a human modification of both the vegetation cover (including local range extensions of the transplanted agaves) and the landform surface (Fish, Fish, and Madsen 1985, 1990, 1992; Fish, Fish, Miksicek, and Madsen 1985). Interspersed with pits for roasting the fruits, as well as with low terraces and check dams for field crops, the rockpiles contributed to impressive agricultural/cultivation complexes (Figure 1.7). Nonetheless, as with formal agricultural fields, the percent of the landscape directly modified by constructed rockpiles is small—they collectively cover only 1.4 percent of the area in the "full-coverage" survey in the northern Tucson Basin—and the acreage of the complexes mapped at a more general scale leave much landscape unmodified (Figure 1.7).

A second classic example of the transplanting of wild plants by Native Americans involves the spreading of fan palms (*Washingtonia filifera*) across the warm deserts of southern California. Useful for both fruits and fronds, the trees easily could have been dispersed to isolated moist canyons and perennial springs by people carrying seeds. The cited evidence is anecdotal (Patencio 1943; Bean and Saubel 1972) but persuasively logical. Moreover, the introduction of the palms transformed ("humanized") the desert oases more or less permanently, a point suggested for transplanted species generally at both local and regional scales (Jennings 1966; Borher 1991). The moist locales that could support palms constitute a tiny part of the southern California desert landscape (virtually all of which remained unaltered by palm introductions), although these palm stands sometimes can be seen from great distances (extending, by one measure, the spatial extent of the humanization) and always are disproportionately valued by people, which may elevate the importance of the palm transplants as elements of humanized nature.

A third, speculative but intriguing illustration of transplanting is suggested by Betancourt et al. (1993; see also Betancourt et al. 1991), who proposes that Native Americans may have been responsible for the spreading of certain genetic characteristics of plants, notably good-masting strains of pinyon pine (*Pinus edulis*) in New Mexico, by the collection of, and returning home with, seeds from particularly productive trees. Such genetic manipulations of food plants by subsistence folk is a time-honored research topic (Sauer 1952; Zimmerer 1996); as an example of the humanization of the natural world, it is more focused on detail and fine-grain than on landscape or ecosystem scale.

ENCOURAGEMENT

The most frequent examples of encouragement, of promoting the health of specific wild plants, involve burning top growth (e.g., Bohrer 1983, 1992; Winter and Hogan 1986; McCarthy 1993), digging roots of herbaceous species (e.g., Peri and Patterson 1993), or pruning stems of shrubs (e.g., Anderson 1993). Two particular instances, often cited, suggest still other types of encouragement. First, Nichols and Smith (1965) documented at Mesa Verde in southwestern Colorado the purposeful bending over, and killing the top of, young Douglas fir to induce vigorous vertical growth of branches, which subsequently could be harvested for long, straight construction timbers. After initial branches were so cut, others would assume the terminal dominance and produce additional building material, probably repeatedly. After using dendrochronological techniques in one ravine, the authors suggest that such manipulations may well have occurred in many canyons in the Mesa Verde area. Second, the Paiute of Owens Valley in eastern California diverted waters from streams issuing from the Sierra Nevada to flood-irrigate upland stands of wild hyacinth (*Dichelostemma pulchella*, a brodiaea) and yellow nutgrass (*Cyperus esculentus*, a sedge), both of which produce edible subterranean material (Stewart 1929; Lawton et al. 1976). An area with dam and ditches along Bishop Creek may have watered 6 to 8 square miles, and extrapolating this magnitude to the ten other nearby streams that may have supported such a system produces a total of about 80 square miles of irrigated land. This total approaches 10 percent of the lowland area of the Owens Valley.

PROTECTION

Activities categorized as protection merge, on the one hand, with encouragement and, on the other, with simple gathering. Several examples serve as illustrations. Clearing debris from the top growth of certain herbaceous plants or removing dead branches, leaf litter, or rocks to protect certain plants from being "crowded out" by other species may represent protection (Ortiz 1993). The realization that mature pinyon pine produce larger crops of cones and seeds than smaller trees may have prompted Anasazi peoples to protect older trees when seeking fuel wood or construction timber (Floyd and Kohler 1990). The effect of spiritual beliefs that preclude overharvesting of acorns might also be classified as protection behavior among California Indians (McCarthy 1993). Still another form of restraint, the Paiute people refraining from burning fire-sensitive pinyon woodlands in the Great Basin—if prompted by the obvious importance of pine nuts as a food source—might be described as a protection activity (Burwell 1999).

OVERALL IMPACTS OF VEGETATION MODIFICATIONS

In sum, the landscape impacts of activities classified as cultivation most closely resemble those of formal agriculture: nature is intensely modified;

the spatial extent of landscape modification is modest; and, depending upon the specific impacts, the change may be ephemeral or persistent through time. Compared with agriculture and cultivation, encouragement and protection to a much lesser degree intrude upon, modify, or change the pristine natural world: in the intensity of alternation, the spatial scale of impact, and the temporal scale of persistence, encouragement and protection activities change nature less than planting crop or wild plant species. For someone seeking human impacts in the pre-European landscape, the above statement invites a response—namely, that subtler character of encouragement and protection activities do not negate their reality, and, in fact, that very reality only confirms a humanized North America in 1492. However, the small acreage modified intensively, the modest area altered in any way, and the often fleeting character of much of the alternations may also suggest that much or most of the continent was essentially free of the impacts of cultivation, encouragement, and protection at the time of European contact.

Tree Cutting

Cutting trees for building material and fuel, with concurrent impacts on forest composition and structure, must have been more common in the densely populated and humid East, although the impacts may have been longer-lasting in the drier West. The cutting and removal of trees in forests and woodlands, itself an alteration of the natural scene, likely leaves an imprint on the woody vegetation that persists even after the immediate evidence of the event fades, and the immense literature on historic logging supports this view (Vale 1982). In the pre-European landscape of North America, native peoples' use of wood resources—which might be seen as analogous to selective silviculture in contemporary times—would have had similar effects. In spite of the celebrated example of the Chaco Canyon Anasazi transporting construction timbers more than 75 kilometers (Betancourt, Dean, and Huyll 1986), wood-cutting impacts would have been greatest in the immediate vicinity of settlements, with decreasing impacts away from the village sites (Whitney 1994; Steller 1995; even Sauer, 1947, seems to have this model in mind), perhaps not unlike the reduced availability of downed wood around contemporary campgrounds inhabited by firewood-collecting recreationists. The forest modifications caused by wood-seeking Native Americans, then, would have created not a uniformly modified and humanized forest, but a mosaic with varying degrees of alternation.

In the West, native folks of the marginally arid Southwest may have deforested pinyon-juniper woodlands in their cutting for material and fuel (as well as through agricultural activities). In Southwestern Colorado, Kohler (1992) cites several lines of evidence suggesting Anasazi deforestation: the declines through time in the uses of pinyon and juniper as fuel (as evidenced by charcoal remains) and as food (pinyon seeds) and in the delayed use of older trees for construction (trees that may have been previously saved for their production of cones and seeds). In New Mexico, Minnis (1978, 1985) similarly argues that prehistoric peoples deforested areas near settlements along the Rio Mimbres. Betancourt and Van Devender (1981), interpreting the record of packrat middens, and Samuels and Betancourt (1982), employing a simulation model of wood use, indicate Anasazi deforestation around Chaco Canyon. More generally throughout the landscape along the current international border, Bahre (1991) concluded that floodplains, with their concentration of human settlements, may have been deforested of riparian trees. These specific studies lead some to observe that deforestation may have been universal, or at least extremely widespread. Even Betancourt, whose published work seems to place him away from the humanized landscape extreme, has stated that "New Mexico woodlands of a thousand years ago were part of a deeply humanized landscape, far from the pristine label commonly assigned to pre-Columbian panoramas" (Betancourt et al. 1993).

Could pre-European humans have deforested the pinyon-juniper woodland? Currently, such vegetation covers 27,547,000 hectares (68 million acres; 106,000 square miles) (Klopatek et al. 1979), an area larger than the state of Colorado. Even given the expansion of juniper woodland in historic times, the total area in pre-European North America was immense. Ignoring the clearing for agriculture—which was locally, even regionally, important—the consumption of wood necessary to achieve widespread deforestation would have had to be substantial. Specifically, if each acre supported 600 to 1,010 cubic feet of wood (Gottfried and Ffolliott 1995, but their number may exceed stocking rates for pinyon-juniper stands over much of the West), the 68 million acres of pinyon-juniper vegetation would have totaled 40–70 billion cubic feet of wood. To consume this biomass, native peoples would have had to exceed by two or three times the current wood usage in the United States (including pulp and paper), admittedly for a single year (about 20 billion cubic feet, according to the USDA Forest Service 1990). Moreover, and again omitting clearing for agriculture, for the woodland to be simultaneously cleared at one time, each of the approximately 700,000 people living within the range of pinyon-juniper woodland at the time of European contact would have had to consume 59,000 to 99,000 cubic feet of wood. Even if distributed over a century of consumption, such a rate exceeds contemporary wood usage in the United States by as much as ten times. In sum, it seems reckless to suggest more than a moderate position: the pinyon-juniper woodland was cleared in the vicinity of settlements, especially in the southwest, but much—most?—of the area of such vegetation could not have been deforested.

To be "deeply humanized," however, the pinyon-juniper woodland may have been more modestly subjected to scattered wood cutting, not total deforestation. The spatial pattern of such impacts, resembling those of forest clearing specifically and human villages generally, probably formed a gradient of decreasing alteration away from settlements. Moreover, the question arises of how much cutting would be necessary to invoke the label of "deeply humanized": heavy cutting in the vicinity of a large and permanent village; cutting several trees in an acre near a temporary settlement; cutting a dead tree near a seasonal camp; collecting dead and downed wood beside an overnight camp; or walking through a woodland, breaking off dead branches that then lie on the ground surface. The question prompts no easy and universal answer, but the generalization that the pinyon-juniper woodland, in its large expanse, was altered by pre-European people, and thus not "pristine" (Cartledge and Propper 1993), seems hyperbole.

Hunting of Wild Animals

If pre-European humans acted as keystone predators, their associated impacts may have been no greater in the West than in the East. The concept of keystone biological species—those animals that disproportionately influence the structure and/or diversity of surrounding biotic communities—continues to enjoy attention and popularity in the ecological literature (Mills, Soulé, and Doak 1993; Power et al. 1996; Knapp et al. 1999). Some observers have suggested that humans may act as critical keystone species—an unassailable assertion for people living in the modern world but a more provocative claim for those subsisting in hunting and gathering societies.

No one has been more outspoken in seeing pre-European peoples in North America as a keystone predator than Kay, particularly in his work on Yellowstone (Chaddle and Kay 1991; Kay and Chaddle 1992; Kay and Wagner 1994; Kay 1995b, 1997d). In this famous region, Kay suggests that excessive hunting by native peoples effectively eliminated elk (*Cervus elaphus*) from the northern part of the present park, an eradication that reduced browsing pressure on such trees and shrubs as aspen (*Populus tremuloides*), willows (*Salix* spp.), serviceberry (*Amelanchier alnifolia*), and chokecherry (*Prunus virginiana*). In turn, animals dependent upon robust stands of these plants, notably beaver (*Castor canadensis*) but perhaps also white-tailed deer (*Odocoileus virginianus*), flourished. By contrast, with protection within the national park, elk numbers have exploded, leading to decreases in the browse species and corresponding declines in related animals. The evidence for this dramatic change in the contemporary Yellowstone ecosystem includes an absence of elk remains in archaeological sites, few references to elk (or the predators dependent on them, wolves [*Canis lupus*]—Kay 1995a) in the journals of early Europeans, tall and healthy stands of browse species in nineteenth-century photographs, vigorous growth of browse species within contemporary grazing enclosures, and apparent abundance of fruits in the lightly browsed shrubs in pre-European times (Kay 1994).

Other researchers offer a different interpretation of the Yellowstone elk situation (Despain et al. 1986; Meagher and Houston 1998). Elk numbers were high in the pre-European landscape, according to this viewpoint, and changes in vegetation represent responses more to climate variability and fire suppression than to browsing pressure. More specifically, Yellowstone offers only marginal habitat for aspen, and thus to beaver, and declines in both species reflect climatic drying and reduction in fire frequency. Moreover, heavy browsing by a large population of elk is to be expected in this environment, leading to different interpretations of the related lines of evidence: elk remains exist in archaeological sites; elk and wolf references abound in early written accounts; nineteenth-century photographs depict vegetation of a cooler and more moist climate (and, in addition, reveal remarkable stability in the plant cover); and vigorous growth of unbrowsed trees and shrubs within grazing enclosures represents vegetation conditions developing in the absence of large browsing animals, an unnatural condition for Yellowstone.

Yellowstone and its elk may be the most studied and the most inflammatory instance of possible "aboriginal overkill" (Kay 1994), but the control of prey numbers by excessive human predation in pre-European North America has been argued for other landscapes. In Rocky Mountain National Park, today's elk numbers may be much larger than those in pre-European times, with cascading negative effects similar to those described for Yellowstone, and Indian hunting—not specifically identified—might be invoked to explain the lower elk populations in the past (Hess 1993). Much the same story has been told for other parts of the Rocky Mountains, notably in Canada, and including not only elk but also moose (*Alces alces*) (Kay 1997a, 1997c). Moreover, Indian hunting on the Plains, according to some observers, reduced the number of bison (*Bison bison*) far below the commonly cited 60 million animals that might have been supported by the forage resource (Kay cites West 1995 and Shaw 1995 in this argument, but both actually tell more complex stories). In the eastern states, Neumann (1989, 1995) argues that Indians, who competed with wild animal species for acorns and other mast foods, excessively killed white-tailed deer, tree squirrels (*Sciurus*), turkey (*Meleagris gallopavo*), and raccoon (*Procyon lotor*), among other species. His most intriguing assertion is that the passenger pigeon (*Ectopistes migratorius*)—one of the great icons of animal abundance in wild America—was actually uncommon in pre-European times because of such competition with native peoples: the birds' numbers exploded only when diseases greatly reduced the human population (Neumann 1985).

To the degree that the "aboriginal overkill" thesis is supported empirically—as some of Kay's work argues effectively—the idea has appeal. The luster of the evidence, however, is too often tarnished by the rhetoric of its presentation. First, although Kay qualifies his argument (i.e., ungulates with environmental refuges such as dense forests or marsh vegetation may have escaped the intense pre-European hunters; humans and other predators may have interacted to limit prey numbers), he clearly wants the mechanism to be a universal or at least the norm: said directly, the extrapolation from the northern range of Yellowstone to the entire continent may weaken the argument, even for locales where the empiricism is persuasive. Second, the tone of the published work is one of strident advocacy, rather than of reflective truth-seeking; a reader might even wonder about a social agenda in Kay's science, indicated by his assertion that the wilderness "myth" was "created, in part, to justify appropriation of aboriginal lands and the genocide that befell native peoples" (Kay 1994:381) and by his recommendation that "we simply permit Native Americans to hunt bison in [Yellowstone]" (Kay 1997b). Finally, the seductiveness of simplicity and single causes, in this case "aboriginal overkill," rests uneasily in the minds of those who find complexity and multiple causes in the natural world, including the effects of ungulate grazing and browsing on vegetation (Mladenoff and Stearns 1993).

The overkill thesis elevates pre-European North American peoples from "children of nature" to a more universal humanity, but it does so by invoking an unflattering story line of excessive resource exploitation. American Indians cannot be described as promoting "ecological integrity" (Czech 1995:568), embracing "conservation . . . as part of their lifeway" (Gomez-Pompa and Kaus 1992:273), or living a "partnership with nature that left the resource base intact" (Anderson 1993:152). The overkill thesis says that Indians ruthlessly, wastefully, and unsustainably slaughtered the wildlife of the continent.

Wildfire

Lightning commonly ignites wildfires in the West, less so in much of the East, raising the possibility that the pre-European fire regime in the American West was more a function of natural ignition and vegetation flammability than of Indian burning. Wildfires require both an ignition source—almost entirely from human activities or lightning strikes—and combustible fuels. Combustibility, in turn, depends upon flammable biomass, often but not necessarily dead and dried leaves and/or twigs and branches, in an atmospheric context of short-term dry weather, perhaps augmented by longer-term drought. These requirements result in a negative feedback mechanism, by which a fire that consumes the combustible fuels reduces the likelihood of a subsequent fire—at least until the fuels have reaccumulated. The time needed for the accumulation of burnable fuels varies greatly, depending upon the vegetation structure; in an annual grassland, it may require but one growing season, whereas in some forests it may take several centuries. A vegetation type, then, can be said to have a fire regime (in a time period of constant climate)—described by a return time or recurrence interval (for a fire to return to a given locale)—dictated by ignition frequency and available fuel.

Ignition frequency or available fuel: either one may limit burning and, thus, determine the fire regime. Those who champion Indian burning as a humanizing influence on landscapes—and their numbers are legion (e.g., Sauer 1950; Denevan 1992; Budiansky 1995; Delcourt et al. 1998)—implicitly stress the importance of the number of ignitions, i.e., native peoples set fires, and these ignitions determined fire regimes. By contrast, other researchers emphasize fuels (e.g., Vogl 1974:148; Despain 1990; Swetnam and Baisan 1996), arguing that ignition sources generally are common through time but what determines whether or not a particular ignition starts a fire is the condition of the vegetation. Whereas the fuel-limited view does not preclude Indian burning as a critical component of fire regimes, it shifts the emphasis toward conditions in the nonhuman world—fuels and weather—and thus appeals to those who argue for "natural" burning characteristics of environments. An intermediate position might recognize the existence of both fuel-limited and Indian-ignition-influenced fire regimes, a reality that would create a mosaic of pristine and humanized conditions in the burned landscape (Baisan and Swetnam 1997).

Whether a product of human agency or natural processes, fire characterized the vegetation dynamics in the American West of pre-European times (Figure 1.8). Return times varied enormously—from more than a 1,000 years on the Arctic tundra, to 400 years in moist coastal forests of the Pacific Coast, to 50 years in some midelevation mountain forests, to 30 years in California chaparral, to several years in some grasslands. The intensity of burns also varied, from light surface fires to stand-initiating crown fires. Burning structured many vegetation types in the eastern states, but fire and western systems were particularly intertwined. The flammability of vegetation, the dryness of summer weather, the prevalence of multiyear drought, the widespread occurrence of lightning without rain—all made (and continue to make) Western vegetation prone to burn (Figure 1.9).

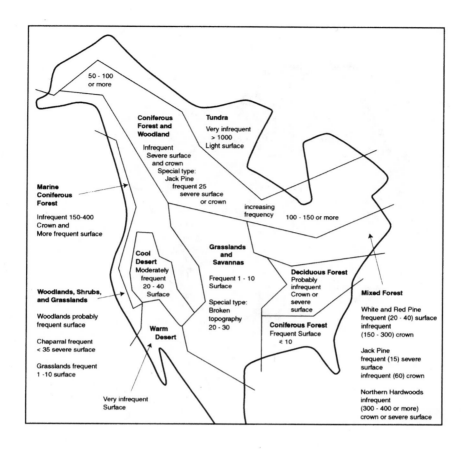

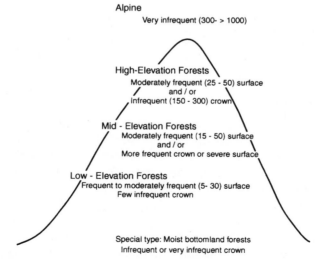

Figure 1.8. Generalized pre-European fire regimes for various areas of North America (Vale 1982).

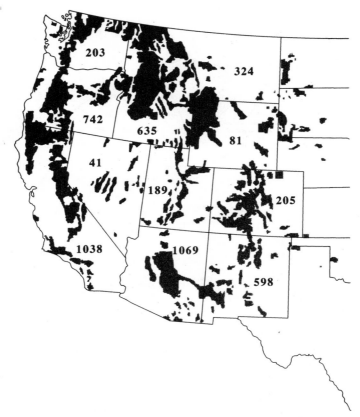

Figure 1.9. National forests and average number of lightning fires per state per year on national forest land in the eleven western states (data from *National Forests Fire Reports* for 11 years between 1971 and 1986).

A Brief Summary

Pre-European peoples humanized areas on the North American continent, including parts of the American West. Although someone seeking human impacts could find them almost anywhere, even in the western states, a more restrained search—one that recognizes that minor human imprints should not be seen as fundamentally modifying the natural world—would turn up humanized effects in a mosaic over the landscape. Evaluated by the three gradients of impact—modification intensity, spatial extent, and temporal persistence—the various humanizing activities altered the natural world differently. Settlements, agricultural landforms, and agricultural fields represent major changes in the landscape, although at modest spatial scales. Of these three impacts, moreover, some dwellings and constructed landforms have persisted long after they were no longer used (today we admire them in some of our National Parks, for example). Nonagricultural plant manipulations illustrate more modest alterations of nature, and at limited spatial and temporal scales (although not always—the planted palms in the southwestern desert persist indefinitely). Wood cutting seems similarly constrained in magnitude (but again, not always), variable in spatial scale, and rather ephemeral in temporal terms. The reduction in numbers of grazing ungulates by excessive hunting not only represents an impact unto itself but also potentially caused vegetation change in more than minor ways and over large areas, although the temporal persistence of such modifications without continued ungulate killing may have been fleeting.

The most likely impact on the landscape—an impact that might be said to alter the fundamental conditions of vegetation and ecosystems—is fire. Moreover, long-lived, fire-dependent trees may testify to a former burning regime centuries after the cessation of conflagrations. These characteristics, then, render Indian burning—identified by generations of anthropologically inclined geographers and other scientists as the human activity that has shaped landscapes for almost as long as people have been around (Stewart 1956)—to be key to those contemporary champions of the pre-European North American humanized landscape, probably because of fire's prehistoric association with people, its apparent ubiquity, and its potential as a landscape-scale factor.

Even so, Indian burning cannot be assumed, a priori, to determine the character of all environments on the continent. In fact, in the very region where fires were, and are, most important—the American West—questions remain as to what factor, fuels or ignitions, determined pre-European fire regimes. If the former, Indian burning may not have been an important modifier of nature; if the latter, Indian burning could have altered the landscape from what otherwise would have occurred.

Since it is both spatially extensive and temporally persistent, anthropogenic fire is the most likely candidate for major human modification of nature in pre-European Western North America, and, as such, it is a key to the pristine-versus-humanized landscape debate. But was Indian burning critical to the appearance of the American West before the arrival of Columbus? It is to this question that the essays in this book are directed.

Literature Cited

Anderson, K. 1993. Native Californians as ancient and contemporary cultivators. Pp. 151–174 in *Before the wilderness: Environmental management by native Californians*, ed. T. C. Blackburn and K. Anderson. Menlo Park, Calif.: Ballena.

Anonymous. 1991. America's crown jewels. *Life* 14 (6):10–28.

Bahre, C. 1991. *A legacy of change: Historic human impact on vegetation in the Arizona borderlands.* Tucson: University of Arizona Press.

Baisan, C., and T. Swetnam. 1997. *Interactions of fire regimes and land use in the central Rio Grande Valley.* Research paper RM-330. Fort Collins, Colo.: USDA Forest Service, Rocky Mountain Forest and Range Experiment Station.

Bakeless, J. 1961. *The eyes of discovery: The pageant of North America as seen by the first explorers.* New York: Dover.

Barbour, M., B. Pavlik, F. Drysdale, and S. Lindstrom. 1993. *California's changing landscapes: Diversity and conversation of California vegetation.* Sacramento: California Native Plant Society.

Bean, L., and S. Saubel. 1972. *Temalpakh (from the Earth): Cahuilla Indian knowledge and usage of plants.* Banning, Calif.: Malki Museum.

Bean, L., and D. Theodoratus. 1978. Western Pomo and northeastern Pomo. Pp. 289–305 in *Handbook of North American Indians,* vol. 8: *California,* ed. R. Heizer. Washington, D.C.: Smithsonian Institution.

Betancourt, J., J. Dean, and H. Hull. 1986. Prehistoric long-distance transport of construction beams, Chaco Canyon, New Mexico. *American Antiquity* 51:370–375.

Betancourt, J., E. Pierson, K. Rylander, J. Fairchild-Parks, and J. Dean. 1993. Influence of history and climate on New Mexico piñon-juniper woodlands. Pp. 42–62 in *Managing pinon-juniper ecosystems for sustainability and social needs,* ed. E. Aldon and D. Snow. General technical report RM-236. Fort Collins, Colo.: USDA Forest Service, Rocky Mountain Forest and Range Experiment Station.

Betancourt, J., W. Schuster, J. Mitton, and R. Anderson. 1991. Fossil and genetic history of a pinyon pine (*Pinus edulis*) isolate. *Ecology* 72:1685–1697.

Betancourt, J., and T. Van Devender. 1981. Holocene vegetation in Chaco Canyon, New Mexico. *Science* 214:656–658.

Blackburn, T., and K. Anderson. 1993. Introduction: Managing the domesticated environment. Pp. 15–26 in *Before the wilderness: Environmental management by native Californians,* ed. T. Blackburn and K. Anderson. Menlo Park, Calif.: Ballena.

Bohrer, V. 1983. New life from ashes: the tale of the burnt bush (*Rhus trilobata*). *Desert Plants* 5:122–124.

———. 1991. Recently recognized cultivated and encouraged plants among the Hohokam. *Kiva* 56:227–235.

———. 1992. New life from ashes II: A tale of burnt brush. *Desert Plants* 10:122–125.

Botkin, D. 1990. *Discordant harmonies: A new ecology for the twenty-first century.* New York: Oxford University Press.

Bradfield, M. 1971. *The changing pattern of Hopi agriculture.* Occasional paper no. 30. London: Royal Anthropological Institute of Great Britain and Ireland.

Budiansky, S. 1995. *Nature's keepers: The new science of nature management.* New York: Free Press.

Burwell, T. 1999. Environmental history of the lower montane pinon (*Pinus monophylla*) treeline, eastern California. Ph.D. diss., University of Wisconsin.

Callaway, D., J. Janetski, and O. Stewart. 1986. Ute. Pp. 336–367 in *Handbook of North American Indians*, vol. 11: *Great Basin*, ed. W. D'Azevedo. Washington, D.C.: Smithsonian Institution.

Callicott, B., and M. Nelson. 1998. *The great new wilderness debate*. Athens: University of Georgia Press.

Cartledge, T., and J. Propper. 1993. Pinon-juniper ecosystems through time: Information and insights from the past. Pp. 63–71 in *Managing pinon-juniper ecosystems for sustainability and social needs*. General technical report RM-236. Fort Collins, Colo.: USDA Forest Service, Rocky Mountain Forest and Range Experiment Station.

Chaddle, S., and C. Kay. 1991. Tall-willow communities on Yellowstone's northern range: A test of the "natural-regulation" paradigm. Pp. 231–262 in *The greater Yellowstone ecosystem: Redefining America's wilderness heritage*, ed. R. Keiter and M. Boyce. New Haven: Yale University Press.

Chase, A. 1987. *Playing God in Yellowstone*. San Diego: Harcourt Brace Jovanovich.

Cordell, L. 1997. *Archaeology of the Southwest*. San Diego: Academic Press.

Cronon, W. 1983. *Changes in the land*. New York: Hill and Wang.

Crown, P. 1987. Classic Period Hohokam settlement and land use in the Casa Grande Ruin area, Arizona. *Journal of Field Archaeology* 14:147–162.

Czech, B. 1995. American Indians and wildlife conservation. *Wildlife Society Bulletin* 23:568–573.

D'Azevedo, W. 1986. Washoe. Pp. 466–498 in *Handbook of North American Indians*, vol. 11: *Great Basin*, ed. W. D'Azevedo. Washington, D.C.: Smithsonian Institution.

deLaguna, F. 1990. Tlingit. Pp. 203–228 in *Handbook of North American Indians*, vol. 7: *Northwest coast*, ed. W. Suttler. Washington, D.C.: Smithsonian Institution.

Delcourt, P., H. Delcourt, C. Ison, W. Sharp, and K. Gremillion. 1998. Prehistoric human use of fire, the eastern agricultural complex, and Appalachian oak-chestnut forests: Paleoecology of Cliff Palace Pond, Kentucky. *American Antiquity* 63:263–278.

Denevan, W., ed. 1976. *The native population of the Americas in 1492*. 1st ed. Madison: University of Wisconsin Press.

———, ed. 1992. *The native population of the Americas in 1492*, 2d ed. Madison: University of Wisconsin Press.

———. 1992. The pristine myth: The landscape of the Americas in 1492. *Annals of the Association of American Geographers* 82:369–385.

Despain, D. 1990. *Yellowstone vegetation: Consequences of environment and history in a natural setting*. Boulder, Colo.: Roberts Rinehart.

Despain, D., D. Houston, M. Meagher, and P. Schullery. 1986. *Wildlife in transition: Man and nature on Yellowstone's northern range*. Boulder, Colo.: Roberts Rinehart.

Doolittle, W. 1992. Agriculture in North America on the eve of contact: A reassessment. *Annals of the Association of American Geographers* 82:386–401.

———. 2000. *Cultivated landscapes of native North America*. New York: Oxford University Press.

34   *Thomas R. Vale*

Fish, S., and P. Fish. 1992. The Marana community in comparative context. Pp. 97–105 in *The Marana community in the Hohokam world*, ed. S. Fish, P. Fish, and J. Madsen. Anthropological research paper no. 56. Tucson: University of Arizona Press.

———. 1994. Prehistoric desert farmers of the southwest. *Annual Review of Anthropology* 23:83–108.

Fish, S., P. Fish, and J. Madsen. 1985. A preliminary analysis of Hohokam settlement and agriculture in the northern Tucson basin. Pp. 75–100 in *Proceedings of the 1983 Hohokam symposium*, part I, ed. A. Dittert and D. Dove. Occasional paper no. 2. Phoenix: Phoenix Chapter of the Arizona Archaeological Society.

———. 1990. Analyzing regional agriculture: A Hohokam example. Pp. 189–218 in *The archaeology of regions: A case for full-coverage survey*, ed. S. Fish and S. Kowalewski. Washington, D.C.: Smithsonian Institution.

———. 1992. Evidence for large-scale agave cultivation in the Marana community. Pp. 73–87 in *The Marana community in the Hohokam world*, ed. S. Fish, P. Fish, and J. Madsen. Anthropological papers no. 56. Tucson: University of Arizona Press.

Fish, S., P. Fish, C. Miksicek, and J. Madsen. 1985. Prehistoric agave cultivation in southern Arizona. *Desert Plants* 7:107–113.

Flores, D. 1997. The west that was, and the west that can be. *High Country News* 29 (15):1, 6–7.

Floyd, M., and T. Kohler. 1990. Current productivity and prehistoric use of Pinon (*Pinus edulis*, Pinaceae) in the Dolores archaeological project area, southwestern Colorado. *Economic Botany* 44:141–156.

Fowler, C., and S. Liljeblad. 1986. Northern Paiute. Pp. 435–465 in *Handbook of North American Indians*, vol. 11: *Great Basin*, ed. W. D'Azevedo. Washington, D.C.: Smithsonian Institution.

Gomez-Pompa, A., and A. Kaus. 1992. Taming the wilderness myth. *BioScience* 42:271–279.

Gottfried, G., and P. Ffolliott. 1995. Stand dynamics on upper elevation pinon-juniper watersheds at Beaver Creek, Arizona. Pp. 38–45 in *Desired future conditions for pinon-juniper ecosystems*, ed. D. Shaw, E. Aldon, and C. LoSapio. General technical report RM-258. Fort Collins, Col.: USDA Forest Service, Rocky Mountain Forest and Range Experiment Station.

Hackenberg, R. 1983. Pima and Papago Ecological Adaptations. Pp. 161–177 in *Handbook of North American Indians*, vol. 10: *Southwest*, ed. A. Ortiz. Washington, D.C.: Smithsonian Institution.

Hajda, Y. 1990. Southwestern coast Salish. Pp. 503–517 in *Handbook of North American Indians*, vol. 7: *Northwest coast*, Washington, D.C.: Smithsonian Institution.

Hammett, J. 1992. The shapes of adaptation: Historical ecology of anthropogenic landscapes in the southeastern United States. *Landscape Ecology* 7:121–135.

Hess, K. 1993. *Rocky times in Rocky Mountain National Park: An unnatural history*. Niwot: University Press of Colorado.

Jennings, J. 1966. *Glen Canyon: A summary.* Anthropological papers no. 81. Salt Lake City: Department of Anthropology, University of Utah.

Kay, C. 1994. Aboriginal overkill: the role of native Americans in structuring western ecosystems. *Human Nature* 5:359–398.

———. 1995a. An alternative interpretation of the historical evidence relating to the abundance of wolves in the Yellowstone ecosystem. Pp. 77–84 in *Ecology and conservation of wolves in a changing world*, ed. L. Carbyn, S. Fritts, and D. Seip. Edmonton: Canadian Circumpolar Institute, University of Alberta.

———. 1995b. Browsing by native ungulates: Effects on shrub and seed production in the greater Yellowstone ecosystem. Pp. 310–320 in *Proceedings: Wildland shrub and arid land restoration symposium*, ed. B. Roundy, E. McArthur, J. Haley, and D. Mann. General technical report INT-315. Ogden, Utah: USDA Forest Service, Intermountain Research Station.

———. 1997a. Aboriginal overkill and the biogeography of moose in western North America. *Alces* 33:141–164.

———. 1997b. Bison myths, "natural regulation," and native hunting: A solution to the Yellowstone bison problem. On the Web at *http://www.webcom.com/gallatin/buffalo/kay.html.*

———. 1997c. The condition and trend of aspen, *Populus tremuloides*, in Kootenay and Yoho National Parks: Implications for ecological integrity. *Canadian Field-Naturalist* 111:607–616.

———. 1997d. Viewpoint: Ungulate herbivory, willows, and political ecology in Yellowstone. *Journal of Range Management* 50:139–145.

Kay, C., and S. Chaddle. 1992. Reduction of willow seed production by ungulate browsing in Yellowstone National Park. Pp. 92–99 in *Proceedings: Symposium on ecology and management of riparian shrub communities*, ed. W. Clary, E. McArthur, D. Bedunah, and C. Wambolt, General technical report INT-289. Odgen, Utah: USDA Forest Service, Intermountain Research Station.

Kay, C., and F. Wagner. 1994. Historical condition of woody vegetation on Yellowstone's northern range: A critical evaluation of the "natural regulation" paradigm. Pp. 151–169 in *Plants and their environments: Proceedings of the first biennial scientific conference on the greater Yellowstone ecosystem*, ed. D. Despain. Technical report NPS/NRYELL/NRTR-93/XX. Denver: National Park Service.

Kloor, K. 2000. Returning America's forests to their "natural" roots. *Science* 287:573–575.

Klopatek, J., R. Olson, C. Emerson, and J. Joness. 1979. Land-use conflicts with natural vegetation in the United States. *Environmental Management* 6:191–199.

Knapp, A., J. Blair, J. Briggs, S. Collins, D. Hartnett, L. Johnson, and E. Towne. 1999. The keystone role of bison in North American tallgrass prairie. *BioScience* 49:39–50.

Kohler, T. 1992. Prehistoric human impact on the environment in the upland North American southwest. *Population and Environment* 13:255–267.

Kohler, T., and M. Matthews. 1988. Long-term Anasazi land use and forest reduction: A case study from southwest Colorado. *American Antiquity* 53:537–564.

Lahren, S. 1998. Kalispel. Pp. 283–296 in *Handbook of North American Indians*, vol. 11: *Great Basin*, ed. W. D'Azevedo. Washington, D.C.: Smithsonian Institution.

Lawton, H., P. Wilke, M. DeDecker, and W. Mason. 1976. Agriculture among the Paiute of Owen's Valley. *Journal of California Anthropology* 3:13–50.

Malinowski, S., ed. 1998a. *Gale encyclopedia of Native American tribes*, vol. 2, *Great Basin, Southwest, Middle America*. Detroit: Gale.

———. 1998b. *Gale encyclopedia of Native American tribes*, vol. 3, *Arctic, Subarctic, Great Plains, Plateau*. Detroit: Gale.

Masse, W. 1981. Prehistoric irrigation systems in the Salt River Valley, Arizona. *Science* 214:408–415.

Matson, R., W. Lipe, and W. Hasse. 1988. Adaptational continuities and occupational discontinuities: The Cedar Mesa Anasazi. *Journal of Field Archaeology* 15:245–264.

McCarthy, H. 1993. Managing oaks and the acorn crop. Pp. 213–228 in *Before the wilderness: Environmental management by native Californians*, ed. T. Blackburn and K. Anderson. Menlo Park, Calif.: Ballena.

Meagher, M., and D. Houston. 1998. *Yellowstone and the biology of time: Photographs across a century*. Norman: University of Oklahoma Press.

Mills, L., M. Soulé, and D. Doak. 1993. The keystone-species concept in ecology and conservation. *BioScience* 43:219–224.

Minnis, P. 1978. Paleoethnobotanical indicators of prehistoric environmental disturbance: A case study. Pp. 347–366 in *The nature and status of ethnobotany*, ed. R. Ford, Ann Arbor: Museum of Anthropology, University of Michigan.

———. 1985. *Social adaptation to food stress: A prehistoric southwestern example*. Chicago: University of Chicago Press.

Mladenoff, D., and F. Stearns. 1993. Eastern hemlock regeneration and deer browsing in the northern Great Lakes region: A re-examination and model simulation. *Conservation Biology* 7:889–900.

Motsinger, T. 1998. Hohokam roads at Snaketown, Arizona. *Journal of Field Archaeology* 25:89–96.

Muir, J. 1901. *Our national parks*. Boston: Houghton, Mifflin. *National Forests Fire Report*. 1971–1986. Washington, D.C.: USDA Forest Service.

Neumann, T. 1985. Human-wildlife competition and the passenger pigeon: Population growth from system destabilization. *Human Ecology* 13:389–410.

———. 1989. Human-wildlife competition and prehistoric subsistence: The case of the eastern United States. *Journal of Middle Atlantic Archaeology* 5:29–57.

———. 1995. The structure and dynamics of the prehistoric ecological systems in the eastern woodlands: Ecological reality versus cultural myths. *Journal of Middle Atlantic Archaeology* 11:125–138.

Nichols, R., and D. Smith. 1965. Evidence of prehistoric cultivation of Douglas-fir trees at Mesa Verde. Pp. 57–64 in Contributions of the Wetherill Mesa archaeological project, ed. H. Osborne, *Memoirs of the Society for American Archaeology*, no. 19. Salt Lake City: Society for American Archaeology.

Orcutt, J. 1986. Climate, population, and resource supply in the Middle Canyon area. Pp. 1051–1088 in *Dolores archaeological program: Anasazi com-*

munities at Dolores: Middle Canyon area, ed. A. Kane and C. Robinson. Denver: Bureau of Reclamation.

Ortiz, B. 1993. Contemporary California basket-weavers and the environment. Pp. 195–211 in *Before the wilderness: Environmental management by native Californians*, ed. T. Blackburn and K. Anderson. Menlo Park, Calif.: Ballena.

Patencio, F. 1943. *Stories and legends of the Palm Springs Indians*. Palm Springs, Calif.: Palm Springs Desert Museum.

Peri, D., and S. Patterson. 1993. "The basket is in the roots, that's where it begins." Pp. 175–193 in *Before the wilderness: Environmental management by native Californians*, ed. T. Blackburn and K. Anderson. Menlo Park, Calif.: Ballena.

Pickett, S. T. A., and M. McDonnell. 1993. Humans as components of ecosystems: A synthesis. Pp. 310–316 in *Humans as components of ecosystem*, ed. M. McDonnell and S. T. A. Pickett. New York: Springer-Verlag.

Pilling, A. 1978. Yurok. Pp. 137–154 in *Handbook of North American Indians*, vol. 8: *California*, ed. R. Heizer. Washington, D.C.: Smithsonian Institution.

Pollan, M. 1991. *Second nature: A gardener's education*. New York: Dell.

Power, M., D. Tilman, J. Estes, B. Menge, W. Bond, L. Mills, G. Daily, J. Castilla, J. Lubchenco, and R. Paine. 1996. Challenges in the quest for keystones. *BioScience* 46:609–620.

Pyne, S. 1982. *Fire in America: A cultural history of wildland and rural fire*. Princeton: Princeton University Press.

Samuels, M., and J. Betancourt. 1982. Modeling the long-term effects of fuelwood harvests on pinyon-juniper woodlands. *Environmental Management* 6:505–515.

Sauer, C. 1947. Early relations of man to plants. *Geographical Review* 37:1–25.

———. 1950. Grassland climax, fire, and man. *Journal of Range Management* 3:16–21.

———. 1952. *Agricultural origins and dispersals*. Bowman Memorial Lectures, Series 2. New York: American Geographical Society. Reprinted 1972 as *Seeds, spades, hearths, and herds: The domestication of animals and foodstuffs*. Cambridge: MIT Press.

Shaw, J. 1995. How many bison originally populated western rangelands? *Rangelands* 17:148–150.

Shipek, F. 1993. Kumeyaay plant husbandry: Fire, water, and erosion control systems. Pp. 379–400 in *Before the wilderness: Environmental management by native Californians*, ed. T. Blackburn and K. Anderson. Menlo Park, Calif.: Ballena.

Silver, S. 1978. Shastan Peoples. Pp. 211–224 in *Handbook of North American Indians*, vol. 8: *California*, ed. R. Heizer, Washington, D.C.: Smithsonian Institution.

Snow, D. 1995. Microchronology and demographic evidence relating to the size of pre-Columbian North American Indian populations. *Science* 268:1601–1604.

Spier, R. 1978a. Foothill Yokuts. Pp. 471–484 in *Handbook of North American Indians*, vol. 8: *California*, ed. R. Heizer. Washington, D.C.: Smithsonian Institution.

————. 1978b. Monache. Pp. 426–436 in *Handbook of North American Indians*, vol. 8: *California*, ed. R. Heizer. Washington, D.C.: Smithsonian Institution.

Statistical abstract of the United States. 1997. Washington, D.C.: U.S. Government Printing Office.

Steller, T. 1995. Dakota impacts on original vegetation of Minnesota. Master's thesis, Department of Geography, University of Wisconsin.

Stevens, W. 1993. An Eden in ancient America? Not really. *New York Times*, March 30.

Stewart, J. 1929. Irrigation without agriculture. *Papers of the Michigan Academy of Science, Arts, and Letters* 12:149–156.

Stewart, K. 1983. Mojave. Pp. 55–70 in *Handbook of North American Indians*, vol. 10: *Southwest*, ed. A. Ortiz. Washington, D.C.: Smithsonian Institution.

Stewart, O. 1956. Fire as the first great force employed by man. Pp. 115–133 in *Man's role in changing the face of the Earth*, ed. W. Thomas. Chicago: University of Chicago Press.

Stiger, M. 1979. Mesa Verde subsistence patterns from Basketmaker to Pueblo III. *Kiva* 44:133–144.

Suttles, W., and B. Lane. 1990. "Southern Coast Salish." Pp. 485–502 in *Handbook of North American Indians*, vol. 7: *Northwest coast*, ed. W. Suttles. Washington, D.C.: Smithsonian Institution.

Swetnam, T., and C. Baisan. 1996. Historical fire regime patterns in the southwestern United States since A.D. 1700. Pp. 11–32 in *Fire effects in southwestern forests*, ed. C. Allen. General technical report RM-286. Fort Collins, Colo.: USDA Forest Service, Rocky Mountain Forest and Range Experiment Station.

Thomas, D., L. Pendleton, and S. Cappannari. 1986. Western Shoshone. Pp. 262–283 in *Handbook of North American Indians*, vol. 11: *Great Basis*, ed. W. D'Azevedo. Washington, D.C.: Smithsonian Institution.

Trombold, C., ed. 1991. *Ancient road networks and settlement hierarchies in the new world*. Cambridge: Cambridge University Press.

Tuggle, H., and J. Reid. 1984. Fourteenth century Mogollon agriculture in the Grasshopper region of Arizona. Pp. 101–110 in *Prehistoric agricultural strategies in the southwest*, ed. S. Fish and P. Fish. Anthropological research paper no. 33. Tempe: Arizona State University Press.

Ubelaker, D. 1988. North American Indian population size, A.D. 1500–1985. *American Journal of Physical Anthropology* 77:289–294.

United States Forest Service. 1990. *An analysis of the timber situation in the United States, 1989–2040*. General technical report RM-99. Fort Collins, Colo.: USDA Forest Service, Rocky Mountain Forest and Range Experiment Station.

Vale, T. 1982. *Plants and people: Vegetation change in North America*. Washington, D.C.: Association of American Geographers.

————. 1998. The myth of the humanized landscape: An example from Yosemite National Park. *Natural Areas Journal* 18:231–236.

————. 2000. Pre-Columbian North America: Pristine or humanized—or both? *Ecological Restoration* 18:2–3.

Vankat, J. 1979. *Natural vegetation of North America: An introduction.* New York: John Wiley.

Vivian, R. 1974. Conservation and diversion: Water-control systems in the Anasazi southwest. Pp. 95–112 in *Irrigation's impact on society*, ed. T. Downing and M. Gibson. Anthropological papers of the University of Arizona. Tucson: University of Arizona Press.

Vogl, R. 1974. Effects of fire on grasslands. Pp. 139–194 in *Fire and ecosystem*, ed. T. Kozlowski and C. Ahlgren. New York: Academic Press.

West, E. 1995. *The way to the West: Essays on the Central Plains.* Albuquerque: University of New Mexico Press.

Whitney, G. 1994. *From coastal wilderness to fruited plain: A history of environmental change in temperate North America from 1500 to the present.* Cambridge: Cambridge University Press.

Williams, M. 1993. An exceptionally powerful biotic factor. Pp. 24–39 in *Humans as components of ecosystem*, ed. M. McDonnell and S. Pickett. New York: Springer-Verlag.

Wilshusen, R., M. Churchill, and J. Potter. 1997. Prehistoric reservoirs and water basins in the Mesa Verde region: Intensification of water collection strategies during the great Pueblo Period. *American Antiquity* 62:664–681.

Wilson, N., and A. Towne. 1978. Nisenan. Pp. 387–397 in *Handbook of North American Indians*, vol. 8: *California*, ed. R. Heizer. Washington, D.C.: Smithsonian Institution.

Winter, J., and P. Hogan. 1986. Plant husbandry in the Great Basin and adjacent northern Colorado Plateau. Pp. 117–44 in *Anthropology of the desert West: Essays in honor of Jesse D. Jennings*, ed. C. Condie and D. Fowler. Anthropological papers no. 110. Salt Lake City: Department of Anthropology, University of Utah.

Woodbury, R. 1961. Prehistoric agriculture at Point of Pines, Arizona. *Memoirs of the Society for American Archaeology*, no. 17. Salt Lake City: Society for American Archaeology.

Wyckoff, D. 1977. Secondary forest succession following abandonment of Mesa Verde. *Kiva* 42:215–231.

Zimmerer, K. 1996. *Changing fortunes: Biodiversity and peasant livelihood in the Peruvian Andes.* Berkeley: University of California Press.

———. 2000. The reworking of conservation geographies: Nonequilibrium landscapes and nature-society hybrids. *Annals of the Association of American Geographers* 90:356–369.

INDIANS AND FIRE IN THE ROCKY MOUNTAINS: THE WILDERNESS HYPOTHESIS RENEWED

William L. Baker

In some sectors, it is commonplace today to hear the generalization that landscapes throughout the world were modified by pre-Euro-American people, and wilderness relatively free of human influences did not exist. Proponents of this view often also suggest that wilderness is an artificial, modern construct, rather than a reality of the preindustrial world, which, they would argue, was nearly everywhere transformed by burning, agriculture, and other aboriginal land uses. This generalization is not supported by the available evidence about use of fire by Indians in the Rocky Mountains. First, ignitions by Indians may often have been ineffective, due to the rarity of suitable conditions for fire to spread following ignition. Ignitions by Indians were also probably numerically insignificant relative to lightning ignitions. These constraints to significant Indian influence on fire regimes are lessened at lower elevations, particularly in the northern Rockies. Second, before widespread Euro-American influence, the Rockies were populated by only about 30,000 people, about three-fourths of whom were living in what is now Montana. Finally, much of the purported evidence suggesting widespread Indian use of fire is from early accounts by Euro-American scientists, explorers, and settlers. These sources are shown here to be unreliable, as Euro-Americans at this time did not understand how frequently fires are ignited by lightning. More reliable Indian oral histories, the few reliable accounts from Euro-Americans, and tree-ring studies all do suggest that Indians influenced the fire regime in low-elevation valleys and along travel routes in the northern Rockies. Reliable evidence of burning by Indians is generally absent throughout the rest of the Rocky Mountains. Given the fragmentary nature of the evidence, it would be premature to draw sweeping conclusions about Indian use of fire, but the burden of proof must shift to those who would counter the most likely hypothesis: Indians were a small part of a large Rocky Mountain wilderness, with a fire regime in much of the mountains essentially free of human influence for millennia.

> In virtually every pre-modern society there has been a part of its territory that was its wildest place, the least-visited, the most mysterious; and that area—on whatever scale—is the working wilderness of that society. When contemporary Indians say "We had no wilderness," they are speaking in terms of recent bureaucratic use of the word. In truth they all had areas which were their "wildest spaces." (Snyder 1998:38)

Introduction

Interpretation of the magnitude and extent of burning of Rocky Mountain forests and grasslands in the United States by Indians is constrained by the fragmentary and uncertain nature of evidence from a brief window of history. Yet, how we interpret Indian fires may be fundamental to the direction and meaning of our land management practices. Some argue that nearly all American lands, including Rocky Mountain ecosystems, were significantly manipulated by Indians, and there was effectively no land free of human influences (e.g., Stewart 1954; Pyne 1982; Denevan 1992a; Schrader-Frechette and McCoy 1995). An implication of this perspective is that we are morally free to manipulate the landscape as we see fit; we may choose a desired future condition based on our likes and dislikes, as there is no moral imperative from the past (e.g., Schrader-Frechette and McCoy 1995). Others, such as Snyder, argue that there was always unmanaged country, wilderness free of Indian influences, even if Indians managed some parts of their environment intensively (e.g., Vale 1998). Proponents of this perspective often suggest that the natural dynamics of pre-Euro-American landscapes should guide our land management (e.g., Swanson et al. 1994). Recently, the Indians themselves have joined the discussion, arguing that they have occupied the country since the beginning, but are not responsible for massive extinctions and land transformations attributed to them by non-native scientists and writers, who may have ulterior motives (Deloria 1995).

Nonnative scientists, explorers, and early settlers are a primary source about Indian influences on the land, and it is thus appropriate to consider their motives and understanding before accepting the information they provide. Nonnatives were probably not disinterested and fully objective observers of people whose land they coveted. However, a more surprising shortcoming of these early observers, elaborated here, is their ignorance of lightning fires. Other sources of information, such as fire history and paleoecological studies, also have limitations. It is difficult, for example, to exclude alternative explanations (e.g., climatic change) for past changes in fire regimes thought to be related to burning by Indians.

Recent summaries, evaluating these and other sources of information, imply widespread Indian influence on vegetation in North America generally and in the American West specifically, including the Rocky Mountains. The perspectives in these summaries may be categorized into four general models. First, the "pervasive significant model" sees burning by Indians as universal in areal extent and consistently significant as an influence on vegetation. For example, Arno et al. (1997:19) conclude: "Recent ecological and anthropological evaluations suggest that aboriginal burning was an important component of many historical fire regimes in western and central North America." This perspective is echoed by Barrett (1994:73–74): "Indians . . . throughout western North America, frequently ignited fires inadvertently and by design." Second, the "spatially varying model" portrays burning by Indians as everywhere important in modifying vegetation but as uneven spatially in the degree of that modification:

> Clearly the most humanized landscapes of the Americas existed in those highland regions where people were the most numerous. . . . Finally, there were the immense grasslands, deserts, mountains, and forests elsewhere, with populations that were sparse or moderate, with landscape impacts that mostly were ephemeral or not obvious but nevertheless significant, as in Amazonia and the northeastern U.S. (Denevan 1992a:379)

Third, the "varying significance model" describes a spatial landscape mosaic, with vegetation conditions in some locales modified in important ways by Indian burning but in other places not so modified or not affected at all. Arno (1980:465), for example, offered an earlier, more qualified synopsis, suggesting that Indian influences were not so pervasive:

> Evidently, in many forests of the western United States, the fire regime in operation for at least several centuries prior to European settlement included both lightning- and Indian-caused ignitions, some of the latter being purposeful burns. Conversely, in many forests, lightning alone may have been the principal ignition source.

Finally, the "enhancing model" argues that Indian burning may have hastened in time, or expanded in space, vegetation transformations primarily brought on by changing climate conditions. For example, Russell (1997:79–80) asserts:

> It is unlikely that humans at the hunter-gatherer stage modified vegetation from fire-resistant to fire-prone without a concomitant change to a climate more favorable to pyrophytic vegetation. On the other hand, humans must have hastened and expanded changes that were stimulated by climatic change.

Questions about pre-Euro-American forests of the Rocky Mountains arise from this characterization of perspectives. Which of these models seems most appropriate for the Rocky Mountain region? Might different parts of the Rocky Mountains conform to different models? Are these models still supported if unreliable Euro-American historical accounts are excluded? It is these questions that are addressed in this chapter.

The effects of burning by Indians are controlled by the burnability of the native vegetation, the local climate, the population density of Indians, and the cultural activities and development of the tribes (Russell 1997). Thus it is important to consider the vegetation and climate contributions to fires in the Rocky Mountains, and the Indians themselves, before reviewing the historical and other evidence of actual burning by Indians.

Climate and Fires in the Rocky Mountains

At the extremes, fire regimes may be controlled by either fuel or fire weather. In dry chaparral and mixed conifer forests of Baja California, the fire regime is thought to be predominantly fuel driven, since ignitions are abundant, but fire can seldom occur until sufficient fuel buildup takes place (Minnich et al. 1993). In contrast, in the more humid environment of subalpine forests in western Canada, fuel buildup is less important, since fires cannot spread until appropriate and rare fire weather arrives (Bessie and Johnson 1995). In fuel-controlled fire regimes, added ignitions by humans are comparatively unimportant, since there are already sufficient ignitions to keep pace with fuel buildup. In weather-controlled fire regimes, supplemental ignitions are probably also relatively unimportant, as ignited fires simply do not spread unless weather conditions are appropriate. However, when weather is suitable for fire spread, additional ignitions can be effective.

Some authors have suggested that lightning is seldom limiting to fire occurrence in some environments (Swetnam and Baisan 1996; chapter 5, this volume), but this is less clear for the Rockies. The Rockies have about 0.5 to 3.0 lightning strikes per square kilometer per year, which is low relative to high lightning areas in the United States, such as Florida and the Midwest (Orville 1994; Orville and Silver 1997). Lightning increases with elevation and toward the south in the Rockies, so the lower elevations, especially in the northern Rockies, may have lightning-limited fire regimes (Baker, in press). The percentage of fires ignited by lightning remains high in the Rocky Mountains (Figure 2.1) relative to more populated areas (Komarek 1967), in spite of the population increase in the Rocky Mountain states since Euro-American settlement.

Several studies identify climate-fire relationships that suggest climate is the predominant factor controlling Rocky Mountain fire regimes, especially in the subalpine zone. In the subalpine zone of the Rocky Mountains, where lodgepole pine, Engelmann spruce, and subalpine fir dominate, ignitions that lead to very small smoldering fires are frequent, but fires seldom spread far until high temperatures, drought, and often windy weather conditions arrive (Kipfmueller 1997; Baker, in press). This suggests a more weather-controlled than fuel- or ignition-controlled fire regime, just as in similar environments in western Canada (Bessie and Johnson 1995). However, this weather control does not prevent human-caused ignitions from having significant impact during suitable drought episodes (e.g., Peirce 1915). In northern Alberta, on the other hand, Indian informants said that they did not burn under drought conditions and seldom burned in boreal forests at all (Lewis 1977).

In the montane zone, where ponderosa pine and Douglas fir dominate, climate control is also evident but less clear. One study in Idaho suggests a fire may ignite for each twenty-four to forty-two lightning strikes in Douglas-fir and ponderosa pine forests (Meisner et al. 1994). In studies in Colorado and elsewhere in the northern Rockies, the number of lightning-ignited fires per 400,000 ha is two to twenty-five times higher in the montane than the subalpine zone (Baker, in press). In a

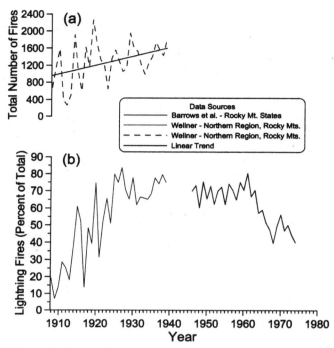

Figure 2.1. Trends in fires in the Rocky Mountains. a. Total number of fires in the northern Rocky Mountains (Wellner 1970) between 1908 and 1939 and a linear trend fit to these data. b. Percentage of total fires that are lightning-ignited fires, occurring in the northern Rocky Mountains (Wellner 1970) between 1908 and 1939 (light line) and in the Rocky Mountain states (Barrows et al. 1976) between 1946 and 1974 (dark line). The Rocky Mountain states are defined by Barrows et al. as Arizona, Colorado, Idaho, Kansas, Montana, Nebraska, Nevada, New Mexico, North Dakota, South Dakota, Utah, and Wyoming.

link with El Niño-Southern Oscillation, high precipitation 1–3 years prior to dry years may lead to abundant fine fuels and increased fires during dry years (Veblen et al. 2000). Certainly, in the montane zone, dry conditions that might allow fires to spread are more frequent than in the subalpine. In similarly dry southwestern montane forests, Swetnam and Baisan (1996) argue that, with the exception of unusual places and time periods, the number of ignitions is not limiting, and the fire regime is controlled by fuels and climate. However, in the northern Rockies, where lightning incidence is about one-third that in the southern Rockies and Southwest (Orville 1994), fires in the montane zone may be much more lightning-limited. In summary, then, the montane zone may be subdivided into distinctive regions: in the southern Rockies, ignitions may not be limiting (and supplemental ignitions by Indians less important), but in the northern Rockies, ignitions might be limiting (and thus additional ignitions by Indians more important).

The Indians and Their Recent History

Indians have occupied the Rocky Mountains, and their populations have fluctuated, since at least the end of the Pleistocene (Larson and Francis 1997). Most relevant to the present discussion, however, are characteristics of these peoples in more recent centuries.

History since A.D. 1500

Indian distribution and cultures in the Rocky Mountains shifted markedly after A.D. 1500. Changes occurred with the introduction of the gun, the horse, and trade goods, as well as Christian missionaries and devastating diseases (Walker and Sprague 1998). Together these led to changes in Indian distribution and cultural practices that may have influenced Indian use of fire (e.g., Fisher et al. 1987). The oldest tree-ring-based fire histories date from about the sixteenth century (Barrett et al. 1997), so the period since A.D. 1500 is an essential period in evaluating Indian influences on Rocky Mountain fire regimes.

Indian inhabitants on the western side of the Rocky Mountains have ancient roots, but many of the Plains Indians arrived more recently, aided by the horse (Box 2.1). In the northern Rockies the Blackfeet,

---

BOX 2.1. Indian Tribes of the Rocky Mountains in the middle 1800s, from north to south (Waldman 1985; D'Azevedo 1986; Walker 1998), by state and culture area (italics).

Western Montana *(Plateau)*	Eastern Montana *(Plains)*
Kootenai	Blackfoot Confederacy
Flathead and Pend d'Oreille	
(Salish)	
Western Wyoming-Eastern	
Idaho *(Great Basin)*	Eastern Wyoming *(Plains)*
Northern Shoshone and Bannock	Crow
Eastern Shoshone	Arapaho
Western Colorado *(Great Basin)*	Eastern Colorado *(Plains)*
Ute	Arapaho
	Cheyenne
	Jicarilla

Cheyenne, and Arapahos share northern origins, but the Blackfeet split from these other tribes long ago. Unlike most other Plains Indians, the Blackfeet lived on the northwestern plains for centuries (Ewers 1958). Origins of the Kootenai are obscure, but they too have long lived in their present location (Hungry Wolf and Hungry Wolf 1989; Brunton 1998). The Salish-speaking Flatheads and Pend d'Oreille have been in their present location since at least the 1600s, although until about 1700 they also occupied mountain areas east of the Continental Divide in Montana (Malouf 1998). The western side of the Continental Divide from the present Montana-Wyoming border south to the New Mexico border has long been dominated (probably since about A.D. 1100–1300) by Shoshone, Bannock, and Utes who all share links to the Aztecs of Mexico (Janetski 1987; Cassells 1997). Navajos may have been present in part of southwestern Colorado between about A.D. 1500 and 1756, when they were pushed south by the Utes (Cassells 1997). On the eastern Plains in Colorado the earliest Indians (since about A.D. 1300 or earlier) were Jicarilla (Apaches) (Crum 1996; Cassells 1997).

Horse acquisition occurred in a wave from Spanish settlements in New Mexico over the period from about 1650 to 1750, but the gun also played a significant role in tribal transformations. The Utes had horses by the 1650s, the Shoshone by 1700–1720, the Flathead and Pend d'Oreille by about 1730, and the Blackfeet by the 1730s (Haines 1938; Shimkin 1986). This acquisition marked the beginning of the nomadic Plains culture, which transformed most tribes in the Rocky Mountain region, but especially on the western Plains. The Crow Indians moved west from the Missouri River into the southern Montana plains about 1776 after the acquisition of the horse (Janetski 1987). The Sioux, from the eastern woodlands, moved west into the Black Hills–Bighorn Mountains region around 1765 (Fisher et al. 1987). The Apaches in eastern Colorado acquired horses early, but not guns, and by about 1730 armed Comanches had forced the Apaches south out of Colorado (Crum 1996). But the Comanches were also forced south and eventually out of Colorado by about 1830 by Arapahos and Cheyennes, who dominated the Plains of Colorado from about 1800 until the beginning of the reservations in the last half of the 1800s (Cassells 1997). The Arapaho, with ancestral roots in the Great Lakes area, probably came south in the late 1700s from the northern Plains in Canada, North Dakota, Montana, and Wyoming. The Cheyenne acquired the horse about 1760, then moved from their former territory on the Missouri River into the area from the Black Hills to the Bighorn Mountains of Wyoming, eventually spreading south into Colorado in the 1830s (Cassells 1997).

What are the ramifications of these cultural and distributional changes for Indian use of fire? It is likely that Indian attitudes toward fire varied

(Russell 1997), but while the Rocky Mountain tribes differed in their use of resources and their mobility, we have little evidence about how these differences may have influenced their use of fire. What evidence is available is indirect. For example, fire apparently was not a formal cultural element of the Salish and Kootenais, and does not show up in their art (Barrett 1980b).

The most significant change, perhaps, was the acquisition of the horse and the rise of the Plains culture, but it remains speculative how these affected Indian use of fire. Barrett (1980b) cites one person's belief that, before 1700, the Sheepeater Indians in central Idaho may have fought fire on the winter game ranges, because they could not afford to lose their forage resource. However, that possibility seems unlikely, given the Indians' apparent inability to extinguish fires effectively in such steep, dry terrain (Personal Communication, S. Barrett, November 1998). While the Salish living east of the Continental Divide long were bison hunters, and their hunting habits were possibly only modified by the arrival of the horse (Malouf 1998), the Kootenais, and perhaps also the western Salish, became more mobile and more often entered the Plains for bison after the arrival of the horse (Brunton 1998). Barrett and Arno (1982) speculated that burning by Indians might have increased after acquisition of the horse, since Indians may have needed to clear more travel corridors and manipulate forage, but these researchers could not detect such an increase in their fire-history analysis. The arrival of the Sioux in the Black Hills around 1770, along with their population increase and an increase in warfare, might explain an increase in fire frequency in that area, since the Sioux were displaced woodland people who used fire in hunting (Fisher et al. 1987).

Population and Depopulation

The potential impact of burning by Indians is not only a matter of culture and distribution, but also the size of the Indian population. Recent estimates of the total population of Indians in the United States or North America north of Mexico around A.D. 1500 vary from less than 2 million to more than 5 million (Thornton 1987; Ubelaker 1988; Denevan 1992b). Perhaps the best estimate is based on accumulating tribe-by-tribe data compiled by authors contributing to a handbook of North American Indians (Sturtevant 1978–1998). This estimate is that the population of North America north of Mexico was about 1.9 million in A.D. 1500 (Ubelaker 1988) (it is this number that Denevan [1992b] doubled to 3.8 million).

The decline in population near the Rockies began with Coronado and the Spanish in 1540. The chief causes were diseases, alcoholism, removal

and relocation, and genocide (Thornton 1987). The Pueblo population
of northern New Mexico had been reduced by about half by the time of
the Pueblo Revolt of 1680 (Thornton 1987). Ubelaker (1988) estimates
that depopulation did not affect the Great Basin and Plateau areas until
the 1700s, but about half the Plains' population was lost before 1600. A
significant smallpox epidemic, on the Plains and into the mountains,
which devastated the Nez Perce, Flathead, and Plains Kootenai, is
known from 1780 to 1781 (Boyd 1998). In 1801–1802 another smallpox epidemic spread along the Missouri River, devastating the Flathead,
Pend d'Oreille, and Crow, and it spread into and destroyed more than
half of the Plains tribes (Thornton 1987; Boyd 1998). An epidemic in
1836–1840 arrived via the Missouri River into the northern Plains,
killing about two-thirds of the Blackfeet and thousands of Crow, and yet
another occurred in this area in 1869–1870 (Ewers 1958). The Kootenai suffered significant outbreaks in 1855 and 1901 (Brunton 1998).
The Ute were affected by outbreaks in 1861–1862 and 1883 (Thornton
1987). The southern Cheyenne lost half their tribe in an 1849 cholera
epidemic (Thornton 1987).

The only estimate of the total Indian population of the Rockies itself
near European contact is Mooney's (1928) estimate for A.D. 1845 of
19,300 for the "Central Mountain Region." However, there was significant depopulation prior to 1845. Ubelaker's (1988) estimates for A.D.
1500 use the cultural areas in Sturtevant's (1978–1998) handbook, in
which the Rocky Mountains are part of the "Great Basin," "Plateau" and
"Plains" cultural areas. Ubelaker estimates the population in 1500 as
37,500 in the Great Basin, 77,950 in the Plateau, and 189,100 in the
Plains, for a total of 304,550, but only a small part of this population was
in the Rockies itself. In 1850, for example, for which Mooney's (1928)
estimate of the population of the Rockies is 19,300, Ubelaker estimates
the total population for the three cultural areas as 175,533. For the three
cultural areas, Ubelaker estimates the range of percent reductions
between 1500 to 1850, about the time of Mooney's (1928) estimate of
19,300 for the Rockies, as varying between 30 and 45 percent of the
1500 population. Assuming the mean percent reduction of 39 percent
also occurred in the Rockies, then the population in the Rockies itself in
A.D. 1500 may have been about 32,000. The Indian population of the
Rocky Mountain states in 1900 was still smaller: Montana, 11,343;
Wyoming, 1,686; and Colorado, 1,437 (Thornton 1987). Assuming
that state proportions in 1500 were similar to those in A.D. 1900, about
25,000 of the 32,000 were in Montana, with the remainder in Wyoming
(3,700) and Colorado (3,300).

Thus, Indian populations were significantly declining in the Rocky
Mountains at about the time that tribal distributions and cultural prac-

tices were adjusting to the acquisition of the horse and gun. The number of Indians is not necessarily directly related to the magnitude of burning, but some previous work has implied that where Indians are abundant their impacts are also abundant (Denevan 1992a). Indians were comparatively few in the Rocky Mountains relative to much of the rest of North America. The greater population in Montana relative to Wyoming and Colorado, if true, might suggest more influence of burning by Indians there, but by the smallpox epidemic of 1801–1802 burning by Indians may have been significantly diminished in any case.

Evidence of Burning by Indians

A variety of evidence is used to reconstruct the importance of burning by Indians. In this section, four different types of evidence are analyzed: accounts by early Euro-Americans, oral histories by Indians, ecological fire history data, and pollen/charcoal data.

Early Historical Accounts by Euro-Americans

Oral histories and records of early explorers and settlers have been used as evidence of burning by Indians. Often researchers identify or use all locations at which early journals and records suggest burning by Indians (Moore 1972; Barrett 1980a, 1980b; Gruell 1985a, 1985b). The number of journal references is suggestive of a general pattern, but there are reasons to question the validity of many of these records, as explained below.

For the Rocky Mountains, there is evidence from early historical accounts by Euro-Americans and Indians themselves that Indians burned intentionally for a variety of reasons and that Indian fires also accidentally escaped (Box 2.2). In western Montana, 77 percent of interviewed Indian descendants and early settlers who claimed knowledge of burning by Indians said Indians intentionally set fires (Barrett 1980a, 1980b). The most commonly cited reasons were to improve hunting and horse grazing, although accidental fires were also common (Barrett 1980a, 1980b). Barrett's (1980a, 1980b) results suggest that fire use by the Salish and Kootenai Indians was largely informal, in part because they roamed a large area and had little reason to manage fires carefully. This contrasts with the observation that Indians were highly systematic users of fire in northern Alberta's boreal forest (Lewis 1985).

BIASED OBSERVERS

There are several reasons to question the reliability of early Euro-American observations of burning by Indians. First, given the antagonism

BOX 2.2. Some reasons cited for burning by Indians in the Rocky Mountains.

Mentioned in the Rockies

Unextinguished campfires	Loope and Gruell 1973
Other accidental fires	Barrett 1980a, 1980b, 1981; Barrett and Arno 1982
Hunting	
Attract game to new vegetation	Barrett 1980a, 1980b, 1981; Barrett and Arno 1982; Arno 1976
Game drives	Houston 1973; Barrett 1980a, 1980b, 1981; Barrett and Arno 1982; Fisher et al. 1987
Stimulate fruiting of desired plants	Barrett 1980a, 1980b, 1981; Barrett and Arno 1982
Warfare	Fisher et al. 1987; Barrett 1981
Hostility toward Euro-Americans	Billings 1969; Gartner and Thompson 1972; Houston 1973; Loope and Gruell 1973; Honaker 1995
Facilitate travel	Barrett 1980a, 1980b, 1981; Barrett and Arno 1982
Improve grazing for horses	Barrett 1980a, 1980b, 1981, 1981; Barrett and Arno 1982
Protect forest from crown fires	Barrett 1980a, 1980b, 1981; Barrett and Arno 1982
Clearing campsites of tall vegetation that could conceal enemies	Barrett 1980a, 1980b, 1981; Barrett and Arno 1982
Communication	Barrett 1980a, 1980b, 1981; Barrett and Arno 1982

between Euro-American settlers and Indians, it is plausible that early Euro-American reports of burning by Indians could have been exaggerated to paint the Indians as reckless savages and poor land stewards who did not deserve to keep their land. Second, Euro-American reports may also have particularly noticed and inadvertently exaggerated burning by Indians because Euro-Americans generally feared and did not understand fire, whereas Indians apparently considered fires unremarkable (Barrett 1980b; Barrett and Arno 1982). These are merely plausible questions about the reliability of early accounts, and some are recognized as limitations by previous researchers (e.g., Barrett 1980a, 1980b; Gruell 1985a, 1980b).

IGNITIONS NOT OBSERVED

More significant than the observer bias, however, is the fact that seldom was the act of ignition actually observed (Gruell 1985b). The mere presence of Indians near fires that were burning is insufficient evidence that they ignited a fire, particularly since they may have been attracted to fires started by lightning (Choquette, Personal Communication, cited in Barrett 1980b) simply to hunt fleeing game or for other reasons. It is plausible that early Euro-Americans may not have been particularly interested in distinguishing the causes of fires and simply made a casual attribution based on circumstantial evidence (i.e., here is a fire; Indians are nearby; therefore, Indians set the fire).

Reliable first-hand accounts of ignition are typically a small percentage of the total accounts. For example, in an analysis of fires in the central grassland, Moore (1972:112) says: "For the 149 fires attributed to Indians, however, only about twenty seem to be based on an equally sound [first-hand] foundation. . . . the informational problem concerning Indian fires was largely a reflection of the fact that whites were rarely present when Indians set fire to the grass." Moore, however, analyzes all 149 ignitions as though they were caused by Indians, simply because Euro-Americans attributed them to Indians, when an argument can be made that only the reliable firsthand accounts should be used. If all 149 fires are used, Indian fires are 35.6 percent (149/418) of the total number of fires, but if only the 20 reliable accounts are used, Indian fires are 4.8 percent (20/418), a very large difference in the potential role of Indians as ignition agents, and undoubtedly in what would be revealed by an analysis of the 20, as opposed to 149, accounts.

IGNORANCE OF LIGHTNING FIRES

The largest problem, suggesting that early historical accounts by Euro-Americans are generally unreliable, is the surprising lack of mention of lightning fires, which implies that early Euro-Americans often failed to correctly identify the cause of fires. Gruell (1985a:102) says that "very likely some lightning fires were inaccurately attributed to Indians." Gruell (1985a, 1985b) analyzed 145 early Euro-American accounts of fires from 1776 to 1900 in the western U.S. (Table 2.1). Gruell finds that "with the exception of a report by Ayres . . . , I found no mention of lightning fires" (Gruell 1985b:69). Similarly, Moore (1972) reports that of 418 records of fire in the central grassland only 1 was attributed to lightning (Table 2.1).

Many early Euro-American accounts, which fail to recognize light-

TABLE 2.1. Number of fires attributed to Indians, Whites, and lightning. Human-set fires are the total of Indian fires and White fires. Non-Indian fires could be either from Whites or lightning. Unknown means a cause was not identified. Numbers for Plummer (1912) and Barrows et al. (1976) are mean number of fires per year on public lands in the Rocky Mountain States, defined as Arizona, Colorado, Idaho, Kansas, Montana, Nebraska, Nevada, New Mexico, North Dakota, South Dakota, Utah, and Wyoming. For Plummer (1912) the National Forests are the only lands, whereas for Barrows et al. (1976) the lands considered are those protected by private, state, and federal agencies. Hough (1882) is for the whole United States.

Author	Gruell (1985a,b)	Moore (1972)	Hough (1882)	Plummer (1912)	Barrows et al. (1976)
Period	1776–1900	1535–1890	1880	1907–1911	1946–1974
Cause					
a. Indians	60 (41%)	149 (36%)			
b. Whites		96 (23%)		2,884 (91.4%)	3,321 (41.0%)
c. Human-set (a + b)		245 (59%)	464 (99%)	2,884 (91.4%)	3,321 (41.0%)
d. Lightning	1 (< 1%)	1 (< 1%)	3 (1%)	273 (8.6%)	4,781 (59.0%)
e. Non-Indian	7 (5%)				
f. Unknown	78 (54%)	172 (41%)			
g. Total	145 (100%)	418 (100%)		3,157 (100%)	8,102 (100%)

ning as a major source of ignition, are from educated, scientific observers and government explorers (see list in Table 1 of Gruell 1985a) who were generally attentive to detail. For example, the failure of an astute scientific observer and government employee (Leiberg 1900) to report the fact that fires could be started by lightning, rather than Indians, was noted earlier by Habeck (1972:27):

> Before the advent of whiteman, the main cause of forest burning is ascribed [by Leiberg] to Indians. Evidently Leiberg never witnessed forest fire ignitions caused by lightning; he fails to mention the possibility anywhere in his report, although frequent mention of fire is provided throughout his lengthy report. It is difficult to know whether Leiberg should be faulted for this serious omission in his observations.

However, Leiberg was not alone among educated and informed observers in failing to recognize the role of lightning. For example, an early U.S. Department of Agriculture Correspondent, who was asked to report to Hough (1882) on the extent and causes of fires in the correspondent's area, said:

> We have no forests in this portion of the West [Colfax County in northern New Mexico], excepting such timber thickets as occur in the mountains, and among these fires will sometimes appear more or less every year. They have been formerly charged to the Indians, and are yet. They are most apt to begin in the fall, and sometimes last for weeks. The Indians have been mostly removed to reservations, except a few stragglers who come back to hunt, but still these fires will rage and we cannot tell how they originate. (Hough 1882:199)

Indeed, all the correspondents reporting to Hough on fires in Dakota, Colorado, Montana, Idaho, Utah, Oregon, and Washington blame these fires on hunters, campers, and Indians, with no mention of lightning (Hough 1882). In the United States as a whole, the total reports from Hough's correspondents as to causes include 464 fires that are "the direct or incidental act of man" and only 3 that are from "natural causes–lightning" (Hough 1882:206). Similarly, in 1901 C. S. Crandall, a forester with the U.S. Department of Agriculture, analyzed fires and tree regeneration in northern Colorado and reported on the causes of forest fires in this area:

> Forest fires, with a few possible exceptions may be traced to human sources. It is claimed that lightning sometimes causes fires, and while this may be true, there is reason to believe that such instances are exceedingly rare. . . . Considering then that human agencies are the only causes deserving attention, forest fires may be started either intentionally or accidentally through carelessness. (Crandall 1901:12)

While it seems difficult for us to understand now, these accounts suggest that even informed observers in the late 1800s and early 1900s did not know how frequently fires could be started by lightning.

Moreover, this knowledge of the role of lightning appears to have grown rather slowly, until about the 1920s. A few decades after Hough's report, there appears to have been increased understanding, but still significant underestimation, of lightning fires in western forests. In the first systematic survey of the lightning fires between 1907 and 1911 in the National Forests of the western states (Plummer 1912), the number of fires and the percentage of fires attributed to lightning are very low relative to data from these same states for 1946–1974 (Barrows et al. 1976) (Table 2.1). The percentage of lightning-ignited fires in the Rocky Mountain states varied between about 40 and 85 percent between 1925 and 1974 (Figure 2.1), and averages about 63 percent (Komarek 1967), whereas early Euro-American accounts suggest that lightning was responsible for 1 percent or less of fires (Table 2.1). The total number of fires reported in the northern Rocky Mountains increased about 50 percent from 1908 to 1939 (Figure 2.1a), perhaps reflecting increasing ability to detect fires, but the percentage of these fires attributed to lightning increased about 700 percent during the same period (Figure 2.1b), suggesting a large increase in knowledge of lightning fires.

Even in the mid-1980s the ability of lightning to ignite fires in grasslands was still underestimated, suggesting that even today the importance of lightning as an agent of ignition may not be appreciated by some researchers evaluating the importance of ignitions by Indians. For example, Gruell (1985b:69), after citing several arguments about why lightning may have difficulty starting fires in grasslands, suggests that "presettlement lightning fires in grasslands were probably infrequent." Similarly, Moore (1972:111) concluded that since early Euro-American accounts rarely mentioned lightning as a cause of fires, then "it would seem that it was not generally regarded as important during the time period considered." Higgins (1984), however, reviewed recent evidence of observed lightning-ignited fires in four locations in the northern Plains and concluded that "these data demonstrate that lightning is a common cause of fires in northern mixed-grass prairie grasslands" (p. 101). Komarek (1964) showed that there were three times as many lightning-ignited fires as human-set fires in eastern Wyoming grasslands in 1960.

An alternative climatic explanation of the low percentage of lightning-ignited fires in early Euro-American accounts can probably be excluded. The Little Ice Age (LIA), from about 1350 to the mid-1800s, was likely cool and dry in the Rockies relative to current conditions (Petersen 1988, Fritz et al. 1994). Cooler, drier conditions may have led to less lightning during the LIA. Temperature and lightning occurrence are correlated, and a 30 percent increase in lightning-ignited fires in the Rocky Mountains can be expected from a 4.2°C rise in temperature (Price and Rind 1994). Since it was only about 0.5°C cooler during the LIA (Houghton et al. 1990), only a small decline in lightning-ignited fires might be expected from the cooler temperatures during the LIA.

Thus it appears that prior to the establishment of the National Forests and the beginning of systematic data collection and careful observation, most Euro-American observers, including early settlers, scientists, government explorers, and government researchers, generally did not appreciate the significance of lightning as a cause of forest fires. Some, perhaps many, clearly did not understand how frequently lightning can cause forest fires. The tendency to underestimate the importance of lightning in starting forest and grassland fires persisted into the early 1900s and even nearly to the present in the case of grassland fires. The consequence is that early Euro-American accounts that attribute fires to Indians are generally unreliable.

WHICH ACCOUNTS ARE RELIABLE?

Two criteria can identify early Euro-American accounts that are reliable enough to use in assessing the extent of burning by Indians. First, to attribute particular ignitions to Indians, Indians should have been actually observed, by disinterested parties with no clear motive for blaming the Indians, in the act of actually setting the fire, or Indians themselves should have reported that they set the fire. Some might object that this first criterion is too severe, as it makes reliable observations rare, but this is exactly the point—reliable observations *are* rare. Barrett (1980a, 1980b), Boyd (1986), Moore (1972), and others have some early accounts that meet this criterion, but a large percentage of Euro-American reports of burning by Indians used by these authors does not meet this criterion. For example, 7 of Barrett's (1981) 58 informants identified locations where burning occurred; of these 7 only 2 reported that Indians were actually seen lighting fires. In Moore's (1972) study, 87 percent of accounts that attribute fires to Indians do not meet this criterion. Second, given the failure of many early Euro-Americans to appreciate the extent to which lightning can cause forest fires, if the fire was not observed being set by Indians, it is essential to establish the credibility of an early observer. This can be done by presenting evidence that the observer was clearly aware that fires could be started by lightning, and that there are logical reasons for attributing the ignition to Indians rather than lightning. For example, if an observer aware of lightning fires detects a fire during a period that lacked lightning, if holdover fires (smoldering in duff) are unknown, and if Indians are observed in the area, then they are likely to have been the ignition source, as the alternative (lightning) can be effectively excluded. Using this second criterion will probably lead to the omission of most records where Indians are not actually observed setting the fire, as few early Euro-Americans appear to have been aware that lightning-ignited fires are common.

These two criteria significantly diminish the number of accounts that reliably indicate the magnitude and extent of burning by Indians in Rocky Mountain forests, but they do not refute that Indians did burn these forests and grasslands. Applying these two criteria may reduce the number of reliable cases so far as to suggest that burning by Indians was insignificant in the Rocky Mountains, but this conclusion is premature. The number of accounts by early Euro-American observers, whether reliable or not, does not indicate the extent and magnitude of burning by Indians, although this inference is commonly made or implied (e.g., Moore 1972; Barrett 1980a, 1980b: Figure 1; Gruell 1985a, 1985b). Early Euro-American observers were not intentionally seeking information about burning by Indians, were clearly uninformed about or not interested in ignition causes, and did not sample the ignition phenomenon to the degree that any sound, much less statistical, inference can be drawn about ignitions in the Rocky Mountains. While rather sweeping conclusions have been drawn in the past from this evidence by many researchers, few early historical accounts by Euro-Americans, whether early settlers, scientists, or government employees, can be reliably used to evaluate the extent to which Indians caused or did not cause fires in western U.S. landscapes.

Indian Oral History Evidence of Burning

To understand, in general, the burning practices of Indians, oral histories directly from Indians clearly provide more compelling information, superior to accounts by early explorers and settlers unaware of the role of lightning and potentially predisposed against Indians (Lewis 1985; Deloria 1995). Of course, just as Whites may have reasons to blame Indians for igniting fires, Indians could exaggerate their burning to underscore claims of traditional use. However, Indians may also be reticent toward and suspicious of non-Indian interviewers, and thus not provide as much information as Euro-American informants (Personal Communication, S. Barrett, November 1998).

Unfortunately, there are few oral histories from Indians, and they address only a few topics. Barrett (1980a) used a mixture of Indian and Euro-American sources, so it is not always possible to separate the Indian oral histories. Referring to the reports clearly attributed to Indians, he says:

> One Salish informant said her mother-in-law and others burned lichens that hang from trees to reduce the threat of wildfires spreading to the forest canopy. (p. 36)
>
> A Kootenai informant claimed fire also was used to protect medicine plants. His father was a shaman ("medicine man") and told him small ground fires were set to burn unwanted vegetation and to fireproof the area from wildfires. (p. 36)
>
> One Salish informant said Indians sometimes cleared overgrown trails with fire. (p. 37)

Romme et al. (1994:6), in discussing the San Juan Mountains in south-western Colorado, says: "Oral histories from elderly Ute people . . . indicates that the Utes set fires throughout the San Juan Mountain country until about the 1920s, when white settlers forced them to stop." Gartner and Thompson (1972:48) said:

> While plains Indians apparently burned the grasslands for various reasons, it appears doubtful that they burned the Black Hills forests. . . . Evidence suggesting that Indians tended to avoid the Black Hills was presented by Dodge. . . . One Indian, interviewed through an interpreter, stated that although he was 50 years old, and had been around the Hills nearly every day of his life, "He had never before ventured inside." He further stated that at times squaws cut lodgepoles and bucks sometimes ventured into the Hills to hunt, "but that these stops are very short." His reasons for Indians not entering the Black Hills were: (1) "The Hills were 'bad medicine,' and the abode of spirits," (2) there was no reason to enter except for lodge-poles; game was scarce and "more difficult to kill than that on the plains," (3) the thickets were "so dense that their ponies were lost if turned loose," and flies so bad that they were "tormented and worried out if kept tied up," (4) frequent rains were not liked by Indians, and (5) "that it thunders and lightnings with terrible force, tearing trees to pieces and setting fire to the woods."

Adequate oral histories require a reasonable sample size (e.g., Barrett 1980a, 1980b), rather than lone informants, as people may recall events and practices differently. Interviewers must also follow standard research protocols, or results may be anecdotal and biased (Personal Communication, S. Barrett, November 1998). Sample size for oral histories is often either not reported or is very small (e.g., Gartner and Thompson's 1972 quote from Dodge above) because isolated information was obtained anecdotally and simply reported uncritically. Now, with the passing of tribal elders born before Euro-American settlement, oral histories must rely upon second- or thirdhand recollections (i.e., offspring), and the opportunity for meaningful oral histories is all but gone. It is tempting to accept even fragmentary evidence from isolated oral history observations, particularly when the explanations that are offered are plausible. However, sample size, interview techniques, and possible bias must always be considered; inadequately sampled oral history explanations that appear plausible and compelling to one person may be rightfully challenged as insufficient by another. In the U.S. Rocky Mountains, only Barrett's (1980a, 1980b, 1981) study contains a large sample.

Fire History Evidence of Burning by Indians

Tree-ring-based fire history analyses are potentially free of many of the problems accompanying accounts by early Euro-Americans. I examined all published and a few unpublished fire histories for the Rocky Mountains. Quotes from those studies that mention burning by Indians, and citations to the studies, are in Box 2.3, and conclusions may be summarized as follows. Fire history evidence, in some cases, suggests that early observers erred in attributing fires to Indians. Fire history researchers have also suggested that, in some places, lightning is sufficient to explain the observed frequency of fires; Indian ignitions are not needed. However, fire frequency in areas of concentrated Indian use may exceed that in more remote, seldom-used areas with similar vegetation. There is some evidence that fires set by Indians were most common in the spring and fall. Ignitions by Indians may have been most common in lower-elevation valleys and hunting or travel zones, but heavily forested canyons and the subalpine zone may have been less or not at all influenced by burning by Indians. Changes in fire frequency may indicate changes in burning by Indians. Several authors remark, however, that it is difficult to partition out the Indian contribution to burning.

Fire history studies rely upon several lines of reasoning to establish the trends reported in Box 2.3 and summarized above. First, many fire history authors begin their discussion of the contribution of Indians to burning by mentioning the long Indian occupancy (i.e., thousands of years) (e.g., Loope and Gruell 1973; Barrett 1994; Arno et al. 1997). This clearly establishes the presence of Indians over the length of time that most post-Pleistocene Rocky Mountain forested landscapes have been in their present distribution (e.g., Whitlock 1993), but does not provide any assessment of the magnitude of impacts by Indians during this time.

Second, the occurrence, abundance, and timing of fire can be compared to expected trends for lightning fires in particular settings or by using spatial comparisons. For example, if fire frequencies are higher than expected, based upon the environmental setting (Arno et al. 1997), then supplemental ignitions by Indians have been suggested to explain the difference. The simple presence of abundant burned area is not evidence of burning by Indians unless the burned area exceeds the amount that could arise from lightning ignitions. Better control is obtained in Barrett's (1980a, 1981) and Barrett and Arno's (1982) comparison of fire frequencies in known areas of high Indian use with

BOX 2.3. Some themes in quotes from Rocky Mountain fire history studies that address Indian fires. I have included all quotes in a particular article where Indian influence or lack of influence is mentioned, rather than selecting quotes. I omitted citations that were in the quoted material. Quotes related to the purposes of Indian burning are not included here, but are summarized in Table 2.2. Where similar quotes are found in Barrett (1980a, 1980b) and Barrett and Arno (1982), I have included only the Barrett (1980a) quote.

Indians may have been blamed for an ignition, but lightning could also have been the cause

Billings 1969:195—southeastern Wyoming

"Hanna . . . states that the largest of these fires was set by the Ute Indians during the Indian wars of the late 1860's . . . my dendrochronologic evidence (from cross-sections of fire-scarred living trees) indicates that these areas were burned earlier (c. 1766, 1774, 1809) by smaller fires probably caused by lightning."

Romme et al. 1994:8—southwestern Colorado

"1879 . . . was also the year of the famous Lime Creek burn near Molas Pass. The Ute people traditionally have been blamed for setting this fire, but, given the weather conditions that must have prevailed that summer, it could easily have been started by lightning instead."

Indian ignitions not needed to explain fire frequencies: lightning and weather are sufficient

Loope and Gruell 1973:434—Jackson Hole, northwestern Wyoming

"Aboriginal man probably started fires, intentionally or inadvertently, but sufficient lightning fires have been ignited by late-Summer storms to assure the existence of fire-influenced forests with periodic cyclic disturbances without human ignition."

Arno and Davis 1980:23—northern Idaho

"On most subunits the period 1750 to 1900 probably reflects the general lightning fire frequencies prior to settlement by European man. The frequency of Indian-caused fires in these forests is unknown, but evidently such fires were of minor importance."

continues

BOX 2.3. *Continued*

Indian ignitions needed to explain fire frequencies that are higher than expected

Arno 1976:7—Bitterroot National Forest, western Montana

"Fires occurred almost twice as frequently throughout the Onehorse area. . . . Several threads of evidence suggest another reason for the higher fire frequency at Onehorse. . . . Indians preferred the main Bitterroot Valley grasslands adjacent to the Onehorse area."

Arno 1980:462—northern Rockies

"The north Bitterroot Valley data seem to represent unusually short fire-free intervals for the northern Rockies, possibly because of frequent Indian-set fires in the adjacent lowlands."

Arno et al. 1997:14—western Montana

"Another anomaly in the relationship of fire frequencies to site moisture arises at site B-4 (table 1). This site had very frequent fires and is immediately adjacent to the Bitterroot Valley where an earlier study suggests that Indian burning played a major role in increasing fire frequencies on the landscape. . . . Similarly, the historical fire regime of stand L-5 [Seeley Lake] may have had an important component of Indian burning for hundreds of years."

Barrett 1994:74—northeastern Yellowstone National Park, northwestern Wyoming

"Native Americans evidently supplemented the fire frequency in YNP's northern range."

Romme et al. 1994:6—southwestern Colorado

"The Turkey Springs area has been the site of human settlements, at least periodically, for several hundreds or even thousands of years. . . . The extremely short median fire intervals at this site during the 1500s and 1600s may reflect a preponderance of human ignitions."

Indian ignitions were most common outside the summer season or are more clearly attributable to Indians in these seasons

Arno 1980:462—northern Rockies

"It seems likely that Indian-set fires in the drier forest types occurred in late spring or early fall—largely outside of the severe mid-summer season."

Higgins 1984:103—foothills of the Black Hills, South Dakota

"Nearly all fires during the fall-winter period (October–March) reported in journals and letters from the Northern Great Plains region since ca. 1750 were probably caused by sources other than lightning strikes, most likely man."

Indian ignitions were most common in lower-elevation valleys and hunting/travel zones

Arno 1976:7—Bitterroot Valley

"According to Dr. C. Malouf, University of Montana, Missoula . . . Indians preferred the main Bitterroot Valley grasslands adjacent to the Onehorse area; therefore aboriginal burning probably would have been more common here than on the rather remote Tolan and West Fork study areas."

Arno 1980:462—northern Rockies

"The north Bitterroot Valley data seem to represent unusually short fire-free intervals for the northern Rockies, possibly because of frequent Indian-set fires in the adjacent lowlands."

Barrett 1980a:35—western Montana

"Most Indian fires occurred in valley grasslands and lower-elevation forests dominated by ponderosa pine, Douglas-fir, or western larch."

Barrett 1994:74—northeastern Yellowstone National Park, northwestern Wyoming

"In fact, early records . . . verify that Native Americans, miners, and others contributed to ignition frequency in YNP [Yellowstone National Park] until at least the turn of the 20th century, particularly in the hunting and travel zones of YNP's northern valleys."

Indian ignitions occurred, but were less important in (1) heavily forested canyons near lower-elevation valleys used by Indians, (2) the subalpine zone, and (3) large areas seldom used by Indians

McCune 1983:215—Bitterroot canyons, southwestern Montana

"The Salish Indians used fire in the Bitterroot Valley before European settlement . . . and it seems likely that some of these fires burned into the canyons. However, their burning practices may not have greatly influenced the fire regime of the canyons, since the Salish used the open valleys more than the heavily timbered canyons."

Romme and Despain 1989:13—Yellowstone National Park, northwestern Wyoming

"Archaeological studies completed to date . . . suggest that aboriginal populations on the high subalpine plateaus were small and transient, although people may have been more

continues

BOX 2.3. *Continued*

numerous at the lower elevations. This certainly suggests to us that the pattern of fires seen in Figure 1 is unrelated to human activities in the area we studied."

Arno 1985:83—western mountains

"Indians occasionally traveled through these habitats, and sometimes lit fires for route clearing or other purposes. In areas where subalpine forests occur directly above the major valleys, Indian fires no doubt spread upslope into them. Overall, however, it appears that lightning was the prevalent cause of fires in these forests simply because of their remoteness."

Change in fire frequency may reflect a change in the tribes occupying a region, warfare with other tribes, or simply increased human use

Fisher et al. 1987:254—Devil's Tower, northeastern Wyoming

"The sharp increase in fire frequency between 1770 and 1900 was unexpected. This period coincided with a time during which the Sioux took possession of the Black Hills from the Cheyenne, Kiowa and Crow. The Sioux entered the Black Hills area about 1765 and by 1823 they controlled the area S of the Missouri from the Black Hills to the Bighorn Mountains. . . . These early plains Sioux were displaced woodland people. They did not have many horses and did not know how to use those they possessed effectively in warfare or hunting. . . . In the prairie-forest border area from which the Sioux had recently migrated fire was widely used to drive game. There are few reports on the habits of the newly arrived Sioux in the Black Hills. We can only surmise that they continued to live in the forest as much as possible. They certainly would have quickly begun to hunt the buffalo. Again we can only surmise that they used the eastern woodland method of driving the animals into a river or over a break into a gully by means of fire. If either or both of these suppositions is true, it would help to account for the increase in fire frequency. The warfare between tribes, and later between the Sioux and Europeans, may have been enough to account for the increase in fires. . . . Before the Sioux migration, the northern plains away from the major rivers were sparingly used by the native people. The Sioux brought a population explosion to the area and dramatically increased use of minor streams. . . . This increased human occupation of the area may have also been a factor in the increased frequency of fires."

Partitioning out the Indian contribution to fire frequency is difficult

Arno et al. 1997:19—western Montana

"Moreover trying to partition out and remove the effects of aboriginal ignitions to define a conceptual 'natural' condition without human influence would no doubt be a highly speculative endeavor."

Houston 1973:1115—northern Yellowstone National Park, Wyoming

"It seems probable that aboriginal man contributed to the frequency of fires on the area, but a quantitative assessment of this contribution is not possible."

Nelson and England 1977:45—eastern Montana

"It is very difficult to reconstruct fire frequency accurately and even more difficult to separate cultural from climatic causes of fire."

Taylor 1974:70–71—Yellowstone National Park, Wyoming

"Undoubtedly, Indians set fires, but little direct evidence is currently available. The only published account of Indians setting fire was in 1886 when a small group from the Lehmi Reservation set two fires on the west border of the park. The role Indians played in causing fires in the park is still in question."

Loope and Gruell 1973:432—Jackson Hole, northwestern Wyoming

"It is possible only to speculate on the importance of aboriginal populations in influencing the past fire frequency in the Jackson Hole area."

that of more remote sites, during the same time period. This spatial comparison, with climate history similar in both areas, excludes the possibility that climatic fluctuations can be the primary cause of the observed differences, although it is difficult to show that climate is the same in both areas. Moreover, Barrett argues against an alternative explanation—that the valley bottoms might have higher fire frequencies simply because they receive more fires that spread into stands than do the more isolated, remote sites he studied. The opposite argument has also been used: if lightning ignitions are sufficient to explain the frequency of fire or abundance of burned area, then burning by Indians may be interpreted to be insignificant (Loope and Gruell 1973). However, fires set by Indians could still be at least minor contributors to fire regimes with abundant lightning, even if Indian-set fires were numerically insignificant.

Third, temporal comparison of fire frequency in the pre-Euro-American era, when lightning and Indians were both potential ignition sources, with fire frequency in a modern period (e.g., 1931–1980), when records allow separation of lightning ignitions, is another way to evaluate the importance of Indian ignitions (Barrett 1980a, 1981; Barrett and Arno 1982). In this comparison in western Montana, the pre-Euro-American era had higher ignitions, suggesting that burning by Indians had supplemented lightning ignitions. However, the use of short periods (e.g., 50 years) to estimate mean fire frequency and the difficulty of estimating which fires might have burned if they had not been suppressed could both lead to poor estimates (Barrett 1980a; Barrett and Arno 1982) that make this method less valuable than spatial comparisons. Moreover, the possibility remains that the difference in fire frequency between the pre-Euro-American and modern period is related to climatic differences. Using a similar temporal comparison approach, if contemporary lightning ignitions are confined to particular months, but pre-Euro-American ignitions occur outside these months, then these atypical ignitions were interpreted to be from Indians or Euro-American explorers (Higgins 1984). However, climatic shifts can also change the seasonality of fires (Grissino-Mayer 1995).

A fourth argument is based on the extent of Indian use of an area. If Indians seldom used an area, then their contribution to that area's fire frequency is assumed to have been less than in heavily traveled zones (Romme and Despain 1969; Arno 1985). This idea also underlies Barrett's (1980a) use of "remote" areas for comparison with areas heavily used by Indians. This argument assumes, however, that Indians do not set large fires on their occasional visits, and also that their effects are definitely not pervasive, yet these conclusions are only suggested by oral histories and logical arguments (Box 2.3), rather than firmly established. Finally, a temporal shift in fire frequency that coincides with a change in tribe, particularly if their cultural practices differ, might provide evidence about burning practices of Indians (e.g., Fisher et al. 1987).

Pollen/Charcoal Evidence of Burning by Indians

Paleoecological data, such as charcoal and pollen records, might also be used to identify past Indian influences on fires. A primary signal of Indian-ignited fires in the charcoal/pollen record is a rise in charcoal that corresponds with pollen indicators of human land use, such as pollen of weedy plant species typical of human environments (e.g., Russell 1997). Rocky Mountain charcoal/pollen studies, however, do not generally identify such a signal. Instead, evidence of burning by Indians has been inferred from a rise in charcoal that is unexpected, based on climatic conditions indicated by pollen (e.g., Hemphill 1983).

Some studies in the Rocky Mountains suggest a change in fire frequency—not accompanied by climate conditions thought to promote fire—that may suggest an influence by Indians. Mehringer et al. (1977:366) suggested that an increase in fires near Lost Trail Pass bog in western Montana over the last 2,000 years might be the result of a contribution from "changing patterns of aboriginal land-use and resource management." Hemphill (1983) similarly identified a significant increase in charcoal, suggesting an unexpected increase in fire frequency, over the last 1,100 years at a bog about 200 km north of Mehringer et al.'s site. She suggested that the charcoal increase is not accompanied by a change in pollen or macrofossils that indicates significant climate change, and that a change in Indian culture or population may have led to increased burning. Petersen (1988) identified an unexpectedly high charcoal influx during a period of increased Anasazi agricultural expansion in southwestern Colorado, which was also a wetter period that he suggests would be less favorable for fires. This charcoal peak, he says, "may reflect aboriginal land use" (p. 101).

Other paleoecological studies in the region did not find this signal, perhaps because Indians did not burn these areas or their burning was insignificant relative to lightning fires. In Yellowstone National Park (Millspaugh and Whitlock 1995) and west-central Colorado (Fall 1997), there are no distinctive signals indicating burning by Indians. Moreover, there is a strong correlation between climate and fires in Yellowstone National Park over the past 17,000 years (Millspaugh et al. 2000). Barrett (1994) also argued, using tree-ring-based fire history evidence, that Indian fires were rare and unlikely in this area, so paleoecological results are consistent with fire history results in identifying this ecosystem as one with little evidence of burning by Indians.

The most significant problem with inferences from charcoal and pollen relationships is that there is strong evidence that climate variation can cause changes in fire regimes during periods when vegetation composition remains unchanged. Large fires in the Rocky Mountains can and often do occur during extended wet periods; even brief (e.g., two-week) droughts during otherwise wet years can lead to very large fires (Barrett et al. 1997; Baker, in press). Wet periods followed 1 to 3 years later by drought may actually increase fires in ponderosa pine forests of the southern Rockies (Veblen et al. 2000). Certainly, brief droughts would be unlikely to change pollen abundances. Even the significant climatically induced changes in fire regimes identified in *Pinus ponderosa* forests in New Mexico (Grissino-Mayer 1995) would be unlikely to change pollen amounts as significantly as charcoal amounts. Thus, it is more likely that past episodes or even extended periods of high charcoal input, which lacked corresponding pollen changes indicative of climate change, represent increases in the frequency of drought-related fire episodes, rather than increases in burning by Indians. This idea is supported by the strong correlation of fire and climate during the length of the Holocene in Yellowstone National Park, when pollen data suggest there was little vegetation change (Millspaugh et al. 2000).

Plausibility and Alternative Hypotheses

Studies of fire history that attribute an influence to Indians often rely on plausibility, without examining and excluding plausible alternative hypotheses. Thus, Moore (1972) concludes that because almost no early Euro-Americans mentioned lightning as a source of ignition in the central grassland, it must have been insignificant. The alternative hypothesis, that early Euro-American accounts are not reliable sources of information about the cause of fires, cannot be excluded and seems more likely. As another example, Fisher et al. (1987) present a plausible Indian-based explanation for increased fire frequency in northeastern Wyoming (Box 2.3). Yet an alternative hypothesis, that fire frequency variations are the result of climatic fluctuations, is not examined or excluded. Similarly, Barrett and Arno (1982) tested the plausible idea that the acquisition of the horse increased Indian mobility and the desire to burn more to clear travel paths and provide forage for horses. Although their test suggested there was no increase in fire frequency after acquisition of the horse, the possibility remains that there was a difference, but it was offset by a change in climate or by depopulation. I argued earlier that an equally plausible interpretation of the paleoecological record of charcoal and pollen, interpreted as burning by Indians, is simply brief episodes of drought. Although some might argue that plausibility may be reasonable in this kind of scholarship, given the fragmentary nature of historical analysis, a similar standard of plausibility must be afforded alternative hypotheses and the evidence for and against these hypotheses.

Generalizing from the Evidence and the Wilderness Hypothesis

Reliable evidence of burning by Indians in the Rocky Mountains is much less than reported previously, as earlier authors uncritically accepted most early Euro-American accounts of burning by Indians, and many studies did not consider and cannot exclude plausible alternative explanations of fire frequency anomalies. A complete reassessment of the early accounts and oral history evidence cannot be completed here, since I lack the original data. However, there are clearly sufficient remaining reliable accounts and fire history evidence to support the reality that at least some Indians in the Rocky Mountains intentionally and accidentally burned vegetation, at least in some dry ecosystems where their uses were concentrated, and that they had a variety of reasons for doing so. Some other ideas that have been suggested, but not confirmed by sufficient evidence, may be useful hypotheses to explore further, but their status as hypotheses rather than conclusions should be made explicit.

Reliable evidence available to evaluate the relevance of the four models for the Rocky Mountains is thus probably not abundant, and an argument could be made that there is insufficient evidence to draw any conclusions beyond those mentioned above. However, what evidence is available clearly does not support the idea that Indians set fire to all of the Rocky Mountains (the "pervasive significant model" of Stewart 1954). The idea of geographically varying but consistently significant burning by Indians (Denevan 1992a) is also not well supported by available evidence, as there is evidence that Indians had little or no significant effect on fire regimes in higher-elevation forests (e.g., Loope and Gruell 1973) and probably even little effect in forested valleys directly adjoining heavy-use areas (e.g., McCune 1983). The "enhancing model" of Russell (1997) is also not well supported, as there is no evidence at the present time that burning by Indians actually enhanced changes that were climatically driven. The best supported model may be the "varying significance model" (Whitney 1994), as there is evidence that ignitions by Indians elevated fire frequencies in some heavy-use areas, but not in most other areas.

What research approaches will be valuable in the future? Early Euro-American accounts may be worthy of reevaluation, but they are too biased and unreliable to be of much value in clarifying the extent of burning by Indians. More reliable oral histories from Indians are becoming infeasible with the passing of time (Lewis 1985). Tree-ring-based fire history studies, such as the spatial comparisons of Barrett (1980a, 1980b), offer evidence that is free of the potential biases inherent in oral and written accounts. However, tree-ring studies are too intensive to apply throughout the region in a way that would allow very complete mapping of the spatial extent of burning by Indians, and tree-ring evidence contained in old, fire-scarred trees is declining. Certainly, further fire history work is warranted and may provide important evidence if carefully directed at specific questions and well-designed to control for potential alternative hypotheses. The montane zone bordering the Plains and lower-elevation travel corridors are most in need of further study, as past work suggests these zones have the most potential of yielding evidence of significant burning by Indians. However, application of the Barrett (1980a, 1981) approach of spatial comparisons will be difficult here, as there is access for Indians with horses everywhere along the border and into mountain canyons. Anthropological work to map the areas most used by Indians would help greatly (Personal Communication, S. Barrett, November 1998). It is difficult to see how paleoecological research using pollen and charcoal can use temporal arguments (e.g., Mehringer et al. 1977) to separate human- and lightning-ignited fires, since more likely alternative explanations based on climate-fire relationships (e.g., Millspaugh et al. 2000) cannot easily be excluded. Perhaps these techniques can help identify human impacts in known heavy-use zones, using the spatial comparison approach of Barrett (1980a, 1980b, 1981).

Shall we conclude that much of the Rocky Mountains outside heavy-use areas contained a fire regime free of significant Indian influences, a wilder landscape than we have today in our designated wilderness areas where fires are still not free to burn? This is the conclusion that I would draw now, were I to generalize freely from limited evidence, as did proponents of the idea that Indians burned extensively (e.g., Stewart 1954). But I have criticized this kind of generalization from limited evidence.

While a strong conclusion is premature, it is time for the burden of proof to shift to those who would counter the hypothesis most suggested by the limited evidence. The hypothesis is that some 30,000 people, living in an enormous mountain range with a strong climate-influenced fire regime, could hardly be expected to have much influence on the pattern of fires outside their heavy-use areas. Imagine them walking alone or in small groups up into the mountains, during the centuries, possibly millennia, wandering on foot in terrain that is even now difficult for the millions of us to fully access by automobile, roads, and trails, and where even today a large percentage of fires is started by lightning. The hypothesis is that Indians were a small part of a large Rocky Mountain wilderness, with a fire regime, in much of the mountains, essentially free of human influence for millennia.

Acknowledgments

This research was supported in part by the Global Change Programs of the National Park Service and U.S. Geological Survey, Biological Resources Division, under Cooperative Agreement No. CA 1268-1-9009. I appreciate reviews of an earlier draft by Stephen Barrett, Stephen Arno, Thomas T. Veblen, and Cathy Whitlock, but I did not heed all their suggestions, and responsibility for the interpretation remains with me.

Literature Cited

Arno, S. F. 1976. *The historical role of fire on the Bitterroot National Forest.* Research paper INT-187. Ogden, Utah USDA Forest Service, Intermountain Forest and Range Experiment Station.

———. 1980. Forest fire history in the northern Rockies. *Journal of Forestry* 78:460–465.

———. 1985. Ecological effects and management implications of Indian fires. Pp. 81–86 in *Proceedings—symposium and workshop on wilderness fire, Missoula, Montana: November 15–18, 1983*, ed. J. E. Lotan, B. M. Kilgore, W. C. Fischer, and R. W. Mutch. General technical report INT-182. Ogden, Utah: USDA Forest Service, Intermountain Forest and Range Experiment Station.

Arno, S. F., and D. H. Davis. 1980. Fire history of western redcedar/hemlock forests in northern Idaho. Pp. 21–26 in *Proceedings of the Fire History Workshop*, ed. M. A. Stokes and J. H. Dieterich. General technical report RM-81. Fort Collins, Colo.: USDA Forest Service, Rocky Mountain Forest and Range Experiment Station.

Arno, S. F., H. Y. Smith, and M. A. Krebs. 1997. *Old growth ponderosa pine and western larch stand structures: Influences of pre-1900 fires and fire exclusion.* Research paper INT-495. Ogden, Utah: USDA Forest Service, Intermountain Research Station.

Baker, W. L. in press. Fires and climate in forested landscapes of the Rocky Mountains: In *Fire and climatic change in temperate ecosystems of the western Americas*, ed. T. T. Veblen, W. L. Baker, G. Montenegro, and T. W. Swetnam. New York: Springer-Verlag.

Barrett, S. W. 1980a. Indian fires in the pre-settlement forests of western Montana. Pp. 35–41 in *Proceedings of the Fire History Workshop*, ed. M. A. Stokes and J. H. Dieterich. General technical report RM-81. Fort Collins, Colo.: USDA Forest Service, Rocky Mountain Forest and Range Experiment Station.

———. 1980b. Indians & fire. *Western Wildlands* 6:17–21.

———. 1981. Relationship of Indian-caused fires to the ecology of western Montana forests. Master's thesis, University of Montana.

———. 1994. Fire regimes on andesitic mountain terrain in northeastern Yellowstone National Park, Wyoming. *International Journal of Wildland Fire* 4:65–76.

Barrett, S. W., and S. F. Arno. 1982. Indian fires as an ecological influence in the northern Rockies. *Journal of Forestry* 80:647–651.

———. 1999. Indian fires in the northern Rockies: Ethnohistory and ecology. Pp. 50–64 in *Indians, fire, and the land in the Pacific Northwest*, ed. R. Boyd. Portland: Oregon State University Press.

Barrett, S. W., S. F. Arno, and J. P. Menakis. 1997. *Fire episodes in the inland northwest (1540–1940) based on fire history data.* General technical report

INT-370. Ogden, Utah: USDA Forest Service, Intermountain Research Station.

Barrows, J. S., D. V. Sandberg, and J. D. Hart. 1976. Lightning fires in northern Rocky Mountain forests. Unpublished report to the U.S. Forest Service, Intermountain Forest and Range Experiment Station, Northern Forest Fire Laboratory by the Department of Forest and Wood Science, Colorado State University. Fort Collins, Colo.

Bessie, W. C., and E. A. Johnson. 1995. The relative importance of fuels and weather on fire behavior in subalpine forests. *Ecology* 76:747–762.

Billings, W. D. 1969. Vegetational patterns near alpine timberline as affected by fire-snowdrift interactions. *Vegetatio* 19:192–207.

Boyd, R. 1986. Strategies of Indian burning in the Willamette Valley. *Canadian Journal of Anthropology* 5:65–86.

———. 1998. Demographic history until 1990. Pp. 467–483 in *Handbook of North American Indians*, vol. 12: *Plateau*, ed. D. E. Walker, Jr. Washington, D.C.: Smithsonian Institution.

Brunton, B. B. 1998. Kootenai. Pp. 223–237 in *Handbook of North American Indians*, vol. 12: *Plateau*, ed. D. E. Walker, Jr. Washington, D.C.: Smithsonian Institution.

Cassells, E. S. 1997. *The archaeology of Colorado*. 2d ed. Boulder: Johnson Books.

Crandall, C. S. 1901. *Natural reforestation and tree growth on the mountains of northern Colorado*. USDA Division of Forestry. Washington, D.C.: U.S. Government Printing Office.

Crum, S. 1996. *People of the red earth: American Indians of Colorado*. Santa Fe: Ancient City Press.

D'Azevedo, W. L., ed. 1986. *Handbook of North American Indians*, vol. 11: *Great Basin*. Washington, D.C.: Smithsonian Institution.

Deloria, V., Jr. 1995. *Red earth, white lies: Native Americans and the myth of scientific fact*. New York: Scribner's.

Denevan, W. M. 1992a. The pristine myth: the landscape of the Americas in 1492. *Annals of the Association of American Geographers* 82:369–385.

———, ed. 1992b. *The native population of the Americas in 1492*. 2d ed. Madison: University of Wisconsin Press.

Ewers, J. C. 1958. *The Blackfeet, raiders on the northwestern Plains*. Norman: University of Oklahoma Press.

Fall, P. L. 1997. Fire history and composition of the subalpine forest of western Colorado during the Holocene. *Journal of Biogeography* 24:309–325.

Fisher, R. F., M. J. Jenkins, and W. F. Fisher. 1987. Fire and the prairie-forest mosaic of Devils Tower National Monument. *American Midland Naturalist* 117:250–257.

Fritz, S. C., D. R. Engstrom, and B. J. Haskell. 1994. "Little Ice Age" aridity in the North American Great Plains: A high-resolution reconstruction of salinity fluctuations from Devils Lake, North Dakota, U.S.A. *The Holocene* 4:69–73.

Gartner, F. R., and W. W. Thompson. 1972. Fire in the Black Hills forest-grass ecotone. *Proceedings of the Tall Timbers Fire Ecology Conference* 12:37–68.

Grissino-Mayer, H. D. 1995. Tree-ring reconstruction of climate and fire history at El Malpais National Monument, New Mexico. Ph.D. diss., University of Arizona, Tucson.

Gruell, G. E. 1985a. Fire on the early western landscape: An annotated record of wildland fires 1776–1900. *Northwest Science* 59:97–107.

———. 1985b. Indian fires in the interior west: A widespread influence. Pp. 68–74 in *Proceedings—Symposium and workshop on wilderness fire, Missoula, Montana: November 15–18, 1983*, ed. J. E. Lotan, B. M. Kilgore, W. C. Fischer, and R. W. Mutch. General technical report INT-182. Ogden, Utah: USDA Forest Service, Intermountain Forest and Range Experiment Station.

Habeck, J. R. 1972. *Fire ecology investigations in the Selway–Bitterroot Wilderness: Historical considerations and current observations*. U.S. Forest Service publication R1-72-001. Missoula: University of Montana.

Haines, F. 1938. Northward spread of horses to the Plains Indians. *American Anthropologist* 40:429–437.

Hemphill, M. L. 1983. Fire, vegetation, and people—charcoal and pollen analyses of Sheep Mountain bog, Montana: The last 2800 years. Master's thesis, Washington State University, Pullman.

Higgins, K. F. 1984. Lightning fires in North Dakota grasslands and in pine-savanna lands of South Dakota and Montana. *Journal of Range Management* 37:100–103.

Honaker, J. J. 1995. Fire history in the Tie Camp area of the Sierra Madre Mountains, Wyoming. Master's thesis, University of Wyoming, Laramie.

Hough, F. B. 1882. *Report on forestry, submitted to Congress by the Commissioner of Agriculture*. Washington, D.C.: U.S. Government Printing Office.

Houghton, J. T., G. J. Jenkins, and J. J. Ephraums. 1990. *Climate change: The IPCC scientific assessment*. Cambridge: Cambridge University Press.

Houston, D. B. 1973. Wildfires in northern Yellowstone National Park. *Ecology* 54:1111–1117.

Hungry Wolf, A., and B. Hungry Wolf. 1989. *Indian tribes of the northern Rockies*. Summertown, Tenn.: Book Publishing Company.

Janetski, J. C. 1987. *The Indians of Yellowstone Park*. Salt Lake City: Bonneville Books, University of Utah Press.

Kipfmueller, K. F. 1997. A fire history of a subalpine forest in southeastern Wyoming. Master's thesis, University of Wyoming, Laramie.

Komarek, E. V., Sr. 1964. The natural history of lightning. *Proceedings of the Tall Timbers Fire Ecology Conference* 3:139–183.

———. 1967. The nature of lightning fires. *Proceedings of the Tall Timbers Fire Ecology Conference* 7:5–41.

Larson, M. L., and J. E. Francis. 1997. *Changing perspectives of the Archaic on the northwest plains and Rocky Mountains*. Vermillion: University of South Dakota Press.

Leiberg, J. B. 1900. The Bitterroot forest reserve. Pp. 317–410 in *U.S. Department of Interior, Geological Survey, 20th Annual Report*, part 5: *Forest Reserves*. Washington, D.C.

Lewis, H. T. 1977. Maskuta: the ecology of Indian fires in northern Alberta. *The Western Canadian Journal of Anthropology* 7:15–52.

————. 1985. Why Indians burned: Specific versus general reasons. Pp. 75–80 in *Proceedings—Symposium and workshop on wilderness fire, Missoula, Montana: November 15–18, 1983*, ed. J. E. Lotan, B. M. Kilgore, W. C. Fischer, and R. W. Mutch. General technical report INT-182. Ogden, Utah: USDA Forest Service, Intermountain Forest and Range Experiment Station.

Loope, L. L., and G. E. Gruell. 1973. The ecological role of fire in the Jackson Hole area, northwestern Wyoming. *Quaternary Research* 3:425–443.

Malouf, C. I. 1998. Flathead and Pend d'Oreille. Pp. 297–312 in *Handbook of North American Indians*, vol. 12: *Plateau*, ed. D. E. Walker, Jr. Washington, D.C.: Smithsonian Institution.

McCune, B. 1983. Fire frequency reduced two orders of magnitude in the Bitterroot Canyons. *Canadian Journal of Forest Research* 13:212–218.

Mehringer, P. J., Jr., S. F. Arno, and K. L. Petersen. 1977. Postglacial history of Lost Trail Pass bog, Bitterroot Mountains, Montana. *Arctic and Alpine Research* 9:345–368.

Meisner, B. N., R. A. Chase, M. H. McCutchan, R. Mees, J. W. Benoit, B. Ly, D. Albright, D. Strauss, and T. Ferryman. 1994. A lightning fire ignition assessment model. *Proceedings of the Conference on Fire and Forest Meteorology* 12:172–178.

Millspaugh, S. H., and C. Whitlock. 1995. A 750-year fire history based on lake sediment records in central Yellowstone National Park, USA. *The Holocene* 5:283–292.

Millspaugh, S. H., C. Whitlock, and P. J. Bartlein. 2000. Variations in fire frequency and climate over the past 17,000 years in central Yellowstone National Park. *Geology* 28:211–214.

Minnich, R. A., E. R. Vizcaino, J. Sosa-Ramirez, and Yue-H. Chou. 1993. Lightning detection rates and wildland fire in the mountains of northern Baja California, Mexico. *Atmósfera* 6:235–253.

Mooney, J. 1928. *The aboriginal population of America north of Mexico*, ed. John R. Swanton. Smithsonian miscellaneous collections 80(7). Washington, D.C.: Smithsonian Institution.

Moore, C. T. 1972. Man and fire in the central North American grassland 1535–1890: A documentary historical geography. Ph.D. diss., UCLA.

Nelson, J. G., and R. E. England. 1977. Some comments on the causes and effects of fire in the northern grasslands area of Canada and the nearby United States, 1750–1900. Pp. 39–47 in *Proceedings of the 1977 rangeland management and fire symposium, presented at the joint Rocky Mountain Fire Council and Intermountain Fire Research Council meeting, November 1–3, 1977, Casper, Wyoming*, ed. C. M. Bourassa and A. P. Brackebusch. Montana Forest and Conservation Experiment Station, Missoula: University of Montana School of Forestry.

Orville, R. E. 1994. Cloud-to-ground lightning flash characteristics in the contiguous United States: 1989–1991. *Journal of Geophysical Research* 99:10833–10841.

Orville, R. E., and A. C. Silver. 1997. Lightning ground flash density in the contiguous United States: 1992–95. *Monthly Weather Review* 125:631–638.

Patterson, W. A., III, and K. E. Sassaman. 1988. Indian fires in the prehistory of New England. Pp. 107–135 in *Holocene human ecology in northeastern North America* , ed. G. P. Nichols. New York: Plenum.

Peirce, E. S. 1915. The regeneration of denuded areas in the Bighorn Mountains by Douglas fir. *Forestry Quarterly* 13:301–307.

Petersen, K. L. 1988. *Climate and the Dolores River Anasazi.* University of Utah anthropological papers no. 113. Salt Lake City: University of Utah Press.

Plummer, F. G. 1912. *Lightning in relation to forest fires.* USDA Forest Service Bulletin No. 111. Washington, D.C.: U.S. Government Printing Office.

Price, C., and D. Rind. 1994. The impact of a 2 × CO_2 climate on lightning-caused fires. *Journal of Climate* 7:1484–1494.

Pyne, S. J. 1982. *Fire in America: A cultural history of wildland and rural fire.* Princeton: Princeton University Press.

———. 1998. Pyre on the mountain. Pp. 38–52 in *Reopening the American West*, ed. H. K. Rothman. Tucson: University of Arizona Press.

Qu, J., and P. N. Omi. 1994. Potential impacts of global climate changes on wildfire activity in the USA. *Proceedings of the Conference on Fire and Forest Meteorology* 12:85–92.

Romme, W. H., and D. G. Despain. 1989. The long history of fire in the Greater Yellowstone ecosystem. *Western Wildlands* 15:10–17.

Romme, W. H., L. Floyd-Hanna, D. Hanna, and H. Grissino-Mayer. 1994. Presettlement range of natural variation in disturbance history and stand structure of ponderosa pine and mixed conifer forests on the San Juan National Forest—Progress report for the first year's work. Unpublished report to the San Juan National Forest. Durango, Colo.: Fort Lewis College.

Russell, E. W. B. 1997. *People and the land through time: Linking ecology and history.* New Haven: Yale University Press.

Schrader-Frechette, K. S., and E. D. McCoy. 1995. Natural landscapes, natural communities, and natural ecosystems. *Forest and Conservation History* 39:138–142.

Shimkin, D. B. 1986. The introduction of the horse. Pp. 517–524 In *Handbook of North American Indians*, vol. 11: *Great Basin*, ed. W. L. D'Azevedo. Washington, D.C.: Smithsonian Institution.

Snyder, G. 1998. A note on *Before the Wilderness. Wild Forest Review*, October/November 1990:38.

Stewart, O. C. 1954. Forest fires with a purpose. *Southwestern Lore* 20:42–45.

Sturtevant, W. C. 1978–1998. *Handbook of North American Indians.* Washington, D.C.: Smithsonian Institution.

Swanson, F. J., J. A. Jones, D. O. Wallin, and J. H. Cissel. 1994. Natural variability—Implications for ecosystem management. Pp. 80–94 in *Eastside forest ecosystem health assessment*, vol. 2: *Ecosystem management: Principles and applications*, ed. M. E. Jensen and P. S. Bourgeron. General technical report PNW-318. Portland, Ore.: USDA Forest Service, Pacific Northwest Research Station.

Swetnam, T. W., and C. H. Baisan. 1996. Historical fire regime patterns in the southwestern United States since A.D. 1700. Pp. 11–32 in *Fire effects in southwestern forests: Proceedings of the second La Mesa fire symposium, Los Alamos, New Mexico, March 29–31, 1994*, ed. C. D. Allen. General technical report

RM-286. Fort Collins, Colo.: USDA Forest Service, Rocky Mountain Research Station.

Taylor, D. L. 1974. Forest fires in Yellowstone National Park. *Journal of Forest History* 18:69–77.

Thornton, R. 1987. *American Indian holocaust and survival: A population history since 1492.* Norman: University of Oklahoma Press.

Ubelaker, D. H. 1976. Prehistoric New World population size: Historical review and current appraisal of North American estimates. *American Journal of Physical Anthropology* 45:661–666.

———. 1988. North American Indian population size, A.D. 1500 to 1985. *American Journal of Physical Anthropology* 77:289–294.

Vale, T. R. 1998. The myth of the humanized landscape: An example from Yosemite National Park. *Natural Areas Journal* 18:231–236.

Veblen, T. T., T. Kitzberger, and J. Donnegan. 2000. Climatic and human influences on fire regimes in ponderosa pine forests in the Colorado Front Range. *Ecological Applications* 10:1178–1195.

Waldman, C. 1985. *Atlas of the North American Indian.* New York: Facts on File Publications.

Walker, D. E., Jr., ed. 1998. *Handbook of North American Indians,* vol. 12: *Plateau.* Washington, D.C.: Smithsonian Institution.

Walker D. E., Jr., and R. Sprague. 1998. History until 1846. Pp. 138–148 in *Handbook of North American Indians,* vol. 12: *Plateau,* ed. D. E. Walker, Jr. Washington, D.C.: Smithsonian Institution.

Wellner, C. A. 1970. Fire history in the northern Rocky Mountains. Pp. 42–64 in *Role of fire in the intermountain West: Proceedings of a symposium.* Missoula: Fire Research Council and University of Montana.

Whitlock, C. 1993. Postglacial vegetation and climate of Grand Teton and southern Yellowstone National Parks. *Ecological Monographs* 63:173–198.

Whitney, G. G. 1994. *From coastal wilderness to fruited plain: A history of environmental change in temperate North America from 1500 to the present.* Cambridge: Cambridge University Press.

PREHISTORIC HUMAN IMPACTS ON FIRE REGIMES AND VEGETATION IN THE NORTHERN INTERMOUNTAIN WEST

Duane Griffin

When the first European explorers entered the vast interior region situated between the Sierra Nevada and the Rocky Mountain cordilleras, they encountered sparse populations of Ute, Paiute, Shoshone, and Washoe hunter-foragers living much as their forebears had for the past 4,500 years. Commercial trappers began exploiting the region in the 1820s, and by 1900 the ecological and biogeographic reorganizations of the region were well under way. The native populations had been decimated by disease and removed to reservations to make way for ranchers, miners, loggers, and farmers. A century later, these and other distinctively modern practices had changed the landscapes of the intermountain West in ways that would have been fundamentally impossible 200 years earlier.

What do these changes represent? Are they modifications of a pristine environment, or are they simply the latest alterations of a region whose human inhabitants have adapted it to suit their needs for over 10 millennia? Did human activities, particularly modification of fire regimes, play a role in setting the structure and composition of vegetation in the intermountain West? If so, where and to what degree? Was the "Sagebrush Ocean" that greeted the first White explorers and settlers (Vale 1975a) the ecological norm for the region? Or was it the successional reflection of altered patterns of burning brought about by demographic collapse (e.g. Cook 1955), as Denevan (1992) has proposed for the Americas as a whole?

These questions have important implications for understanding both the past and the future ecology of the intermountain region, but answering them with any degree of specificity and confidence is currently impossible. Despite a rich tradition of anthropological, historical, ecological, and biogeographic research in the intermountain region, we know almost nothing about its past fire regimes and prehistoric human impacts on its environments (Rhode 1999).

This chapter is directed at framing a series of hypotheses about the role of humans in prehistoric fire regimes and suggesting some ways that they can be tested. I begin by reviewing what we know about premodern populations and subsistence in the Great Basin and comparing this information with our understanding of fire ecology in modern plant communities. The results of this exercise suggest that the aboriginal inhabitants of the region likely benefited from periodic fires in the primary habitats they utilized. The next step is to ask if there were times and places when and where anthropogenic burning would have been both necessary and sufficient to alter vegetation patterns. I use modern fire occurrence data as a basis for positing null hypotheses about human impacts on fire regimes and biota in the past. I conclude by suggesting approaches to testing these hypotheses and identifying opportunities for future research in the intermountain West.

The Region

Broadly defined, the northern intermountain West includes the Columbia Plateau, the Wyoming Basin, the Colorado Plateau, and the Great Basin (Fenneman 1931). Most of this area falls within the Great Basin Culture Area identified by d'Azevedo (1986). The area where these physiographic and cultural regions overlap north of the Mojave Desert corresponds to the floristic Great Basin defined by Cronquist et al. (1972); see Figure 3.1.

The spatial distribution of vegetation communities in the intermountain region reflects two primary climatic gradients that are modified locally by topography (see Shreve 1942; Billings 1951; Holmgren 1972; Harper et al. 1978; Harper 1986; West 1988; Trimble 1989; Hidy and Klieforth 1990; Grayson 1993). Average temperature and evaporation rates decrease regionally from southwest to northeast and locally with

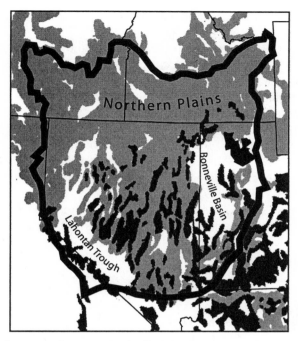

Figure 3.1. Major vegetation types in the floristic Great Basin (from Küchler 1985). Pinyon and juniper woodland is shown in dark gray, and sagebrush shrubland in light gray. White areas are barren desert, saltbrush-greasewood shrubland, and montane vegetation. Riparian forests and tule marshes constitute less than 1 percent of the surface area. For regional vegetation descriptions, see Grayson (1993), Harper (1986), Harper et al. (1978), Holmgren (1972), Trimble (1989), and West (1988).

elevation. The cordilleras to the east and west block the flow of moisture into the region, so precipitation everywhere is low. The eastern part of the region receives the bulk of its precipitation as rainfall produced by summer intrusions of Gulf moisture. The west is dominated by winter moisture from the Pacific that falls as rain in the south and snow in the north.

The broad-scale physiographic structure of the Great Basin is that of a great arch. The Lahontan trough on the west side and the Bonneville Basin in the east form the ends of the arch, while the high central plateau of central and eastern Nevada represents the peak. Superimposed on this structure are a multitude of generally north-south-oriented mountain ranges and intervening basins. Few of these ranges reach elevations greater than 3,000 meters, and only three peaks extend above 3,500 meters. On the northern end of the region, the fault-block mountains of the physiographic Great Basin give way to the plains of the Columbia Plateau.

Forests in the intermountain West are rare and limited to high elevations and the riparian strips that connect them with the extensive barren playas that occupy the floors of enclosed valleys. Between these extremes, moderate elevations and cool winters favor the development of three primary plant communities that dominate most of the region: (1) shadscale (*Atriplex*) shrubland, (2) sagebrush (*Artemisia*) shrubland, (3) and pinyon-juniper (*Pinus* and *Juniperus*) woodland. These correspond to Küchler's (1985) saltbush-greasewood (*Atriplex-Sarcobatus*), Great Basin sagebrush and sagebrush steppe, and juniper-pinyon woodland vegetation types (Figure 3.1).

Saltbush-greasewood shrubland reaches its greatest extent in low-lying basins (principally in the Lahontan, Bonneville, and Uinta basins), generally at elevations below ca. 1,000 meters. Sagebrush, especially big sagebrush (*Artemisia tridentata*), replaces saltbush and greasewood as the dominant shrub at elevations above ca. 1,000 meters (and extending to elevations as high as 3,050 meters in some places). South of 41°N, in Küchler's Great Basin sagebrush type, *Artemisia* plants rarely exceed 1 meter in height, and total cover rarely exceeds 40 percent (Knapp 1997). As effective moisture increases, the stature of sagebrush increases but its abundance decreases relative to perennial grasses and forbs, which more or less codominate the sagebrush steppe communities north of 41°N. Cover in these communities typically exceeds 80 percent and approaches 200 percent on mesic sites (Wright and Bailey 1982; West 1988). In the eastern part of the region, where summer precipitation is relatively abundant, perennial bunchgrasses may make up the bulk of both cover and phytomass (Küchler 1985; West 1988) and may have even dominated many landscapes prior to Euro-American settlement (Cottam 1961; Christensen and Johnson 1964; Hull and Hull 1974).

In the southeastern two-thirds of the region, temperature inversions caused by nighttime radiative heat loss and cold-air drainage create a band of relatively warm temperature between ca. 1,500 and 2,000 meters. These inversion layers enable pinyon-juniper woodland to develop between the upper and lower limits of the sagebrush zone, effectively creating lower- and upper-elevation sagebrush communities (Billings 1951, 1954; Hidy and Klieforth 1990). Above ca. 2,800 meters, the upper sagebrush communities generally give way to montane brush, conifer and aspen woodlands, or, more rarely, conifer forests. These forests have depauperate tree floras (particularly in the western part of the region) with floristic affinities to the Rocky Mountains (Axelrod 1976; Harper et al. 1978; Wells 1983).

The Great Basin's Aboriginal Inhabitants

Prior to European contact with the New World, most of the northern intermountain West was home to Ute, Paiute, Shoshone, and Washoe hunter-foragers. With the exception of the Washoe, whose territory was relatively small and centered on Lake Tahoe, these tribes spoke mutually intelligible dialects of Numic, a Uto-Aztecan language from which they derive their collective name.

Leland (1986) estimates the population of the entire Great Basin Culture Area to have been around 40,000 (but perhaps as high as 57,000) when the first Spanish explorers entered the eastern Great Basin in 1776. Using the 900,000 square km areal extent of the region given in Vale, chapter 1, Leland's lower estimate yields a human occupancy rate of one person per 23 square km. Even assuming a high estimate of 75,000 people (Vale, chapter 1 of this volume), the mean occupancy rate for the region as a whole was only one person per 12 square km, comparable to sparsely inhabited parts of Alaska today. Populations were not, however, evenly distributed through the region. Locally, occupation rates are estimated to have been as high as one person per 6 square km in the relatively rich riverine and marsh settings where resources were diverse, abundant, and reliable and as low as 90 square km for every person living in the Harsh Bonneville Basin (Grayson 1993) (Figure 3.2).

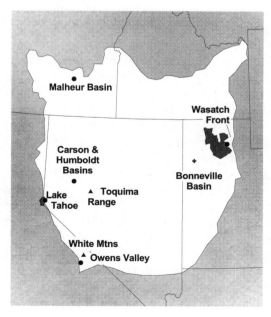

Figure 3.2. Locales where human populations are known to have been concentrated in prehistoric times (Grayson 1993).

Based on his ethnographic work among the Owens Valley Paiute and the Western Shoshone, Julian Steward (1938) proposed the basic tenets of what has become the "standard model" of Great Basin subsistence. He argued that the overall scarcity and highly variable spatial and temporal distribution of resources in the Great Basin favored a generalized subsistence strategy that was spatially, socially, and ecologically flexible and extensive (Steward 1938).

Steward's model is broadly consistent with historical accounts of Great Basin peoples (e.g., Fowler 1982) and with archeological evidence from the period since ca. 4,500 B.P. (Thomas 1973). As such, we can assume that it provides a reasonable approximation of Great Basin lifeways during the late Holocene, especially since ca. 2,000 B.P., when Great Basin landscapes began to look much as they did at the time of European contact (Grayson 1993; Bettinger 1999).

Historic Subsistence Patterns

Great Basin subsistence patterns were strongly seasonal. During the warm season, small, generally kin-based bands of people ("camp groups" in Fowler's [1982] terminology) migrated between relatively rich, but scattered and ephemeral, resource patches collecting whatever foods were abundant at each locale. Each group would travel long distances, traversing from low-elevation *Atriplex* shrublands to montane highlands. Their particular route would have varied from year to year depending on resource abundances and the highly variable rainfall patterns characteristic of the region.

At various times throughout the year, several groups would join together to cooperatively hunt pronghorn (*Antilocapra americana*) or mountain sheep (*Ovis canadensis*), as well as small game such as sage grouse (*Centrocercus urophasianus*), coots (*Fulica americana*), ducks (*Anatidae*), and rabbits and hares (*Leporidae*) (Fowler 1986; Grayson 1993). These gatherings rarely lasted for more than a few days. Longer-term gatherings occurred each fall, when multiple family groups congregated in semipermanent winter villages.

Winter village sites depended on access to wood, water, and key staples (roots and berries in the northern plains and pinyon pine [*Pinus monophylla*] nuts elsewhere), together with other foods that had been cached during the warm season. The lower treeline in pinyon-juniper woodlands and canyon mouths and riparian areas with abundant fish were favored locations (Grayson 1993). Because the availability of the key resources varied from year to year, so too did the location and size of the winter village. Where resources were especially abundant, the villages might have had populations of 100 or more; in leaner years and less favorable environments, villages of 25 to 30 were more common (Grayson 1993).

In a few places on the margins of the Great Basin, resources were abundant and reliable enough to support relatively dense concentrations of people in permanent or semipermanent villages (Figure 3.2). Owens Valley, California, had more than 30 permanent villages, some of which may have been home to as many as 200 people (Grayson 1993). Like their kinfolk living in more marginal areas, inhabitants of these well-watered locales also dispersed during the warm season to exploit peripheral resource zones. In the case of Owens Valley and the Reese River Valley, they even established seasonally occupied residential villages in the alpine zone of the White Mountains and the Toquima range (Grayson 1993).

Resource Use

Most of what we know about aboriginal resource use and environmental manipulation in the Great Basin comes from ethnographic research that Steward and his colleagues conducted between the 1920s and the 1940s (Downs 1966) and from ethnobotanical fieldwork and archival research conducted since the 1960s (Fowler 1986, 2000). Based on this body of research, Fowler (1986, 2000) has identified 470 plant and 178 animal species that Great Basin peoples used. Given the late date and incomplete coverage of the early ethnographic work, she estimates that these values may underestimate the full Great Basin ethnoecological repertoire by at least 300 species.

The relative importance of plant and animal foods in Great Basin diets varied considerably. Fowler (1986) estimates that plant resources constituted as little as 20 percent of the diet in riverine and lake settings to as much as 70 percent in the arid southwestern part of the region. Animal protein made up the rest of the diet. In addition to pronghorn and mountain sheep, Great Basin peoples hunted mountain goats (*Oreamnos americanus*), deer (*Odocoileus heminonus* and *O. virginianus*), elk (*Cervus elaphus*), and other large game where they were available. Probably more important than big game species were small game animals and fish. Fowler (1986) lists 57 mammal species, 73 bird species, and 48 species of fish that Numic peoples hunted. They also collected insects (sometimes using fire drives) and larvae (Fowler 1986, 2000; Grayson 1993).

Among the 344 species of food plants that Fowler (1986) lists, the majority (216 species or 63 percent) are herbaceous terrestrial species belonging to 11 families (Table 3.1). Pinyon pine was the most important tree species used. Great Basin foragers also harvested the fruits of

TABLE 3.1. Great Basin food plants as listed by Fowler (1986).

Family	No. of Species
Aster (*Asteraceae*)	41
Grass (*Poaceae*)	39
Lily (*Lilaceae*)	27
Goosefoot (*Chenopodaceae*)	22
Parsley (*Apiaceae*)	22
Mustard (*Brassicacea*)	15
Buckwheat (*Polygonaceae*)	14
Phlox (*Polemoniaceae*)	14
Amaranth (*Amaranthaceae*)	8
Blazing Star (*Losaceae*)	8
Purslane (*Portulaceae*)	6
Total	**216**

montane shrubs (*Rosaceae* and *Saxifragaceae* spp.) and the seeds of salt-bush, greasewood, and sagebrush species from low-elevation sites.

Environmental Manipulation

The people that Steward and his colleagues interviewed identified a broad range of plant management strategies that included pruning, coppicing, clearing, broadcast seeding, wild plant irrigation (Lawton et al. 1976), and burning. Archeologists have added agriculture (Wilde and Newman 1989) and surface modifications related to water harvesting (Irwin-Williams et al. 1990) to the list. Given the low population densities in the Great Basin and the labor-intensive nature of most of these practices, it is unlikely that they could have affected more than a small fraction of the landscape. The only environmental manipulation capable of widespread ecological change that was available to the aboriginal inhabitants of the Great Basin was intentional burning. Given the extensive nature of both fire-prone shrubland and pinyon woodland habitats and native subsistence patterns, intentional burning could potentially have affected vast areas of the region (cf. Vale 1975a).

Steward's ethnographic sources reported setting fires for the same reasons that other hunter-foragers do: principally to increase the availability of desirable plants, to maintain favorable habitats for important animals, and to drive game in hunting (Downs 1966; Fowler 1986). The ethnographic data indicate that the practice was widespread, but not universal. Downs (1966) notes that only two-thirds of the Numic groups interviewed in the 1930s reported using intentional burning as a management strategy. The Washoe even specifically denied setting fires.

Two related problems arise when assessing the degree to which the ethnographies reflect prehistoric practices. The first is the question of accuracy: how closely did ethnographic informants' interview responses reflect actual practice? The second is the question of representativeness: to what degree did the ethnographic data reflect practices used in other places and, especially, at other times?

Both accuracy and representativeness are limited by the late date at which data collection began. By the time extensive ethnographic work began in the 1930s, most native populations in the Great Basin had been moved to reservations and were at their historic nadirs (Leland 1986). Reservation dwellers continued to hunt and collect wild plants (or remembered having done so), but many traditional practices had been modified, abandoned, and forgotten (Service 1962). Others—including intentional burning—had been vilified by white culture, which may have affected responses to the ethnographers' questions (Downs 1966). As such, it is impossible to determine what, exactly, the ethnographic data represent. On the one hand, they may record the ancient practice of intentional burning as it was in the process of dying away. On the other, Great Basin people may have used intentional burning as an intensification strategy in response to changes in ecology, mobility, population density, and even climate that occurred in the protohistoric and early historic periods.

Historical sources (e.g., Shinn 1980; Gruell 1985) suggest that intentional burning was not entirely a post-nineteenth-century practice. Indeed, the first written description of the region, the log of the Dominguez-Escalante expedition, records the intentional firing of once-extensive grasslands (see Cottam 1961) as the party passed through the eastern Great Basin in the autumn of 1776 (Chavez and Warner 1976). Subsequent visitors recorded Indian-set fires as well. Gruell (1985) identified early historical descriptions of forty-three fires in the Great Basin, twenty-six of which (60 percent) were reported as having been set intentionally.

As with the ethnographic record, questions of accuracy and representativeness make it impossible to know what these descriptions represent in terms of premodern fire regimes. As Baker (chapter 2 of this volume) notes, awareness of the commonness of lightning as an ignition source is a twentieth-century phenomenon, and most historical accounts of wildland fire ignitions are likely to be biased. Furthermore, even if the historical record is accurate, it may reflect postcontact changes in aboriginal society and ecology. For example, unlike most historical fire reports, the Dominguez-Escalante account appears to be based on the friars' direct observations and corroborated by their translator and guide. Thus we can reasonably assume it to be an accurate and reliable account of intentional burning by local Paiutes. It may not, however, be representative. Dominguez and Escalante speculated that the local Paiute, seeing mounted riders approaching, assumed their expedition was a group of Comanches and fired the grasslands to deprive their party of forage (Chavez and Warner 1976).

This interpretation reflects the fact that the effects of European colonization preceded face-to-face contact between the colonists and inhabitants of the Great Basin. Among the earliest impacts of contact were the introduction of European diseases and adoption of the horse by the Ute, northern Paiute, northern Shoshone, and neighboring tribes to the north, south, and west of the region by 1700 (Arkush 1990). The first disease epidemics may have predated European incursions into the region by more than a century (Grayson 1993), affecting the demographic structure of Great Basin societies. Similarly, the presence of fleet, highly mobile, horse-mounted hunting and raiding parties affected many aspects of life in the Great Basin, including the availability of game animals and patterns of conflict. It is possible that the pressures these changes induced led the Paiute and other Great Basin peoples either to alter their ecological practices (increased dependence on grasslands and intensifying fire regimes to support or expand them) or to set fires as a defensive strategy.

Fowler (1986) suggests that Dominguez and Escalante witnessed the annual (or semiannual) practice of autumn burning rather than a protohistoric Paiute defensive tactic. She bases this interpretation on that fact that everything we know about aboriginal subsistence practices, vegetation dynamics, and fire ecology in the intermountain West suggests that Great Basin peoples and their prehistoric forebears had very good reasons to set fires if they did not occur naturally.

Fire and Succession

Contemporary range management and fire control issues have guided research on fire ecology in the northern intermountain West (e.g., Wright and Bailey 1982; Britton and Clark 1985; Bunting 1985; Winward 1985; Whisenant 1990; Knapp 1997, 1998). Little empirical research has been conducted on past fire regimes, especially in low-elevation and foothill communities in the Great Basin (Heyerdahl et al. 1995; Miller 2000). Most of what we do know of fire history in sagebrush and pinyon-juniper ecosystems comes from studies focused on understanding the historic expansion of pinyon-juniper woodland (e.g.,

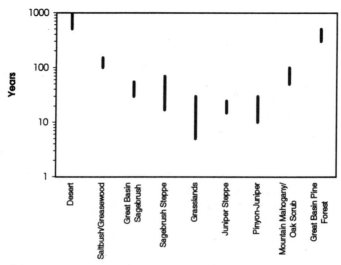

Figure 3.3. Fire return intervals for regional Küchler vegetation types arrayed along a generalized moisture gradient (data from Leenhouts 1998; Vale 1982; Whisenant 1990; Wright and Bailey 1982; and Young and Tipton 1990).

Houston 1973; Burkhardt and Tisdale 1976; Mehringer 1985; Miller and Wigand 1994; Miller and Rose 1995; Burwell 1998, 1999).

Fire return intervals for the dominant Küchler vegetation types in the region exhibit a characteristic U-shaped trend when plotted along a moisture gradient (Figure 3.3)(cf. Martin 1982). The longest return intervals (greater than 100 years) are in xeric communities where plant cover is too sparse to carry fire and in high-elevation forests where moist conditions and/or rocky substrates inhibit burning. The shortest return intervals (less than 10 years) are in grasslands. Return intervals for sagebrush communities are typically 20 to 50 years (Wright and Bailey 1982) but range from as low as 17 years in moist settings (Houston 1973) to 110 years in xeric communities (Winward 1985; Whisenant 1990).

Postfire successional patterns in contemporary sagebrush communities are generally predictable, though the specific composition of postfire communities varies considerably (Harniss and Murray 1973; Wright and Bailey 1982; Bunting 1985). With the exception of silver sage (*Artemisia tripartita*) and threetip sage (*A. nova*), all sagebrush species readily succumb to even low-intensity fires (Britton and Clark 1985). Sagebrush reestablishes readily from seeds, but recovery is often slow. Annual plants increase following fire, but the productivity of all other species generally decreases in the first few years following a burn. After this initial recovery period, grasses, forbs, and sprouting shrub species (such as horsebrush [*Tetradymia* spp.] and rabbitbrush [*Chrysothamnus* spp.]) show marked biomass and productivity increases that may persist for up to 20 years. Sagebrush recovers slowly, reaching preburn levels of biomass and productivity after 30 to 50 years, with concomitant decreases in grasses, forbs, and other shrub species. If no further burns occur, sagebrush communities (except those on the driest sites) tend either to grow into dense thickets or to be invaded by trees (e.g., Vale 1975b; Wright and Bailey 1982).

Above the sagebrush zone, higher effective moisture supports the growth of pinyon and juniper trees as well as greater fine-fuel productivity. The likelihood of lightning ignitions also increases with elevation (Reap 1986). As a result, fire return intervals are generally shorter in pinyon and juniper woodlands than they are in the sagebrush communities, at least in the absence of domestic livestock grazing (Wright and Bailey 1982; Agee 1993).

Succession in the understory of pinyon and juniper woodland is similar to that in sagebrush communities. A flush of annual forbs (and resprouting shrubs, if present) appears in the first 3 years, followed by increases in perennial grasses and forbs. Sagebrush and other nonsprouting shrubs begin to reestablish after 6 years and can, barring further fires, eventually develop into thickets and dominate sites until overtopped by trees (Wright and Bailey 1982). Small pinyon and juniper trees (less than 1.2 meters tall) are readily killed by fire, though mature trees are rarely susceptible to ground fires unless fine-fuel accumulations are exceptionally heavy (Bruner and Klebenow 1978; Wright and Bailey 1982). Fire return intervals of 10 to 30 years—variable enough to ensure reproduction but short enough to suppress both seedling survival and dense shrubs—served to keep pinyon and juniper woodlands open and savanna-like and limited to steep, rocky, and/or dissected terrain (West et al. 1975; West 1984, 1988; Burwell 1998, 1999).

Prehistoric Human Impacts on Fire Regimes: Hypotheses

The ecological and ethnographic generalizations described above suggest that frequent to intermediate disturbance rates in both shrub communities and pinyon woodlands would have supported the subsistence patterns that Steward and other anthropologists have described.

In shrublands, patchy mosaics of early- and midsuccessional communities would have supported a greater range of economically useful plant species (and the animals that fed upon them; Klebenow 1985; Nydegger and Smith 1986) than senescent stands of sagebrush. In pinyon woodlands, the ideal fire regime would presumably have allowed stands of nut-bearing trees to develop and persist wherever suitable habitats existed while maintaining an herbaceous understory as well. Annual forbs such as sunflower (*Helianthus annuus*) and wild tobacco (*Nicotiana atenuata*) thrive in the early- and midsuccessional pinyon pine communities, as do Great Basin wildrye (*Elimus cinereus*), Indian rice-grass (*Oryzopsis hymenoides*), and other useful perennial species (Wright and Bailey 1982). Frequent, low-intensity fires would have ensured the availability of these resources while killing off tree seedlings and shrubs and thus reduced the possibility of catastrophic fires.

That Great Basin peoples benefited from periodic fires does not, of course, mean that they needed to set them. Fires will not burn unless fuel loads are sufficient to support their spread. It is entirely possible that natural ignition sources were sufficient to maintain the types of landscapes on which aboriginal hunter-foragers depended.

Some authors (e.g., Shinn 1980; Harper 1986) have assumed that Indian burning was both widespread and ecologically significant. Others (e.g., West 1988) assume that native burning could not have been important and contend that the vegetation of the intermountain region was pristine at the time of European contact. In fact, with the exception of a few studies from the northern sagebrush steppes (Burkhardt and Tisdale 1976; Mehringer 1985; Wigand 1987; Miller and Wigand 1994; see Whitlock and Knox, chapter 6 of this volume), we know little about the prehistoric distribution of fires in the region and almost nothing about prehistoric environmental manipulation in the region (Rhode 1999). Our knowledge of past ignition sources is similarly thin. Using tree-ring evidence, Wadleigh and Jenkins (1996) suggested that the paucity of fires in the montane forests of northern Utah before 1859 indicates that fire regimes there had been ignition-limited prior to Mormon settlement of the area. However, it is not clear what this might imply for prehistoric fire regimes in the lower-elevation shrublands and woodlands, especially since their data only extend back to 1700, and they did not consider the possibility of climate change as an alternative explanation for the change in fire frequency.

Modern fire regimes reflect the effects of dramatically altered biotic landscapes (Knapp 1998) and thus are poor analogs for pre-Columbian conditions. But because the simplest hypothesis about past patterns is that they are similar to those we see today, contemporary data provide a basis for positing testable null hypotheses about past conditions. The National Fire Occurrence Database (Schmidt et al., forthcoming) is a compilation of all available records from federal and state land management agencies from 1986 through 1996. More than 14,500 fires occurred on federal lands within the study area during this period (Figure 3.4), and their spatial and temporal distributions provide an overview of regional patterns of fire ignitions in the intermountain West.

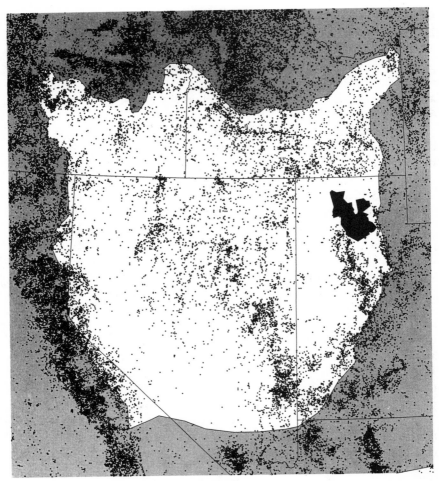

Figure 3.4. Locations of all fires on federal lands from 1986 through 1996 listed in the National Fire Occurrence Database (Schmidt et al., forthcoming). State agency records are less uniform than federal sources and are not included.

Fires were most common in the mountains surrounding the region, along the central arch of the Great Basin, and in the northern plains (cf. Knapp 1997). Lightning associated with thunderstorm activity between June and September (Figure 3.5) ignited most fires (65 percent), though there is little correlation between lightning-ignited fires and published maps of cloud-to-ground lightning flash densities (Orville 1991; Orville and Silver 1997). Flash densities decrease from 1–3 flashes per square km in Utah to 0–0.5 flash per square km in western Nevada and California. The relative proportion of "hot" lightning strikes (i.e., positive cloud-to-ground flashes with a continuing current) trends in the opposite direc-

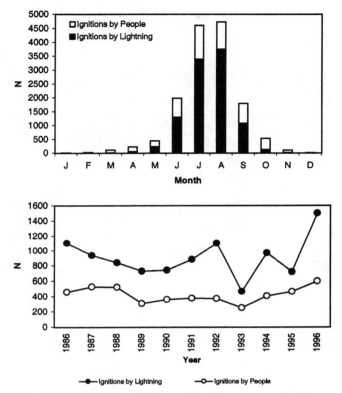

Figure 3.5. Temporal distribution of fires and ignition sources in the study area, 1986–1996 (by month and year).

tion. These strikes, which are more likely to result in ignitions, are proportionally higher (3.1 percent to as high as 12.5 percent of lightning flashes) in the northwest and the lowest (1.6 to 3.1 percent) in the southeast. Neither pattern corresponds to the pattern of lightning-ignited fires in the region. This is consistent with Knapp's (1997, 1998) findings that fuel conditions and topography seem to be the primary controls on both ignitions and area burned.

Anthropogenic ignitions account for 32 percent of all fires, but accounted for most ignitions (80 percent) between October and April, and the annual number of fires attributed to people shows greater year-to-year constancy than lightning ignitions (Figure 3.5). The relative importance of anthropogenic ignitions is greatest in the northern half of the region, particularly near populated areas such as the Wasatch Front and the Snake River Plains (Figure 3.6). Linear concentrations of ignitions caused by people are evident along the Snake and Humboldt Rivers and the highways that follow their courses.

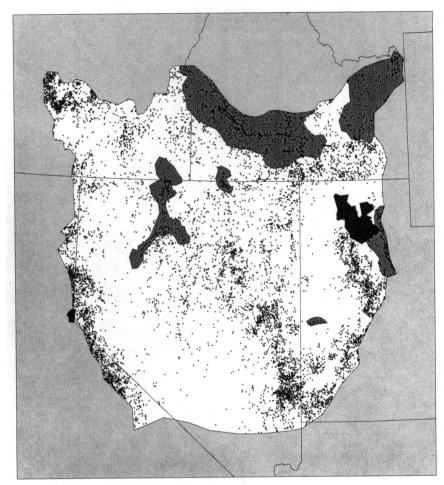

Figure 3.6. Areas where human activities ignited more than half of all fires on federal lands from 1986 through 1996 (values calculated using a 40-km-radius filter).

These patterns suggest at least four hypotheses about aboriginal impacts on prehistoric fire regimes. First, anthropogenic ignitions were less important than lightning ignitions across most of the region, and few fires occurred outside of sagebrush shrubland, pinyon-juniper woodland, and montane forest communities. Second, anthropogenic burning was locally most important in the northern part of the region, particularly in areas with high population densities, including transportation corridors, waterways, and water bodies. Third, aboriginal fire practices served to keep year-to-year ignition frequencies more constant then they would have been without human intervention. Finally, human alteration in fire regimes ensured that more fires burned during the autumn, winter, and spring than would have occurred under natural conditions.

Evaluation

These four hypotheses are, at least in principle, testable. The first two may be amenable to empirical investigation. The third and fourth can probably only be addressed through some combination of empirical work and modeling. Conducting such tests, if it is to be done at all, will require a great deal of interdisciplinary collaboration. A reasonable first step would be to collect and integrate existing information and knowledge that is currently scattered across various academic disciplines, government agencies, and other institutions. The goal of this effort should be to identify the gaps in our knowledge of both human and ecological prehistory at spatial scales, time frames, and levels of resolution appropriate to the questions being addressed. Once identified, we can begin filling in these gaps as needed.

The primary difficulty in evaluating human impacts on fire regimes in the distant past is arriving at independent estimates of fire and lightning frequencies. Such estimates have proven difficult to obtain using the standard approaches to paleoecological reconstruction. Dendrochronological methods allow tremendously detailed fire histories for some types of forest communities. Analyses of microfossils, macrofossils, charcoal, and chemical clues from lake sediments, packrat middens, and caves provide insight into past ecological communities and environmental conditions. But none of these methods can tell us anything about ignition sources. It may, however, be possible to reconstruct past frequencies of lightning strikes and past fire regimes geomorphologically.

One of the key limitations to reconstructing fire histories in the intermountain West is simply the paucity of forests and trees available for fire-scar analysis. The periodic drying and alkaline chemistry of its playa lakes similarly limit the effectiveness of pollen analysis, though charcoal records should be less affected and probably deserve greater attention. The most promising approach to reconstructing fire histories in the region may be geomorphic. Fires are geomorphic as well as biological events, and alluvial fan sediments should record those events (e.g., Meyer and Wells 1997). It may, therefore, be possible to reconstruct past fire frequencies and spatial distributions through careful stratigraphic work.

Cloud-to-ground lightning strikes sometimes fuse silica particles in soils to form hollow glass tubes called fulgurites. Sponholz et al. (1993) used excavated fulgurites to reconstruct Holocene thunderstorm frequencies in the Sahara. It might be possible to adapt their approach to

Great Basin environments to reconstruct past lightning frequencies. Combined with archeological and paleoecological data, such reconstructions might make it possible to identify patterns of fire, lightning activity, and human activity that tell us a great deal about prehistoric relationships between Great Basin peoples and the environments they inhabited.

An assessment of these relationships is long overdue. In a recent review of the rich relationship between Great Basin paleoecology and archeology, David Rhode (1999) notes that anthropologists have generally assumed that native environmental modifications have been minor and possibly recent. He comments (pp. 44–45):

> The fact is that we have little idea how much native peoples managed and shaped parts of the prehistoric environment. Obviously people have influenced many ecosystems in many different and significant ways, they have not been passive recipients of whatever Nature dishes out. The prehistoric inhabitants of the Great Basin could have exerted, and probably did exert, very significant environmental effects at some times and in certain areas.

After listing several possible impacts (altered wildlife populations, the possible role of humans in dispersing pinyon pine, and the use of fire), he concludes (p. 44) by saying that

> Documenting whether people had important environmental effects in the prehistoric Great Basin will not be an easy task; indeed, it may be very difficult. But if we were to try and find out, we might learn an awful lot about how Great Basin environments work, now and in the past, and we might learn much more about the people who worked those environments.

Just as the Great Basin was the last great blank space to be filled by American cartographers, its late Holocene ecological history and biogeography remain underexplored in comparison with other parts of the continent. The significance of this lacuna is not merely academic.

Visually, much of the modern northern intermountain West still resembles the landscapes described in early accounts of the region (Vale 1975a), but this superficial resemblance is deceiving (Rogers 1982). Plant macrofossils and pollen from packrat middens collected from Capitol Reef National Park, Utah, indicate that vegetation changes in the past two centuries have been more severe than any in the past 5,400 years (Cole et al. 1997). The same is likely to be true for most, if not all, lands in the northern intermountain West. Livestock grazing, range conversions, mining, timber harvesting, fire suppression, hunting and game management, military testing and training, road building, urbanization, interbasin water transfers, atmospheric pollution and (possibly) carbon dioxide fertilization, the introduction of exotic plant and animal species and the extinction or extirpation of native ones, and other modern human activities and impacts have altered the intermountain West's biophysical landscapes, fundamentally and probably irreversibly (D'Antonio and Vitousek 1992; Turner et al. 1993; Knapp 1996). However intensive native peoples' landscape manipulations might have been, they fade to insignificance in comparison.

More than 90 percent of the northern intermountain West is federally managed land, and the future biological status of this vast area will, to a great degree, reflect the policy and management decisions made in the next few decades. Better understanding of past human manipulations in the northern intermountain West may allow us to understand better its regional ecology as it continues to organize itself in the context of biophysical conditions and constraints that have never before existed.

Acknowledgments

I would like to thank Kirsten Schmidt of the USDA Forest Service, Rocky Mountain Research Station, Fire Sciences Laboratory in Missoula, Montana, and Cindy Savoie of the Western Great Basin Coordination Center in Reno, Nevada, for providing data. I would also like to thank Tom Vale and two reviewers for their comments on earlier drafts of the manuscript, and Eric Olmanson and Anne Griffin for their help. This research was supported in part by the NSF Postdoctoral Fellowship in Science, Mathematics, and Engineering Education program (DGE–9714534).

Literature Cited

Agee, J. K. 1993. *Fire ecology of Pacific Northwest forests.* Washington, D.C.: Island Press.

Arkush, B. S. 1990. The protohistoric period in the western Great Basin. *Journal of California and Great Basin Anthropology* 12:28–36.

Axelrod, D. I. 1976. *History of the coniferous forests, California and Nevada.* Berkeley: University of California Press.

Bettinger, R. L. 1999. What happened in the Medithermal. Pp. 62–74 in *Models for the millennium: Great Basin archeology today,* ed. C. Beck. Salt Lake City: University of Utah Press.

Billings, W. D. 1951. Vegetational zonation in the Great Basin of western North America. Pp. 101–122 in *Les bases écologiques de la régénération de la végétation des zones arides.* International Union of Biological Sciences, series B, no. 9.

————. 1954. Temperature inversions in the pinyon-juniper zone of a Nevada mountain range. *Butler University Botanical Studies* 11:112–118.

Blackburn, W. H., and P. Tueller. 1970. Pinyon and juniper invasion in black sagebrush communities in east central Nevada. *Ecology* 51:841–848.

Britton, C. M., and R. G. Clark. 1985. Effects of fire on sagebrush and bitter-brush. Pp. 22–26 in *Rangeland fire effects: A symposium*, ed. K. Sanders and J. Durham. Boise: USDI Bureau of Land Management, Idaho State Office.

Bruner, A. D., and D. A. Klebenow. 1978. *A technique to burn pinyon-juniper woodlands in Nevada*. General technical report INT-219. Ogden, Utah: USDA Forest Service, Intermountain Forest and Range Experiment Station.

Bunting, S. C. 1985. Fire in sagebrush-grass ecosystems: Successional change. Pp. 7–11 in *Rangeland fire effects: A symposium*, ed. K. Sanders and J. Durham. Boise: USDI Bureau of Land Management, Idaho State Office.

Burkhardt, J. W., and E. W. Tisdale. 1976. Causes of juniper invasion in south-western Idaho. *Ecology* 76:472–484.

Burwell, T. 1998. Successional patterns of the lower montane treeline, eastern California. *Madroño* 45:12–16.

————. 1999. Environmental history of the lower montane pinyon (*Pinus monophylla*) treeline, eastern California. Ph.D. diss., University of Wisconsin.

Chavez, F. A., and T. J. Warner, eds. 1976. *The Dominguez-Escalante journal: Their expedition through Colorado, Utah, Arizona and New Mexico in 1776*. Provo, Utah: Brigham Young University Press.

Christensen, E., and H. Johnson. 1964. Presettlement vegetation and vegetation change in three valleys in central Utah. *Brigham Young University Science Bulletin* 4:5–16.

Cole, K. L., N. Henderson, and D. S. Shafer. 1997. Holocene vegetation and historic grazing impacts at Capitol Reef National Park reconstructed using packrat middens. *Great Basin Naturalist* 57:315–326.

Cook, S. F. 1955. The epidemic of 1830–1833 in California and Oregon. *University of California Publications in American Archeology and Ethnology* 43:303–326.

Cottam, W. P. 1961. *Our renewable wild lands—A challenge*. Salt Lake City: University of Utah Press.

Cronquist, A., A. H. Holmgren, N. H. Holmgren, and J. L. Reveal. 1972. *Intermountain flora: Vascular plants of the intermountain West, U.S.A.* New York: Hafner Publishing.

D'Antonio, C. M., and P. M. Vitousek. 1992. Biological invasions by exotic grasses, the grass/fire cycle, and global change. *Annual Review of Ecology and Systematics* 23:63–87.

D'Azavedo, W., ed. 1986. *Handbook of North American Indians*, vol. 11: *Great Basin*. Washington, D.C.: Smithsonian Institution.

Denevan, W. M. 1992. The pristine myth: The landscape of the Americas in 1492. *Annals of the Association of American Geographers* 82:369–385.

Downs, J. F. 1966. The significance of environmental manipulation in Great basin cultural development. Pp. 39–55 in *The current status of anthropological research in the Great Basin: 1964*, ed. W. L. d'Azevedo et al. University of Nevada Desert Research Institute social sciences and humanities publication 1.

Fenneman, N. M. 1931. *Physiography of western United States.* New York: McGraw-Hill.

Fowler, C. 1982. Food-named groups among Northern Paiute in North America's Great Basin: An ecological interpretation. Pp. 113–129 in *Resource managers: North America and Australia hunter-gatherers,* ed. N. M. Williams and E. S. Hahn. Boulder: Westview Press.

———. 1986. Subsistence. Pp. 64–97 in *Handbook of North American Indians,* vol. 11: *Great Basin,* ed. W. D'Azavedo. Washington, D.C.: Smithsonian Institution.

———. 2000. We live by them: Native knowledge of biodiversity in the Great Basin of western North America. Pp. 99–132 in *Biodiversity and Native America,* ed. P. E. Minnis and W. J. Elisens. Norman: University of Oklahoma Press.

Grayson, D. K. 1993. *The desert's past: A natural prehistory of the Great Basin.* Washington, D.C.: Smithsonian Institution.

Gruell, G. E. 1985. Fire on the early western landscape: An annotated record of wildland fires 1776–1900. *Northwest Science* 59:97–107.

Harniss, R. O., and R. B. Murray. 1973. Thirty years of vegetational change following burning of sagebrush-grass range. *Journal of Range Management* 26:320–325.

Harper, K. T. 1986. Historical environments. Pp. 51–63 in *Handbook of North American Indians,* vol. 11: *Great Basin,* ed. W. D'Azavedo. Washington, D.C.: Smithsonian Institution.

Harper, K. T., D. L. Freeman, W. K. Ostler, and L. G. Klikoff. 1978. The flora of Great Basin mountain ranges: Diversity, sources, and dispersal ecology. Pp. 81–104 in *Intermountain biogeography: A symposium,* ed. K. T. Harper and J. L. Reveal. Great Basin naturalist memoirs 2.

Heyerdahl, E. K., D. Berry, and J. K. Agee. 1995. Fire history database of the Western United States. Interagency Agreement DW12934530. U.S. Environmental Protection Agency, USDA Forest Service, University of Washington. On the Web at *http://www.fsl.orst.edu/lter/datafr.htm,* July 1998.

Hidy, G. M., and H. E. Klieforth. 1990. Atmospheric processes affecting the climate of the Great Basin. Pp. 17–45 in *Plant biology of the basin and range,* ed. C. B. Osmond, L. F. Pitelka, and G. M. Hidy. New York: Springer-Verlag.

Holmgren, N. H. 1972. Plant geography of the Intermountain region. Pp. 77–161 in *Intermountain flora: Vascular plants of the intermountain West, U.S.A.,* vol. 1, ed. A. Cronquist, A. H. Holmgren, N. H. Holmgren, and J. L. Reveal. New York: Hafner Publishing.

Houghton, J. G., C. M. Sakamoto, and R. O. Gifford. 1975. *Nevada's weather and climate.* Reno: Nevada Bureau of Mines and Geology (special publication 2).

Houston, D. B. 1973. Wildfires in northern Yellowstone National Park. *Ecology* 54:1111–1114.

Hull, A. C., Jr., and M. K. Hull. 1974. Presettlement vegetation of Cache Valley, Utah and Idaho. *Journal of Range Management* 27:27–29.

Irwin-Williams, C. C., C. B. Osmond, A. J. Dansie, and L. F. Pitelka. 1990. Man and plants in the Great Basin. Pp. 1–15 in *Plant biology of the basin and range*, ed. C. B. Osmond, L. F. Pitelka, and G. M. Hidy. Berlin: Springer-Verlag.

Jennings, J., and E. Norbeck. 1955. Great Basin prehistory: A review. *American Antiquity* 21:1–11.

Klebenow, D. A. 1985. Big game response to fire in sagebrush-grass rangelands. Pp. 53–57 in *Rangeland fire effects: A symposium*, ed. K. Sanders and J. Durham. Boise: USDI Bureau of Land Management, Idaho State Office.

Knapp, P. A. 1996. Cheatgrass (*Bromus tectorum* L) dominance in Great Basin Desert. *Global Environmental Change* 6:37–52.

———. 1997. Spatial characteristics of regional wildfire frequencies in intermountain West grass-dominated communities. *Professional Geographer* 49:39–51.

———. 1998. Spatio-temporal patterns of large grassland fires in the intermountain West, U.S.A. *Global Ecology and Biogeography Letters* 7:259–272.

Küchler, A. W. 1985. Potential natural vegetation. *National atlas of the United States of America* (1:7,500,000 scale map). Reston, Va.: Department of the Interior, U.S. Geological Survey.

Lawton, H. W., P. J. Wilke, M. DeDedker, and W. M. Mason. 1976. Agriculture among the Paiute of Owens Valley. *Journal of California Anthropology* 3:13–50.

Leenhouts, B. 1998. Assessment of biomass burning in the conterminous United States. *Conservation Ecology* 2. On the Web at *http://www.consecol.org/vol2/iss1/art1*.

Leland, J. 1986. Population. Pp. 608–619 in *Handbook of North American Indians*, vol. 11: *Great Basin*, ed. W. D'Azavedo. Washington, D.C.: Smithsonian Institution.

Lewis, H. T. 1981. Hunter-gatherers and problems for fire history. Pp. 115–119 in *Proceedings of the fire history workshop*, ed. M. A. Stokes and J. H. Dieterich. General technical report RM-81. Fort Collins, Colo.: USDA Forest Service, Rocky Mountain Forest and Range Experiment Station.

Martin, R. E. 1982. Fire history and its role in succession. Pp. 92–99 in *Forest succession and stand development in the northwest*, ed. J. E. Means. Corvallis: Forest Research Laboratory, Oregon State University.

Mehringer, P. J., Jr. 1985. Late-Quaternary pollen records form the interior Pacific Northwest and Northern Great Basin of the United States. Pp. 167–190 in *Pollen records of late-Quaternary North American sediments*, ed. V. M. Bryant, Jr., and R. G. Holloway. Dallas: American Association of Stratigraphic Palynologists.

Meyer, G. A., and S. G. Wells. 1997. Fire-related sedimentation events on alluvial fans, Yellowstone National Park, USA. *Journal of Sedimentary Research A: Sedimentary Petrology and Processes* 67:776–791.

Miller, R. F. 2000. Fire history in the intermountain sagebrush steppe. Project description, U.S. Geological Survey Forest and Rangeland Ecosystem Science Center Project No. 70-88. On the Web at *http://webdata.fsl.orst.edu*, July 31, 2000.

Miller, R. F., and J. A. Rose. 1995. Historic expansion of *Juniperus occidentalis*

PREHISTORIC HUMAN IMPACTS ON FIRE REGIMES 99

(western juniper) in southeastern Oregon. *Great Basin Naturalist* 55(1):37–45.

Miller, R. G., and P. E. Wigand. 1994. Holocene changes in pinyon-juniper woodlands: Response to climate, fire, and human activities in the U.S. Great Basin. *BioScience* 44:465–474.

Muir, J. 1911. *The mountains of California.* New York: Century.

Nydegger, N. C., and G. W. Smith. 1986. Prey populations in relation to *Artemisia* vegetation types in southwestern Idaho. Pp. 152–156 in *Proceedings—Symposium on the biology of Artemisia and Chrysothamnus,* ed. E. D. McArthur, E. Durant, and B. L. Welch. General technical report INT-200. Ogden, Utah: USDA Forest Service, Intermountain Research Station.

Orville, R. E. 1991. Lightning ground flash density in the contiguous United States—1989. *Monthly Weather Review* 119:573–577.

———. 1994. Cloud-to-ground lightning flash characteristics in the contiguous United States: 1989–1991. *Journal of Geophysical Research* 99:10833–10841.

Orville, R. E., and A. C. Silver. 1997. Lightning ground flash density in the contiguous United States: 1992–95. *Monthly Weather Review* 125:631–638.

Reap, R. M. 1986. Evaluation of cloud-to-ground lightning data from the western United States for 1983–84 summer seasons. *Journal of Climate and Applied Meteorology* 25:785–799.

Rhode, D. 1999. The role of paleoecology in the development of Great Basin archeology, and vice versa. Pp. 29–49 in *Models for the millennium: Great Basin archeology today,* ed. C. Beck. Salt Lake City: University of Utah Press.

Rogers, G. F. 1982. *Then and now: A photographic history of vegetation change in the central Great Basin desert.* Salt Lake City: University of Utah Press.

Schmidt, K. M., J. P. Menakis, C. C. Hardy, D. L. Bunnell, and N. Sampson. Forthcoming. Development of coarse-scale spatial data for wildland fire and fuel management. General technical report RMRS-CD-000. Ogden, Utah: USDA Forest Service, Rocky Mountain Research Station.

Service, E. R. 1962. *Primitive social organization.* New York: Random House.

Shinn, D. E. 1980. Historical perspectives on range burning in the inland Pacific Northwest. *Journal of Range Management* 33:415–423.

Shreve, F. 1942. The desert vegetation of North America. *Botanical Review* 8:195–246.

Sponholz, B. R. Baumhauer, and P. Felix-Henningsen. 1993. Fulgurites in the southern central Sahara, Republic of Niger, and their paleoenvironmental significance. *The Holocene* 3:97–104.

Steward, J. H. 1938. Basin-Plateau aboriginal sociopolitical groups. *Bureau of American Ethnology Bulletin* 120.

Thomas, D. H. 1973. An empirical test for Steward's model of Great Basin settlement patterns. *American Antiquity* 38(2):155–176.

Trimble, S. 1989. *The sagebrush ocean: A natural history of the Great Basin.* Reno: University of Nevada Press.

Turner, M. G., W. H. Romme, R. H. Gardner, R. V. O'Neill, and T. K. Kratz. 1993. A revised concept of landscape equilibrium: Disturbance and stability on scaled landscapes. *Landscape Ecology* 8:213–227.

Vale, T. R. 1975a. Presettlement vegetation in sagebrush/grass area of the intermountain West. *Journal of Range Management* 28:32–36.

———. 1975b. Invasion of big sagebrush (*Artemisia tridentata*) by white fir (*Abies concolor*) on the southeastern slopes of the Warner Mountains, California. *Great Basin Naturalist* 35:319–324.

———. 1982. *Plants and people: Vegetation change in North America.* Washington, D.C.: Association of American Geographers.

———. 1998. The myth of the humanized landscape: An example from Yosemite National Park. *Natural Areas Journal* 18:231–236.

Wadleigh, L., and M. J. Jenkins. 1996. Fire frequency and the vegetative mosaic of a spruce-fir forest in northern Utah. *Great Basin Naturalist* 56:28–37.

Wigand, P. E. 1987. Diamond Pond, Harney County, Oregon—Vegetation history and water-table in the eastern Oregon desert. *Great Basin Naturalist* 47:427–458.

Wells, P. V. 1983. Paleobiogeography of montane islands in the Great Basin since the last glaciopluvial. *Ecological Monographs* 53:341–382.

West, N. E. 1984. Successional patterns and productivity potentials of pinyon-juniper ecosystems. Pp. 1302–1332 in *Developing strategies for rangeland management*, National Research Council/National Academy of Sciences, Boulder: Westview Press.

———. 1988. Intermountain deserts, shrub steppes, and woodlands. Pp. 211–230 in *North American terrestrial vegetation*, ed. M. G. Barbour and W. D. Billings. Cambridge: Cambridge University Press.

West, N. E., K. H. Rhea, and T. I. Tausch. 1975. Basic synecological relationships in juniper-pinyon woodlands. Pp. 41–53 in *The pinyon-juniper ecosystem: A symposium*, ed. G. F. Gifford and F. E. Busby, Utah Agricultural Experiment Station.

Whisenant, S. J. 1990. Changing fire frequencies on Idaho's Snake River plains: Ecological and management implications. Pp. 4–10 in *Proceedings—Symposium on cheatgrass invasion, shrub die-off, and other aspects of shrub biology and management*, ed. E. D. McArthur, E. M. Romney, S. D. Smith, and P. T. Tueller, General technical report INT-276. Ogden, Utah: USDA Forest Service, Intermountain Research Station.

Wilde, J. D., and D. E. Newman. 1989. Late Archaic corn in the eastern Great Basin. *American Anthropologist* 91:712–720.

Winward, A. H. 1985. Fire in the sagebrush-grass ecosystem—The ecological setting. Pp. 2–6 in *Rangeland fire effects: A symposium*, ed. K. Sanders and J. Durham. Boise: USDI Bureau of Land Management, Idaho State Office.

Wright, H. A., and A. W. Bailey. 1982. *Fire ecology, United States and southern Canada.* New York: John Wiley.

Young, J. A., and F. Tipton. 1990. Invasion of cheatgrass into arid environments of the Lahontan basin. Pp. 37–40 in *Proceedings—Symposium on cheatgrass invasion, shrub die-off, and other aspects of shrub biology and management*, ed. E. D. McArthur, E. M. Romney, S. D. Smith, and P. T. Tueller. General technical report INT-256. Ogden, Utah: USDA Forest Service, Intermountain Research Station.

FIRE IN THE PRE-EUROPEAN LOWLANDS OF THE AMERICAN SOUTHWEST

Kathleen C. Parker

Historic accounts of Native American–ignited fires during the early European settlement of the Southwest (Bahre 1985) have fostered claims that
pre-Columbian inhabitants of this region were masters at manipulating
their habitat through the use of fire (Dobyns 1981). Ethnographic studies of modern aboriginal cultures that use fire to manage the environment
have been extrapolated to faraway regions (Stewart 1956; Pyne 1982),
including the prehistoric Southwest, thereby fueling these claims. This
chapter debates the validity of these arguments, with an emphasis on
southern Arizona and New Mexico, where the pre-Columbian cultures
have been more thoroughly investigated than in northern Chihuahua and
Sonora (Spoerl and Ravesloot 1995). In lowland semiarid and arid parts
of the intermountain region, where trees that record fires through scar-
ring and wetlands that record fires in clear pollen/charcoal stratigraphies
are rare, there is little direct material evidence that indicates prehistoric
fire regimes. Even where charred plant remains have been found in an
archaeological context, solid clues about the associated cultural practices
are scarce. Consequently, this chapter explores the aboriginal use of fire
in southern intermountain lowlands by first addressing several related
indirect questions, then synthesizing the resulting lines of evidence. The
specific questions addressed are: (1) What is the reference fire regime for

the lowlands of the Southwest—i.e., based on lightning ignitions alone, how frequently have the lowlands burned in the recent past? (2) What indigenous cultures inhabited the region before European contact; how did their population levels fluctuate over time and space; and how did the livelihoods of the different cultures vary, particularly with respect to the use of fire? (3) How did past climates and vegetation differ from those of today in ways that would have led to long-term variation in the natural fire regime? Finally, these are integrated to address the question: (4) How did the likely past frequency of aboriginal burning in this region compare to the frequency of lightning ignitions over time—i.e., when, where, and to what extent might human activities have altered the natural fire regime?

From available data that are relevant to these questions, several key points emerge. The southern intermountain lowlands have been characterized by a rich cultural history since humans first occupied this region of the continent. Throughout the period of human occupancy, the use of fire has varied both spatially and temporally in this area as population densities, settlement patterns, and cultural practices have shifted with the evolution of the different cultural traditions. Once the modern climatic regime, with frequent summer thunderstorms, became established relatively early in the human settlement of the Southwest, any use of fire by indigenous peoples occurred against a backdrop of frequent lightning fires. For several millennia, fires ignited by lightning strikes during dry summer thunderstorms have been sufficiently frequent and extensive to account for the existence of vegetation shaped by fire where it has dominated the landscape. In certain places and during certain periods, burning by native peoples may have significantly affected the vegetation at a local scale by altering the seasonality or frequency of fire; these effects were more likely in desert grasslands than in desertscrub because of their much shorter natural fire return interval. Nonetheless, it is unlikely that intentional burning by indigenous inhabitants profoundly altered the vegetation at a broad spatial scale.

The Physical Environment in Historic Times

Environmental systems display a variety of characteristics that vary in both space and time. Two such characteristics, climate and vegetation, are particularly important influences on a third, the natural fire regime.

Climate

Although some regional variation in temperature and precipitation exists, the Southwest has four distinctive climatic periods throughout the year (Burgess 1998). May and June are consistently hot, dry months,

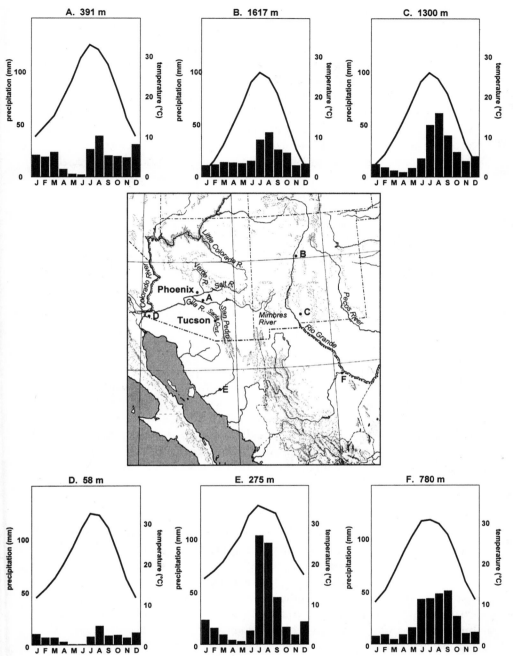

Figure 4.1. Map of the study area showing place-names mentioned and climate diagrams for selected locations within the southern intermontane region: a. Sacaton, Arizona; b. Albuquerque, New Mexico; c. Jornada, New Mexico; d. Yuma, Arizona; e. El Oregano, Sonora; and f. Presidio, Texas. (Climatic data from NCDC's Global Historical Climatology Network, version 1, dataset for El Oregano, and from NCDC's TD 9641 Clim 81 1961–1990 Normals dataset for all other stations, both available from *http://www.worldclimate.com*, visited May 5, 1999.)

with the highest water deficits of the year (Figure 4.1). The summer monsoon follows this dry period, when the influx of moist air from primarily the Gulf of California (Hales 1974) and increased convective activity lead to the occurrence of spatially disparate, but locally intense, thunderstorms. The autumn is more unpredictable than the previous two periods; in most years conditions are dry, but occasional tropical storms make landfall to the south in Mexico and pass over the region, bringing enormous amounts of rainfall that can profoundly influence the vegetation of the region. In winter, cyclonic storms track through the region and associated widespread frontal precipitation recharges soil moisture. Overall, the region exhibits a bimodal precipitation regime, with a general decrease in both the summer and annual rainfall from east to west (Figure 4.1). During El Niño–Southern Oscillation (ENSO) phenomena, the penetration of moist air into the Southwest during fall and spring is enhanced, and rainfall tends to be higher than in non-ENSO years (Andrade and Sellers 1988; Swetnam and Betancourt 1990).

Vegetation

The southern intermountain lowlands include primarily desertscrub and semidesert grassland. Together these vegetation types constitute over 70 percent of the Southwest (Lowe and Brown 1982). Chaparral, woodlands, and forests at higher elevations in the mountains and localized wetlands are the main inclusions of other vegetation within the region.

The desertscrub of the Southwest has traditionally been divided into the Sonoran and Chihuahuan Deserts on the basis of key components of the vegetation and their relationship to the environment (Figure 4.2; Shreve 1964). The Chihuahuan Desert (Figure 4.3a) extends from its main area of occurrence in northern Mexico into southeastern Arizona, southern New Mexico along the Rio Grande, and western Texas. Chihuahuan desertscrub occurs primarily from 400 to 1,600 m in elevation; most of these areas receive 200 to 300 mm of rainfall per year, with a strong summer concentration. Creosotebush (*Larrea tridentata*) is dominant throughout the Chihuahuan Desert; the codominant species vary locally (Brown 1982a). On the plains, creosotebush occurs with tarbush (*Flourensia cernua*) or whitethorn acacia (*Acacia neovernicosa*). At higher elevations and on steeper slopes, succulents are more common, including lecheguilla (*Agave lecheguilla*) and several species of yucca (*Yucca* spp.), agave (*Agave* spp.), sotol (*Dasylirion* spp.), and beargrass (*Nolina* spp.; Brown 1982a). The Rio Grande and its tributaries drain to the sea, but most other basins in the Chihuahuan Desert are internally drained. Many of the basin floors support semidesert grasslands of

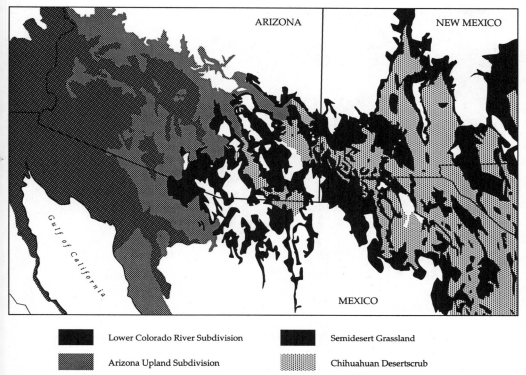

Figure 4.2. Map of the different types of lowland vegetation in the southern inter-montane region (from Brown and Lowe 1983).

tobosa (*Hilaria mutica*) or sacaton (*Sporobolus wrightii, S. airoides*), with occasional individuals of shrub species that are common in the grasslands (e.g., mesquite, *Prosopis glandulosa* and *P. juliflora*). In contrast to the Sonoran Desert, smaller stream courses lack physiognomically distinctive riparian vegetation (Brown 1982a).

The northern Sonoran Desert includes both the open, floristically simple Lower Colorado River Valley and the more diverse, structurally complex Arizona Upland (Figures 4.3b and 4.3c); additional subdivisions occur farther south in Mexico (Shreve 1964). The Lower Colorado River Valley, which includes terrain primarily below 600 m elevation, is the most extensive subdivision of the Sonoran Desert. With annual precipitation ranging from less than 50 mm to 240 mm, this subdivision includes some of the most arid parts of the Sonoran Desert (Turner and Brown 1982). Creosotebush and white bursage (*Ambrosia dumosa*) strongly dominate vast expanses of the Lower Colorado River Valley. In lower landscape positions with finer soil, saltbush (*Atriplex* spp.) was his-

Figure 4.3. Representative vegetation: a. Chihuahuan Desert, b. Lower Colorado River Valley, and c. Arizona Upland (both within the Sonoran Desert), and d. semidesert grassland.

torically more common, but the extent of this species has declined in valley bottoms that have been converted to cultivation. Small trees line waterways in the Lower Colorado River Valley; these include western honey mesquite (*Prosopis glandulosa* var. *torreyana*), ironwood (*Olneya tesota*), blue paloverde (*Cercidium floridum*), and smoketree (*Psorothamnus spinosa*).

The Arizona Upland occurs east of the Lower Colorado River Valley, where elevations are typically higher (300–1,000 m) and rainfall is greater (200–425 mm) and more strongly concentrated in the summer monsoon season (Turner and Brown 1982). Moisture is sufficiently abundant to support a low woodland with intervening shrubs and succulents, making this subdivision the most diverse in the northern Sonoran Desert. Creosotebush and triangle-leaf bursage (*Ambrosia deltoidea*) are dominant shrubs throughout the Arizona Upland; common associates include foothill paloverde (*Cercidium microphyllum*), ironwood, saguaro (*Carnegiea gigantea*), and numerous other cactus species. Streams on valley floors and bajadas support diverse tree growth that includes whitethorn (*Acacia constricta*), catclaw acacia (*A. greggii*), blue paloverde, mesquite, and desert willow (*Chilopsis linearis*; Turner and Brown 1982).

At a regional scale, the semidesert grasslands of the Southwest (Figures 4.2 and 4.3d) occur farther east than the Sonoran Desert. At a landscape scale, the distribution of semidesert grasslands is naturally fragmented by controls imposed by elevation, topography, soil texture, and carbonate-layer development (Burgess 1995). Grasslands typically occur at 900–1,525 m elevation, between desertscrub at lower elevations and evergreen woodland, chaparral, or plains grassland at higher elevations (Martin 1975). They also occupy basins, where grasses are especially suited to the shallow wetting zone characteristic of these fine-textured soils (McAuliffe 1995; McClaran 1995). Most grassland locations receive 250 to 450 mm of precipitation per year, with over half of this occurring from April through September (Brown 1982b). Semidesert grasslands include a dynamic assemblage of grasses, subshrubs, shrubs, and stem succulents; the success of each changes temporally and spatially with variation in disturbance regime, edaphic conditions, or climate (Burgess 1995). The importance of different grass species varies regionally, but most are summer-active species. Black grama (*Bouteloua eriopoda*) dominates the semidesert grasslands throughout New Mexico and western Texas, especially on gravelly upland soils (Dick-Peddie 1993:107), whereas Rothrock grama (*B. rothrockii*) and curly mesquite grass (*Hilaria belangeri*) are more widespread in Arizona (Humphrey 1958; Martin 1975). Other common grasses include three-awns (*Aristida* spp.), other grama species (*Bouteloua* spp.), Arizona cottontop (*Trichachne californica*), and bush muhly (*Muhlenbergia porteri*) (Bahre 1991). Sacaton and tobosa grasslands are more common on finer-textured soils in swales and along waterways (Brown 1982b). Important woody components of the semidesert grassland include mesquite, Mormon tea (*Ephedra trifurca*), false mesquite (*Calliandra eriophylla*), ocotillo (*Fouquieria splendens*), snakeweed (*Gutierrezia sarothrae*), creosotebush, yucca, and beargrass.

The Historic Fire Regime

Although the greatest frequency of cloud-to-ground lightning strikes in the United States occurs over peninsular Florida in a typical year (Orville 1994; Orville and Silver 1997), the Southwest leads the country in the incidence of lightning-caused fires (Komarek 1967; Schroeder and Buck 1970:168). Within Arizona, studies based on news accounts and Forest Service records have reported that fewer fires (both lightning and human-set) occur in semidesert grasslands and desertscrub than in ponderosa pine (*Pinus ponderosa*) forests at higher elevations (Barrows 1978; Baisan and Swetnam 1990; Bahre 1991—but see Kaib 1998). Most lightning fires in this region occur from May through August. To burn, vegetation needs an ignition source, an accumulation of fine, dry fuel, and appropriate meteorological conditions; the peak fire frequency in the southwestern grasslands and deserts occurs prior to the initiation of the summer monsoon when dry thunderstorms easily ignite any accumulated fine fuels cured by preceding spring drought (Wooton 1916; Bahre 1991). Gosz et al. (1995) found that although cloud-to-ground lightning strikes are more numerous over the uplands of New Mexico in the initial stages of the monsoon, strikes typically extend to lower elevations and across Arizona as the monsoon progresses (Figures 4.4a and

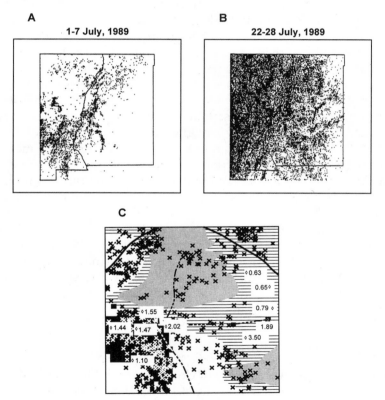

Figure 4.4. The incidence of cloud-to-ground lightning strikes over the Southwest. a. and b. The extension of cloud-to-ground lightning strikes over New Mexico as the monsoon develops from the week of July 1–7, 1989, through the week of July 22–28 (from Gosz et al. 1995). c. The location of 533 cloud-to-ground lightning strikes in a 40 square km area around Tucson from 0400 to 1100 MST on July 24, 1990, with Tucson shown in black, elevations from 915–1,525 shown with lines, and elevations greater than 1,525 m shown in gray (from Holle and Bennett 1997).

4.4b). Consequently, there is no absence of natural ignition sources at lower elevations during the height of the monsoon (Figure 4.4c). Natural ignitions are rare in the winter; previous studies based on Forest Service records have attributed all cool-season fires to human ignition (Barrows 1978; Schmid and Rogers 1988). Although grasslands vary in their rate of fuel accumulation depending on their composition and previous rainfall (Wright 1980; Cox et al. 1990), they generally accumulate sufficient biomass to carry a fire much more quickly than desertscrub and, consequently, have a greater fire frequency, or shorter fire return interval (Humphrey 1974).

Dramatic shifts in the composition and structure of semidesert grasslands since the late 1800s, coupled with concurrent land-use changes and climatic fluctuations, have obfuscated attempts to determine the natural fire regime prior to, or even immediately after, European settlement. The cover of shrubs and low trees has increased substantially in certain areas, often with a simultaneous decrease in the cover of grasses (Buffington and Herbel 1965; Gross and Dick-Peddie 1979; Hennessey et al. 1983). Scholars have attributed changes in vegetation structure to several causes: grazing, which limits the accumulation of fine fuels, disseminates seeds, and increases soil erosion (Buffington and Herbel 1965; York and Dick-Peddie 1969); fire suppression, which interacts with grazing to reduce the fire frequency further and allow woody plants to become established (Griffiths 1910; Humphrey 1958; Wright 1990; Bahre 1991); climatic change or carbon dioxide fertilization, both of which shift the competitive balance from grasses (many C_4 plants) to shrubs and trees (mostly C_3 plants) (Hastings and Turner 1965; Neilson 1986; Idso 1992); and complex interactions among these processes (Archer 1989; Grover and Musick 1990; Schlesinger 1990).

Range scientists generally agree that fire was more frequent prior to the 1900s, which helped maintain the grasslands by controlling woody growth (McPherson 1995); however, there is still debate over what that frequency was. For many years, scientists had considered the fire return interval before the late 1800s to be approximately 10 years in the semidesert grasslands of Arizona (Griffiths 1910; Leopold 1924; Hastings and Turner 1965; Wright 1980), although others felt that grasslands of New Mexico and Texas burned less frequently because of generally slower fuel accumulation and the relative fire sensitivity of black grama, the dominant species in this area (Wright and Bailey 1982; Dick-Peddie 1993). These estimates were surmised from historic newspaper accounts and journals, charred stumps within grassland areas, and purported responses of individual grass species to natural or prescribed fire. More recently, Kaib and others (Kaib et al. 1996, 1998; Kaib 1998:61–62) have reported shorter fire return intervals (4–12 years, depending on fire size) for semidesert grasslands in southeastern Arizona based on fire chronologies reconstructed from fire-scarred trees in adjacent canyons. This frequency is similar to the very short fire return intervals that Swetnam and others have reported for ponderosa pine forests in numerous uplands of the southern intermountain region (Swetnam and Dieterich 1985; Grissino-Mayer and Swetnam 1995; Swetnam and Baisan 1996a, 1996b; Touchan et al. 1996), which often ignited from fires that spread from the adjacent grasslands below (Caprio and Zwolinski 1995). Fires in the semidesert grasslands often burned large areas; Kaib (1998:62) reported a mean fire return interval of 9 to 12 years for fires that extended beyond a single basin in southeastern Arizona and burned hundreds to thousands of square kilometers. Historical accounts of grassland fires in this area (Dobyns 1981:31) indicate that some fires burned for several days. The frequent occurrence of large fires suggests that even a small number of natural ignitions is capable of burning vast tracts of semidesert grassland every several years; such ignitions are likely common under typical summer monsoonal conditions.

Recent vegetation changes in desertscrub have been more subtle, and the historic incidence of lightning fires in this vegetation probably reflects the natural fire regime more closely than in semidesert grasslands. The occurrence of fire in desertscrub communities is limited by an insufficient accumulation of fine fuels in most years (Humphrey 1963). When fires do occur, they are most common in years that follow two wet winters. These conditions are often associated with ENSO events in the Southwest (Grissino-Mayer and Swetnam 2000). Added moisture increases the productivity of annuals active during the preceding winters (Patten 1978), which leads to more rapid fuel accumulation (McLaughlin and Bowers 1982; Rogers and Vint 1987). Pockets of grass-dominated communities embedded within desertscrub (e.g., tobosa grass swales) accumulate sufficient fuel to carry a fire more quickly, but their position within a less flammable matrix probably makes them burn less frequently than semidesert grasslands (Humphrey 1963).

Several studies have estimated fire frequencies and mean fire size in desertscrub by synthesizing historical fire records maintained by different governmental agencies (Rogers and Steele 1980; Schmid and Rogers 1988). Although these estimates have shortcomings that reflect inconsistent criteria for inclusion of individual fires among different agencies, they can be used to provide a first approximation of the historical fire regime in southwestern desertscrub environments. Typical fire size in desertscrub is much smaller than in semidesert grasslands. Published estimates of mean fire size for the Sonoran

Desert range from 25.7 ha/fire in the Tonto National Forest in the Arizona Upland (including 1,611 fires from 1955 to 1983, Schmid and Rogers [1988]) to 174.4 ha/fire on Bureau of Land Management land in the Lower Colorado River Valley and Arizona Upland (210 fires from 1973 to 1979, Rogers and Steele [1980]). Based on fire records from a 29-year period for Tonto National Forest, Arizona, Schmid and Rogers (1988) estimated a fire return interval of 274 years for desertscrub habitats in the Arizona Upland. The fire frequency for the Lower Colorado River Valley may be similar, despite the less dense perennial shrub cover, because the winter annuals and other herbaceous plants are probably the most important determinants of fuel adequacy, and they can be quite prolific in these habitats after a sequence of rainy winters. Rogers and others (Schmid and Rogers 1988; Wilson et al. 1996) have noted a slight rise in fire frequency over time, which they attributed to increased cover of flammable exotic annuals and greater rainfall near the end of their study periods. The fire return interval reported by Schmid and Rogers (1988) should be interpreted as a rough estimate, given the limited data on which it is based; nonetheless, it does indicate that the natural fire return interval is far longer in desertscrub than in semidesert grasslands. The fire intolerance of many desertscrub plant species offers further testimony to the infrequency of fire in this type of vegetation under a natural regime. Although some shrubs and trees resprout after fire (Ahlstrand 1982; Cave and Patten 1984), many woody species experience reduced biomass or mortality after fire, including many cacti and other succulents (Wright 1980; Wilson et al. 1996). For some, such as saguaro, the mortality rate from fire may be 50 to 100 percent under certain conditions (Thomas 1991).

Pre-Columbian Cultures of the Southern Intermountain Lowlands

The southwestern lowlands have been a region of tremendous cultural diversity since soon after humans initially settled the area (Nabhan 1995). From the beginning of the Archaic period (ca. 7.5 ka) onward, several major cultural traditions have coexisted in this region (Figure 4.5; Cordell 1997). Even within what is generally viewed as a single tradition, there often was considerable geographic variability in pottery style, architecture and settlement pattern, means of livelihood, and other cultural practices (Doelle and Wallace 1991; McGuire 1991). This section examines some of the dominant pre-Columbian cultural traditions of the arid and semiarid lowlands over time, as well as the changing environmental backdrop against which they existed.

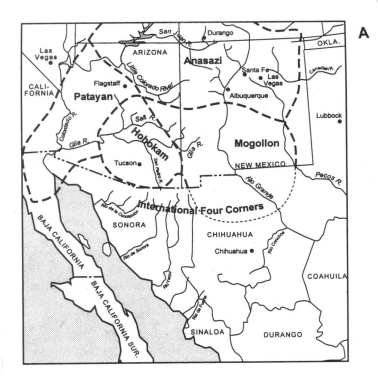

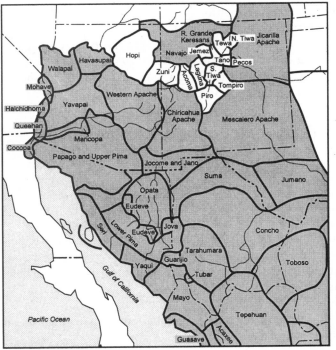

Figure 4.5. Native cultures of the southwestern lowlands during the agricultural zenith (a) and modern times (b) (Cordell 1997).

Paleoindians (ca. 11.5–7.5 ka)

Although there are many reports of earlier human occupation of North America, the first undisputed Paleoindians inhabited parts of this continent by ca. 11.5 ka. Within the southwestern lowlands, material evidence indicates their presence in valleys of the San Pedro River, the Little Colorado River, and the Rio Grande (Cordell 1997:98). No accurate population estimates exist for Paleoindians; the population probably grew throughout the period, but the density remained much lower than during later periods in the Southwest. Modern hunters and gatherers usually occur in groups of less than fifty, but Cordell (1997:97) cautioned that they may not serve as valid ethnographic analogs for southwestern Paleoindians, as some evidence from Paleoindian kill sites is inconsistent with hunting groups that small. Paleoindians were generally nomadic and collected a somewhat diverse diet of both plant and animal foods. There apparently was a trend towards decreasing size of game taken over the period, due in part to the extinction of the Pleistocene megafauna in the early Holocene. The size of game pursued varied geographically, as well; Paleoindians in the eastern part of the region specialized more in large game, including bison, while hunters to the west tended to take a greater percentage of small animals (Cordell 1997:93). Although we have very little information on their means of subsistence, it is reasonable, albeit speculative, to posit that Paleoindians used fire to drive large game in their hunting (S. Fish 1996).

When Paleoindians inhabited the southern intermountain lowlands, the physical environment was very different from the way it is now. Humans who arrived in North America near the end of the Pleistocene encountered a climate in the lowlands that was cooler and wetter, with precipitation more concentrated in the winter, than today (Betancourt et al. 1993; Thompson et al. 1993). Summer temperatures and summer rainfall increased after the Pleistocene (Van Devender 1990a, 1990b; Davis and Shafer 1992; Anderson 1993). During the early Holocene (ca. 11–8.9 ka), conditions were drier (on an annual basis) than they had been previously, but wetter than in the present day (Thompson et al. 1993). Mixed juniper (*Juniperus* spp.) and oak (*Quercus* spp.) woodlands dominated throughout the northern Chihuahuan and Sonoran Deserts; and desert riparian species were also present in some sites in the Sonoran Desert (Van Devender 1990a, 1990b). Many packrat middens from this period and cores from lakes near the Mogollon Rim (which bounds the Sonoran Desert on the north) offer evidence of abundant grasses in the vegetation of the early Holocene.

By the mid-Paleoindian period (ca. 9 ka), the summer monsoon had become well established as a consequence of the maximum summer insolation and enhanced land/sea temperature contrasts that promoted onshore air flow during this period (Thompson et al. 1993). Whether monsoon circulation and associated precipitation patterns were in place before this, as Spaulding and Graumlich (1986) suggested, is not clear (Thompson et al. 1993). By ca. 6 ka, late in the period of occupation of this region by Paleoindians, the monsoon had weakened. According to packrat data, the Chihuahuan semidesert grassland reached its maximum areal extent in the middle Holocene (ca. 8.9–4 ka) after the transition from a winter-dominated precipitation regime, which favors woody C_3 plants, to a summer-rainfall regime, which favors C_4 grasses (Neilson 1986). At the same time, desertscrub became established at lower elevations of the Sonoran and Chihuahuan Deserts (Van Devender 1990a, 1990b). The grass cover in early to middle Holocene woodlands and grasslands yielded an abundance of fine fuels; and, with increased summer convective activity providing a consistent source of ignition, frequent lightning fires were probably an integral component of the landscape—at least during the later Paleoindian occupation of this area.

The Archaic Period (ca. B.C. 7.5 ka through 200)

The Archaic period marked the dawn of the agricultural era in the Southwest. Populations grew throughout the Archaic period, and although there was always some degree of mobility, those populations became increasingly sedentary (Wills and Huckell 1994). Early Archaic peoples were hunters and gatherers. In the middle Archaic, however, as populations grew and settled, the need to extract more food from the available land coincided with the roots of agriculture in this region. By 3.5–3 ka, corn and squash were cultivated at many sites throughout the Chihuahuan and Sonoran Deserts (P. Fish and S. Fish 1994), initially in small gardens rather than large fields, which were more common later (Ford 1981). S. Fish (1996) suggested that preagriculturalists of the middle Archaic were the most likely prehistoric southwestern group to use fire in landscape management. Ethnographic analyses indicate that such a practice is common when populations are concentrating and surrendering mobility, land use is intensifying to support greater densities, and settlements are still sufficiently sparse to permit safe and efficient burning.

By the early Archaic period (ca. 6 ka), the climate approached modern conditions, but with more frequent winter freezes and rainfall more concentrated in the summer (Thompson et al. 1993). The reduced severity of winters in the late Holocene (ca. 4 ka) permitted more of the subtropical floristic elements common in the hot deserts today to migrate northward, thereby establishing modern vegetation patterns

(Van Devender 1990a, 1990b; Betancourt et al. 1993). This change occurred earlier at lower elevations and gradually progressed to higher-elevation desert locations. There is some dendrochronological and paly-nological evidence for wetter conditions later in the Archaic period to the north of the desert lowlands (Euler et al. 1979; Grissino-Mayer 1996), but whether this occurred regionally is not clear. The hydrologic record indicates that ca. 4.5–4 ka, widespread aggradation occurred in some valleys of southeastern Arizona; this preceded human occupation of those valleys (Cordell 1997:115–17).

The Agricultural Zenith (ca. A.D. 1–200 through 1250–1450)

The Archaic period in the southern intermountain lowlands was followed by the expansion and sophistication of agriculture. As agriculture developed throughout the region, populations grew. It was a time of cultural diversity, as many different cultural traditions, each with their own characteristics, existed contemporaneously (Figure 4.5). Some of the core areas of different traditions were the Phoenix and Tucson Basins (the Hohokam), the Rio Grande Valley (the Mogollon), the Mimbres River Valley (the Mimbres, which was part of the Mogollon tradition), and the Colorado River Valley (the Patayan). In these valleys, farming was closely tied to the use of supplemental water. More dispersed settlements dotted the lower Sonoran Desert in Arizona, Chihuahua, and Sonora. The following discussion focuses on the Hohokam cultural tradition, for several reasons. First, probably more is known about the Hohokam than any other southwestern lowland culture of this period (P. Fish and S. Fish 1994). Second, the Hohokam comprised more people and occupied more land than other lowland cultures (Dean et al. 1994). The Hohokam tradition occurred across the northern Sonoran Desert, except the driest western reaches. Settlements were located primarily in valleys and on lower bajadas below 1,065 m elevation (S. Fish and Nab-han 1991). Finally, the Hohokam's diverse means of subsistence, certain aspects of which were shared by other contemporaneous cultures, serve to focus any discussion about the likelihood of widespread use of fire to manage the landscape.

Regionally, the population of the Southwest grew from ca. A.D. 1 to 1000, fluctuated until ca. A.D. 1200, then declined precipitously (Dean et al. 1994; Figure 4.6). The population decline for the Hohokam probably occurred later than for other major southwestern cultures, including the Anasazi or the Mimbres. As the Hohokam population grew throughout this period, the occupied area expanded, the population became more aggregated, and land use intensified—all resulting in many changes in culture and overall economic structure (Cordell et al. 1994). The Hohokam were unique among southwestern traditions in their long-term occupation of certain sites, even in habitats away from elaborate riverine irrigation systems (P. Fish and S. Fish 1994). Despite the stability of some Hohokam sites, the period was also characterized by population flux. Local populations often abandoned an area that ceased to meet their subsistence needs, given the environmental, demographic, and cultural constraints prevalent at the time, and moved to a new location (Doelle and Wallace 1991). For example, Waters (1988a, 1988b) described population shifts to nearby bajadas where dry farming and agave production were possible (S. Fish et al. 1985) after channel downcutting along the Santa Cruz River disrupted floodwater farming in the riverine environment (Figure 4.7). At the height of their culture, the Hohokam occupied 120,000 square km in the desert lowlands of central Arizona (S. Fish and P. Fish 1992), where they constructed one of the most extensive irrigation networks of aboriginal North America. The Salt River Valley alone, which was one of the most densely populated Hohokam areas, had 12,100 to 24,200 ha of irrigated land (Nials et al. 1989) dissected by 579 km of canals (Cordell 1997:269). Accurate population estimates for the Hohokam are elusive; estimates range from 25,000 to 80,000 (Haury 1976; Cordell et al. 1994; Dean et al. 1994; Figure 4.6). During the last century or so of a clearly defined Hohokam tradition, regionally integrated settlements encompassing more than 200 ha and supporting 600–2000 people and smaller, more dispersed, mobile settlements with only 100 people simultaneously occupied the landscape (Cordell et al. 1994).

During the same time period, the Mimbres culture developed in the Mimbres River Valley in southwestern New Mexico (Minnis 1985). Like the Hohokam, they employed stream-fed irrigation along the floodplain, but also occupied smaller sites on bajadas where only dry farming and collection of wild foods were the primary means of subsistence. The Mimbres became more sedentary and experienced more rapid population growth than other Mogollon cultures in the northern Rio Grande Valley, although evidence of them as a distinct culture disappears from the archaeological record after A.D. 1150 (Minnis 1985). Mogollon populations along the northern Rio Grande never reached the size and sedentariness of Hohokam populations in the Phoenix Basin as a consequence of generally greater-magnitude floods along the Rio Grande and the shorter growing season, which increased the risks associated with agriculture (Cordell 1997:301). There were still other cultures who contemporaneously inhabited this region, but archaeological sites have been less thoroughly excavated and we have less material evidence of their cul-

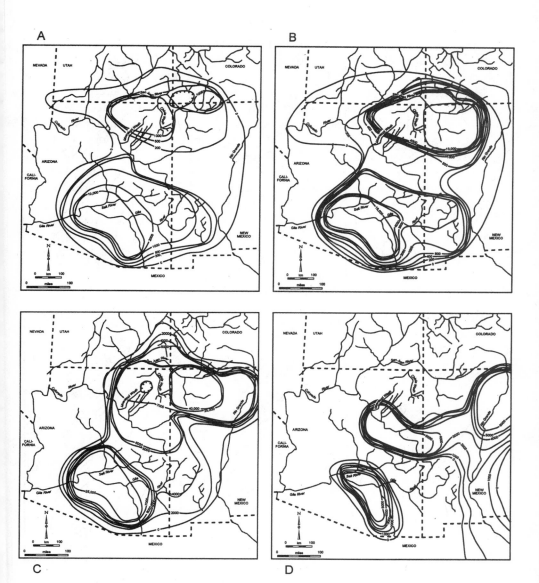

Figure 4.6. Estimated population shifts in the southwestern lowlands. Dean et al. (1994) emphasized that they have little confidence in the absolute accuracy of the estimates; rather, they should be viewed as providing a general portrayal of temporal fluctuations and spatial shifts in populations in a. A.D. 400, b. A.D. 800, c. A.D. 1200, and d. A.D. 1500 (adapted from Dean et al. 1994).

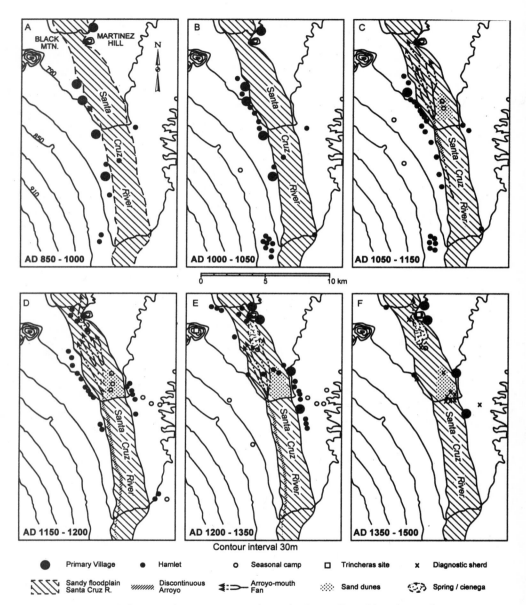

Figure 4.7. Shifts in settlement pattern along the Santa Cruz River in southeastern Arizona from A.D. 800 to A.D. 1450 in response to changes in the hydrologic regime and associated means of subsistence (adapted from Waters 1988a).

ture, particularly the ways in which they interacted with the environment.

The Hohokam and other riverine agriculturalists altered their local environment in many ways that affected the distribution of plants and animals. Overall, they constructed settlements with pithouses, ballcourts, and courtyards; introduced water to their fields, increasing plant biomass; planted both native and cultivated crops; encouraged weedy species in their fields along with crops; altered their immediate habitat in a way that favored smaller game species; and removed wood for fuel (Szuter 1991; S. Fish and P. Fish 1992). How these effects were felt in a certain location varied greatly, however, as a consequence of both geographic variation in population density and the tremendous spatial heterogeneity in culture and livelihood even within the Hohokam tradition (Doyel 1991; Gasser and Kwiatkowski 1991a, 1991b). In some areas, Hohokam were intimately tied to irrigation farming; in others, they relied more heavily on floodwater and dry farming and the collection of wild foods. Often these contrasts were apparent within the same community.

Crown (1987) characterized Hohokam communities as consisting of zones that differed in the intensity of land use and infrastructural investment, and S. Fish (1996) evaluated the probability that populations used fire as a management tool in each zone (Figure 4.8). The central area of riverine communities included intensively used land that was irrigated for agriculture, with dwellings and other structures adjacent but typically separated from fields by canals (Crown 1987). Even in smaller ephemeral drainages, there were networks of ditches from streams to fields. Charred plant remains, including several weedy species associated with disturbed ground, have been found in this zone at many archaeological sites[1] (Bohrer et al. 1969; Miksicek 1983, 1984; Bohrer 1984; S. Fish 1984b). These have been interpreted as evidence of intentional burning to clear fields and irrigation ditches (Miksicek 1983; Bohrer 1991) and to encourage weedy species that were used for food (Bohrer 1992). S. Fish (1996) agreed that some spot burning may have been used to clear canals and ditches and dispose of trash, but argued that widespread use of fire in this zone was unlikely because it would have posed too great a threat to dwellings, other structures, and valuable food resources. In addition, fire would have threatened nearby firewood sources, for which there was a substantial need in long-term settlements.

Upslope from residential areas, dry farming plots were located in close proximity to dwellings; farther up the bajada and piedmont, the Hohokam used floodwater farming (Crown 1987). Structures built in conjunction with these activities included short terraces, check dams across shallow streams, rockpiles that reduced evaporative water losses

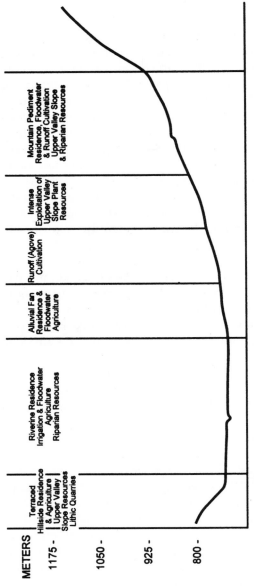

Figure 4.8. Zones of land use around riverine Hohokam communities, which probably differed in the likelihood of the use of fire as a management tool (adapted from S. Fish and P. Fish 1992).

from the soil, and brush structures designed to divert floodwater to the fields and control erosion (Miksicek 1984; see Figures 1.7a and 1.9a). The use of fire, as in the intensively used riverine environment, was improbable in these zones as well (S. Fish 1996). Flammable structures would have been damaged by fire; furthermore, bajadas and alluvial fans were habitats where the Hohokam harvested wild cactus and planted native agave, both of which are often killed by fire (Thomas 1991). Beyond this zone were more remote, higher-elevation areas where activities were limited to hunting and gathering wild foods. S. Fish (1996) noted that many intensive gathering cultures use fire to encourage useful species in a small area, but she felt that widespread use of fire by the Hohokam in these remote areas was unlikely. They would have had little time to burn these areas in addition to the other tasks necessary to maintain the structures associated with their more intense land use. As was the case on lower slopes, higher elevations supported many fire-intolerant species that constituted valuable food and medicinal resources, which fire would have destroyed. Furthermore, fallow fields and field margins provided areas to grow useful weedy species closer to their dwellings (S. Fish 1996).

The Hohokam supplemented the food raised through farming by hunting small game. Most small animals were collected near their irrigated land and dwellings. Women and children hunted most of the game in the size range (Szuter 1991) and were not likely to have used fire in the process. Men were more involved in hunting larger species, and S. Fish (1996) felt that the Hohokam probably did use fire to drive these larger animals during hunting in more remote areas. Szuter (1991) found a decreasing use of large game (e.g., deer and sheep) by the Hohokam over time, a trend similarly reported for the Mimbres (Minnis 1985), which may have been associated with constraints placed on the availability of game and related hunting practices by increasing population densities and land-use intensification.

After the Archaic period, our understanding of environmental fluctuations improves, although there are still many uncertainties about the regional synchroneity of certain precipitation anomalies and hydrologic periods, as most high-resolution proxy climatic records (e.g., tree-ring chronologies) come from higher forested terrain embedded within the desert or around its periphery (Dean et al. 1994). Existing evidence indicates that the Hohokam and other agriculturalists of the first millennium A.D. inhabited a landscape with climates and vegetation similar to those of today; nonetheless, they experienced short- and long-term fluctuations in climatic and hydrologic regimes. Short-term variation in the expression of the summer monsoon and ENSO events was likely part of that climatic fluctuation (Grissino-Mayer 1995); this, in turn, was probably associated with variation in the frequency and timing of lightning-caused fires (Swetnam and Betancourt 1998; Grissino-Mayer and Swetnam 2000).

Several hydrologic reconstructions have been made for streams in the Salt River Valley, the Tucson Basin, and the Colorado Plateau, and each shows periods of aggradation and degradation from ca. A.D. 500 through the time of widespread abandonment (A.D. 1250–1450). Despite the asynchrony of major hydrologic events among the three areas,[2] several patterns are common across the region. First, very infrequent episodes of high discharge likely destroyed irrigation structures (Waters 1988a; Nials et al. 1989). Second, channel entrenchment along a certain reach disrupted riverine agriculture by reducing the effectiveness of irrigation structures built when channel beds were higher. In contrast, relatively stable periods after valley filling were favorable for riverine farming. Third, the numerous analyses of underlying causes of local and regional abandonment have revealed complex links between population dynamics and environmental variation. Several authors have maintained that population growth and dislocation were closely tied to climatic and hydrologic fluctuations (Waters 1988a, 1988b; Nials et al. 1989; Doyel 1991; Dean et al. 1994; Grissino-Mayer 1996), but the local manifestation of such variation differed given the local environmental constraints, the cultural practices and carrying capacity of the local population, and the regional interactions among settlements (P. Fish et al. 1994; S. Fish and P. Fish 1994).

Post-Abandonment/Pre-European Contact (ca. A.D. 1250–1450 to 1536)

From ca. A.D. 1200–1450, there was widespread dislocation of people in the Southwest (Figure 4.9), which included both regional emigration and movement from one community to another within the region (Cordell 1997:368). Although attempts have been made to link regional abandonment with environmental fluctuation, strong evidence for regional synchroneity of abandonment coupled with environmental degradation is lacking (P. Fish et al. 1994; S. Fish and P. Fish 1994). The Hohokam core area in the Phoenix Basin experienced a population decline after 1450 and clear evidence of their existence is not apparent in the archaeological record after this date (S. Fish and P. Fish 1992). Population decline evidently occurred later in this area than in other areas of the Southwest (e.g., the Mimbres, other Mogollon peoples, the Anasazi). Some have noted that Hohokam abandonment followed hydrologic changes in the Salt River Valley during the mid-1300s, and somewhat later in the Tucson Basin, which likely disrupted irrigation

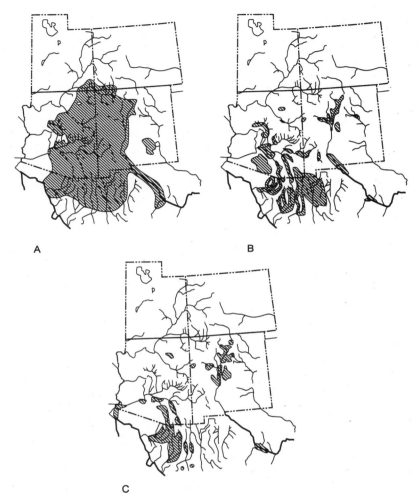

Figure 4.9. Changes in the distribution of agricultural peoples in the southern intermontane region. a. A.D. 1275–1300, b. A.D. 1400–1425, and c. A.D. 1600–1700 (adapted from P. Fish et al. 1994).

structures (Waters 1988a; Nials et al. 1989; Dean et al. 1994). However, there is considerable debate about the underlying causes of abandonment.

Between the time of widespread abandonment and the arrival of Europeans in the southwestern lowlands over a century later, native cultures present in the region today were evident. In some cases, their ancestral roots can be traced to earlier cultural traditions; in other cases, relationships between modern cultures and those of the past are unclear

(Crosswhite 1981). The Navajo and Apache played a prominent role in early interactions with European settlers in the Southwest. The history of these Athapaskan-speaking peoples in the Southwest is poorly understood. They apparently immigrated from outside the region shortly before Spanish explorers entered the Southwest; dependable radiocarbon dates link Navajo sites to the 1500s (Cordell 1997:217). Both cultures were significantly influenced by changes associated with European settlement of the area; consequently, their livelihoods differed greatly from those of previous inhabitants of the area. The Apache were less sedentary than many other groups. In contrast to either their contemporaries, the O'odham, or the Hohokam, the Apache inhabited the uplands more than the valleys. They supplemented their hunting and gathering with resources acquired through raiding and warfare (Kaib et al. 1996; Seklecki et al. 1996); in fact, a significant part of the livelihood of the Apache (as well as the Navajo) centered on domesticated livestock. Historical accounts describe the frequent use of fire by the Apache to drive game, to improve game habitat, and to provide an advantage during conflicts (Dobyns 1981; Bahre 1985, 1991).

The O'odham lived in the northern Sonoran Desert during the precontact period and continue to reside there today. Their ancestry is not clear. Some have argued that they are descendants of the Hohokam, whereas others maintain that their ancestors were another culture that coexisted with the Hohokam in the Sonoran Desert (Crosswhite 1981; Cordell 1997:435). From west to east, along a gradient of increasing rainfall, the O'odham differed in their means of subsistence and various related cultural characteristics. The westernmost O'odham (i.e., the Hiach-eD O'odham, at one time called the Sand Papago but no longer extant as a distinct culture) were nomadic and eked out an existence in the western, most arid reaches of the Sonoran Desert by using a broad array of native plants and animals, including a number of marine species from the Gulf of California (Felger 1980; Crosswhite 1981). They obtained water from tinajas and the few perennial springs that occur in the western Sonoran Desert. The O'odham who inhabited the intermediate terrain farther east (i.e., the Tohono O'odham, formerly called the Papago) were more sedentary, moving primarily on a seasonal basis. During summer, they used rock structures and brush dams to divert runoff during flash floods onto fields on lower slopes and flat areas to grow crops, interspersed with weeds and other encouraged native plants (Nabhan 1979; Fontana 1983). In winter, they lived in smaller family groups in the uplands and consumed more wild foods, which accounted for 80 percent of their diet on an annual basis (Castetter and Bell 1942:57). In addition, the Tohono O'odham set up temporary "cactus camps" on bajadas when saguaro were in fruit to harvest this wild resource, which constituted ca. 20 percent of their food supply (Cross-white 1981). At the eastern edge of the Sonoran Desert and extending into the grasslands beyond, the O'odham (i.e., the Akimel O'odham, formerly called the Pima) inhabited riverine environments that typically had a reliable water source to raise crops (Hackenberg 1983). Like the other O'odham, they incorporated many native foods into their diet; but they relied much more heavily on cultivated crops (50–60 percent of their diet; Castetter and Bell 1942:56) than their neighbors farther west. In historic times, they encouraged fencerows of native species between fields, which increased the diversity of small game species (Rea 1983) near their dwellings; but whether this practice predated the introduction of domesticated livestock is uncertain (Miksicek 1984).

The use of intentional burning by the O'odham before European contact likely varied geographically. The Hiach-eD O'odham and Tohono O'odham, who inhabited the western and central reaches of the northern Sonoran Desert, relied heavily on cacti and other fire-intolerant wild species. Any intentional fires they set were likely localized in habitats with dense herbaceous cover, away from areas where fire-sensitive ethnobotanical resources would have been damaged. The potential use of fire by the Akimel O'odham, who inhabited riverine environments and grasslands, is less certain. Ethnographic studies have described the use of fire by the O'odham during historic times to clear fields and control crop pests (Castetter and Bell 1942:125, 177), to limit woody encroachment in grasslands (Dobyns 1981:39), and to drive game (Rea 1979). However, Fontana (1983) discussed the pitfalls of using the modern O'odham as an ethnographic analog to inform us of their prehistoric cultural practices. European contact was a dynamic period for the O'odham. The upheavals associated with European settlement accompanied appreciable hydrologic and climatic fluctuation (Hackenberg 1983; Grissino-Mayer 1996). The period was also marked by the intrusion of the Apache into the eastern fringes of Akimel O'odham territory, which brought frequent raids and warfare. Although the Akimel O'odham clearly used irrigation to grow wheat in riverine environments after its introduction, it is not clear whether they irrigated crops before European contact, at a time before Apache confrontations contracted the sphere of Akimel O'odham hunting and gathering around villages (Hackenberg 1983). Therefore, modern ethnographic studies that describe the use of fire to clear fields or irrigation ditches are of debatable relevance. As S. Fish (1996) noted for the Hohokam, the widespread use of fire to manage resources close to O'odham settlements was improbable in view of the flammable structures and other valuable resources located in the immediate vicinity. Only more remote locations were likely to have been intentionally burned. Of these, grasslands in localized low areas and near the

eastern limits of O'odham lands, which were relatively sparsely populated (Fontana 1983), would have more dependably carried a fire than
desertscrub, the predominant type of vegetation throughout O'odham
country.

In 1536, the precontact era came to a close in the Southwest when
Alvar Nuñez Cabeza de Vaca encountered indigenous peoples in the
lower Yaqui Valley (Cordell 1997:429). A party led by Francisco
Vasquez de Coronado followed four years later, and a wave of European
settlement slowly moved over the area from south to north as missions
were established throughout the region over the next 150 years (Hastings and Turner 1965:28). Soon after contact, European diseases, new
crops, and domesticated animals were introduced; Spanish policies
became the rule of the land; and the original inhabitants of the region
were profoundly affected.

Discussion

Many historic newspaper and journal reports of aboriginal conflagrations
in the southwestern lowlands involved the Apache after Europeans
began to settle southeastern Arizona (Dobyns 1981; Bahre 1985, 1991).
Dendrochronologic analyses have similarly attributed periods of unusually frequent fire in several southwestern upland forests to wartime
incendiarism by the Apache, who inhabited those areas at the time, or
their enemies (Morino 1996; Seklecki et al. 1996; Kaib 1998; Kaye and
Swetnam 1999). S. Fish (1996) and others (Seklecki et al. 1996; Kaib
1998) admonished that historic use of fire by the Apache fails to provide
a valid analog for fire-related practices of most pre-Columbian southwestern cultures, for two reasons. First, most historic reports of fire use
by the Apache came during periods of hostile relations with early European settlers. Therefore, early news accounts of fires attributed to the
Apache were not necessarily free of bias (Kaye and Swetnam 1999), as
the tone in the following report from the *Arizona Daily Star*, May 21,
1882, conveys:

> Immense forest fires are still prevailing in some parts of
> western New Mexico and southern Arizona. They are
> believed to have been set out by Indians. Next to the pleas-
> ures of killing, burning appears to be the favorite amuse-
> ment of the savages. (Bahre 1991:134)

Kaib (1998) found that during peaceful periods, news accounts of fire
use by the Apache declined dramatically. Ethnographic data indicate that
the Apache used many fire-sensitive plants for food and fibers; therefore
Kaib concluded that the Apache were cautious with their use of fire in

order to protect their ethnobotanical resources, unless they were at war (Seklecki et al. 1996; Kaib 1998).

Second, our understanding of the Apache culture in this region is from the postcontact era, which undoubtedly reflects the dramatically altered political, socioeconomic, and cultural atmosphere of the region for indigenous peoples. The livelihood of the Apache following contact differed greatly from that of more sedentary agriculturalists inhabiting the region for centuries before their arrival. Yet many of the claims of universal aboriginal burning (e.g., Stewart 1956; Pyne 1982, 1995), including authors who apply ethnographic data from distant portions of the globe to the Southwest, have failed to take these cultural differences into account. Nabhan (1995:91) discusses this problem of "cultural parallax":

> Despite such diversity within and between North American cultures, it is still quite common to read statements implying a uniform "American Indian view of nature"—as if all the diverse cultural relations with particular habitats on the continent can be swept under one all-encompassing rug. Whether one is prejudiced toward the notion of Native Americans as extirpators of species or assumes that most have been negligible or respectful harvesters, there is a shared assumption that all Native Americans have viewed and used the flora and fauna in the same ways. This assumption is both erroneous and counterproductive in that it undermines any respect for the realities of cultural diversity.

Dobyns at least considered ethnographic evidence for more southwestern native cultures than just the Apache; nonetheless, his comments about aboriginal burning exemplify cultural parallax in the Southwest:

> The Western Apaches and Northern Pimans were representative of all Indoamerican tribes inhabiting the Sonoran Desert in this frequent use of fire-drives. . . . Now the time has arrived to point to the desert-wide distribution of this cultural pattern. (1981:40)

Suppositions about the widespread use of fire by aboriginal peoples of the Southwest have also been based on archeological evidence. Although fire was likely used in certain contexts (Miksicek 1983, 1984), some claims of the ubiquitous use of fire by native peoples have been more sweeping than the underlying data warrant (e.g., Bohrer 1983). S. Fish (1984a, 1984b) and Miksicek (1983, 1984) found charred plant remains and pollen assemblages indicative of human disturbance in agricultural fields and other archaeological contexts along the Salt-Gila Aqueduct in central Arizona. Their published descriptions led Bohrer (1991, 1992) to assert that the Hohokam were skilled pyrotechnicians who used fire to manage weedy species and clear irrigation ditches: "Pollen and flotation evidence in the Queen Creek area suggests that they used fire as deliberately as irrigation in the deserts surrounding their villages," and "[this evidence] combines with what we know of desert fire ecology to propose that large tracts of desert were burned to promote the grasses and cool season herbs so important to Hohokam economy" (Bohrer 1991:233). The original authors of those studies, however, were more guarded in their interpretations. Miksicek (1984:55) noted that they had "some evidence that fire may have been used for field clearing or field hunting," as well as clearing irrigation ditches; but he avoided claims that the Hohokam burned vast areas of the desert. S. Fish attributed the ubiquitous charred remains of weedy species at many sites she examined to more general manipulation of the environment by the Hohokam: "Desirable plants were collected, undesirable competitors were removed as time permitted, and mature plants were left to insure seeding" (1984a:126). She reported weed seeds and pollen in kitchen gardens adjacent to dwellings and agave remains in fields—both places where fire would have threatened valuable resources. The presence of weedy species is not necessarily indicative of fire; they are also associated with various other types of disturbance, such as overbank flooding of streams or canals (Gasser and Kwiatkowski 1991a), disruption associated with valley filling or downcutting (Martin and Mehringer 1965), or soil disturbance associated with agriculture (Minnis 1985). S. Fish (1996) later addressed the question of intentional burning by the Hohokam and concluded that it was unlikely that they used fire in the heart of their settlements near structures and fields containing crops, or in plant communities where fire-susceptible, ethnobotanically valuable species were common.

In assessing whether the pre-European settlement vegetation was a product of native peoples manipulating their environment with fire, we must consider not only the pattern of fire use by native cultures in the Southwest during their occupancy of the region, but also whether human-ignited fires altered the frequency of ignitions from lightning strikes (Minnich et al. 1993; Swetnam and Baisan 1996a). If the natural fire regime (in terms of frequency and seasonality) alone could account for the precontact vegetation patterns, we need not invoke human ignitions to explain those patterns, regardless of aboriginal landscape-burning practices (Vale 1998). Under typical monsoonal conditions, characterized by frequent convective thunderstorms, the Southwest experiences a high incidence of cloud-to-ground lightning strikes (Gosz et al. 1995; Holle and Bennett 1997). Any aboriginal burning done during summer under a monsoonal regime would likely have had little effect on the frequency of fire (Bahre 1991; Swetnam and Baisan 1996a). In desertscrub and some of the grasslands of New Mexico, where relatively slow biomass accumulation limits the occurrence of fire (Schmid and Rogers 1988; Dick-Peddie 1993), the frequency of lightning strikes far exceeds the frequency of fire. Even in the semidesert grasslands of Arizona, where the pre-1900 fire frequency was much greater (Kaib 1998), lightning strikes undoubtedly provided numerous opportunities for natural ignition (although Minnich et al. [1993] noted that fire frequency in grasslands that quickly accumulate sufficient biomass to burn tends to be limited more by ignition sources than fuel buildup). The occurrence of fires that burned hundreds to thousands of square kilometers in southeastern Arizona grasslands every decade or so before 1900 (Kaib 1998) indicates that large areas could have burned frequently with relatively few ignitions.

Perhaps the most likely period for human-enhanced fire frequency was before the development of the summer monsoon in the Southwest, when natural sources of ignition would have been greatly reduced; however, the duration of this period is not clear. Paleoenvironmental evidence indicates that the monsoon was well established by ca. 9 ka (Thompson et al. 1993), although there is some indication of an earlier expression of monsoonal conditions in parts of the Southwest (Spaulding and Graumlich 1986). Before summer thunderstorms characterized this region, increased fire frequency through human ignitions could have caused localized shifts in the composition of the herbaceous understory in woodlands, favoring fire-tolerant grasses and forbs at the expense of fire-sensitive species (Wright 1969; Cable 1972). Whether this effect would have been regionally pervasive, however, is debatable, because early Paleoindian populations were probably the smallest of any in the history of human occupancy in the Southwest. There is little likelihood that human-set fires were responsible for the extensive grass cover in the early Holocene woodlands, as has been suggested previously (Sauer 1950); the diversity of herbivores within the Pleistocene megafauna attests to a long period of coevolution of grazing animals and grasses in North America before human immigration to the continent.

By the mid-Paleoindian period (i.e., early to middle Holocene), the summer monsoonal regime was apparently well established in the lowlands (Van Devender 1990a, 1990b; Thompson et al. 1993), which undoubtedly increased the frequency of natural fire ignitions. Even for Archaic preagriculturalists, which S. Fish (1996) identified as some of the more likely practitioners of prehistoric prescribed burning, any human-set fires were occurring against a backdrop of frequent natural ignitions, when fire occurrence was probably governed more by cycles of fuel accumulation than ignition frequency. A possible exception to this might have been short- to intermediate-term episodes of reduced monsoonal strength (and associated changes in lightning ignitions), but more research is needed to determine how monsoonal expression has varied temporally and what effect this had on fire frequency (e.g., weaker monsoon conditions could have *increased* fire frequency if dry thunderstorms that brought little fire-extinguishing rainfall were common). The potential effects of aboriginal burning on vegetation during periods of reduced natural ignitions would be difficult to assess, in view of the complex direct and indirect influences of variation in monsoonal expression—and associated changes in the lightning regime—on vegetation patterns. For example, Neilson (1986) found that the population dynamics of black grama, the modern dominant throughout the grasslands of New Mexico, is closely tied to the balance between summer and winter rainfall; and the species may indeed be out of equilibrium with the modern climate. During the Little Ice Age (ca. 1400–1800), the reduced winter but consistent summer rainfall provided more favorable conditions for establishment of black grama (a C_4 summer-active plant) from seed; the increased frequency of wet winters since then has tipped the competitive balance in favor of C_3 plants, and black grama regeneration has been primarily asexual (Neilson 1986). Prehistoric intermediate-term fluctuations in rainfall seasonality may have been accompanied by similar compositional shifts in the semidesert grasslands, thereby changing the mosaic of fuels that carry fire. Therefore, attempts to determine effects of altered natural ignitions associated with monsoonal fluctuation on grasslands would have to isolate the direct influence of changes in precipitation seasonality on vegetation composition from the indirect effects (i.e., associated changes in the lightning regime).

Aboriginal use of fire under a monsoonal climate may have affected the fire regime in more subtle ways than altering the fire frequency. Interannual variation in the occurrence of fire in many southwestern ponderosa pine forests from ca. 1600 until ca. 1900 shows a strong relationship to antecedent climatic conditions, which govern the accumulation of fine fuel (Swetnam and Betancourt 1990; Swetnam and Baisan 1996a, 1996b; Touchan et al. 1996). In some mountain ranges, however, reconstructed fire chronologies apparently reflect the augmentation of climatically governed natural ignitions with aboriginal fires during the postcontact period (Swetnam et al. 1992; Morino 1996; Swetnam and Baisan 1996a, 1996b; Baisan and Swetnam 1997; Kaib 1998; Kaye and Swetnam 1999). Some of these fires were set earlier in the spring, when natural ignitions are less common (Seklecki et al. 1996; Kaye and Swetnam 1999). Morino (1996) postulated that such fires might interrupt

the climatically induced cycle of fuel accumulation by igniting the vegetation at times when it would not normally burn, thereby potentially
affecting the subsequent occurrence of fire.

Whether such effects may have been felt in the lowlands is inconclu-
sive. Most of the enhanced burning recorded in the uplands were conflagrations set by warring Apache, whose incendiary habits were unpar-
alleled among early agriculturalists. The settlement patterns of the
Hohokam and other riverine agriculturalists likely precluded more than
a limited, controlled use of fire within the main area of settlement (S.
Fish 1996). The need to protect fire-sensitive, valuable ethnobotanical
resources, as well as an inconsistent fuel accumulation in the desertscrub,
probably restricted the use of fire in peripheral areas of Hohokam settlements or in terrain used by less sedentary peoples. Nonetheless, it is possible (albeit speculative, in the absence of firm evidence) that some fires
used to clear irrigation ditches or drive game were set at a time of the
year when fires would have been easier to control than during the dry
premonsoon period. Experimental work has shown that the effect of fire
on many individual grassland and desertscrub species varies seasonally
(e.g., black grama: Reynolds and Bohning 1956; Cable 1972; Bock and
Bock 1978; Martin 1983); consequently, the use of fire during the cool
season might have induced subtle compositional changes reflecting these
interspecific differences. As was probably the case in earlier periods, however, it is unlikely that any human alterations of the natural fire regime
were pervasive throughout the precontact landscape or that they were
the dominant controls of vegetation patterns where they did occur.

Conclusion

At certain times and in some locations, various pre-Columbian cultures of
the Southwest made use of fire to manage their resources; but the evidence certainly does not warrant the general conclusion that "Indoamer-
ican hunting with fire basically determined the distribution of plant
species Euroamericans encountered in the Sonoran Desert" (Dobyns
1981:43). Early in their occupation of the area, human populations were
probably too small and scattered—leaving large portions of the landscape
temporarily uninhabited—to have been a dominant force in shaping vegetation patterns through the use of fire. Later, as their numbers grew and
land use intensified, social constraints probably precluded indiscriminate
burning of the landscape in many places, while an insufficient fuel accumulation limited fire in others. Throughout most of the human occupancy of the southern intermountain lowlands, monsoonal circulation has
provided a nonlimiting source of ignitions during the early summer. What
prescribed burning did occur before European settlement was not likely

to have enhanced the already high potential ignition frequency, although changes in seasonality of burning may have produced localized changes in vegetation composition. Clearly the tendency of prehistoric southwestern peoples to burn their habitat varied among different cultures, and probably both temporally and geographically within cultures, as well. In any event, an understanding of the Native American use of fire to manipulate the pre-European landscape requires an appreciation of the diverse cultural history of the area. Hastings and Turner's remarks (1965:22) about landscape changes in the last century echo the cultural complexity of previous human-vegetation relations: "What we have to consider, then, is . . . a fluid environment shifting with the centuries under the impact of a succession of cultures, each differing somewhat from the preceding in its relation to the life around it." Generalizations about aboriginal environmental manipulation that ignore this cultural richness and natural environmental variation fail to provide an accurate vision of the past.

Notes

1. Miksicek (1983) noted that even in arid climates where decomposition is relatively slow, prehistoric plant remains are not preserved and later recovered from open archaeological sites unless they are charred.
2. The Salt River heads in the Mogollon Highlands, whereas the streams in the Tucson Basin head farther to the south at lower elevation. Therefore, hydrologic conditions are often out of phase in the two basins, despite their relatively close proximity (Dean et al. 1994). Furthermore, within a single stream system, the locus of aggradation or degradation shifts over time, and adjustments ripple through the drainage network (Waters 1988a).

Literature Cited

Ahlstrand, G. M. 1982. Response of Chihuahuan Desert mountain shrub vegetation to burning. *Journal of Range Management* 35:62–65.

Anderson, R. S. 1993. A 35,000 year vegetation and climate history from Potato Lake, Mogollon Rim, Arizona. *Quaternary Research* 40:351–359.

Andrade, E. R., and W. D. Sellers. 1988. El Niño and its effect on precipitation in Arizona and western New Mexico. *Journal of Climatology* 8:403–410.

Archer, S. 1989. Have southern Texas savannas been converted to woodlands in recent history? *American Naturalist* 134:545–561.

Bahre, C. J. 1985. Wildfire in southeastern Arizona between 1859 and 1890. *Desert Plants* 7:190–194.

———. 1991. *A legacy of change: Historic human impact on vegetation of the Arizona borderlands.* Tucson: University of Arizona Press.

Baisan, C. H., and T. W. Swetnam. 1990. Fire history on a desert mountain range: Rincon Mountain Wilderness, Arizona, U.S.A. *Canadian Journal of Forest Research* 20:1559–1569.

Barrows, J. S. 1978. Lightning fires in southwestern forests. Final unpublished report to USDA Forest Service Rocky Mountain Forest and Range Experiment Station, Fort Collins, Colo., cooperative agreement 16-568-CA.

Betancourt, J. L., E. A. Pierson, K. A. Rylander, J. A. Fairchild-Parks, and J. S. Dean. 1993. Influence of history and climate on New Mexico piñon-juniper woodlands. Pp. 42–62 in *Managing piñon-juniper ecosystems for sustainability and social needs*, tech. coord. E. F. Aldon and D. W. Shaw. General technical report RM-236. Fort Collins, Colo.: USDA Forest Service.

Bock, C. E., and J. H. Bock. 1978. Response of birds, small mammals, and vegetation to burning sacaton grasslands in southeastern Arizona. *Journal of Range Management* 31:296–300.

Bohrer, V. L. 1983. New life from ashes II: The tale of the burnt brush (*Rhus trilobata*). *Desert Plants* 5:122–124.

———. 1984. Domesticated and wild crops in the CAEP study area. Pp. 183–259 in *Prehistoric cultural development in central Arizona: Archaeology of the Upper New River Region*, ed. P. M. Spoerl and G. J. Gumerman. Southern Illinois University at Carbondale Center for Archaeological Investigations occasional paper no. 5. Carbondale: Southern Illinois University.

———. 1991. Recently recognized cultivated and encouraged plants among the Hohokam. *Kiva* 56:227–235.

———. 1992. New life from ashes II: A tale of burnt brush. *Desert Plants* 10:122–125.

Bohrer, V. L., H. C. Cutler, and J. D. Sauer. 1969. Carbonized plant remains from two Hohokam sites, Az. BB:13:41 and Az. BB:13:50. *Kiva* 35:1–10.

Brown, D. E. 1982a. Chihuahuan desertscrub. Pp. 169–179 in *Biotic communities of the American Southwest—United States and Mexico*, ed. D. E. Brown. Vol. 4 of *Desert Plants*. Tucson: University of Arizona.

———. 1982b. Semidesert grassland. Pp. 123–131 in *Biotic communities of the American Southwest—United States and Mexico*, ed. D. E. Brown. Vol. 4 of *Desert Plants*. Tucson: University of Arizona.

Brown, D. E., and C. H. Lowe. 1983. *Biotic communities of the American Southwest*, rev. ed. (map). General technical report RM-78. Fort Collins, Colo.: USDA Forest Service.

Buffington, L. C., and C. H. Herbel. 1965. Vegetational changes on a semidesert grassland range from 1858 to 1963. *Ecological Monographs* 35:139–164.

Burgess, T. L. 1995. Desert grassland, mixed shrub savanna, shrub steppe, or semidesert scrub: The dilemma of coexisting growth forms. Pp. 31–67 in *The desert grassland*, ed. M. P. McClaran and T. R. Van Devender. Tucson: University of Arizona Press.

———. 1998. Norwestern Apacherian savannas: A description and review of issues concerning human inhabitation. Pp. 3–10 in *The future of arid grasslands: Identifying issues, seeking solutions*, ed. B. Tellman, D. M. Finch, C. Edminster, and R. Hamre. Proceedings RMRS-P-3. Fort Collins, Colo.: USDA Forest Service.

Cable, D. R. 1972. Fire effects on southwestern semidesert grass-shrub communities. *Proceedings of the Tall Timbers Fire Ecology Conference* 12:109–127.

Caprio, A. C., and M. J. Zwolinski. 1995. Fire and vegetation in a Madrean oak woodland, Santa Catalina Mountains, southeastern Arizona. Pp. 389–398 in *Biodiversity and management of the Madrean Archipelago: The sky islands of southwestern United States and northwestern Mexico*, tech. coord. L. F. DeBano, G. J. Gottfried, R. H. Hamre, C. B. Edminster, P. F. Ffolliott, and A. Ortega-Rubio. General technical report RM-264. Fort Collins, Colo.: USDA Forest Service.

Castetter, E. F., and W. H. Bell. 1942. *Pima and Papago agriculture*. Albuquerque: University of New Mexico Press.

Cave, G. H., and D. T. Patten. 1984. Short-term vegetation responses to fire in the upper Sonoran Desert. *Journal of Range Management* 37:491–496.

Cordell, L. 1997. *Archaeology of the Southwest*, 2d ed. San Diego: Academic Press.

Cordell, L. S., D. E. Doyel, and K. W. Kintigh. 1994. Processes of aggregation in the prehistoric Southwest. Pp. 109–133 in *Themes in Southwest prehistory*, ed. G. J. Gumerman. Santa Fe: School of American Research Press.

Cox, J. R., F. A. Ibarra-F, and M. H. Martin-R. 1990. Fire effects on grasses in semiarid deserts. Pp. 43–49 in *Effects of fire management of southwestern natural resources*, tech. coord. J. S. Krammes. General technical report RM-191. Fort Collins, Colo.: USDA Forest Service.

Crosswhite, F. S. 1981. Desert plants, habitat and agriculture in relation to the major pattern of cultural differentiation in the O'odham people of the Sonoran Desert. *Desert Plants* 3:47–76.

Crown, P. L. 1987. Classic period Hohokam settlement and land use in the Casa Grande Ruins area, Arizona. *Journal of Field Archaeology* 14:147–162.

Davis, O. K., and D. S. Shafer. 1992. A Holocene climatic record for the Sonoran Desert from pollen analysis of Montezuma Well, Arizona, USA. *Palaeogeography, Palaeoclimatology, Palaeoecology* 92:107–119.

Dean, J. S., W. H. Doelle, and J. D. Orcutt. 1994. Adaptive stress, environment, and demography. Pp. 53–86 in *Themes in Southwest prehistory*, ed. G. J. Gumerman. Santa Fe: School of American Research Press.

Dick-Peddie, W. A. 1993. *New Mexico vegetation: Past, present and future*. Albuquerque: University of New Mexico Press.

Dobyns, A. F. 1981. *From fire to flood*. Anthropological paper 20. Socorro, N. Mex.: Ballena.

Doelle, W. H., and H. D. Wallace. 1991. The changing role of the Tucson Basin in the Hohokam regional system. Pp. 279–345 in *Exploring the Hohokam: Prehistoric desert peoples of the American Southwest*, ed. G. J. Gumerman. Albuquerque: University of New Mexico Press.

Doyel, D. E. 1991. Hohokam cultural evolution in the Phoenix Basin. Pp. 231–278 in *Exploring the Hohokam: Prehistoric desert peoples of the American Southwest*, ed. G. J. Gumerman. Albuquerque: University of New Mexico Press.

Euler, R. C., G. J. Gumerman, T. N. V. Karlstrom, J. S. Dean, and R. H. Hevly. 1979. The Colorado Plateau: Cultural dynamics and paleoenvironment. *Science* 205:1089–1101.

Felger, R. S. 1980. Vegetation and flora of the Gran Desierto, Sonora, Mexico. *Desert Plants* 2:87–114.

Fish, P. R., and S. K. Fish. 1994. Southwest and Northwest: Recent research at the juncture of the United States and Mexico. *Journal of Archaeological Research* 2:3–44.

Fish, P. R., S. K. Fish, G. J. Gumerman, and J. J. Reid. 1994. Toward an explanation for southwestern "abandonments." Pp. 135–163 in *Themes in Southwest prehistory*, ed. G. J. Gumerman. Santa Fe: School of American Research Press.

Fish, S. K. 1984a. Agriculture and subsistence implications of the Salt-Gila Aqueduct pollen analysis. Pp. 111–138 in *Hohokam archaeology along the Salt-Gila Aqueduct, Central Arizona Project*, vol. 7: *Environment and subsistence*, ed. L. S. Teague and P. L. Crown. Arizona State Museum, Archaeological Series 150. Tucson: University of Arizona.

———. 1984b. Appendix A: Pollen from agricultural features. Pp. 575–603 in *Hohokam archaeology along the Salt-Gila Aqueduct, Central Arizona Project*, vol. 3: *Specialized activity sites*, ed. L. S. Teague and P. L. Crown. Arizona State Museum archaeological series 150. Tucson: University of Arizona.

———. 1996. Modeling human impacts to the Borderlands environment from a fire ecology perspective. Pp. 125–134 in *Effects of fire on Madrean Province ecosystems: A symposium proceedings, March 11–15, 1996, Tucson, Arizona*, tech. coord. P. F. Ffolliott, L. F. DeBano, M. B. Baker, G. J. Gottfried, G. Solis-Garza, C. B. Edminster, D. G. Neary, L. S. Allen, and R. H. Hamre. General technical report RM-289. Fort Collins, Colo.: USDA Forest Service.

Fish, S. K., and P. R. Fish. 1992. Prehistoric landscapes of the Sonoran Desert Hohokam. *Population and Environment* 13:269–283.

———. 1994. Prehistoric desert farmers of the Southwest. *Annual Review of Anthropology* 23:83–108.

Fish, S. K., and G. P. Nabhan. 1991. Desert as context: The Hohokam environment. Pp. 29–60 in *Exploring the Hohokam: Prehistoric desert peoples of the American Southwest*, ed. G. J. Gumerman. Albuquerque: University of New Mexico Press.

Fish, S. K., P. R. Fish, C. Miksicek, and J. Madsen. 1985. Prehistoric agave cultivation in southern Arizona. *Desert Plants* 7:107–112, 100.

Fontana, B. L. 1983. Pima and Papago: Introduction. Pp. 125–136 in *Handbook of North American Indian*, vol. 10: *Southwest*, ed. A. Ortiz. Washington, D.C.: Smithsonian Institution.

Ford, R. I. 1981. Gardening and farming before A.D. 1000: Patterns of prehistoric cultivation north of Mexico. *Journal of Ethnobiology* 1:6–27.

Gasser, R. E., and S. M. Kwiatkowski. 1991a. Food for thought: Recognizing patterns in Hohokam subsistence. Pp. 417–459 in *Exploring the Hohokam: Prehistoric desert peoples of the American Southwest*, ed. G. J. Gumerman. Albuquerque: University of New Mexico Press.

———. 1991b. Regional signatures of Hohokam plant use. *Kiva* 56:207–226.

Gosz, J. R., D. I. Moore, G. A. Shore, and H. D. Grover. 1995. Lightning estimates of precipitation location and quantity on the Sevilleta LTER, New Mexico. *Ecological Applications* 5:1141–1150.

Griffiths, D. 1910. *A protected stock range in Arizona*. USDA Bureau of Plant Industry bulletin no. 177. Washington D.C.: U.S. Government Printing Office.

Grissino-Mayer, H. D. 1995. Tree-ring reconstructions of climate and fire history at El Malpais National Monument, New Mexico. Ph.D. diss., University of Arizona, Tucson.

———. 1996. A 2129-year reconstruction of precipitation for northwestern New Mexico, USA. Pp. 191–204 in *Tree rings, environment, and humanity*, ed. J. S. Dean, D. M. Meko, and T. W. Swetnam. Tucson, Ariz.: Radiocarbon.

Grissino-Mayer, H. D., and T. W. Swetnam. 1995. Effects of habitat diversity on fire regimes in El Malpais National Monument, New Mexico. Pp. 195–200 in *Proceedings of the symposium on fire in wilderness and park management, Missoula, Mont., March 30–April 1, 1993*, ed. J. K. Brown, R. W. Mutch, C. W. Spoon, and R. H. Wakimoto. General technical report INT-320. Ogden Utah: USDA Forest Service.

———. 2000. Century-scale climate forcing of fire regimes in the American Southwest. *The Holocene* 10:213–220.

Gross, F. A., and W. A. Dick-Peddie. 1979. A map of primeval vegetation in New Mexico. *Southwestern Naturalist* 24:115–122.

Grover, H. D., and H. B. Musick. 1990. Shrubland encroachment in southern New Mexico, U.S.A.: An analysis of desertification processes in the American Southwest. *Climatic Change* 17:305–330.

Hackenberg, R. A. 1983. Pima and Papago ecological adaptations. Pp. 161–177 in *Handbook of North American Indians*, vol. 10: *Southwest*, ed. A. Ortiz. Washington, D.C.: Smithsonian Institution.

Hales, J. E., Jr. 1974. Southwestern United States summer monsoon source—Gulf of Mexico or Pacific Ocean? *Journal of Applied Meteorology* 13:331–342.

Hastings, J. R., and R. M. Turner. 1965. *The changing mile: An ecological study of vegetation change with time in the lower mile of an arid and semiarid region*. Tucson: University of Arizona Press.

Haury, E. W. 1976. *The Hohokam, desert farmers and craftsmen: Excavations at Snaketown, 1964–1965*. Tucson: University of Arizona Press.

Hennessy, J. T., R. P. Gibbens, J. M. Tromble, and M. Cardenas. 1983. Vegetation changes from 1935 to 1980 in mesquite dunelands and former grasslands of southern New Mexico. *Journal of Range Management* 36:370–374.

Holle, R. L. and S. P. Bennett. 1997. Lightning ground flashes associated with summer 1990 flash floods and streamflow in Tucson, Arizona: An exploratory study. *Monthly Weather Review* 125:1526–1536.

Humphrey, R. R. 1958. *The desert grassland—A history of vegetational change and an analysis of causes*. Arizona Agricultural Experiment Station bulletin 299. Tucson: University of Arizona.

———. 1963. The role of fire in the desert and desert grassland areas of Arizona. *Proceedings of the Tall Timbers Fire Ecology Conference* 2:45–61.

———. 1974. Fire in deserts and desert grassland of North America. Pp. 365–400 in *Fire and ecosystems*, ed. T. T. Kozlowski and C. E. Ahlgren. New York: Academic Press.

Idso, S. B. 1992. Shrubland expansion in the American Southwest. *Climatic Change* 22:85–86.

Kaib, J. M. 1998. Fire history in riparian canyon pine-oak forests and the inter-vening desert grasslands of the southwest borderlands: A dendroecological, historical, and cultural inquiry. Master's thesis, University of Arizona, Tucson.

Kaib, M., C. H. Baisan, H. D. Grissino-Mayer, and T. W. Swetnam. 1996. Fire history in the gallery pine-oak forests and adjacent grasslands of the Chiri-cahua Mountains of Arizona. Pp. 253–264 in *Effects of fire on Madrean Province ecosystems: A symposium proceedings, March 11–15, 1996, Tucson, Arizona*, tech. coord. P. F. Ffolliott, L. F. DeBano, M. B. Baker, G. J. Gottfried, G. Solis-Garza, C. B. Edminster, D. G. Neary. L. S. Allen, and R. H. Hamre. General technical report RM-289. Fort Collins, Colo.: USDA Forest Service.

Kaib, M., C. H. Baisan, and T. W. Swetnam. 1998. Historical patterns of sur-face fire in canyon pine-oak forests, savannas, and intervening semiarid grass-lands of the Southwest borderlands. Pp. 101–106 in *The future of arid grass-lands: Identifying issues, seeking solutions*, ed. B. Tellman, D. M. Finch, C. Edminster, and R. Hamre. Proceedings RMRS-P-3. Fort Collins, Colo.: USDA Forest Service.

Kaye, M. W., and T. W. Swetnam. 1999. An assessment of fire, climate, and Apache history in the Sacramento Mountains, New Mexico. *Physical Geogra-phy* 20:305–330.

Komarek, E. V. 1967. The nature of lightning fires. *Proceedings of the Tall Tim-bers Fire Ecology Conference* 7:5–41.

Leopold, A. 1924. Grass, brush, timber, and fire in southern Arizona. *Journal of Forestry* 22:1–10.

Lowe, C. H., and D. E. Brown. 1982. Introduction. Pp. 8–16 in *Biotic com-munities of the American Southwest—United States and Mexico*, ed. D. E. Brown. Vol. 4 of *Desert Plants*. Tucson: University of Arizona Press.

Martin, P. S., and P. J. Mehringer, Jr. 1965. Pleistocene pollen analysis and bio-geography of the Southwest. Pp. 433–451 in *The Quaternary of the United States*, ed. H. E. Wright, Jr., and D. G. Frey. Princeton: Princeton University Press.

Martin, S. C. 1975. Ecology and management of southwestern semidesert grass-shrub ranges: The status of our knowledge. Research paper RM-156. Fort Collins, Colo.: USDA Forest Service.

———. 1983. Responses of semidesert grasses and shrubs to fall burning. *Jour-nal of Range Management* 36:604–610.

McAuliffe. J. R. 1995. Landscape evolution, soil formation, and Arizona's desert grasslands. Pp. 100–129 in *The desert grassland*, ed. M. P. McClaran and T. R. Van Devender. Tucson: University of Arizona Press.

McClaran, M. P. 1995. Desert grasslands and grasses. Pp. 1–30 in *The desert grassland*, ed. M. P. McClaran and T. R. Van Devender. Tucson: University of Arizona Press.

McGuire, R. H. 1991. On the outside looking in: The concept of periphery in Hohokam archaeology. Pp. 347–382 in *Exploring the Hohokam: Prehistoric desert peoples of the American Southwest*, ed. G. J. Gumerman. Albuquerque: University of New Mexico Press.

McLaughlin, S. P., and J. E. Bowers. 1982. Effects of wildfire on a Sonoran Desert plant community. *Ecology* 63:246–248.

McPherson, G. R. 1995. The role of fire in the desert grasslands. Pp. 130–151 in *The desert grassland*, ed. M. P. McClaran and T. R. Van Devender. Tucson: University of Arizona Press.

Miksicek, C. H. 1983. Appendix B: Plant remains from agricultural features. Pp. 604–620 in *Hohokam archaeology along the Salt-Gila Aqueduct, Central Arizona Project*, vol. 3: *Specialized activity sites*, ed. L. S. Teague and P. L. Crown. Arizona State Museum Archaeological Series 150. Tucson: University of Arizona.

————. 1984. Historic desertification, prehistoric vegetation change, and Hohokam subsistence in the Salt-Gila Basin. Pp. 53–80 in *Hohokam archaeology along the Salt-Gila Aqueduct, Central Arizona Project*, vol. 7: *Environment and subsistence*, ed. L. S. Teague and P. L. Crown. Arizona State Museum Archaeological Series 150. Tucson: University of Arizona.

Minnich, R. A., E. F. Vizcaíno, J. Sosa-Ramirez, and Y.-E. Chou. 1993. Lightning detection rates and wildland fires in the mountains of northern Baja California, Mexico. *Atmósfera* 6:235–253.

Minnis, P. E. 1985. *Social adaptation to food stress: A prehistoric southwestern example*. Chicago: University of Chicago Press.

Morino, K. A. 1996. Reconstruction and interpretation of historical patterns of fire occurrence in the Organ Mountains, New Mexico. Master's thesis, University of Arizona, Tucson.

Nabhan, G. P. 1979. The ecology of floodwater farming in arid southwestern North America. *Agro-Ecosystems* 5:245–255.

————. 1995. Cultural parallax in viewing North American habitats. Pp. 87–101 in *Reinventing nature? Responses to postmodern deconstruction*, ed. M. E. Soulé and G. Lease. Washington, D.C.: Island Press.

Neilson, R. P. 1986. High-resolution climatic analysis and Southwest biogeography. *Science* 232:27–34.

Nials, F. L., D. A. Gregory, and D. A. Graybill. 1989. Salt River streamflow and Hohokam irrigation systems. Pp. 59–76 in *The 1982–1984 excavations at Las Colinas: Environment and subsistence*. Archaeological series no. 162, vol. 5. Tucson: Cultural Resource Management Division, Arizona State Museum, University of Arizona.

Orville, R. E. 1994. Cloud-to-ground lightning flash characteristics in the contiguous United States: 1989–1991. *Journal of Geophysical Research* 99(D5):10833–10841.

Orville, R. E., and A. C. Silver. 1997. Lightning ground flash density in the contiguous United States: 1992–1995. *Monthly Weather Review* 125:631–638.

Patten, D. T. 1978. Productivity and production efficiency of an upper Sonoran Desert ephemeral community. *American Journal of Botany* 65:891–895.

Pyne, S. J. 1982. *Fire in America: A cultural history of wildland and rural fire*. Princeton: Princeton University Press.

————. 1995. *World fire: The culture of fire on earth*. New York: Henry Holt.

Rea, A. M. 1979. Hunting lexemic categories of the Pima Indians. *Kiva* 44:113–119.

————. 1983. *Once a river: Bird life and habitat changes on the Middle Gila*. Tucson: University of Arizona Press.

Reynolds, H. G., and J. W. Bohning. 1956. Effects of burning on a desert grass-shrub range in southern Arizona. *Ecology* 37:769–777.

Rogers, G. F., and J. Steele. 1980. Sonoran desert fire ecology. Pp. 15–19 in *Proceedings of the Fire History Workshop*, tech. coord. M. A. Stokes and J. H. Dieterich. General technical report RM-81. Fort Collins, Colo.: USDA Forest Service.

Rogers, G. F., and M. K. Vint. 1987. Winter precipitation and fire in the Sonoran Desert. *Journal of Arid Environments* 13:47–52.

Sauer, C. O. 1950. Grassland climax, fire, and man. *Journal of Range Management* 3:16–21.

Schlesinger, W. H., J. F. Reynolds, G. L. Cunningham, L. F. Huenneke, W. M. Jarrell, R. A. Virginia, and W. G. Whitford. 1990. Biological feedbacks in global desertification. *Science* 247:1043–1048.

Schmid, M. K., and G. F. Rogers. 1988. Trends in fire occurrence in the Arizona Upland subdivision of the Sonoran Desert, 1955 to 1983. *Southwestern Naturalist* 33:437–444.

Schroeder, M. J., and C. C. Buck. 1970. *Fire weather: A guide for application of meteorological information to forest fire control operations*. Agricultural handbook 360. Washington, D.C.: USDA Forest Service.

Scurlock, D. 1998. *From the rio to the sierra: An environmental history of the middle Rio Grande Basin*. General technical report RMRS-5. Fort Collins, Colo.: USDA Forest Service.

Seklecki, M. T., H. D. Grissino-Mayer, and T. W. Swetnam. 1996. Fire history and the possible role of Apache-set fires in the Chiricahua Mountains of southeastern Arizona. Pp. 238–246 in *Effects of fire on Madrean Province ecosystems: A symposium proceedings, March 11–15, 1996, Tucson, Arizona*, tech. coord. P. F. Ffolliott, L. F. DeBano, M. B. Baker, G. J. Gottfried, G. Solis-Garza, C. B. Edminster, D. G. Neary, L. S. Allen, and R. H. Hamre. General technical report RM-289. Fort Collins, Colo.: USDA Forest Service.

Shreve, F. 1964. Vegetation of the Sonoran Desert. Vol. 1, part 1 of *Vegetation and flora of the Sonoran Desert*, F. Shreve and I. L. Wiggins. Stanford: Stanford University Press.

Spaulding, W. G., and L. J. Graumlich. 1986. The last pluvial climatic episodes in the deserts of southwestern North America. *Nature* 320:441–444.

Spoerl, P. M., and J. C. Ravesloot. 1995. From Casas Grandes to Casa Grande: Prehistoric human impacts in the sky islands of southern Arizona and northwestern Mexico. Pp. 492–501 in *Biodiversity and management of the Madrean Archipelago: The sky islands of southwestern United States and northwestern Mexico*, tech. coord. L. F. DeBano, G. J. Gottfried, R. H. Hamre, C. B. Edminster, P. F. Ffolliott, and A. Ortega-Rubio. General technical report RM-264. Fort Collins, Colo.: USDA Forest Service.

Stewart, O. C. 1956. Fire as the first great force employed by man. Pp. 115–133 in *Man's role in changing the face of the earth*, ed. W. L. Thomas, Jr. Chicago: University of Chicago Press.

Swetnam, T. W., and C. H. Baisan. 1996a. Fire histories of montane forests in the Madrean borderlands. Pp. 15–36 in *Effects of fire on Madrean Province ecosystems: A symposium proceedings, March 11–15, 1996, Tucson, Arizona,* tech. coord. P. F. Ffolliott, L. F. DeBano, M. B. Baker, G. J. Gottfried, G. Solis-Garza, C. B. Edminster, D. G. Neary, L. S. Allen, and R. H. Hamre. General technical report RM-289. Fort Collins, Colo.: USDA Forest Service.

———. 1996b. Historical fire regime patterns in the southwestern United States since A.D. 1700. Pp. 11–32 in *Fire effects in southwestern forests: Proceedings of the second La Mesa Fire symposium, March 29–31, 1994, Los Alamos, New Mexico*, ed. C. D. Allen. General technical report RM-286. Fort Collins, Colo.: USDA Forest Service.

Swetnam, T. W., and J. L. Betancourt. 1990. Fire-southern oscillation relations in the southwestern United States. *Science* 249:1017–1020.

———. 1998. Mesoscale disturbance and ecological response to decadal climatic variability in the American Southwest. *Journal of Climate* 11:3128–3147.

Swetnam, T. W., and J. H. Dieterich. 1985. Fire history of ponderosa pine forests in the Gila Wilderness, New Mexico. Pp. 390–397 in *Proceedings of the symposium and workshop on wilderness fire, Nov. 15–18, 1983, Missoula, Mont.*, ed. J. E. T. C. Lotan, B. M. Kilgore, W. C. Fischer, and R. W. Mutch. General technical report INT-182. Ogden, Utah: USDA Forest Service.

Swetnam, T. W., C. H. Baisan, A. C. Caprio, and P. M. Brown. 1992. Fire history in a Mexican oak-pine woodland and adjacent montane conifer gallery forest in southeastern Arizona. Pp. 165–173 in *Ecology and management of oak and associated woodlands: Perspectives in the southwestern United States and northern Mexico*, tech. coord. P. F. Ffolliott, G. J. Gottfried, D. A. Bennett, V. M. Hernandez, A. Ortega-Rubio, and R. H. Hamre. General technical report RM-218. Fort Collins, Colo.: USDA Forest Service.

Szuter, C. R. 1991. Hunting by Hohokam desert farmers. *Kiva* 56:277–291.

Thomas, P. A. 1991. Response of succulents to fire: A review. *International Journal of Wildland Fire* 1:11–22.

Thompson, R. S., C. Whitlock, P. J. Bartlein, S. P. Harrison, and W. G. Spaulding. 1993. Climatic changes in the western United States since 18,000 yr B.P. Pp. 468–513 in *Global climates since the last glacial maximum*, ed. H. E. Wright, Jr., J. E. Kutzback, T. Webb III, W. F. Ruddiman, F. A. Street-Perrott, and P. J. Bartlein. Minneapolis: University of Minnesota Press.

Touchan, R., C. D. Allen, and T. W. Swetnam. 1996. Fire history and climatic patterns in ponderosa pine and mixed-conifer forests of the Jemez Mountains, northern New Mexico. Pages 33–46 in *Fire effects in southwestern forests: Proceedings of the second La Mesa Fire symposium, March 29–31, 1994, Los Alamos, New Mexico*, ed. C. D. Allen. General technical report RM-286. Fort Collins, Colo.: USDA Forest Service.

Turner, R. M., and D. E. Brown. 1982. Sonoran desertscrub. Pp. 181–221 in *Biotic communities of the American Southwest—United States and Mexico*, ed. D. E. Brown. Vol. 4 of *Desert Plants*. Tucson: University of Arizona Press.

Vale, T. R. 1998. The myth of the humanized landscape: An example from Yosemite National Park. *Natural Areas Journal* 18:231–236.

Van Devender, T. R.. 1990a. Late Quaternary vegetation and climate of the Chihuahuan Desert, United States and Mexico. Pp. 104–133 in *Packrat mid-*

dens: The last 40,000 years of biotic change, ed. J. L. Betancourt, T. R. Van Devender, and P. S. Martin. Tucson: University of Arizona Press.

————. 1990b. Late Quaternary vegetation and climate of the Sonoran Desert, United States and Mexico. Pp. 134–165 in *Packrat middens: The last 40,000 years of biotic change*, ed. J. L. Betancourt, T. R. Van Devender, and P. S. Martin. Tucson: University of Arizona Press.

Van Devender, T. R., J. L. Betancourt, and M. Wimberly. 1984. Biogeographic implications of a packrat midden sequence from the Sacramento Mountains, south-central New Mexico. *Quaternary Research* 22:344–360.

Vogl, R. J. 1974. Effects of fire on grasslands. Pp. 139–194 in *Fire and ecosystems*, ed. T. T. Kozlowski and C. E. Ahlgren. New York: Academic Press.

Waters, M. R. 1988a. Holocene alluvial geology and geoarchaeology of the San Xavier reach of the Santa Cruz River, Arizona. *Geological Society of America Bulletin* 100:479–491.

————. 1988b. The influence of late quaternary landscape processes on Hohokam settlement patterning in southern Arizona. Pp. 79–130 in *Hohokam archaeology along phase B of the Tucson Aqueduct Central Arizona project*. Archaeological series no. 178. Tucson: Cultural Resource Management Division, Arizona State Museum, University of Arizona.

Wills, W. H., and B. B. Huckell. 1994. Economic implications of changing land-use patterns in the late Archaic. Pp. 33–52 in *Themes in Southwest prehistory*, ed. G. J. Gumerman. Santa Fe: School of American Research Press.

Wilson, R. C., M. G. Narog, B. M. Corcoran, and A. L. Koonce. 1996. Postfire saguaro injury in Arizona's Sonoran Desert. Pp. 247–252 in *Effects of fire on Madrean Province ecosystems: A symposium proceedings, March 11–15, 1996, Tucson, Arizona*, tech. coord. P. F. Ffolliot, L. F. DeBano, M. B. Baker, G. J. Gottfried, G. Solis-Garza, C. B. Edminster, D. G. Neary, L. S. Allen, and R. H. Hamre. General technical report RM-289. Fort Collins, Colo.: USDA Forest Service.

Wooton, E. O. 1916. *Carrying capacity of grazing ranges in southern Arizona*. USDA Bureau of Plant Industry bulletin no. 367. Washington, D.C.: U.S. Government Printing Office.

Wright, H. A. 1969. Effect of spring burning on tobosa grass. *Journal of Range Management* 22:425–427.

————. 1980. *The role and use of fire in the semidesert grass-shrub type*. General technical report INT-85:1–24. Ogden, Utah: USDA Forest Service.

————. 1990. Role of fire in the management of southwestern ecosystems. Pp. 1–5 in *Effects of fire management of southwestern natural resources*, tech. coord. J. S. Krammes. General technical report RM-191. Fort Collins, Colo.: USDA Forest Service.

Wright, H. A., and A. W. Bailey. 1982. *Fire ecology: United States and southern Canada*. New York: John Wiley.

York, J. C., and W. A. Dick-Peddie. 1969. Vegetation changes in southern New Mexico during the past hundred years. Pp. 157–166 in *Arid lands in perspective*, ed. W. G. McGinnies and B. J. Goldman. Tucson: University of Arizona Press.

CHAPTER 5

LOTS OF LIGHTNING AND PLENTY OF PEOPLE: AN ECOLOGICAL HISTORY OF FIRE IN THE UPLAND SOUTHWEST

Craig D. Allen

Was the pre-European Southwest a region of wild landscapes, shaped primarily by natural processes like lightning-ignited fire, or did people substantially mold these lands into regional-scale artifacts through their use of fire and other means? Perspectives on this question have varied markedly through time and between scholars, as evident from the quotes interspersed through this chapter (see Box 5.1). As the American frontier closed around the turn of the nineteenth century, lightning was rarely considered a primary cause of fire, with most fires in western forests assumed to be human-ignited. Native Americans were thought to have been the primary source of burning in the Southwest until Euro-Americans usurped that role after ca. 1850. Today, lightning-ignited fire is widely acknowledged to be an ancient and essential ecological process in the American Southwest (Pyne 1995a:282–283; Swetnam and Baisan 1996a; Bogan et al. 1998), for millennia structuring landscapes from low-elevation desert grasslands to montane forests. However, because the Southwest has been home to people for more than 12,000 years, with large human populations for over 1,000 years (Plog et al. 1988), some scholars continue to assert the dominance of aboriginal burning in the fire regimes of this region (Dobyns 1981; Pyne 1995a, 1996, 1997). This essay focuses on the roles of lightning versus human ignitions in pre-1900 fire regimes of the upland forests and woodlands of the Southwest. Given the regional abundance of long-term paleoecological and archaeological information, the Southwest provides unique opportunities to assess the relative importance of both natural and cultural factors in the ecological history of fire (Swetnam et al. 1999).

The American Southwest as discussed here is centered on Arizona and New Mexico, extending into adjoining portions of Mexico, the Colorado Plateau in Utah and Colorado, and western Texas. The emphasis of this chapter is on upland settings in the mountains and plateaus of this region, ranging from isolated mountain "sky islands" in the deserts of northern Sonora to the extensive subalpine forests of the southern Rocky Mountains in New Mexico. The forests and woodlands that cloak the Southwestern uplands provide the most extensive and detailed regional-scale network of fire history data available in the world (Swetnam and Baisan 1996a; Swetnam et al. 1999). I will give particular attention to the Jemez Mountains area in northern New Mexico (Figure 5.1), as this landscape exemplifies one of the most humanized portions of the prehistoric Southwest, with abundant fire history and land use information available. It is also the landscape I know and love best.

Multiple lines of evidence contribute to the southwestern fire and land use histories used here (Allen et al. 1998; Swetnam et al. 1999):

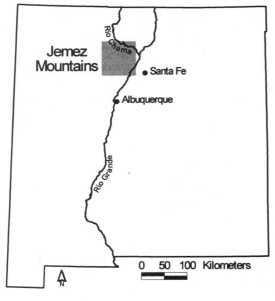

Figure 5.1. Location of the Jemez Mountains in New Mexico. The box outlines the area displayed in Figures 5.2, 5.4, and 5.5.

dendrochronological reconstructions of fire history, forest age structures, and climate; charcoal from bogs and other sedimentary records; repeat photography; modern observations of lightning and fire activity; documentary archives; and a variety of data from archeological surveys and excavations. This review begins with a consideration of the natural history of fire in the Southwest, then addresses the role of humans in modifying the fire regimes of this region's landscapes. I assert that frequent fire is an intrinsic, natural feature of the uplands of the Southwest, primarily driven by nonhuman factors such as climate, availability of surface fuels, and lightning ignitions. Modern claims of extensive aboriginal burning of southwestern landscapes are shown to be based upon broad overgeneralizations and uncritical extrapolations from a few historical reports of localized fire use. Yet within the overall regional context of generally natural fire regimes, people have significantly modified patterns of fire during particular times and in particular places. Since the ecological history of southwestern fire involves interactions among both natural and cultural histories, generalizations about "pristine" versus "humanized" landscape conditions need to consider the particulars of variation in the relative effects of people through time and space.

The Natural History of Fire in the Southwest

> Fire belongs in the mountain Southwest, and unless the peaks flatten, the monsoon evaporates, the seasons homogenize, or the biota vanishes, those fires will continue. (Pyne 1995a:295)

The paleoecology of the southwestern United States, including records of fire occurrence, is documented as well as for any region on Earth (Betancourt et al. 1990; Swetnam et al. 1999). Packrat middens (Van Devender and Spaulding 1979; Betancourt et al. 1990) and pollen deposits (R. S. Anderson 1993; Weng and Jackson 1999) show that modern climate/vegetation patterns basically developed in the Southwest during the early Holocene, ca. 11,000 to 8,000 years ago. Substantial fire activity apparently emerged in the Southwest during that time, as evidenced by the contemporaneous and rapid spread of fire-adapted ponderosa pine forests across the region (Anderson 1989) and by the abundant charcoal deposits found in lake and bog sediments (Petersen 1988; Brunner-Jass 1999; Weng and Jackson 1999). For example, Weng and Jackson (1999) link increases in fire activity to the establishment of ponderosa pine forests on the Kaibab Plateau between about 10,000 and 11,000 years ago, while charcoal sediments from Alamo Bog in the Jemez Mountains indicate essentially continuous fire activity extending back to at least 8,000 years ago (Brunner-Jass 1999). Other evidence includes a regional network of dendrochronologically dated fire-scar chronologies that documents the patterns of frequent and extensive fire which have characterized most southwestern forests over at least the past 300 to 500 years (Swetnam and Baisan 1996a; Swetnam et al. 1999), while the fire suppression records of land management agencies provide a direct record of abundant fire activity during the twentieth century (Barrows 1978; Snyderman and Allen 1997; Rollins et al. 1999). It is apparent that the uplands of the Southwest have experienced widespread and recurrent fires for thousands of years. Although fire-using people were present in the Southwest throughout this time period, the dominant view among fire ecologists is that most of the regional patterns of fire occurrence across the prehistoric and historic Southwest are adequately explained by natural factors (Swetnam and Baisan 1996a), including an abundance of lightning ignitions (Barrows 1978) and receptive climate/fuel conditions (Swetnam and Betancourt 1998).

A key feature of the southwestern environment that naturally fosters the occurrence of fire is a plentiful source of fire ignitions through high levels of lightning activity (Barrows 1978; Orville and Silver 1997). Convectional thunderstorms that generate lightning occur frequently in the Southwest, particularly during the summer monsoon season when warm temperatures and influxes of moist maritime air trigger near-daily cloud buildups over mountain areas. For example, 62 thunderstorm-days per year are observed in the Jemez Mountains at Los Alamos (U.S. DOE 1979), generating large numbers of lightning strikes. An automated lightning detection system (Krider et al. 1980) recorded 165,117 cloud-to-ground lightning strikes over a 775,554 ha area centered on the Jemez Mountains during the period 1985–1994. The annual number of recorded lightning strikes varied between 9,410 and 23,317 (see Figure 5.2). Although lightning activity clearly peaks during the summer monsoon (Figure 5.3), strikes were recorded in every month. Particularly important for fire ignitions is the substantial lightning activity during the warm, dry, foresummer months of April through June (Figure 5.3), when many lightning strikes occur from sporadic storms or clouds generating only virga (rain that evaporates while falling and thus fails to reach the Earth's surface). These strikes are the most significant sources of fire ignition because lightning is much more likely to start a spreading fire if it strikes dry fuels. Because lightning ignitions are so frequent and ubiquitous in the Southwest (Barrows 1978), climate and fuel conditions are the main drivers of fire regime dynamics in this region (Swetnam and Betancourt 1990, 1998; Swetnam and Baisan 1996a).

Patterns of precipitation variability in the Southwest favor frequent and extensive fire activity. The generally dry climate of this interior conti-

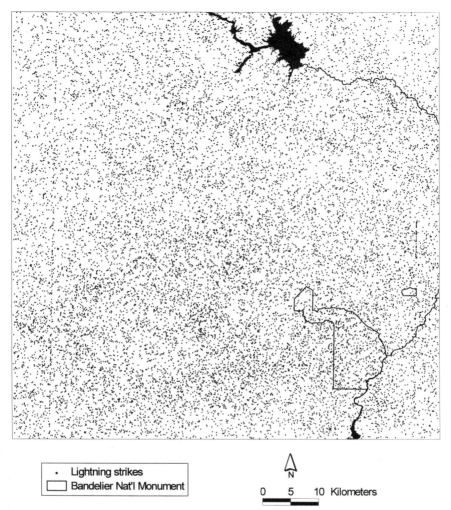

Figure 5.2. Lightning strikes in the Jemez Mountains, 1986. Map of 23,317 light-ning strikes recorded across 775,554 ha in the Jemez Mountains area during 1986 by the national automated lightning detection system. The nominal resolution of the locational data is approximately 2 km. Surprisingly little difference in lightning strike frequencies is evident across the 1,800-meter elevational gradient present in this field of view, which is also the same in Figures 5.4 and 5.5.

nental region permits fuels to burn readily much of the year, especially during the warmer months of April through October (Barrows 1978). Dry seasons typically occur in the spring and fall between the winter period of cyclonic storms and the summer monsoon, with most precipi-tation received during the monsoon (Figure 5.3). The spring dry season

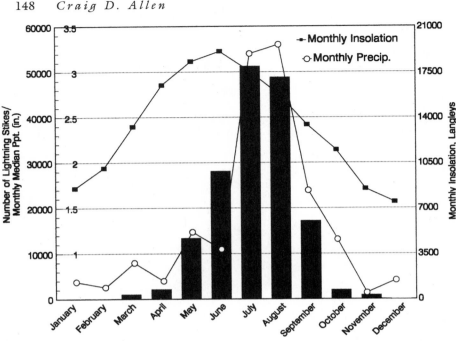

Figure 5.3. Monthly patterns of lightning strikes, insolation, and precipitation in the Jemez Mountains area. Lightning data from 165,117 cloud-to-ground strikes during 1985–1994 over 775,554 ha centered on the Jemez Mountains (Figure 5.2). Insolation and precipitation data for Los Alamos, New Mexico, from Bowen (1990).

(April through June) is particularly conducive to fire activity due to the common persistence of drought throughout much of this period, the long and warm days of this high-sun period, and the occurrence of lightning. While dry conditions are also common for multiweek periods in the fall, few natural ignitions occur at this time due to low levels of lighting activity. Fall burning conditions are also constrained by the shorter day lengths, the cooler temperatures, and the interruption of dry spells by cyclonic storms. In addition, substantial variability in regional precipitation happens at annual and decadal time scales due to the El Niño–Southern Oscillation phenomenon and other factors. This regionalized precipitation variability tends to synchronize fire activity and other disturbances across the Southwest, with the highest levels of fire activity occurring after dry winters (Swetnam and Betancourt 1990, 1998). Dendrochronological reconstructions of climate show that these patterns of substantial precipitation variability, including severe and sustained droughts, have characterized the Southwest for at least the past 2,000 years (Dean and Funkhouser 1995; Meko et al. 1995; Grissino-Mayer 1996). Overall, the climatic regime of recurrent dryness in the Southwest provides frequent and extended opportunities for the ignition and spread of fires. To the north, into southern Colorado and Utah, the distinctive climate of the Southwest grades into a colder and more continental pattern dominated by fall-to-spring moisture from cyclonic storms embedded in the polar front jet stream, without pronounced spring drought and with less lightning activity (as a result, fire occurrence begins to shift from spring to midsummer, and natural fire frequencies decrease [Brown et al. 1999]). To the south, down the continental spine of the Sierra Madre Occidental into Durango (Mexico), key fire-enhancing features of the southwestern climate remain evident, including the pattern of warm, dry spring conditions broken by the influx of lightning-yielding summer moisture from the tropics (Fulé and Covington 1999).

Fuel conditions in the Southwest also promote fire activity. The buildup of herbaceous and woody plant materials through plant growth and slow decay processes provides sufficient fuel periodically to support spreading fires in most Southwestern ecosystems. However, fuel types (e.g., grass versus logs), quantities (tons/ha), flammabilities, and rates of buildup depend upon patterns of vegetation structure, productivity, and species composition—these vary considerably across the major topographic, elevational, and ecological gradients that characterize southwestern landscapes (cf. Bogan et al. 1998). General zonational patterns can be discerned (Merriam 1890; Brown 1982): low-elevation grasslands grade upslope into woodlands of pinyon (*Pinus edulis*) and juniper (*Juniperus*) species, then into open ponderosa pine (*Pinus ponderosa*) forests, then become denser forests of mixed-conifer species (including *Pseudotsuga menziessi* and *Abies concolor*), ending with the high, cold, wet forests of spruce (*Picea engelmanni*) and corkbarkfir (*Abies lasiocarpa* var. *arizonica*), which in turn grade into subalpine and alpine vegetation on the highest peaks. The high frequency of spreading surface fires observed in the fire-scar record (Swetnam and Baisan 1996a) indicates that fine fuels (grasses and needle litter) have long been primary fuels in many southwestern ecosystems. Prior to changes initiated by the heavy grazing of introduced sheep and cattle (Leopold 1924; Cooper 1960; Baisan and Swetnam 1997; Bogan et al. 1998), herbaceous understories dominated by perennial grasses were present from valley grasslands up through ponderosa pine forests and into many highland mixed-conifer forests. Herbaceous plants create fine-textured surface fuels that dry out quickly (hours to days), particularly when exposed to sun and wind in open forest settings; as a result such fuels are often in suitable condition to burn. Since fire-adapted perennial grasses and herbs regenerate rapidly after fire, fuel quantities and continuities can often recover sufficiently to allow fire to recur in just a few years. Similarly, the needle litter from long-needled ponderosa pine trees dries out quickly, contains highly flammable terpenoid compounds, and rebuilds a surface litter cover within 3 to 7 years of removal as senescent needles drop from the trees—all characteristics that support high-frequency surface fires.

The factors of ignition, climate, and fuels combine to create a regional pattern where fire frequencies are greatest at the middle elevations along montane topographic gradients in the upper ponderosa pine zone (Swetnam and Baisan 1996a). Since high fire frequencies feed back to maintain relatively open forest structures that favor persistent herbaceous ground cover and long-needled ponderosa pines, these conditions generally co-occurred in the Southwest. At lower elevations (e.g., pinyon-juniper woodlands) herbaceous productivity declines due to drier conditions, thereby reducing fuel continuities and increasing the time needed for fuels to recover between fires. In contrast, vegetation productivity is enhanced at higher elevations, but the cooler, moister climate is only suitable for burning during shorter time windows, resulting in less frequent and patchier fires, denser mixed-conifer and spruce-fir forests, stifled herbaceous understories, and the dominance of slower-drying woody fuels (including the more compacted and less flammable litter of these shorter-needled conifers).

Twentieth-century records of fire suppression efforts illustrate the fire-prone nature of southwestern ecosystems. During the period 1960–1975, 80 percent of the fires on the national forests of Arizona and New Mexico were ignited by lightning, averaging 1,873 lightning fires per year (ranging from 1,184 to 2,841) for the highest rate of lightning fire ignition in the United States (Barrows 1978); for all protected private, state, and federal lands the regional average was 2,371 lightning fires per year. In southwestern national forests between 1940 and 1975, more than 1,000 lightning fires occurred during all but two fire seasons, 1941 and 1955; 187 lightning fires were ignited on the Gila National Forest alone in a 7-day period in 1974 (Barrows 1978:34). Area burned by lightning-caused wildfires peaks in June before the onset of the summer rains, although lightning ignitions are at a maximum in July (Barrows 1978). Southwestern fire activity is generally enhanced by drought (Barrows 1978; Rollins et al. 1999), with higher levels of regionally synchronized fire activity occurring in dry La Niña years (Swetnam and Betancourt 1990, 1998). Fires would have repeatedly burned across widespread portions of the Southwest during the twentieth century if these numerous lightning-ignited fires had not been vigorously suppressed by fire-fighting actions. Fuel availability has become less of a limiting factor in recent decades due to the landscape-wide buildups of woody fuels associated with a century of fire suppression (Covington et al. 1997; Bogan et al. 1998). As a result the frequency and severity of wildfire activity (including lightning-ignited fires) has been escalating despite increasing human suppression efforts, as the mean number of lightning fires per year in the Southwest grew by more than 50 percent from 1940 to 1975 (Barrows

1978); the mean annual acreage burned in the Southwest has increased continuously since ca. 1960 (Swetnam and Betancourt 1998); and unnatural stand-replacing conflagrations like the 1977 La Mesa Fire (Allen 1996a) and the 2000 Cerro Grande Fire are occurring more often in overdense ponderosa pine forests (Covington and Moore 1994).

These regional patterns of twentieth-century fire activity are also apparent in the suppression records from the Jemez Mountains (Figure 5.4). The point locations of 4,487 wildfires recorded between 1909 and 1996

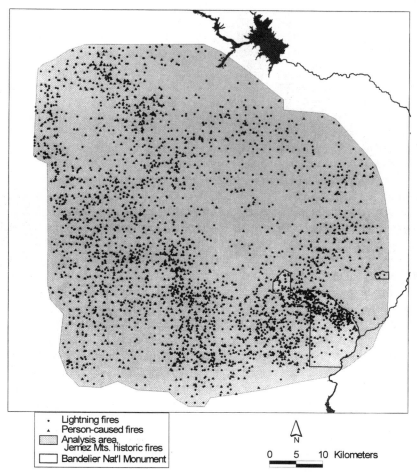

- Lightning fires
▲ Person-caused fires
Analysis area,
Jemez Mts. historic fires
Bandelier Nat'l Monument

N

0   5   10 Kilometers

Figure 5.4. Point locations of historic fires in the Jemez Mountains, 1909–1996. Point locations of 4,487 historic wildfires in the Jemez Mountains, 1909–1996, compiled from the administrative records of land management agencies (Snyderman and Allen 1997). The shaded analysis area covers 380,691 ha. The gridlike pattern results from a subset of the data that were recorded only to the nearest section corner. Person-caused fires cluster near major roadways, campgrounds, habitations, and other human use areas.

across a 380,691 ha area in the Jemez Mountains, compiled from an array of administrative records (Snyderman and Allen 1997), suggest a high frequency of lightning fires in the most flammable vegetation types. Lightning caused 68 percent of the fires, with human ignitions clustered about roadways, campgrounds, habitations, and other human use areas. Area burned is greatest in June, while July records the most lightning-fire ignitions, consistent with local lightning occurrence and precipitation data (Figure 5.3). In contrast, area burned by management-ignited "prescribed" fires is greatest in the fall after the end of the summer monsoon, when conditions are often dry enough to sustain fire but controllability is greater than in the spring. Note that this record of modern fire occurrence in the Jemez Mountains is certainly conservative and substantially underestimates the actual occurrence of fire during this time period, as many small fires were likely never reported (especially prior to ca. 1945) and the database is riddled with multiple large gaps where data are obviously incomplete or missing (Snyderman and Allen 1997). For example, it is visually apparent that the greatest concentration of lightning fires is recorded in the southeastern flank of the Jemez Mountains at Bandelier National Monument (Figure 5.4), where a more complete administrative record of fires since 1934 has survived (yet even the Bandelier record lacks any data for 9 years since 1941). The Bandelier fire record indicates a per ha rate of lightning fire ignitions five times greater than the Jemez Mountains–wide data, reflecting the incompleteness of the overall Jemez record. Still, consistent patterns emerge from the large total number of fires in these records. From 1934 to 1997, lightning caused 341 fires at Bandelier (86 percent of all wildfires), with ignitions peaking in July and higher levels of fire activity occurring in dry years (Foxx and Potter 1978). Lightning ignited at least one fire per 2,134 ha per year during this period at Bandelier, with the greatest frequency of fires occurring in ponderosa pine forests at mid-elevations. Many of these fires would have spread widely in the absence of suppression efforts. The data from Bandelier, moreover, are not unique: despite a variety of problems with the completeness of fire suppression records, high levels of lightning-ignited fire are clearly observed in the modern landscapes of the Southwest (Barrows 1978; Snyderman and Allen 1997).

The extensive regional network of fire-scar chronologies (Fulé and Covington 1996; Swetnam and Baisan 1996a, 1996b; Touchan et al. 1996; Abolt 1997; Baisan and Swetnam 1997; Fulé et al. 1997; Allen et al. 1998; Kaib 1998; Kaufmann et al. 1998; Morino et al. 1998; Wolf and Mast 1998; Fulé et al. 2000; Swetnam et al. 2001) provides a precisely dated, multicentury perspective on fire regimes in the Southwest that is strikingly consistent with modern observations of lightning-caused wildfire activity. While substantial variability existed in pre-1900 fire regimes (Swetnam and Baisan 1996a), high-frequency, low-intensity surface fires were common in the Southwest, with the shortest intervals between fires found in mid-elevation ponderosa pine forests. Extensive fire activity was often recorded in the same year across landscape and regional scales, indicating that fires spread widely in the absence of active human suppression and artificial fuelbreaks like livestock trails and road networks (Allen et al. 1998; see also *http://biology.usgs.gov/luhna/ chap9.html*). The absence of spreading fires in consecutive years from stand-scale fire histories in the Southwest indicates that rates of fuel recovery were one constraint on maximum fire frequencies. The landscape context of topographic and fuel conditions could enhance or inhibit the spread of fire into particular stands (Swetnam and Baisan 1996b).

Climate variability acted to synchronize regional fire activity, as major fire years were clearly associated with drought conditions, while wet periods recorded little fire activity (Swetnam and Betancourt 1990). The most extensive fire activity in ponderosa pine forests occurred in dry years that followed within 1 to 3 years of wet conditions; this pattern of major fire years suggests the importance of both fuel production and fuel moisture in these fire regimes, with antecedent wet conditions stimulating the buildup of continuous fuels and subsequent drought conditions enabling the fuels to burn widely. The common occurrence of persistent drought conditions in the Southwest likely allowed some fires to burn for months, potentially allowing even a few ignitions to cause extensive fire activity. The importance of climate in determining southwestern fire regimes is highlighted by evidence from fire-scar chronologies of responses to climate variations at annual, decadal, and centennial time scales (Swetnam and Baisan 1996a; Swetnam and Betancourt 1998; Grissino-Mayer and Swetnam 2000).

In most cases the seasonality of fire occurrence can be inferred by the relative position of a fire scar within the annual growth rings (Baisan and Swetnam 1990). The regional patterns of fire seasonality developed from prehistoric fire scars and modern fire records are generally indistinguishable (Swetnam et al. 2001), indicating that prehistoric fires occurred during the same seasons as modern lightning-ignited fires—predominantly in the spring and summer (Grissino-Mayer and Swetnam 2000). Unusual patterns of "excess" fall fires have been found in fire-scar histories only for brief time periods at a few localities (e.g., Secklecki et al. 1996).

Overall, regional fire-scar chronologies show that pre-1900 fire regimes in upland forests were characterized by frequent, widespread fires that favored the open forest stand structures and abundant herbaceous vegetation that have been well documented across the Southwest by early photographs, historical writings, early land surveys, and dendrochronological reconstructions of stand conditions (Weaver 1951; Cooper 1960; Bahre 1991; Covington and Moore 1994; Fulé et al. 1997; Allen et al. 1998; Kaufmann et al. 1998; Swetnam et al. 1999). At higher elevations and in more mesic forests, surface fire regimes became patchier and increasingly mixed with more intense fires occurring at longer return intervals (Grissino-Mayer et al. 1995; Touchan et al. 1996; Romme et al. 1999b), eventually grading into the (little-studied) stand-replacing fire regimes that apparently characterized subalpine spruce-fir forests in the absence of spreading surface fires. Historic records, synchronous fire-scar dates from canyon forest stringers linked by semi-desert grasslands, and ecological inferences suggest a substantial role for fire prior to the late 1800s in some lowland ecosystems in the Southwest (e.g., Humphrey 1974; Bahre 1991; Archer 1994; Swetnam et al. 2001). In contrast, ecosystems where fires were apparently scarce include deserts and some subalpine and alpine communities.

The fire-scar record from the Jemez Mountains (Allen 1989; Allen et al. 1996; Touchan et al. 1996; Morino et al. 1998) is consistent with regional patterns. Dendrochronologically dated fire-scar collections have been made from forty-two localities in and adjoining the Jemez Mountains (Figure 5.5), with more than 4,000 pre-1900 fire-scar dates determined from more than 600 sampled trees, snags, logs, and stumps. Fire dates extend back to A.D. 1422. Sampled forest types and landscape settings range from low-elevation stands of ponderosa pine intermixed with semiarid pinyon and juniper woodlands up to high-elevation montane forests dominated by Engelmann spruce. The Jemez Mountains fire-scar chronologies show that high-frequency fire (with mean return intervals of 6 to 15 years) characterized the pre-1900 fire regimes at most sites (Touchan et al. 1996), with maximum frequencies found in upper-elevation ponderosa pine stands (e.g., Figure 5.6). Fire activity commonly occurred over extensive areas (Figure 5.5; Allen et al. 1998); for example, watershed-wide fires occurred approximately every 16 years across the 15-km-long Frijoles watershed in Bandelier (Allen 1989). Stand-level fire frequencies were affected by topographic features that would inhibit or enhance the spread of fires into the site from the larger surrounding landscape (e.g., reduced frequencies where rocky cliffs act as isolating barriers, versus greater frequencies on the upper portions of a large smooth plateau slope), indicative of natural controls on fire regimes (Allen and Snyderman 1997). Years with extensive fire activity were tied to dry conditions in all forest types, with lagged relationships to wet years in ponderosa pine forests (Touchan et al. 1996). The fire-scar seasonality data show that most prehistoric fire scars in the Jemez Mountains formed during the dry spring and early summer months (about 94

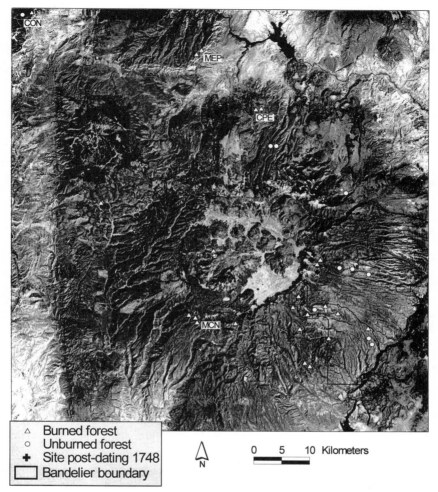

Figure 5.5. Jemez Mountains, extent of fires in 1748. Map of fire-scar sample site locations in the Jemez Mountains, showing the extent of widespread fires in 1748. Sites where at least 10 percent of the sampled trees recorded a fire in 1748 are shown as burned. Three clusters of sites in the northern Jemez Mountains area are labeled: CON (Continental Divide), MEP (Mesa Prieta), and CPE (Cerro Pedernal). Also marked is Monument Canyon (MCN) in the south.

percent formed by July), and fall fires were rare (Allen 1989 and unpublished data; Touchan and Swetnam 1995). Abundant fire activity clearly was a major determinant of ecosystem patterns and processes in the pre-1990 landscape of the Jemez Mountains (Allen 1989; Touchan et al. 1996; Morino et al. 1998). As elsewhere in the Southwest, the surface fire regimes collapsed by ca. 1900 at most sites in the Jemez area (Fig-

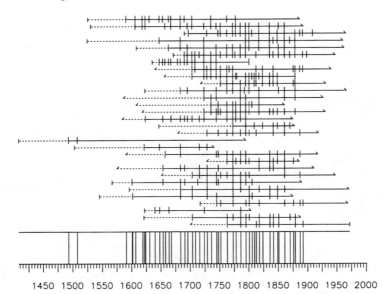

1450 1500 1550 1600 1650 1700 1750 1800 1850 1900 1950 2000

Figure 5.6. Fire-scar chronology, Monument Canyon Research Natural Area. Horizontal lines represent the life spans of individual trees, whereas fire-scar events are shown by short vertical bars. The longer vertical lines at the bottom of each chronology indicate the years in which at least 10 percent of the recording trees (i.e., previously scarred trees) recorded a fire.

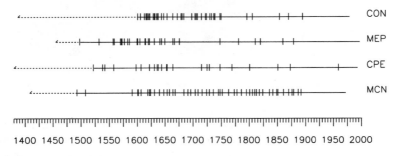

1400 1450 1500 1550 1600 1650 1700 1750 1800 1850 1900 1950 2000

Figure 5.7. Composite fire-scar chronologies from four sites, Jemez Mountains. Each of the four labeled horizontal lines represents the composite fire chronology from a different site (labels match Figure 5.5), and the vertical bars are the fire dates recorded by at least 10 percent of the fire-scarred trees within that site. Fire frequency patterns before ca. 1600 are reduced by small sample sizes (cf. Figure 5.6).

ures 5.6 and 5.7), due to the effects of domestic grazing on fuel availability and human suppression activities (described below in the section titled Historic Human Effects on Southwestern Fire Regimes).

Overall, the patterns of lightning-ignited fire observed in the modern landscapes of the Southwest are strikingly consistent with, and generally sufficient to explain, the prehistoric and historic fire regimes indicated by the fire-scar record. This natural history of frequent lightning-ignited fires in most upland ecosystems, modulated by climate and fuel conditions, provides the context against which potential human alteration of southwestern fire regimes though time and space must be assessed.

The Cultural History of Fire in the Southwest

The natural history of southwestern fires overlaps with a history of human occupancy. The two worlds of nature and people interact to give a history of southwestern landscapes.

Prehistoric Human Effects on Southwestern Fire Regimes (11,000 B.C.–A.D. 1600)

> That extraordinary fire load is not simply a product of natural processes. For millennia humans have busily restructured the geography and seasonality of Southwestern fire— sometimes complementing and sometimes countering the natural order. Lightning had to compete not only with rain but with aboriginal firesticks. Human inhabitants added other sources of ignition in the service of hunting, raiding, foraging, and horticulture, and as an inadvertent by-product of a seasonal nomadism whose routes became trails of smoke from camp fires, signal fires, and escaped fires of diverse origins. (Pyne 1995a:284)

The American Southwest has a long record of occupation by humans (Cordell 1997), the fire-using species (Pyne 1995a), extending back to the Clovis Paleoindian sites that document Native American presence here for more than 11,000 years. These first known people of the Southwest were apparently big-game hunters who likely moved frequently as they pursued their primary food resources. Their small populations and mobile way of life likely caused few lasting changes to regional ecosystems, although it is possible that these early hunters contributed to the extinction of the "Pleistocene megafauna" through overhunting (Martin and Klein 1984), which indirectly had substantial ecological effects. Paleoindian use of fire to manipulate southwestern landscapes is possible (e.g., as a hunting method), but entirely speculative at this point. "It is difficult to reconstruct the impact of early humans, whose firesticks coincided with the colossal climatic fluctuations that ended the last ice age" (Pyne 1995a:294).

With the development of foraging lifeways during the Archaic period (ca. 5500 to 500 B.C.), hunting and gathering by small, mobile groups of people became the norm. The primary ecological effects of these people were likely localized, with frequent movements allowing any over-harvested resources to recover. Based upon cross-cultural surveys of fire use by hunting and gathering societies in the western United States and the rest of the world, Fish (1996) has suggested that Archaic peoples of the Southwest may have made substantial use of fire to modify vegetation, although direct supporting evidence is absent.

By ca. 2000 B.C., cultigens from Mexico (e.g., maize) initially appear in the Southwest, beginning the slow transition toward sedentary agricultural societies with higher populations. With increasing reliance on agriculture, human populations and societal complexity increased, as did their ability to modify landscapes to support their growing resource demands. By ca. A.D. 800, substantial human populations had developed across much of the Southwest; population growth in the Colorado Plateau area accelerated (Euler 1988); and evidence of human effects on at least local environments can be discerned in various paleorecords (Plog et al. 1988), such as in the Dolores River Valley of southwestern Colorado (Kohler and Mathews 1988). By ca. A.D. 1100, large populations of sedentary agriculturalists were found across the Southwest, including the Hohokam irrigators of the Arizona desert river valleys, the Mogollon of the Mogollon Rim uplands (e.g., Mimbres), and the Anasazi of the Colorado Plateau (e.g., the Chaco region and Mesa Verde). Anasazi (ancestral Puebloan) occupations were focussed on pinyon-juniper ecosystems, which occur widely across the upland mesas, plateaus, and mountain footslopes of the Four Corners region. With the decline of the Chacoan system in the 1100s and the general abandonment of the Colorado Plateau by the late 1200s, these ancestral Puebloan populations largely shifted toward the northern Rio Grande valley, including the Jemez Mountains. Throughout the late prehistoric period (A.D. 1200–1600) the northern Rio Grande region was the center of large Puebloan populations; at the time of European settlement in A.D. 1598, the Pueblo world consisted of about 100,000 people associated with about 100 communities (Schroeder 1992). While greatly reduced over the next several centuries by diseases and other impacts of the Spanish Entrada, their descendants are the modern Puebloan peoples who continue to live in this region (Hopi, Zuni, and the numerous pueblos of the northern Rio Grande watershed). Most of these contemporary communities have been occupied since before European contact. In addition, unknown numbers of more nomadic peoples were present in the Southwest by the 1400s, including the ancestors of the modern Utes, Paiutes, Navajos, and Apaches (Towner 1997).

The Jemez Mountains contain much evidence of large Anasazi populations. For example, Bandelier National Monument (Figure 5.5) may have the highest density of cultural resource sites in the entire National Park Service system, with over 2,400 archeological sites recorded from the approximately 6,500 hectares inventoried to date (Powers and Orcutt 1999, unpublished data at Bandelier National Monument). Site densities are greatest in the pinyon-juniper and lower ponderosa pine zones. Intensive utilization of the Bandelier landscape by ancestral Puebloans occurred during the period A.D. 1150–1550, with estimated populations of between 1,000 and 3,500 people across some 10,000 ha during the period A.D. 1225–1450 (Bracker 1996; Orcutt 1999). Similar densities of late prehistoric archeological sites are found around much of the Jemez country, including several dozen huge communal pueblos (1,000–3,000 rooms) in the Chama and Jemez River drainages (Elliott 1993; Anschuetz 1998).

Human populations of this magnitude and extent could substantially modify their environment in many ways (Butzer 1990; Denevan 1992; Spoerl and Ravesloot 1995; Fish 1996), including through the use of fire. Since southwestern agriculturalists like the Anasazi utilized about 0.5 ha per person per year to raise staple foods (Kohler et al. 1996; Trierweiler 1990), large areas were farmed to raise staple foods, with abundant archeological evidence still visible today of agricultural terraces, cobble mulch gardens, and even irrigation infrastructure (Doolittle 1992; Periman 1996; Anschuetz 1998). The broad extent of prehistoric agricultural influence in landscapes like the Pajarito Plateau (on the eastern flank of the Jemez Mountains) is also indicated by the abundance of "field houses" found dispersed across potential agricultural areas, as these small structures (one to ten rooms) were probably used seasonally for purposes that included tending crops. Wood scarcities likely developed over extensive areas as the Anasazi and other farmers overharvested pinyon-juniper woodlands to meet their substantial needs for cleared agricultural land, firewood for cooking and winter heating, and building materials. Evidence of deforestation has been detected from such areas as Mesa Verde (Wyckoff 1977) and Dolores in southwestern Colorado (Kohler and Matthews 1988), Chaco Canyon (Samuels and Betancourt 1982; Betancourt et al. 1986), and Bandelier (Huber and Kohler 1993; Allen, in review). The shifting of agricultural field locations through time, and the frequent relocations of human populations at local and regional scales (Euler 1988), amplified the total area affected by these cultural activities.

While significant land-altering activities surely occurred near human settlements, anthropogenic effects at more expansive landscape and regional scales are less certain, particularly in mountain areas remote from permanent habitations. We know that aboriginal southwesterners certainly were capable of utilizing remote resources, such as transporting thousands of logs more than 75 km from mountain source areas to "great houses" in Chaco Canyon (Betancourt et al. 1986). Another indication of extensive human influence is the evidence that populations of large mammals, particularly elk, may have been depleted over broad areas by prehistoric southwestern hunters (Lang and Harris 1984; Osborn 1993; Allen 1996b; cf. Kay 1994; Martin and Szuter 1999).

How might the various aboriginal peoples of the Southwest have modified fire regimes in the late prehistoric period (ca. A.D. 1200–1600)? Since prehistoric documentation of specific burning practices does not exist, most of our perspectives about the effects of early Indian burning in the Southwest must be inferred from indirect lines of evidence ranging from archeological and paleoecological information to historic accounts of aboriginal fire use (cf. Fish 1996; Kaib 1998). Although an extensive ethnographic literature describes cultural uses of fire by Native Americans from many regions of North America (Hough 1926; Stewart 1951, 1955, 1956, 1963; Day 1953; Lewis 1973, 1985; Sauer 1975; Barrett and Arno 1982; Boyd 1986; M. K. Anderson 1993, 1996; Gottesfeld 1994; Clark and Royall 1995; Pyne 1997; Williams 1997, 2000; Delcourt and Delcourt 1998; Bonnicksen 2000), relatively little information exists for the Southwest (but see the thorough review of fire use in Apacheria by Kaib [1998]). General reasons given for Indian burning in North America (Pyne 1997; Kaib 1998; Williams 2000) include hunting, crop management, improvement of plant growth and yield, insect collection, pest management, fireproofing areas, warfare and signaling, clearing areas for travel, and felling trees. The substantial Native American populations of the prehistoric Southwest may have used fire for all these purposes, (Dobyns 1981; Bahre 1991; Pyne 1997), but a paucity of region-specific data renders speculative most of our conclusions about the effects of aboriginal burning at landscape scales (areas at least several kilometers in extent).

Yet some scholars have painted a region-wide picture of substantial aboriginal burning effects by extrapolating broadly from a few historical anecdotes and statements of questionable authority or accuracy (cf. Forman and Russell 1983). For example, influential overviews by Cooper (1960:138) and Pyne (1995a:284–285, 1987:519) extensively quote Holsinger (1902) (see Box 5.1) as important evidence for widespread Indian burning in the Southwest, even though the Holsinger article (1) cites no evidence for its assertions of Native Americans as primary sources of fire ignition; (2) clearly views fire as a negative influence that degraded forest cover and thereby worked against a utilitarian vision of preserving desired watershed conditions; (3) emphasized fire as unnatu-

BOX 5.1. Varied perspectives on the cause of early fires in the Southwest.

"These prehistoric aborignes [sic] must have exerted a marked influence upon the vegetation of the country. Their fires, and those of the historic races, unquestionably account for the open condition of the forests. . . . From Puget Sound to the Gulf of California these strange people rambled at will, but their abiding place was . . . in the southwest. The extensive ruins indicate that they inhabited the fringe, so to speak, of the forests which, like vanguards, were working their way down from the mountain tops to the plains. The most potent and powerful weapon in the hands of these aborigines was the firebrand. It was alike used to capture the deer, the elk, and the antelope, and also to rout or vanquish the enemy. It cleared their mountain trail and destroyed the cover in which their quarry took refuge. . . . How far the occupancy of the prehistoric and historic tribes has retarded the progress of foresting it is impossible to say, but it must have been no small factor. . . . Were it not for the long Indian occupancy and the ravages of fire incident to their habitancy, vast territories now barren desert wastes might be covered with a forest growth." (Holsinger 1902:23, 24)

"Given the high incidence of lightning-caused fires, reliably documented by modern data, the relative importance of fires set by Indians is probably moot." (Bahre 1991:128)

"Under aboriginal rule, fine fuels blossomed, and the Southwest burned easily and often. Lightning and firestick competed to see which would burn a particular site or in what season." (Pyne 1995a:285)

ral and thus preventable, displaying an obvious bias toward blaming all fires, past and present, on people, particularly Indians; and (4) primarily, though loosely, focuses on undocumented ancient burning practices of southwestern Native Americans who left obvious architectural ruins (e.g., the Anasazi), rather than Apaches or other contemporary historic tribes. Cooper (1960:138) indicates that "There is abundant evidence that Indians were responsible for many fires," but the sources that he cites convey largely hearsay claims of Indian burning in the Southwest. Pyne's footnotes (1995a:359–360, 1997:615) indicate only a few other anecdotal sources that hardly provide solid support for his assertions that prehistoric Native American burning was important in the Southwest. The fact is that archaeological, anthropological, and historic sources contain little evidence for widespread anthropogenic alteration of prehistoric fire regimes in the Southwest.

For example, consider the use of fire for prehistoric agricultural purposes in the Southwest, where new plots were likely cleared and prepared using fire (Wyckoff 1977). Indians also may have burned to enhance the productivity of a variety of favored wild resources (M. K. Anderson 1993, 1996), such as herbs with edible seeds in pinyon-juniper woodlands (Sullivan 1992). These probable uses of fire represent the potential for abundant wildfire starts to have occurred from human ignitions, given the dependence of large prehistoric human populations on agriculture in this region, the shifting nature of their enterprises, and the probability that some fires escaped from human control. Petersen (1988:101) suggests that high charcoal concentrations dating to about A.D. 900 in a bog at 3,060 m elevation in the La Plata Mountains of southwestern Colorado are due to charcoal influx from Anasazi land uses (presumably agriculture-related fire in the adjoining valleys), although natural forest fires might be a more plausible explanation. Fish (1996) suggests that prehistoric agriculturalists in southeastern Arizona would have carefully controlled or avoided burning practices in their zones of intensive settlement, agriculture, and fuelwood procurement in order to protect residences, crops, and fuel supplies. These rationales to constrain the application of fire are equally valid elsewhere in the Southwest. Localized burning by agriculturalists may have caused little change in the natural fire regimes of extensive upland areas.

Similarly, the use of fire as a hunting strategy is commonly presented as a potential means by which fire regimes could have been altered across broad areas by aboriginal peoples (Stewart 1956), including prehistoric southwesterners (Holsinger 1902; Cooper 1960; Dobyns 1981). Cabeza de Vaca's early description of Indian fire use from southeastern Texas in the 1520s is often quoted in support of this idea: "[They] fire the plains and forests within reach with brands, both to drive the mosquitoes away and at the same time drive lizards and like things from the earth to eat. They also kill deer [antelope] by encircling fires; deprived of pasturage, the animals are forced to seek it where the Indians may trap them" (Cabeza de Vaca, in Covey 1993). The idea that western Indians extensively used fire in hunting has been widely asserted by many influential people, ranging from John Wesley Powell (1890, "Before the white man came the natives systematically burned over the forest lands with each recurrent year as one of their great hunting economies") and Aldo Leopold (1920, "As is well known to all old-timers, the Indian fired the forests with the deliberate intent of confusing and concentrating the game so as to make hunting easier") to Stephen Pyne (1987:74, "Of all Indian uses for fire, the most widespread was probably the most ancient: fire for hunting"). However, in the Southwest the idea of land-scape-scale hunting fires is based upon an insubstantial foundation of minimal documentation. For example, although Pyne (1987:519) specifically propagates the view of extensive Apache fire use in the Southwest for purposes that included hunting, an extremely thorough review of Apache fire use in the U.S./Mexico-borderlands portion of the Southwest finds only evidence for localized fire use for small game drives, not widespread fire-drive hunting (Kaib 1998:140). While Kaib's review documents that historic-era Apaches certainly used fire for a variety of other purposes (most significantly warfare), he emphasizes that they had good reasons and sufficient skills to control the spread of most fires. Fish (1996) also downplays the idea of extensive burning by pre-historic southwestern hunters, as it would work against "attracting and concentrating game in a precise, predictable location for hunters," defeating the supposed aboriginal purpose. Primary evidence for land-scape-scale burning for hunting purposes is nearly nonexistent in the Southwest, and supporting rationales are weak.

A lack of archeological or ethnographic evidence on aboriginal use of fire is similarly apparent in the Jemez Mountains area, despite an overall wealth of archaeological information (e.g., Powers and Orcutt 1999) and the continuity of relatively intact native Puebloan cultural traditions since prehistoric times (Henderson and Harrington 1914; Harrington 1916; Robbins et al. 1916). For example, a detailed "Ethnographic Literature Search and Consultation" to document traditional Indian uses of the cultural and natural resources of Bandelier National Monument uncovered no information on fire use (Levine and Merlan 1997). Surprisingly little information is available on cultural uses of fire by ancestral Puebloan peoples (cf. Hough 1926).

Overall, the archeological and ethnographic evidence in the Southwest supports the notion that human-set fires likely enhanced prehistoric fire frequencies in localized areas, as fire-using people were present throughout the region. However, there is little evidence of landscape-scale burning practices in the Southwest, as aboriginal peoples likely emphasized "controlled rather than comprehensive [i.e., broadcast] uses of fire" (Fish 1996). There are severe limitations on our ability to reliably infer the prehistoric ecological effects of cultural fire use from anthropological information sources alone in a region where the rate of natural fire occurrence is so high. Assertions that emphasize aboriginal burning as a major ecological process in the Southwest are largely based upon overgeneralized amplifications of anecdotal information or biased and unsubstantiated statements in historical writings.

However, another emerging source of evidence exists—the detailed temporal and spatial records of past fire activity contained in dendrochronologically dated fire-scar chronologies may provide indications of aboriginal burning during certain periods in particular southwestern localities. Although relatively few fire-scar chronologies have been developed that overlap documented prehistoric human use areas in both time and space, those that exist provide opportunities to test some hypotheses about prehistoric Indian burning, to see if a signal of human burning can be distinguished. For example, Fish (1996) suggests that "cultural practices could have accelerated vegetational responses by introducing fire in seasons of low natural ignition and by increasing frequencies to the extent that fuel buildups allowed," while Pyne (2000) asserts that "Anthropogenic (human-caused) fire comes with a different seasonal signature and frequency than natural fire." Clues of human influences on the fire regime recorded in a fire-scar chronology might include periods with unusual patterns of fire frequency, stand-level fire synchroneity, fire seasonality, or decreased correlation with climatic conditions (Baisan and Swetnam 1997; Swetnam et al. 2001), providing the potential for linkages to documented patterns of human land use. For example, fire-scar chronologies from two sites in the mountains near Albuquerque display early periods (1500s to 1680) with frequent, patchy fires and inconsistent fire-climate relationships that indicate the possibility that local Native Americans were starting fires in these areas during this time (Baisan and Swetnam 1997). In the Jemez Mountains area, chronologies from the three northernmost clusters of sites display patchy, frequent fires in the late 1500s and early 1600s that may reflect enhanced ignition rates by protohistoric people (Figure 5.7). For example, the Continental Divide cluster of sites (Figure 5.5) shows high fire frequencies and less synchronous fire dates in the period prior to 1750 (Figure 5.7), and fire-climate relationships are weaker here than at any other site sampled so far in the Jemez Mountains (Touchan et al. 1995; Allen et al., unpublished data). Perhaps these fire scars record excess ignitions by early Navajos around this area before their acquisition of substantial numbers of sheep disrupted surface fire frequencies in this dry ponderosa pine/pinyon-juniper transition area (Touchan et al. 1995, 1996). In these cases the fire-scar record does provide limited evidence of possible aboriginal alteration of southwestern fire regimes in the late prehistoric to early historic period.

Still, these unusual site histories belie the consistency of the general patterns found in fire-scar chronologies at all scales across the Southwest (Swetnam and Baisan 1996a; Swetnam et al. 1999). Climate relationships are strong and persistent at most fire-scar chronology sites. Although pre-1900 fire regimes were dynamic, most chronologies are like Monument Canyon (Figure 5.6), showing no obvious fire frequency changes across the late prehistoric to early historic divide despite the continued occupation of Jemez Puebloan peoples near this forested highland site until as late as ca. 1620, when the Spanish forcibly resettled them in the adjoining Jemez Valley (Elliott 1993). Similarly, early fire-scar chronologies from other areas near prehistoric or historic Puebloan communities (e.g., the Frijoles watershed in Bandelier, near Cochiti and San Ildefonso Pueblos, and Gallina Mesa near Santa Clara and San Juan Pueblos) also do not show higher fire frequencies in the late prehistoric or early historic eras (Touchan et al. 1996; Allen et al., unpublished data). Although fire-scar sample sizes are generally small for prehistoric time periods, in the Jemez Mountains alone there are currently six fire-scar chronologies with earliest fire dates in the 1400s and six more with initial dates between A.D. 1503 and 1601. If human burning was an important ignition source, one would expect to see declines in fire frequencies in the early historic period with decreased Puebloan use of the mountains, but most fire chronologies in the Jemez Mountains show no sustained decline in fire frequencies from ca. 1600 to 1850 (although perhaps increased use of the mountains by Navajo and Apaches added a compensatory set of new aboriginal ignition sources).

The fire-scar record can be used to directly test some claims about Indian burning practices. For example, Lewis (1985:76) expansively asserts that "there are four general considerations used by hunter-gatherers that distinguish their fire regimes from natural ones: the seasonality of burning, the frequency with which fires are set, the intensity of fires, and the selection of preferred sites. These . . . considerations are shown from North American Indians across a broad range of habitats . . ." (see also Bonnicksen et al. 1999:444). Overall, the extensive fire-scar record in the Southwest is strikingly consistent with modern patterns of lightning fire ignition, revealing few indications of early human modification to natural fire-regime patterns of seasonality, frequency, intensity, or locality. For example, Stevenson (1881) "stated that Indians set fire to the timber on the mountain ranges of New Mexico each fall in order to drive deer down into the canyons" (in Cooper 1960:138). However, this claim is not supported by the abundant fire-scar seasonality data from New Mexico's mountains, as fall fire scars were rarely recorded in the pre-1900 period, and the proportion of late-season fire scars actually declines in the 1800s relative to preceding centuries (Allen 1989:91–94; Grissino-Mayer 1995:199–201), likely due to a shift in regional climate (Grissino-Mayer and Swetnam 2000). Indeed, the fire-scar record across the Southwest shows that prehistoric fires generally occurred in the same April to July window as modern fires (Baisan and Swetnam 1990; Touchan and Swetnam 1995; Swetnam and Baisan 1996a; Grissino-Mayer and Swetnam 2000; Swetnam et al. 2001). Given the suitability of fall conditions for human-ignited burning, the near absence of fall fires in the fire-scar record suggests that aboriginal ignitions were unimportant in the Southwest, or that for unknown reasons they restricted their burning to the same spring-to-early summer period as natural lightning ignitions.

Tree-ring fire reconstructions cannot directly determine the cause of ignition for recorded fires. So it is possible that prehistoric people set spring fires that spread widely when fuels and climatic conditions allowed, leaving fire scars and ecological outcomes indistinguishable from the natural lightning fires that otherwise would have occurred. Thus, while the simplest explanation of the available data is that lightning started essentially all extensive prehistoric fires in the uplands of the Southwest, Indian-set fires could have been substituting for some natural ignitions to varying degrees through time and space without altering natural fire regimes.

Overall, the notion of landscape-scale burning by prehistoric Indians in the Southwest lacks archaeological and ethnographic support, and the regional network of fire-scar chronologies generally records patterns of prehistoric fire that are consistent with natural control of fire regimes by climate and fuels. Although long-term use by large populations of prehistoric Native Americans likely had substantial impacts on pinyon-juniper woodlands and lowland riverine environments in many areas, the available evidence indicates that Indians likely had minimal effects on the fire regimes of most upland ecosystems in the Southwest prior to European contact.

Historic Human Effects on Southwestern Fire Regimes (Since A.D. 1600)

> The character of Southwestern fire reflects the changing character of its human occupation. (Pyne 1995a:294)

> The region boasts an ideal formula for natural fires. Its dramatic terrain and well-defined wet-dry cycles, both annular and secular, have long established it as an epicenter for lightning fires. But the real narrative of Southwest fire history belongs to its human firebrands, who have co-existed, if not co-evolved, with the regional biota throughout the Holocene. Different waves of human colonization have shaped distinctive fire regimes. (Pyne 1996)

The American Southwest has one of the longest histories of European exploration and settlement of any part of the United States. Prehistoric and historic eras and land uses grade into one another here, with sporadic Spanish exploration from the 1530s onward (e.g., Cabeza de Vaca, Coronado, Espejo), culminating in Oñate's colonizing settlement at the foot of the Jemez Mountains in 1598 and the establishment of Santa Fe in 1610. For the purposes of this overview, A.D. 1600 will be used to mark the approximate divide between the prehistoric and historic eras when Euro-Americans began markedly reshaping the Southwest, even though their Old World diseases, livestock, and cultures likely started to affect the region during the 1500s. Still, large portions of this region remained outside Euro-American control (and written documentation) until the last half of the nineteenth century, and some prehistoric land use patterns persisted among the diverse Indian lifeways of the historic Southwest. For example, although the subjugated Puebloan farmers were greatly reduced in numbers, concentrated in river valleys, and incorporated into the colonial Spanish economy of farming and livestock husbandry, they also maintained much of their indigenous culture and undoubtedly continued to utilize adjoining upland areas for resource procurement (medicinal plants, game) and other traditional uses (Henderson and Harrington 1914; Harrington 1916; Robbins et al. 1916; Levine and Merlan 1997). At the other extreme, some nomadic peoples (e.g., Apaches and Utes) held onto their independence and many aspects of their prehistoric hunter-gatherer-raider lifeways through the middle to late 1800s, while enhancing their mobility with horses. Navajo hunters and farmers developed along a somewhat intermediate path, also maintaining their freedom through mobility and warfare, while adding sheep husbandry and raiding to their economies. There was also a blending of land use practices here at the frontier of the Spanish Empire—by trade and warfare among these groups, including commerce in captive slaves; by Spanish settlement of Europeanized Indians in peripheral genizaro communities as buffers against warring tribes; and by intermarriage between Euro-Americans and Native Americans (Meinig 1971; deBuys 1985; Scurlock 1998). The presence of such diverse cultures suggests that fire use likely varied markedly through time and space across the historic Southwest.

Given the 400-year duration of the historic period here, it is conceivable that intermingled Native American and Euro-American impacts on southwestern fire regimes have been going on long enough to appear natural to many modern observers. However, assertions of landscape-scale burning by southwestern peoples during the historic era are subject to the same criticisms as the prehistoric claims reviewed above. Overall these claims are largely speculative due to the paucity of firm information on this topic found in archaeological, anthropological, and historic sources (with some exceptions reviewed here). Eyewitness accounts of broadcast burning by Indians are quite rare in the Southwest (Kaib

1998). In addition, the regional network of fire-scar chronologies shows relatively consistent patterns of pre-1900 fire occurrence through time and space, indicating that the fire regimes at most sampled sites were primarily driven by natural and synoptic climatic factors rather than by local and ephemeral cultural burning practices. However, unique local fire histories that differ markedly from regional patterns provide some indications of probable human interactions with southwestern surface fire regimes during the historic period.

As noted above, some southwestern fire-scar chronologies (e.g., Figure 5.7) hint that human ignitions were raising fire frequencies above natural levels during the transition between late prehistoric times and the early historic era (Baisan and Swetnam 1997). Interestingly, the abrupt end of the higher fire-frequency period at several sites in New Mexico is roughly coincident with the Pueblo Revolt of 1680 (Baisan and Swetnam 1997; Figure 5.7). The 1600s were a tumultuous time in New Mexico, likely with lots of undocumented Indian use of upland areas around the Spanish-dominated valley settlements, perhaps including use of fire. On the other hand, the 1600s and 1700s were generally a time of relatively high frequency and less well synchronized fires across the Southwest, and after ca. 1800 increased synchronization and lower frequencies are regionally evident, regardless of local Indian site histories (Grissino-Mayer and Swetnam 2000).

One of the strongest cases for extensive aboriginal burning in the Southwest is associated with the use of fire during historic warfare periods by Apachean peoples, or their enemies, in the U.S./Mexico borderlands region. Several recent fire-scar studies document enhanced fire frequencies or partially altered fire seasonalities, in concert with weaker fire/climate relationships, suggesting anthropogenic ignitions in particular localities frequented by Apaches during documented times of raiding and warfare. At Fillmore Canyon in the Organ Mountains, Morino (1996) found high fire frequencies and weak correlations with climate during the 1700s, a time of known Apache use and warfare in this area. Kaye and Swetnam (1999) interpret atypical occurrences of late-season fires, in concert with tree peel scars, as clues of probable Apache war-related fires near Dog Canyon in the Sacramento Mountains during the late 1700s, although they note that alternative explanations exist. Secklecki et al. (1996) suggested that an unusually large proportion of late winter or early spring fires, in concert with a high fire frequency during the period 1760–1786, may indicate Apache burning in a high-elevation portion of the Chiricahua Mountains during this brief time of local warfare. Kaib (1998) more broadly reviews fire histories for several mountain ranges in Apacheria along the U.S./Mexico border, finding evidence for warfare-related burning in parts of the Chiricahua Mountains during two historical warfare periods (1748–1790 and 1831–1886). Kaib (1998) also found indications of Apache burning from the Animas Mountains and Sierra de los Ajos during the later warfare period (1831–1886). Kaib (1998:145) concludes: "Common and indiscriminate burning practices that influenced extensive areas were associated with documented raiding and wartime periods."

Although burning related to warfare between historic Apaches and their enemies has apparently left a fire history signal in some localities, the regional fire-scar record indicates that such burning had limited overall effect on southwestern fire regimes. Evidence of warfare fire use cited above is constrained to a narrow set of particular times and places. The anthropogenic signal noted at some fire history sites is often lacking from adjoining sites within the same mountain range, indicative of the restricted geographic scope of the possible human burning. The fire-scar and documentary evidences are primarily linked to brief periods of historic conflict between the Apaches and European settlers, both relative newcomers to the Southwest.

The most vigorous and best documented claims for widespread aboriginal use of fire in the Southwest are related to various Apache groups in the historic period: "The Apaches worked to create and perpetuate a grassland environment. . . . The uses of broadcast fire by the Apaches were those typical of grassland tribes" (Pyne 1997:519). While there is more evidence of Apache burning practices than for other regional Indian cultures (Hough 1926; Kaib 1998; Kaye and Swetnam 1999; Swetnam et al. 2001), assertions of widespread ("broadcast") fire use are weakly supported overall. The extent of warfare burning was limited to particular times and places, and there is little tangible support for the idea that Apaches or other historic southwestern Indians burned at landscape scales for hunting purposes (as reviewed in the prehistory section above). Kaib believes that the Chiricahua Apaches applied controlled fires on fine scales, particularly for hunting small game in localized grassland settings (Kaib 1998 and personal communication). However,

> Overall, the documentary and ethnoecological evidence suggests that neither widespread nor local burning practices were used to promote forest or grassland resources. . . . Non-warfare burning practices were also more likely controlled spatially and limited in use because of (a) enemy detection, (b) inherent problems with fire control, (c) threats to life and property. And (d) because increasing fire frequencies beyond the normal fire regimes would probably have been detrimental to the majority of important ethnobotanical resources including fuelwood. (Kaib 1998: 144–145)

Historic Euro-Americans and Fire

How did historic Euro-Americans influence southwestern fire regimes? The best evidence for ecologically significant enhanced ignition rates comes from the period of initial Anglo-American rule during the last half of the 1800s, a time of Euro-American-set conflagrations elsewhere in the United States (e.g., Veblen and Lorenz 1991:25; Agee 1993; Pyne 1997). Some historical evidence suggests that large even-aged forests of aspen, mixed conifer, and spruce-fir may have regenerated after crown fires dating to this period throughout the southern Rocky Mountains and farther into the Southwest (Personal Communication, W. de Buys). Anglo settlement and exploitation of the Southwest in the last half of the 1800s likely contributed to higher frequencies of large stand-replacing fires in high-elevation mixed-conifer and spruce-fir forests, where the availability of ignitions during brief dry periods may have been a limiting factor (Box 5.2). However, fire history and age structure studies in aspen and spruce-fir forests by Romme et al. (1996, 1999a, 1999b) do not show anomalously high rates of disturbance for this period in the San Juan Mountains of southwestern Colorado, and Baker (in review) has found frequent lightning ignitions (but infrequent weather-controlled fire spread) in Rocky Mountain spruce-fir forests farther north.

In an odd twist, Kay (1997) broadly asserts that western aspen is "doomed" due to the European suppression of earlier fire regimes that he attributes to Indians ("The very presence of aspen, for instance, indicates that aboriginal burning was once widespread. . . . Unlike lightning fires, which tend to be infrequent, high-intensity infernos, native burning produced a higher frequency of lower-intensity fires."). However, Kay's paradigm is historically and ecologically incorrect in the Southwest, where lightning ignitions are frequent and aspen stands generally develop by resprouting from clonal rootstocks after high-intensity crown fires free them from the competition of more shade-tolerant conifers.

The apparent pulse of careless burning by early Euro-Americans in the late nineteenth and early twentieth centuries notwithstanding, there appears to have been a substantial bias among Anglo observers at that time toward a belief in human ignition as the primary cause of fire in the western United States, including the Southwest (Box 5.3). Fire was generally considered to be an unnatural agent of destruction that wasted timber resources, degraded the ability of forests to regenerate and protect essential watersheds, and threatened the ability of foresters to exert management control over the newly created forest reserves. Human-caused fires were considered preventable, and pressure was building to protect forests from purposeful underburning as well as wildfire conflagrations. Perhaps the late-1800s prejudice that Indians set many fires

BOX 5.2. John Wesley Powell (1890:919) provides a confessional description of a Colorado crown fire in a plea to protect western forests from human-set burns.

"More than two decades ago I was camped in a forest of the Rocky Mountains. The night was arched with the gloom of snow-cloud: so I kindled a fire at the trunk of a great pine, and in the chill of the evening gazed at its welcome flame. Soon I saw it mount, climbing the trunk, crawling out along the branches, igniting the rough bark, kindling the cones, and setting fire to the needles, until in a few minutes the great forest pine was all one pyramid of flame, which illumined a temple in the wilderness domed by a starless night. Sparks and flakes of fire were borne by the wind to other trees, and the forest was ablaze. On it spread, and the lingering storm came not to extinguish it. Gradually the crackling and roaring of the fire became terrific. Limbs fell with a crash, trees tottered and were thrown prostrate; the noise of falling timber was echoed from rocks and cliffs; and here, there everywhere, rolling clouds of smoke were starred with burning cinders. On it swept for miles and scores of miles, from day to day, until more timber was destroyed than has been used by the people of Colorado for the last ten years.

"I have witnessed more than a dozen fires in Colorado, each one of which was like that described. Compared with the trees destroyed by fire, those used by man sink into insignificance. Some years ago I mapped the forests of Utah, and found that about one-half had been thus consumed since the occupation of the country by civilized man. So the fires rage, now here now there, throughout the Rocky Mountains and through the Sierras and the Cascades. They are so frequent and of such vast proportions that the surveyors of the land who extend the system of triangulation over the mountains often find their work impeded or wholly obstructed by clouds of smoke. A haze of gloom envelops the mountain land and conceals from the eye every distant feature. Through it the rays of the sun can scarcely penetrate, and its dull red orb is powerless to illumine the landscape."

was also related to a "Manifest Destiny" mind-set that sought to justify removing some tribes from their native forest lands. These biases affected even many of the most perceptive and knowledgeable observers of the time (Box 5.4), from utilitarian conservationist Gifford Pinchot to the aesthetic-minded preservationist John Muir (Pyne 1997).

Sheep grazing was one of the economic mainstays of the historic Southwest (Denevan 1967; Baxter 1987). During the long period of

BOX 5.3. Selected historical references on fire causation in the western United States (emphasis added to first quote).

<u>1897</u>: "Fires are particularly destructive to the forests of western North America. . . . Fires in western forests are started by careless or ignorant hunters and campers, who often leave their camp fires burning or, in utter wantonness, ignite coniferous trees to enjoy the excitement of the conflagration. **They can be occasionally traced to the effects of lightning, which locally is held responsible for many forest fires, although in reality fires set in this way are very rare**, as lightning is usually accompanied or followed by copious rains, which extinguish them before they can gain headway; **and very rarely they are produced by the rubbing together of adjacent trees swayed by the wind**. The right of way of every railroad crossing the Rocky Mountains and the other interior ranges of the continent is marked by broad zones of devastation due to fires which have started from the camps of construction gangs or the sparks of locomotives; and thousands of acres of timber are destroyed annually by the spread of fires lighted by settlers to clear their farms.

"Prospectors in search of valuable minerals frequently set fires in wooded regions to uncover the rocks and facilitate their operations; and the shepherds who drive their flocks to pasture during the summer months in the mountain forests . . . make fires in the autumn to clear the ground and improve the growth of forage plants the following year.

". . . Such conflagrations have occurred in the West since it was settled, and they will always menace the prosperity of that part of the country." (National Academy of Sciences 1897:44)

<u>1898</u>: "It has often been claimed that many forest fires are due to lightning. Little credence was at first given to this. . . . It is possible that lightning fires may be much more frequent in the Cascades than has been supposed, and the subject is certainly one worthy of further investigation." (Coville 1898:32, 33, Cascade Forest Reserve, Ore.)

<u>1900</u>: "The origin of the oldest fires is unknown. They are not even accredited, as in the White River region, to the Ute Indians. . . . While the general belief among settlers that most fires are due to careless campers is true in the main, there are also other agencies. The extensive coal mining carried on at various points in and near the reserve, with the constantly burning 'slag piles,' can not fail to be a prolific source of ignition. . . . Sheep men are charged with starting fires to improve the pasture. Hunters, cattlemen, sheep herders, sawmill operators, logging crews, ranchmen, settlers, and transient travelers are the people responsible for fires originating in the reserve. Doubtless some are blameless, while others are guilty of neglecting camp fires. . . . Circumstantial evidence, at least, points to these par-

ties as the most likely perpetrators, as recent fires of greater or lesser extent were found in close connection with their work. It is reasonable, therefore, to conclude that the greatest danger from fire lies in the presence of these people." (Sudworth 1900:228–231, Battlement Mesa Forest Reserve, Colo. [today's Grand Mesa National Forest])

1900: "Of all the reserves established by the federal government, the three under consideration have probably been the most damaged by fire. . . . Probably at least 75 per cent of the total area of the reserves clearly shows damage by fire, much of it within the last half century or since the advent of white settlers in the region." (Jackson 1900:43, 44, Pike's Peak, Plum Creek, and South Platte Forest Reserves, Colo. [today's Pike National Forest])

1900: "It (the large fire) was said to have originated from the burning of a heap of brush by one of the early settlers; but other information placed the responsibility for the fire upon the Indians, who probably are charged with more than their share of such occurrences." (Jackson 1900:97, South Platte Forest Reserve, Colo. [today's Pike National Forest])

1900: "Several cases of fires started by lightning were reported." (Jackson 1900:77, Plum Creek Forest Reserve, Colo. [today's Pike National Forest])

1900: "The early fires which devastated a great part of the forest land are said to have taken place when the country was first explored, about half a century ago; and it is claimed that they were started by Indians, who thus attempted to drive out the game before them when they were compelled to leave this region for more distant reserves." (Jackson 1900:69, Pike's Peak Forest Reserve, Colo. [today's Pike National Forest])

1900: "The fires which burned during Indian occupancy and soon after the arrival of the present settlers in the region were far more widespread and destructive than those of recent years. . . .

"The origin of fires in recent years may, in part, be ascribed to carelessness of sheep herders, in part to sparks from the engines on the Atchison, Topeka and Santa Fe Railroad. The region is not good hunting or camping ground and few fires originate from the camps of hunting parties. But by far the larger number of fires are due to lightning strokes, and this cause has, of course, always operated. Electric storms are very numerous in this region during July and August. . . . While most of the thunder showers are accompanied by rain, some are not and when a tree is struck by lightning during a storm of this sort, a fire of more or less severity is sure to follow." (Leiberg et al. 1904:266–268, San Francisco Mountains Forest Reserve, Ariz. [today's Coconino National Forest])

continues

BOX 5.3. *Continued*

<u>1910</u>: "It is probably unjust, however, to attribute all the fires to man. During two summers' work nearly a dozen fires were noted which were due to lightning." (Clements 1910:8, Estes Park, Colo.).

<u>1912</u>: "That lightning is one of the chief causes of forest fires is now an established fact. Careful observations on the National Forests have shown that there it ranks second only to sparks from locomotives as a source of conflagration. . . . Lightning may bring about a forest fire by igniting the tree itself, or the humus at its base. Most forest fires caused by lightning probably start in the humus." (Plummer 1912b:5, 36)

<u>1912</u>: "In order of their importance, the following are the chief known causes of fires on the National Forests: ([R])ailroads; lightning; campers; brush burning; incendiary; sawmills. Lightning is responsible for about 17.5 per cent of the fires." (Plummer 1912a:9).

<u>1955</u>: "Almost all of the forests of California, Oregon, and Washington have indicators, either in the scars on living trees or in the sub-climax nature of the types of trees, showing that fires set by Indians have frequently run through them.

"Many foresters and plant ecologists have been reluctant to attribute to the aborigines the amount of vegetation burning evident from the record in the trees. They seem to prefer a natural cause, lightning, rather than human cause for such widespread conflagrations. . . . In a few sections of the mountains, lightning starts dozens of fires each year, but over the major part of the west fires started by lightning are unknown. Thus, there are millions of acres of forest, brushland, and grassland on which Indian fires were the factor determining what kind of vegetation survived or dominated." (Stewart 1955:6)

<u>1978</u>: "Lightning is the leading cause of fires in southwestern forests. On all protected private, state and federal lands in Arizona and New Mexico, nearly 80 percent of the forest, brush and range fires are ignited by lightning. The Southwestern region leads all other regions of the United States both in total number of lightning fires and in the area burned by these fires. Lightning fires are an important factor in the management of wildland resources in all of the western United States. . . . These fires are a natural element in wildland ecosystems." (Barrows 1978:1)

BOX 5.4. Historic views of fire in the Southwest by the U.S. Bureau of Biological Survey.

Vernon Bailey of the U.S. Bureau of Biological Survey spent major portions of at least nine field seasons between 1889 and 1908 conducting biological inventories in the Southwest, including efforts to synthetically describe these landscapes in the life-zone system developed by C. H. Merriam (1890). Bailey noticed the obvious signs of past fire occurrence in many southwestern landscapes, and he consistently attributed these to human causes, particularly to efforts to burn off forests to create better pastures during this era of peak livestock grazing intensities. In 1903, Bailey described extensive evidence of fire in the high elevation forests of today's Pecos Wilderness in the Sangre de Cristo Mountains, which he linked to the influence of people: "The forest (now included in the Pecos River Forest Reservation) has been sadly thinned by burning, fully three fourths of it having been burned over and a large part of the coniferous forest replaced by poplars [aspen] or kept open by repeated burning for grazing land" (Bailey 1903).

In 1904 Bailey spent over two weeks reconnoitering the "Gallinas Mountains" (actually, the northwest portion of the Jemez Mountains, including the San Pedro Parks plateau), noting: "Canadian Zone covers the tops and upper slopes of the mountains and is marked by both dense forests and extensive grassy parks. Its timber . . . has been burned over as far as possible & replaced to a great extent by Populus tremuloides." (Bailey 1904a). On this trip Bailey provided a classic description of widespread fire-structured ponderosa pine forests: "Transition Zone is the most extensive in the mountains and includes the most extensive and perfect yellow pine (Pinus ponderosa) forest that I have ever seen. It covers the broad basal slopes of the range from 8,000 to 9,700 feet on S.W. slopes or 7,000 to 9,000 on N.E. slopes and is generally an open park like forest with well spaced trees and clean grama turf beneath. The trees are large and symmetrical, often 5 feet in diameter and 80 to 100 feet high with beautifully smooth trunks. . . . Fire has left little havoc in this open forest" (Bailey 1904a).

Yet Bailey's field notes for this same expedition show that he viewed fire to be a relatively recent anthropogenic intrusion rather than a long-term natural disturbance process in these mountain forests: "The timber has been burnt off as far as possible, but fortunately the yellow pines stand burning pretty well and have not been injured much while much of the higher spruce forest will not burn. This leaves much of the forest in good condition" (Bailey 1904b). In contrast, dendrochronological fire histories developed in the past decade from this northern portion of the Jemez Mountains provide evidence of frequent surface fires extending back into the late 1400s at Mesita del Cañoncito Seco, into the mid-1500s at three other sites, and back to ca. A.D. 1600 at four additional sites (Touchan et al. 1996). These early fires precede the Spanish colonization and introduction of livestock into this region, and thus were not set by people to create grazing lands.

Spanish and Mexican rule there is very little documentation of fire use, although burning to improve pasturage for livestock seems likely given Spanish traditions (Pyne 1997:137). By 1890 there were more than 5 million sheep in New Mexico alone (Wooton 1908); shepherds, like Indians, clearly became another favorite target of the late 1800s "establishment," which accused them of causing many uncontrolled resource and social problems, including setting destructive fires (National Academy of Sciences 1897). Third-generation shepherd Leandro Salazar recalled his father telling of fires set by shepherds to enlarge pastures in the northeastern Jemez Mountains in the late 1800s—fires that created meadows still present today (Allen 1984:131–132). But since one might expect shepherds to burn in fall as they retreated from the mountains toward the valleys, to improve next year's grazing without damage to the current year's potential, the absence of fall fires in fire-scar chronologies from the Jemez Mountains (including from near the area described by Salazar) fails to support claims of shepherd ignitions. However, perhaps efforts to convert southwestern forests into grass would have been focused on the natural spring burning window, when higher fire intensities can occur.

If shepherd burning had been important, pressure on the sheep industry to improve its image and the imposition of severe penalties against even accidental ignition of wildland fires must have reduced the frequency of human-set fires by ca. 1900 (Allen 1984:130–132). Consider this report by Coville (1898:34, 36), who was sent to inspect for shepherd impacts in the Cascade Forest Reserve in Oregon:

> It has been alleged that sheep herders systematically set fire to the forest in order to burn off the timber so that a growth of weeds and grass will spring up to furnish grazing in succeeding years. . . . It is clear that the extent of the practice among sheepmen of systematically setting forest fires has been overestimated. It is interesting to note that during the progress of the season's investigation, while no fires were found that could be traced by positive evidence to sheepmen, camp fires were seen abandoned by travelers, by campers and by Indians, fires set by road builders and by lightning, and fires set for the purpose of creating smudges.

Similarly, there is no evidence that shepherds were more important than many other human causes of fire in the historic Southwest. Indeed, dendrochronological fire histories show precipitous declines in fire frequencies concurrent with the introduction of extensive sheep herds—not an increase. Although early fire suppression records on the Santa Fe

National Forest (1910–1920) occasionally noted "goatherders" and "brushburning" as causes of fire, Leandro Salazar told me that shepherds certainly no longer set fires by 1922, when he began herding sheep in the Jemez Mountains (Allen 1984:131).

Associated with the late-1800s emphasis on the human role in setting destructive fires (cf. Agee 1993) was the downplaying of a natural role for lightning ignitions (Box 5.4). Although many people knew that lightning started fires, they did not recognize the commonness of lightning ignitions. The turn-of-the-twentieth-century references that are cited today as evidence for the importance of human ignitions in southwestern fire regimes are tainted by the prevailing bias that people started almost all fires. However, evidence regarding the importance of lightning-caused fires was eventually assembled, especially after the establishment of the U.S. Forest Service (in 1905), which quickly developed a firefighting organization that systematically collected data on fire causes (Plummer 1912a, 1912b). Improvements in fire-detection methodologies during the 1930s and 1940s (Swetnam 1990) also increased the incidence of reported lightning fires by picking up many small lightning-strike ignitions in remote locations. Eventually, over the course of several decades, the discussion of fire as a natural disturbance process in the Southwest began to emerge above the insistent utilitarian mantra of universal fire control (Leopold 1937; Weaver 1951; Pyne 1997). The evolution of perspectives on fire causation, from emphasis on human ignitions to recognition of lightning as a dominant source, is evident from a review of written accounts through time (Box 5.4). It is now apparent that lightning is the leading cause of fires throughout the West, igniting more than 64 percent of all recorded fires (an average of 6,253 lightning fires per year) in western national forests from 1960 to 1975 (Barrows 1978:5).

The relative importance of lightning fires in the pre-1900 Southwest is further confirmed by the observation that surface fire frequencies in ponderosa pine and many mixed-conifer forests generally declined somewhat by ca. 1840 (Grissino-Mayer and Swetnam 2000), decades before the onset of suppression, despite the turn-of-the-nineteenth-century perception that Anglo ignitions were the main cause of fires after ca. 1850. This suggests that Euro-American ignitions were insignificant relative to background levels of lightning-ignited surface fires in these ecosystems even during this "Wild West" period of fire use.

Further, cessation of spreading surface fires occurred at most southwestern fire-scar sites between ca. 1880 and 1900 (Swetnam et al. 1999), despite continued Euro-American fire sources and a general lack of organized suppression activities until ca. 1910 (Pyne 1997). Indeed, the greatest impacts of historic people on southwestern fire patterns have involved suppression rather than ignition of fires. The region-wide collapse of surface-fire regimes by ca. 1900 (e.g., Figures 5.6 and 5.7) is closely linked to major reductions in fuel quantities and continuities due to intense overgrazing and trailing effects by livestock, especially sheep in the mountains. Livestock numbers soared in the uplands of the Southwest with the pacification of the mobile raiding tribes (Apache, Navajo, and Ute) and the entry of railroads into the region by ca. 1880. The fire-suppressing effects of overgrazing were well recognized by some contemporary observers (Leopold 1924)—consider this description by Powell (1890):

> There is a practical method by which the forests can be preserved. All of the forest areas that are not dense have some value for pasturage purposes. Grasses grow well in the open grounds, and to some extent among the trees. If herds and flocks crop these grasses, and trample the leaves and cones into the ground, and make many trails through the woods, they destroy the conditions most favorable to the spread of fire.

Early interruptions in fire regimes, likely due to localized livestock grazing by Indians or Hispanics, are evident in some fire-scar chronologies from the Chuska Mountains (Savage and Swetnam 1990; Savage 1991) and the Sandia and Manzano Mountains (Baisan and Swetnam 1997). Fire-scar histories from the northern Jemez area (Figure 5.5) tend to show early gaps or interruptions in fire regimes that follow an initial period of highest fire frequency (Figure 5.7). Grazing by Navajo and Puebloan peoples likely occurred at these sites, which include Continental Divide and Cerro Pedernal (Touchan et al. 1995, 1996), and Mesa Prieta along an old "Navajo Trail" (Figure 5.7; Allen and Riser, unpublished data). Some Indians adopted sheep husbandry early on (Puebloans in the 1600s and Navajo by ca. 1700 [Bailey 1980; Baxter 1987:13, 25])—the Puebloans even kept sheep through the Pueblo Revolt of 1680–1696 when many other aspects of Spanish culture were violently rejected (e.g., "During the April 1694 battle for the heights above Cochití, Spanish forces captured nine hundred sheep" [Baxter 1987:13]). Old Spanish documents record non-Navajo sheep/goat numbers in New Mexico of 112,000 in 1757, with 58 percent of those owned by Pueblo and Hopi Indians (Baxter 1987:42), and at least localized overgrazing of ranges noted in the 1730s and 1810s (Baxter 1987:24, 92). As a result, it is hard to confidently attribute grazing suppression effects in fire-scar chronologies to Indian, Hispanic, or even later Anglo cultures without firm knowledge of local land use histories.

By the 1880s millions of sheep and cattle grazed across the Southwest

(Wooton 1908; Bogan et al. 1998; Frederickson et al. 1998), and surface fire regimes collapsed in most places (Swetnam et al. 1999). In the Jemez Mountains area, spreading surface fires cease earliest near the encircling river valleys and latest in the most interior portions (Allen, unpublished data), consistent with the spread of livestock from valley settlements up into more remote and dangerous uplands. Fire cessation dates at particular sites correspond to the local initiation of intense livestock grazing, not to the cessation of human ignitions associated with local declines in Indian activities. For example, fire activity (and thus ignitions) continued for decades in many mountain ranges of the U.S./Mexico borderlands region after Apache removals, with subsequent declines associated with either overgrazing impacts on fine fuels or the start of active fire suppression (Swetnam et al. 2001). In contrast, relatively natural fire regimes persisted in the few areas of the Southwest where heavy livestock grazing and active fire suppression were excluded by topography or land use history, such as forested kipuka islands amidst forbidding lava-flow seas at El Malpais National Monument (Grissino-Mayer 1995), an inaccessible butte summit at Zion National Park (Madany and West 1983), isolated plateaus in the Grand Canyon (Fulé et al. 2000), portions of the rugged and remote Animas Mountains of the New Mexico bootheel (Swetnam et al. 2001), and the Sierra de los Ajos and other isolated mountains in northern Mexico (Swetnam et al. 2001). These unique local situations show that natural lightning ignitions can sustain surface fire regimes even where human ignitions have been inconsequential, particularly where Indians and their potential firesticks are long gone.

Inadvertent disruption of fire regimes by livestock graded into active fire suppression across the American Southwest in the early 1900s (Pyne 1997), with suppression methods becoming increasingly effective through ca. 1950 (Swetnam 1990). The resultant fuel buildups have promoted increased numbers of large and intense fires (Swetnam and Betancourt 1998), while the negative ecological effects of long-term fire suppression have become ever more apparent across the Southwest (Weaver 1951; Cooper 1960; Covington and Moore 1994; Bogan et al. 1998). In recent decades a consensus has emerged among federal wildland managers that the strategy of suppressing all fires has become counterproductive and that "wildland fire use" has many benefits (USDI/USDA 1995). Powell would likely grant himself a smile at the current popularity of prescribed burning, taking it as confirmation of his once maverick position in support of "Pauite forestry" (Powell 1890; Pyne 1997). However, vigorous debate persists over the notion that fire can be used to restore more natural conditions in wilderness areas (Pyne 1995b; Swetnam et al. 1999).

Conclusion: How Important Was Native American Burning in Shaping the Upland Ecosystems of the Southwest?

> How can anyone dismiss anthropogenic fire as inconsequential or indistinguishable from lightning fire? Biotas are adapted not just to fire but to fire regimes, and all the regimes of Holocene America have emerged within the context of anthropogenic burning or that negotiated matrix between lightning and humans. . . . Together lightning and people made the elastic matrix that defined the fire regime. (Pyne 1995b:16, 21)

> It is unnecessary in most cases to invoke human-set fires as an explanation or cause of fire regime patterns in the Southwest. We contend that, even if humans had never crossed the land bridge from Asia to North America, historical fire regimes in most Southwestern forests would still have been similar in most respects to the fire regimes that we have documented. (Swetnam and Baisan 1996a:29)

It is possible to believe and appreciate the eloquent scholarship of Sauer (1975), Stewart (1956), and Pyne (1995a) regarding aboriginal modification of *many* landscapes through fire use without accepting the premise that *all* landscapes are artifacts of ancient human burning practices. Indeed, it is appropriate to "dismiss anthropogenic fire as inconsequential or indistinguishable from lightning fire" in most times and places in the uplands of the American Southwest. Multiple lines of evidence from this region overwhelmingly suggest that in A.D. 1850, as in A.D. 1580, most mountain landscapes were "natural" and "wild" with regard to fire regimes and associated vegetation patterns. Evidence of landscape-scale fire use by aboriginal people in the Southwest is scanty to nonexistent, and most assertions of aboriginal burning are based upon anecdotal accounts or sources subject to substantial historical bias. The high levels of lightning-ignited fire observed today in the Southwest are easily sufficient to generate the frequent return intervals indicated for many forest types by the fire-scar record, given pre-1900 landscapes where fires would have spread widely in dry years through continuous and quick-regenerating fine fuels in the absence of active human suppression and artificial fuelbreaks. The strong consistencies between the multicentury fire-scar record of prehistoric fire regimes and modern observations of lightning-caused wildfire activity suggest that pre-1900 fire regimes can largely, if not wholly, be attributed to natural factors. Since ignitions are generally not a limiting factor in this region, the factors of climate and

fuels are magnified as the primary drivers of southwestern fire regimes—
it is unnecessary to invoke human agency. Mid-elevation wild lands in
the Southwest naturally included frequent fires, regardless of human
burning practices.

Proponents of aboriginal modification of North America through fire
use are generally well aware of the age-old importance of lightning fires
in the American Southwest: "It is more difficult to interpret fire in the
Southwest, where lightning, not humans, normally supplies ignition"
(Pyne 1995a:295). Yet some would cast a humanistic perspective across
the entire continent, transposing a global view of the dominance of landscape-scale aboriginal burning to the Southwest, despite much contrary
evidence and only meager support from a few historic documents about
localized fire use.

Still, anthropogenic effects on fire regimes are discernable in particular times and places in the southwestern uplands. Human-set fires likely
enhanced natural fire frequencies in local areas over the already high levels initiated by lightning. Yet, even during these limited time periods
only a few localities show irregularities consistent with possible anthropogenic enhancement of fire frequencies, such as periods with unusually
high fire frequencies, less within-stand synchrony of fire dates, weaker
fire-climate relationships, aberrant patterns of fire seasonality, or drastic
changes in fire regime through time. As summarized by Swetnam et al.
(2001) for the Apacheria Borderlands situation: "quantitative fire history
studies in the region . . . all conclude that, if Apaches or Europeans influenced pre-1900 fire regime patterns, these influences were probably very
time and place specific, and not generalizable across broader temporal
and spatial scales." Native American burning practices, by Apaches or
other Indians, had little regional effect on pre-1900 fire regimes in the
Southwest. Overall, the most profound anthropogenic effects on southwestern fire regimes are the pervasive but relatively modern impacts of
fire suppression.

Of course, it is possible that prehistoric Native Americans used fire
widely in the Southwest, but little evidence has survived to our current
day due to the "fading record" problem (Swetnam et al. 1999). This
presumption has likely contributed to the casually documented claims
about the essential role of aboriginal burning in the Southwest and elsewhere (e.g., Bonnicksen et al. 1999:443; Krech 1999:113; Bonnicksen
2000:355; Pyne 2000; Williams 2000). Yet even if we assume that substantial, undocumented aboriginal fire use occurred, the potential ecological effects of prehistoric Indian burning in the Southwest are greatly
diminished by the intrinsic natural background of frequent lightning
fires.

The role of people in southwestern fire regimes relates to a larger question: Were the pre-European landscapes of the Southwest in the 1500s pristine wildernesses or humanized culturescapes? The relative effects of people upon wild nature in the Southwest were contingent upon the particulars of time and place and culture, with spatial gradients of impacts associated with the varying intensities of human occupation and use. For example, the extensive portions of the Pajarito Plateau on the eastern flank of the Jemez Mountains that sustained large Anasazi populations into the mid-1500s are likely still in recovery from prehistoric land uses that cleared mesatops for agriculture and consumed large quantities of wood, suggested by the modern lack of old-growth pinyon-juniper woodland in the area. In general, prehistoric aboriginal impacts in the Southwest were greater at lower elevations, in woodland and valley settings where many people lived year-round (and where a dendrochronological record of human land uses is usually poorly preserved due to centuries of human wood use). Still, despite a variety of early human land uses, most mountains in the Southwest retained a dominantly wilderness character until the advent of Anglo-American exploitation in the late nineteenth century, as evidenced by the persistence of natural fire regimes until this time.

While available evidence asserts the long-term primacy of lightning-ignited fires, we will never know for certain the varied roles of aboriginal Americans in the fire regimes of the prehistoric Southwest. However, precise determination of Indian burning effects is unnecessary to justify wildland fire programs in this region, for we can be sure that "lots of lightning" and frequent fire naturally characterize the mesas and mountains of the Southwest, even in the absence of burning by "plenty of people."

Acknowledgments

This chapter draws heavily on long-term collaborations with Tom Swetnam's fire history research group at the University of Arizona Laboratory of Tree-Ring Research, especially interactions with Tom, Chris Baisan, Kiyomi Morino, Ramzi Touchan, Henri Grissino-Mayer, and Tony Caprio. I thank Bill deBuys for historic reference materials and thoughtful discussions on this topic. James Riser, Dave Snyderman, and John Hogan of the USGS Jemez Mountains Field Station conducted essential fieldwork, tree-ring dating, and mapping of historic fires, while most figures were created by Kay Beeley. This research was supported by the U.S. Geological Survey (Biological Resources Division), the National Park Service (particularly Bandelier National Monument), and the Santa Fe National Forest. For helpful review comments I thank Tom O'Shea, Bill deBuys, Tom Swetnam, Tom Vale, and Mark Kaib. The views expressed here are those of the author and do not represent an official position of the USGS.

Literature Cited

Abolt, R. A. P. 1997. Fire histories of upper elevation forests in the Gila Wilderness, New Mexico Via fire scar and stand age structure analyses. M.S. thesis, University of Arizona, Tucson.

Agee, J. K. 1993. *Fire ecology of Pacific Northwest forests.* Washington, D.C.: Island Press.

Allen, C. D. 1984. Montane grasslands in the landscape of the Jemez Mountains, New Mexico. Master's thesis, University of Wisconsin.

————. 1989. Changes in the landscape of the Jemez Mountains, New Mexico. Ph.D. diss., University of California, Berkeley.

————, tech. ed. 1996a. *Fire effects in southwestern forests: Proceedings of the second La Mesa fire symposium.* General technical report RM-286. Fort Collins, Colo.: USDA Forests Service.

————. 1996b. Elk response to the La Mesa fire and current status in the Jemez Mountains. Pp. 179–195 in *Fire effects in southwestern forests: Proceedings of the second La Mesa fire symposium,* ed. C. D. Allen. General technical report RM-286. Fort Collins, Colo.: USDA Forest Service.

————. 1998. Sensitivity of semiarid woodlands and forests to climate-induced disturbances in the southwestern U.S. Unpublished proposal to USGS Global Change Research Program on file at USGS Jemez Mts. Field Station.

————. In review. Ecological patterns and environmental change in the Bandelier landscape. Chapter 2 in *Village formation on the Pajarito Plateau, New Mexico: The archaeology of Bandelier National Monument,* ed. T. A. Kohler. Albuquerque: University of New Mexico Press.

Allen, C. D., J. L. Betancourt, and T. W. Swetnam. 1998. Landscape changes in the southwestern United States: Techniques, long-term datasets, and trends. Pp. 71–84 in *Perspectives on the land use history of North America: A context for understanding our changing environment,* ed. T. D. Sisk. U.S. Geological Survey, biological science report USGS/BRD/BSR-1998-0003.

Allen, C. D., and D. Snyderman. 1997. Spatial patterns of prehistoric and historic fires in the Jemez Mountains, New Mexico (abstract). Bulletin of the Ecological Society of America 78:44.

Allen, C. D., R. Touchan, and T. W. Swetnam. 1996. Overview of fire history in the Jemez Mountains, New Mexico. Pp. 35–36 in *New Mexico Geological Society guidebook, 47th field conference, Jemez Mtns. Region,* ed. F. Goff, B. S. Kues, M. A. Rogers, L. D. McFadden, and J. N. Gardner. New Mexico Geological Society.

Anderson, M. K. 1993. The mountains smell like fire. *Fremontia* 21:15–20.

————. 1996. Tending the wilderness. *Restoration and Management Notes* 14:154–166.

Anderson, R. S. 1989. Development of the southwestern ponderosa pine forests: What do we really know? Pp. 15–22 in General technical report RM-185. Fort Collins, Colo.: USDA Forest Service.

————. 1993. A 35,000 year vegetation and climate history from Potato Lake, Mogollon Rim, Arizona. *Quaternary Research* 40:351–359.

Anschuetz, K. F. 1998. Not waiting for the rain: Integrated systems of water management by pre-Columbian Pueblo farmers in north-central New Mexico. Ph.D. diss., University of Michigan, Ann Arbor.

Archer, S. 1994. Woody plant encroachment into southwestern grassland and savannas: Rates, patterns and proximate causes. Pp. 13–68 in *Ecological implications of livestock herbivory in the West*, ed. M. Vavra, W. A. Laycock, and R. D. Pieper. Denver, Colo.: Society for Range Management.

Bahre, C. J. 1991. A legacy of change: Historic human impact on vegetation in the Arizona borderlands. Tucson: University of Arizona Press.

Bailey, L. R. 1980. If you take my sheep: The evolution and conflicts of Navajo pastoralism, 1630–1868. Pasadena: Westernlore Publications.

Bailey, V. O. 1903. Unpublished physiography report—Pecos River Mountains. Transcribed and annotated by William deBuys, on file at USGS Jemez Mts. Field Station, Los Alamos, N. Mex.

————. 1904a. Unpublished physiography report—Gallinas Mountains. Transcribed and annotated by William deBuys, on file at USGS Jemez Mts. Field Station, Los Alamos, N. Mex.

————. 1904b. Unpublished field notes, Gallinas Mountains, October 4–20, 1904. Transcribed and annotated by William deBuys, on file at USGS Jemez Mts. Field Station, Los Alamos, N. Mex.

Baisan, C. H., and T. W. Swetnam. 1990. Fire history on a desert mountain range: Rincon Mountain Wilderness, Arizona, U.S.A. *Canadian Journal of Forest Research* 20:1559–1569.

————. 1997. *Interactions of fire regimes and land use in the central Rio Grande valley*. Research paper RM-330. Fort Collins, Colo.: USDA Forest Service.

Baker, W. L. (In review.) Fires and climate in forested landscapes of the Rocky Mountains. In *Fire and climatic change in the Americas*, ed. T. W. Swetnam, G. Mongenegro, and T. T. Veblen.

Barrett, S. W., and S. F. Arno. 1982. Indians fires as an ecological influence in the northern Rockies. *Journal of Forestry* 8:647–651.

Barrows, J. S. 1978. Lightning fires in southwestern forests. Final report to USDA Forest Service Intermountain Forest and Range Experiment Station. Fort Collins, Colo.

Baxter, J. O. 1987. Las carnerada: Sheep trade in New Mexico, 1700–1860. Albuquerque: University of New Mexico Press.

Betancourt, J. L., J. S. Dean, and H. M. Hull. 1986. Prehistoric long-distance transport of construction beams, Chaco Canyon, New Mexico. *American Antiquity* 5:370–375.

Betancourt, J. L., and T. R. Van Devender. 1981. Holocene vegetation in Chaco Canyon, New Mexico. *Science* 214(6):656–658.

Betancourt, J. L., T. R. Van Devender, and P. S. Martin, eds. 1990. *Packrat middens: The last 40,000 years of biotic change*. Tucson: University of Arizona Press.

Bogan, M. A., C. D. Allen, E. H. Muldavin, S. P. Platania, J. N. Stuart, G. H. Farley, P. Melhop, and J. Belnap. 1998. Southwest. Pp. 543–592 in *National status and trends report*, ed. M. J. Mac, P. A. Opler, and P. D. Doran. Washington, D.C.: U.S. Geological Survey.

Bonnicksen, T. M. 2000. *America's ancient forests.* New York: John Wiley.

Bonnicksen, T. M., M. K. Anderson, H. T. Lewis, C. E. Kay, and R. Knudson. 1999. Native American influences on the development of forest ecosystems. Pp. 439–470 in vol. 2 of *Ecological stewardship: A common reference for ecosystem management*, ed. R. C. Szaro, N. C. Johnson, W. T. Sexton, and A. J. Malk. Oxford: Elsevier Science Ltd.

Bowen, B. M. 1990. *Los Alamos climatology.* LA-11735-MS UC-902. Los Alamos: Los Alamos National Laboratory.

Boyd, R. 1986. Strategies of Indian burning in the Williamette Valley. *Canadian Journal of Anthropology* 5:65–96.

Bracker, S. B. 1996. How many people lived at Bandelier? Unpublished report on file at Bandelier National Monument, N. Mex.

Brown, D. E., ed. 1982. Biotic communities of the American Southwest— United States and Mexico. *Desert Plants* 4(1–4):1–342.

Brown, P. M., M. R. Kaufmann, and W. D. Shepperd. 1999. Long-term landscape patterns of past fire events in a montane ponderosa pine forest of central Colorado. *Landscape Ecology* 14:513–532.

Brunner-Jass, R. 1999. Fire occurrence and paleoecology at Alamo Bog and Chihuahueños Bog, Jemez Mountains, New Mexico, USA. Master's thesis, Northern Arizona University, Flagstaff.

Butzer, K. W. 1990. The Indian legacy in the American landscape. Pp. 27–50 in *The making of the American landscape*, ed. M. P. Conzen London: Harper-Collins Academic.

Clark, J. C., and P. D. Royall. 1995. Transformation of a northern hardwood forest by aboriginal (Iroquois) fire: Charcoal evidence from Crawford Lake, Ontario, Canada. *The Holocene* 5:1–9.

Clements, F. E. 1910. *The life history of lodgepole burn forests.* USDA Forest Service Bulletin 79. Washington, D.C.: U.S. Government Printing Office.

Cooper, C. F. 1960. Changes in vegetation, structure, and growth of southwestern pine forests since white settlement. *Ecological Monographs* 30(2):129–164.

Cordell, L. S. 1997. *Archaeology of the Southwest.* San Diego: Academic Press.

Covey, C., ed. and trans. 1993. Cabeza de Vaca's "Adventures in the unknown interior of America." Albuquerque: University of New Mexico Press.

Coville, F. 1898. *Forest growth and sheep grazing in the Cascade Mountains of Oregon.* USDA Division of Forestry bulletin no. 15. Washington, D.C.: U.S. Government Printing Office.

Covington, W. W., P. Z. Fulé, M. M. Moore, S. C. Hart, T. E. Kolb, J. N. Mast, S. S. Sackett, and M. R. Wagner. 1997. Restoring ecosystem health in ponderosa pine forests of the Southwest. *Journal of Forestry* 95:23–29.

Covington, W. W., and M. M. Moore. 1994. Southwestern ponderosa pine forest structure: Changes since Euro-American settlement. *Journal of Forestry* 92:39–47.

Day, G. M. 1953. The Indian as an ecological factor in the northeastern forest. *Ecology* 34:329–346.

Dean, J. S. 1988. Dendrochronology and paleoenvironmental reconstruction on the Colorado Plateaus. Pp. 119–167 in *The Anasazi in a changing environment*, ed. G. J. Gummerman. Cambridge: Cambridge University Press.

Dean, J. S., and G. S. Funkhouser. 1995. Dendroclimatic reconstruction for the southern Colorado Plateau. Pp. 85–104 in *Climate change in the four corners and adjacent region: Implications for environmental restoration and land-use planning*, ed. W. J. Waugh. Grand Junction, Colo.: U.S. Department of Energy, Grand Junction Project Office.

DeBuys, W. 1985. *Enchantment and exploitation: The life and hard times of a New Mexico mountain range*. Albuquerque: University of New Mexico Press.

Delcourt, H. R., and P. A. Delcourt. 1998. Pre-Columbian Native American use of fire on southern Appalachian landscapes. *Conservation Biology* 11:1010–1014.

Denevan, W. M. 1967. Livestock numbers in nineteenth-century New Mexico and the problem of gullying in the Southwest. *Annals of the Association of American Geographers* 57(4):691–703.

———. 1992. The pristine myth: The landscape of the Americas in 1492. *Annals of the Association of American Geographers* 82:369–385.

Dobyns, H. E. 1981. *From fire to flood: Historic human destruction of Sonoran Desert riverine oases*. Ballena Press anthropology papers no. 20. Socorro, N. Mex.: Ballena.

Doolittle, W. E. 1992. Agriculture in North America on the eve of contact: A reassessment. *Annals of the Association of American Geographers* 82:386–401.

Elliott, M. L. 1993. *Jémez*. Santa Fe: Museum of New Mexico Press.

Euler, R. C. 1988. Demography and cultural dynamics on the Colorado Plateaus. Pp. 192–229 in *The Anasazi in a changing environment*, ed. G. J. Gummerman. New York: Cambridge University Press.

Fish, S. K. 1996. Modeling human impacts to the Borderlands environment from a fire ecology perspective. Pp. 125–134 in *Effects of fire on Madrean Province ecosystems: A symposium proceedings*, tech. coord. P. F. Ffolliott et al. General Technical Report RM-289. Fort Collins, Colo.: USDA Forest Service.

Forman, R. T. T., and E. W. B. Russell. 1983. Evaluation of historical data in ecology. *Bulletin of the Ecological Society of America* 64:5–7.

Foxx, T. S., and L. D. Potter. 1978. Fire ecology at Bandelier National Monument. Unpublished report on file at Bandelier National Monument.

Frederickson, E., K. M. Havstad, and R. Estelle. 1998. Perspectives on desertification: Southwestern United States. *Journal of Arid Environments* 39:191–207.

Fulé, P. Z., and W. W. Covington. 1996. Changing fire regimes in Mexican pine forests: Ecological and management implications. *Journal of Forestry* 94:33–38.

———. 1999. Fire regime changes in La Michilía Biosphere Reserve, Durango, Mexico. *Conservation Biology* 13:640–652.

Fulé, P. Z., W. W. Covington, and M. M. Moore. 1997. Determining reference conditions for ecosystem management of southwestern ponderosa pine. *Ecological Applications* 7:895–908.

Fulé, P. Z., T. A. Heinlein, W. W. Covington, and M. M. Moore. 2000. Continuing fire regimes in remote forests of Grand Canyon National Park. Pp. 242–248 in *Proceedings: Wilderness science in a time of change conference*, vol. 5: *Wilderness ecosystems, threats, and management, May 23–27, 1999, Missoula, Mont.*, comp. D. N. Cole, S. F. McCool, W. T. Borrie, and F. O'Loughlin. Ogden, Utah: USDA Forest Service, Rocky Mountain Research Station, Proceedings RMRS-P-15-VOL-5.

Gottesfeld, L. M. J. 1994. Aboriginal burning for vegetation management in northwest British Columbia. *Human Ecology* 22:171–188.

Grissino-Mayer, H. D. 1995. Tree-ring reconstructions of climate and fire history at El Malpais National Monument, New Mexico. Ph.D. diss., University of Arizona.

———. 1996. A 2129-year reconstruction of precipitation for northwestern New Mexico, USA. Pp. 191–204 in *Tree rings, environment and humanity*, ed. J. S. Dean, D. M. Meko, and T. W. Swetnam. Tucson, Ariz.: Radiocarbon.

Grissino-Mayer, H. D., C. H. Baisan, and T. W. Swetnam. 1995. Fire history in the Pinaleño Mountains of southeastern Arizona: Effects of human-related disturbances. Pp. 399–407 in *Biodiversity and management of the Madrean Archipelago: The sky islands of southwestern United States and northwestern Mexico*, tech. coord. L. F. DeBano et al. General technical report RM-264. Fort Collins, Colo.: USDA Forest Service.

Grissino-Mayer, H. D., and T. W. Swetnam. 2000. Century-scale climate forcing of fire regimes in the American Southwest. *The Holocene* 10(2):207–214.

Harrington, J. P. 1916. *The ethnogeography of the Tewa Indians.* The 29th annual report of the Bureau of American Ethnology—1907–1908. Washington, D.C.: U.S. Government Printing Office.

Henderson, J., and J. P. Harrington. 1914. *Ethnozoology of the Tewa Indians.* Washington, D.C.: Smithsonian Institution, Bureau of American Ethnology.

Holsinger, S. J. 1902. The boundary line between the desert and the forest. *American Forests* 8:21–27.

Hough, W. 1926. *Fire as an agent in human culture.* Smithsonian Institution, U.S. National Museum bulletin 139. Washington, D.C.: U.S. Government Printing Office.

Huber, E. K., and T. A. Kohler. 1993. Pollen Analysis, Kiva, Area 1, Burnt Mesa Pueblo (LA 60372). Pp. 121–129 in *Papers on the early classic period prehistory of the Pajarito Plateau, New Mexico.* Pullman: Department of Anthropology, Washington State University.

Humphrey, R. R. 1974. Fire in the deserts and desert grassland of North America. Pp. 365–400 in *Fire and Ecosystems*, ed. T. T. Kozlowski and C. E. Ahlgren. New York: Academic Press.

Jackson, J. G. 1900. Pikes Peak, Plum Creek, and South Platte forest reserves. Pp. 39–116 in *Twentieth annual report of the U.S. Geological Survey, 1898–1899*, part 5: *Forest Reserves.* Washington, D.C.: U.S. Government Printing Office.

Kaib, J. M. 1998. Fire history in the riparian canyon pine-oak forests and the intervening desert grasslands of the Southwest borderlands: A dendroecological, historical, and cultural inquiry. Master's thesis, University of Arizona, Tucson.

Kaufmann, M. R., L. S. Huckaby, C. M. Regan, and J. Popp. 1998. *Forest reference conditions for ecosystem management in the Sacramento Mountains, New Mexico.* General technical report RMRS-19. Fort Collins, Colo.: USDA Forest Service.

Kay, C. E. 1994. Aboriginal overkill: The role of North Americans in structuring western ecosystems. *Human Nature* 5:359–398.

———. 1997. Is aspen doomed? *Journal of Forestry* 95:4–11.

Kaye, M., and T. W. Swetnam. 1999. An assessment of fire, climate, and Apache history in the Sacramento Mountains, New Mexico. *Physical Geography* 20:305–330.

Kohler, T. A., and M. A. Matthews. 1988. Long-term Anasazi land use and forest reduction: A case study from southwest Colorado. *American Antiquity* 53(3):537–564.

Kohler, T. A., J. D. Orcutt, K. L. Petersen, and E. Blinman. 1986. Anasazi spreadsheets: The cost of doing agricultural business in prehistoric Dolores. Pp. 525–538 in *Dolores archaeological program: Final synthetic report*, comp. D. A. Breternitz, C. K. Robinson, and G. T. Gross Denver: Bureau of Reclamation.

Krech, S., III. 1999. *The ecological Indian: Myth and history.* New York: W. W. Norton.

Krider, E. P., R. C. Noggle, A. E. Pifer, and D. L. Vance. 1980. Lightning direction-finding systems for forest fire detection. *Bulletin of the American Meteorological Society* 61:980–986.

Lang, R. W., and A. H. Harris. 1984. *The faunal remains from Arroyo Hondo Pueblo, New Mexico: A study in short-term subsistence change.* Santa Fe: School of American Research Press.

Leiberg, J. B., T. F. Rixon, and A. Dodwell. 1904. Forest conditions in the San Francisco Mountains Forest Reserve, Arizona. U.S. Geological Survey Professional Paper No. 22, Series H, Forestry, 7. Washington, D.C.: U.S. Government Printing Office.

Leopold, A. 1920. "Piute forestry" vs. forest fire protection. *Southwestern Magazine* 2(3):12–13.

———. 1924. Grass, brush, timber and fire in southern Arizona. *Journal of Forestry* 22:1–10.

———. 1937. Conservationist in Mexico. *American Forests* 43 (3):118–120, 146.

Levine, F., and T. Merlan. 1997. Bandelier National Monument: Ethnographic literature search and consultation. Unpublished report on file at Bandelier National Monument.

Lewis, H. T. 1973. *Patterns of Indian burning in California: Ecology and ethnohistory.* Anthropological papers no. 1. Ramona, Calif.: Ballena.

———. 1985. Why Indians burned: Specific versus general reasons. Pp. 75–80 in *Proceedings—Symposium and workshop on wilderness fire*, tech. coord. J. E. Lotan et al. General technical report INT-182. Ogden, Utah: USDA Forest Service.

Madany, M. H., and N. W. West. 1983. Livestock grazing–fire regime interactions within montane forests of Zion National Park. *Ecology* 64:661–667.

Martin, P. S., and R. G. Klein, eds. 1984. *Quaternary extinctions: A prehistoric revolution.* Tucson: University of Arizona Press.

Martin, P. S., and C. R. Szuter. 1999. War zones and game sinks in Lewis and Clark's West. *Conservation Biology* 13:36–45.

Meinig, D. W. 1971. Southwest: Three peoples in geographical change 1600–1970. New York: Oxford University Press.

Meko, D. M., C. W. Stockton, and W. R. Boggess. 1995. The tree-ring record of severe sustained drought. *Water Resource Bulletin* 31:789–801.

Merriam, C. H. 1890. *Results of a biological survey of the San Francisco Mountains region and desert of the Little Colorado in Arizona.* North America fauna no. 3. Washington, D.C.: USDA

Morino, K., C. H. Baisan, and T. W. Swetnam. 1998. Expanded fire regime studies in the Jemez Mts., New Mexico. Unpublished report on file at USGS Jemez Mts. Field Station.

Morino, K. A. 1996. Reconstruction and interpretation of historical patterns of fire occurrence in the Organ Mountains, New Mexico. Master's thesis, University of Arizona, Tucson.

National Academy of Sciences. 1897. *Report of the commission appointed by the National Academy of Sciences upon a forest policy for the forested lands of the United States.* 55th U.S. Cong., 2d sess., S. Doc. 57, pp. 28–73.

Orcutt, J. D. 1999. Demography, settlement, and agriculture. Pp. 219–308 in *The Bandelier archeological survey* (vols. 1 and 2), ed. R. P. Powers and J. D. Orcutt. USDI National Park Service, Intermountain Cultural Resources Management professional paper no. 57.

Orville, R. E., and A. C. Silver. 1997. Lightning ground flash density in the contiguous United States: 1992–1995. *Monthly Weather Review* 125:631–638.

Osborn, A. J. 1993. Snowblind in the desert Southwest: Moisture islands, ungulate ecology, and alternative prehistoric overwintering strategies. *Journal of Anthropological Research* 49(2):135–164.

Periman, R. D. 1996. The influence of prehistoric Anasazi cobble-mulch agricultural features on northern Rio Grande landscapes. Pp. 181–188 in *Desired future conditions for southwestern riparian ecosystems,* tech. coord. D. Shaw and D. Finch. General technical report RM-272. Fort Collins, Colo.: USDA Forest Service.

Petersen, K. L. 1988. *Climate and the Dolores River Anasazi.* University of Utah anthropological papers no. 113. Salt Lake City: University of Utah Press.

Plog, F., G. J. Gummerman, R. C. Euler, J. S. Dean, R. H. Hevly, and T. N. V. Karlstrom. 1988. Anasazi adaptive strategies: The model, predictions, and results. Pp. 230–277 in *The Anasazi in a changing environment,* ed. G. J. Gummerman. New York: Cambridge University Press.

Plummer, F. G. 1912a. *Forest fires: Their causes, extent and effects, with a summary of recorded destruction and loss.* USDA Forest Service bulletin 117. Washington, D.C.: U.S. Government Printing Office.

———. 1912b. *Lightning in relation to forest fires.* USDA Forest Service bulletin 111. Washington, D.C.: U.S. Government Printing Office.

Powell, J. W. 1890. The non-irrigable lands of the arid region. *Century Magazine* (April 1, 1890):915–922.

Powers, R. P., and J. D. Orcutt, eds. 1999. *The Bandelier archeological survey* (vols. 1 and 2). USDI National Park Service, Intermountain Cultural Resources Management professional paper no. 57.

Pyne, S. J. 1995a. *World fire: The culture of fire on earth.* Seattle: University of Washington Press.

———. 1995b. Vestal fires and virgin lands: A reburn. Pp. 15–21 in *Proceedings: Symposium on fire in wilderness and park management,* tech. coord. J. K. Brown et al. General technical report INT-320. Ogden, Utah: USDA Forest Service.

———. 1996. Nouvelle Southwest. Pp. 10–16 in *Conference on adaptive ecosystem restoration and management: Restoration of cordilleran conifer landscapes of North America,* tech. coord. W. Covington and P. K. Wagner. General technical report RM-278. Fort Collins, Colo.: USDA Forest Service.

———. 1997. *Fire in America: A cultural history of wildland and rural fire.* Seattle: University of Washington Press.

———. 2000. Where have all the fires gone? *Fire Management Today* 60:4–6.

Robbins, W. W., J. P. Harrington, and B. Freire-Marreco. 1916. *Ethnobotany of the Tewa Indians.* Washington, D.C.: Smithsonian Institution, Bureau of American Ethnology.

Rollins, M. G., T. W. Swetnam, and P. Morgan. 1999. Twentieth-century fire patterns in the Selway-Bitterroot Wilderness Area in Idaho/Montana and the Gila/Aldo Leopold Wilderness Areas in New Mexico. Unpublished final report to Aldo Leopold Wilderness Research Institute, Missoula, Mont.

Romme, W. H., D. Hanna, L. Floyd-Hanna, and E. J. Bartlett. 1996. Fire history and successional status in aspen forests of the San Juan National Forest: Final report. Unpublished report on file at USGS Jemez Mts. Field Station.

Romme, W. H., L. Floyd-Hanna, D. Hanna, and E. J. Bartlett. 1999a. Chapter 5: Aspen forests. Landscape condition analysis for the south central highlands section, southwestern Colorado and northwestern New Mexico. Unpublished final report on file at USGS Jemez Mts. Field Station.

Romme, W. H., L. Floyd-Hanna, D. Hanna, J. S. Redders, K. McGarigal, and M. Crist. 1999b. Chapter 6: Spruce-fir forests. Landscape condition analysis for the south central highlands section, southwestern Colorado and northwestern New Mexico. Unpublished final report on file at USGS Jemez Mts. Field Station.

Samuels, M. L., and J. L. Betancourt. 1982. Modeling the long-term effects of fuelwood harvests on pinyon-juniper woodlands. *Environmental Management* 6:505–515.

Sauer, C. O. 1975. Man's dominance by use of fire. *Geoscience and Man* 10:1–13.

Savage, M. 1991. Structural dynamics of a southwestern pine forest under chronic human disturbance. *Annals of the Association of American Geographers* 81:271–289.

Savage, M., and T. W. Swetnam. 1990. Early and persistent fire decline in a Navajo ponderosa pine forest. *Ecology* 70(6):2374–2378.

Schroeder, A. H. 1992. Protohistoric Pueblo demographic changes. Pp. 29–35 in *Current research on the late prehistory and early history of New Mexico*, ed. B. J. Viera New Mexico Archaeological Council special publication 1. Albuquerque, N. Mex.

Scurlock, D. 1998. *From the rio to the sierra: An environmental history of the middle Rio Grande Basin.* General technical report RMRS-5. Fort Collins, Colo.: USDA Forest Service.

Secklecki, M. T., H. D. Grissino-Mayer, and T. W. Swetnam. 1996. Fire history and the possible role of Apache-set fires in the Chiricahua Mountains of southeastern Arizona. Pp. 238–246 in *Effects of fire on Madrean Province ecosystems*, tech. coord. P. F. Ffolliott et al. General technical report RM-289. Fort Collins, Colo.: USDA Forest Service.

Snyderman, D., and C. D. Allen. 1997. Fire in the mountains: Analysis of historical fires for Bandelier National Monument, Santa Fe National Forest, and surrounding areas, 1909–1996. Unpublished report on file at USGS Jemez Mts. Field Station.

Spoerl, P. M., and J. C. Ravesloot. 1995. From Casas Grandes to Casa Grande: Prehistoric human impacts in the sky islands of southern Arizona and northwestern Mexico. Pp. 492–501 in *Biodiversity and management of the Madrean Archipelago: The sky islands of southwestern United States and northwestern Mexico*, tech. coord. L. F. DeBano et al. General technical report RM-264. Fort Collins, Colo.: USDA Forest Service.

Stevenson, J. J. 1881. Report upon geological examinations in southern Colorado and northern New Mexico, during years 1878 and 1879. U.S. Geographic Survey west of 100th Meridian Vol. 3 (supp.).

Stewart, O. C. 1951. Burning and natural vegetation in the United States. *Geographical Review* 41:317–320.

———. 1955. Forest and grass burning in the Mountain West. *Southwestern Lore* 21:5–9.

———. 1956. Fire as the first great force employed by man. Pp. 115–133 in *Man's role in changing the face of the earth*, ed. W. L. Thomas, Jr. Chicago: University of Chicago Press.

———. 1963. Barriers to understanding the influence of use of fire by aborigines on vegetation. *Proceedings of the Tall Timbers Fire Ecology Conference* 72:117–126.

Sudworth, G. B. 1900. Battlement Mesa Forest Reserve. Pp. 181–244 in *Twentieth Annual Report of the U.S. Geological Survey, 1898-1899*, part 5: *Forest Reserves*. Washington D.C.: U.S. Government Printing Office.

Sullivan, A. P., III. 1992. Pinyon nuts and other wild resources in Western Anasazi subsistence economies. *Research in Economic Anthropology* (supp.) 6:195–239.

Swetnam, T. W. 1990. Fire history and climate in the southwestern United States. Pp. 6–17 in *Effects of fire management of southwestern natural resources*, tech. coord. J. S. Krammes. General technical report RM-191. Fort Collins, Colo.: USDA Forest Service.

Swetnam, T. W., C. D. Allen, and J. L. Betancourt. 1999. Applied historical ecology: Using the past to manage for the future. *Ecological Applications* 9:1189–1206.

Swetnam, T. W., and C. H. Baisan. 1996a. Historical fire regime patterns in the southwestern United States since A.D. 1700. Pp. 11–32 in *Fire effects in southwestern forests: Proceedings of the second La Mesa fire symposium*, tech. ed. C. D. Allen. General technical report RM-286. Fort Collins, Colo.: USDA Forest Service.

———. 1996b. Histories of montane forests in the Madrean Borderlands. Pp. 15–36 in *Effects of fire on Madrean Province ecosystems*, tech. coord. P. F. Ffolliott et al., General technical report RM-289. Fort Collins, Colo.: USDA Forest Service.

Swetnam, T. W., C. H. Baisan, and J. M. Kaib. 2001. Forest fire histories of the sky islands of La Frontera. Pp. 95–119 chapter in *Changing Plant Life of La Frontera*, ed. G. Webster and C. J. Bahre. Albuquerque: University of New Mexico Press.

Swetnam, T. W., and J. L. Betancourt. 1990. Fire–southern oscillation relations in the southwestern United States. *Science* 249:1017–1020.

———. 1998. Mesoscale disturbance and ecological response to decadal climatic variability in the American Southwest *Journal of Climate* 11:3128–3147.

Touchan, R., C. D. Allen, and T. W. Swetnam. 1996. Fire history and climatic patterns in ponderosa pine and mixed-conifer forests of the Jemez Mountains, northern New Mexico. Pp. 33–46 in *Fire effects in southwestern forests: Proceedings of the second La Mesa fire symposium*, tech. ed. C. D. Allen. General technical report RM-286. Fort Collins, Colo.: USDA Forest Service.

Touchan, R., and T. W. Swetnam. 1992. Fire history of the Jemez Mountains: Fire scar chronologies from five locations. Unpublished report on file at Bandelier National Monument, N. Mex.

———. 1995. Fire history in ponderosa pine and mixed-conifer forests of the Jemez Mountains, Northern New Mexico. Unpublished report on file at Bandelier National Monument, N. Mex.

Touchan, R., T. W. Swetnam, and H. D. Grissino-Mayer. 1995. Effects of livestock grazing on pre-settlement fire regimes in New Mexico. Pp. 268–272 in *Proceedings: Symposium on fire in wilderness and park management*, tech. coord. J. K. Brown et al. General technical report INT-320. Ogden, Utah: USDA Forest Service.

Towner, R. H. 1997. The dendrochronology of the Navajo Pueblitos of Dinétah. Ph.D. diss., University of Arizona Press, Tucson.

Trierweiler, W. N. 1990. Prehistoric Tewa economy: Modeling subsistence production on the Pajarito Plateau. Pp. 1–296 in *The evolution of North American Indians*, ed. D. H. Thomas. New York: Garland.

U.S. Department of Energy. 1979. *Final environmental impact statement: Los Alamos scientific laboratory site, Los Alamos, New Mexico*. DOI/EIS-0018. Springfield, Va.: National Technical Information Service.

U.S. Department of the Interior/U.S. Department of Agriculture. 1995. *Federal wildland fire management—Policy and program review*. Boise, Idaho: National Interagency Fire Center.

Van Devender, T. R., and W. G. Spaulding. 1979. Development of vegetation and climate in the southwestern United States. *Science* 204:701–710.

Veblen, T. T., and D. C. Lorenz. 1991. *The Colorado front range: A century of ecological change*. Salt Lake City: University of Utah Press.

Weaver, H. 1951. Fire as an ecological factor in southwestern ponderosa pine forests. *Journal of Forestry* 49(2):93–98.

Weng, C., and S. T. Jackson. 1999. Late Glacial and Holocene vegetation history and paleoclimate of the Kaibab Plateau, Arizona. *Palaeogeography, Palaeoclimatology, Palaeoecology* 153:179–201.

Williams, G. W. 1997. American Indian use of fire in ecosystems: Thousands of years of managing landscapes. Unpublished paper presented at the annual meeting of the Ecological Society of America in Albuquerque, N. Mex., August 1997.

———. 2000. Introduction to aboriginal fire use in North America. *Fire Management Today* 60:8–12..

Wolf, J. J., and J. N. Mast. 1998. Fire history of mixed-conifer forests on the North Rim, Grand Canyon National Park, Arizona. *Physical Geography* 19:1–14.

Wooton, E. O. 1908. *The range problem in New Mexico*. Agriculture Experiment Station Bulletin No. 66. Las Cruces: New Mexico College of Agriculture and Mechanic Arts.

Wyckoff, D. G. 1977. Secondary forest succession following abandonment of Mesa Verde. *Kiva* 42(3-4):215–231.

PREHISTORIC BURNING IN THE PACIFIC NORTHWEST: HUMAN VERSUS CLIMATIC INFLUENCES

Cathy Whitlock and Margaret A. Knox

When Europeans first arrived in the Pacific Northwest, the region was occupied by several indigenous cultural groups that were adapted in diverse ways to a wide range of environments. The archaeological record indicates that these lifeways developed early in the Holocene in response to the environmental complexity of the region, and that prehistoric activities were probably not substantially different from those at the time of European contact (Aikens 1993). Throughout the Holocene (the last 11,000 years), changes in environment that occurred seasonally, annually, and on longer time scales affected the availability and utilization of resources, including the plants and animals that existed in the region, and these resources, in turn, influenced human land-use patterns. But what of the reverse? To what extent did early peoples change the environment, not only through their possible role in faunal extinctions (sensu Martin 1984), but also through their alteration of the vegetation and significant ecological processes? Was the vegetation encountered by Euro-Americans a reflection of conditions determined by climate and natural disturbance alone or was it highly modified by humans? Denevan (1992) and others (Pyne 1982, 2000; Chase 1987; Butzer 1990; Cronon 1995; Flores 1997; Williams 2000) argue that North America was widely disturbed by human activity prior to the time of Euro-American exploration. In their view, a desire for wilderness preservation has led to denial of this human imprint and a false belief that landscapes at the time of European contact were pristine (Denevan 1992). Others maintain that much of North America, especially in the western United States, was not significantly altered by prehistoric peoples, and the vegetation at the time of European contact was more natural than humanized (Vale, chapter 1 of this volume). In this chapter, we consider the evidence of human alteration in the Pacific Northwest, where paleoecological, archeological, and historical data are available to describe the relations between humans and their environment.

The Pacific Northwest was apparently fairly populated at the time of Spanish exploration in the 1770s, and estimates of population size along the Northwest coast from southeastern Alaska to northern California vary from 200,000 (Boyd 1990) to 102,000 (minimum estimate of Ubelaker 1988). Regardless of the exact number, population centers were largest along the coast and western valleys, with about 35,000–40,000 people on the Pacific slope of Oregon and Washington and about 16,000 in the Willamette Valley (Boyd 1990). Populations east of the Cascade Range were smaller because resources were scarce and geographically isolated. Interior basins of the Pacific Northwest may have supported up to several hundred people in large salmon-fishing encampments, but less than a few dozen people in individual remote settlements (Aikens 1993).

Native Americans prior to European contact undoubtedly disturbed vegetation in the vicinity of permanent settlements and seasonal encampments, and fishing, hunting, and gathering activities inevitably had some ecological impact as well. The issue of most intense debate with respect to the "pristine myth," however, is the scale of environmental alteration caused by human use of fire. Did anthropogenic burning occur to the extent that it created new vegetation types? For example, were low-elevation savanna and woodland created by deliberate burning practices or were they a consequence of climate, soils, and natural (i.e., nonanthropogenic) disturbances? To address these questions requires information on the activities of Native Americans, and a means of separating the impact of human-set fires on prehistoric vegetation from that caused by a natural disturbance regime.

Today, lightning fires in the Pacific Northwest start in summer and early fall during convectional storms associated with interior high-pressure cells. Because of strong easterlies, fires often spread from east to west (Agee 1993). For example, the large Tillamook Fire of 1933, which burned large tracts of the Coast Range, was started in the western edge of the Willamette Valley and moved westward into the Coast Range (Oregon Department of Forestry 1970). The highest number of light-

TABLE 6.1. Fire return intervals for the Pacific Northwest based on dendrochronological methods for the last few centuries (from Agee 1993 and references therein).

Forest Type	Oregon			Washington		
	Area in type (1,000 ha)	Fire cycle (yr)	Area burned per year (1,000 ha)	Area in type (1,000 ha)	Fire cycle (yr)	Area burned per year (1,000 ha)
Cedar/spruce/ hemlock	292	400	0.7	1,291	937	1.4
Douglas fir	4,444	150	29.6	3,068	217	14.1
Mixed conifer	399	30	13.3	504	50	10.1
Lodgepole pine	757	80	9.4	211	110	1.9
Woodland	1,001	25	40.0	12	25	0.5
Subalpine	1,075	800	1.2	935	500	1.9
Ponderosa pine	3,142	15	209.4	1,438	15	95.8
Other	2,397	133	18.0	1,949	298	6.5

ning strikes today occurs at middle and high elevations in the Cascade Range, in the mountains of eastern Oregon and Washington, and the Klamath region, but, in Oregon, strikes are recorded in all counties (Oregon Department of Forestry 1997).

Modern estimates of fire return intervals for Oregon and Washington are based on forest-cover types and definitions drawn from the first regional forest surveys of the region. On average, Oregon has more dry forests, which burn more frequently than those in Washington, where it is cooler and moister (Agee 1993). The mean fire frequency, based on tree-ring and documentary evidence, varies considerably among forest types (Table 6.1). Ponderosa pine forests burn almost every decade, and the fires are generally of low severity, while subalpine and coastal forests may burn once in a millennium, and the fires tend to be stand-replacing events.

Information on prehistoric vegetation comes from pollen and plant macrofossil records collected from lakes and natural wetlands and from plant assemblages preserved in packrat (Neotoma) middens. A network of paleovegetation sites (Figure 6.1) is available from the Pacific Northwest, and, despite some gaps in coverage, the climate and vegetation history of the region is fairly well known for the last 20,000 years (see reviews by Heusser 1977, 1983; Baker 1983; Mehringer 1985; Barnosky et al. 1987; Whitlock 1992; Thompson et al. 1993). The chronology for paleoecological records comes from radiocarbon dating of organic sediment or individual plant remains. Because radiocarbon years depart from

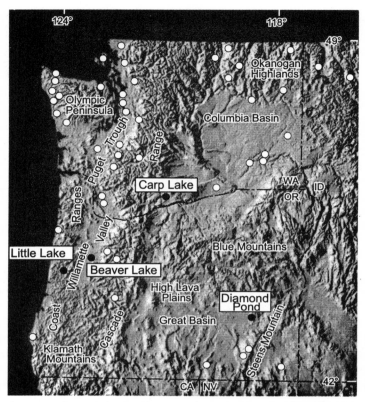

Figure 6.1. Map of geographic regions referred to in text. Open circles show the location of radiocarbon-dated pollen records that have been published in the region. The black circles refer to the sites with high-resolution charcoal data.

calendar years in the early and middle Holocene, it is necessary to convert a radiocarbon-based chronology to calendar years using calibration tables (Stuiver and Reimer 1993; Stuiver et al. 1998). All ages presented in this chapter as "years ago" are radiocarbon dates converted to calendar years.

Two types of records provide prehistoric fire reconstructions: dendrochronological data and lake-sediment data. Dendrochronological records are based on fire-scarred tree-rings as well as the age of forest stands that colonize areas of high-severity fires. Tree rings preserve the scars of low-severity ground fires that do not kill the trees, and from these data it is possible to know exactly where and in what year such fires occurred. Stand-age analysis is used to map the size and age of stand-replacement fires, particularly in boreal and montane forests, where infrequent large fires of high severity characterize the fire regime. Successively younger fires, however, erase the evidence of older fires in stand-age analysis, and, as with fire-scar methods, the reconstruction period is as old as the oldest living trees. Few dendrochronological studies extend beyond the last 500 years, and, in the Pacific Northwest, the longest reliable chronologies span the last 600 years (Agee 1993).

Fire history on longer time scales is obtained from fire proxy preserved in lake-sediment records (see Whitlock and Larsen, in press, for discussion of methods). Particles of charcoal, introduced to a lake during and shortly after a fire, provide information on past fires. Recent refinements have been made in the study of past fires based on charcoal records from laminated and nonlaminated lake sediments (Patterson et al. 1987; Clark 1990; Millspaugh and Whitlock 1995; Clark and Royal 1996; Long et al. 1998). By selecting a site carefully, constraining the size of the charcoal particles examined, and discriminating between the local and extralocal components of the charcoal record, it is possible to reconstruct variations in local fire frequency with fair confidence. The interpretation of the charcoal data is based on calibration studies following recent and historic fires (Whitlock and Millspaugh 1996; Clark et al. 1998; Ohlson and Tryterud 2000; Gardner and Whitlock, in review). Charcoal particles more than 100 microns in size are tallied in contiguous 1-cm-long core intervals, and layers with abundant charcoal (charcoal peaks) are assumed to represent a fire "event." An event is defined as one or more fires occurring during the deposition of that core interval. Depending on the sedimentation rate, a fire event can be dated with decadal precision, although sometimes the peak spans a few centimeters of the core and thus is the equivalent of a few decades of sediment deposition. High-resolution charcoal analysis is time-consuming, and only a few such records are currently available from the Pacific Northwest (Long et al. 1998; Pearl 1999; Mohr et al. 2000). Less detailed charcoal records have been described from the Puget Trough (Sugita and Tsukada 1982; Cwynar 1987) and Cascade Range (Dunwiddie 1986).

Climate and Vegetation Changes Since the Last Ice Age

In the last 20,000 years, the Earth system has undergone a shift from glacial conditions to the present interglacial period, the Holocene (the last 11,000 years). These climatic changes profoundly affected ecosystems as species adjusted their ranges and abundance. Fire regimes were also altered, and it is likely that fire was the proximal cause of many of the vegetation changes. The end of the glacial period is also the time when humans spread across North America. The archeological record in the Pacific Northwest extends back about 11,000 years in the interior region (Aikens and Jenkins 1994) and 10,000 years along the coast (Suttles and Ames 1997).

Environmental changes occurring on millennial time scales were governed by large-scale changes in the climate system that affected western North America (Thompson et al. 1993). One control was the declining influence of North American ice sheets on the climate after 16,000 years ago. The presence of an ice sheet prior to that time steepened the latitudinal temperature gradient south of its margin and shifted the jet stream south of its present position. The Pacific Northwest, as a result, was relatively cold and dry in full-glacial time, and the American Southwest was more humid. As the ice sheets wasted, temperatures warmed, the jet stream shifted northward, and the climate of the Pacific Northwest became warmer and wetter.

Another important control of climate relates to changes in the seasonal cycle of insolation caused by slow variations in the timing of perihelion (when Earth is closest to the sun) and in the amount of tilt of Earth's axis (Kutzbach and Guetter 1986). Between about 14,000 and 7,000 years ago, perihelion was in July and the tilt of Earth's axis was greater than at present. As a result, summer insolation was 8.5 percent greater and 10 percent less in winter in the Pacific Northwest during the early Holocene (about 11,000–7,800 years ago). Greater-than-present insolation led directly to increased summer temperatures and drought. Indirectly, it gave rise to a strengthening of the eastern Pacific subtropical high in the Pacific Northwest, which further intensified summer drought. Paleoclimatic reconstructions suggest that annual precipitation west of the Cascade Range was 40–50 percent less than today and annual temperature was 1–3°C higher. In the Great Basin, increased insolation may have led to stronger-than-present monsoonal circulation and thus wetter summers in the early Holocene. In the middle Holocene (some 7,800–4,400 years ago), summer insolation was less than before and the effects of drought and monsoonal precipitation were attenuated. Summers became cooler and wetter across most of the Pacific Northwest, except in the Great Basin, where the climate became more arid (with the loss of summer precipitation). As the seasonal cycle of insolation approached modern values in the late Holocene (the last 4,400 years), the entire region became cooler than before and the modern climate regime was established.

Paleoecological records indicate that these large-scale climate changes were responsible for major reorganizations of vegetation in the last 20,000 years. The summary of the vegetation history that follows is based on Whitlock (1992, and references therein), as well as new pollen records from the Puget Trough (McLachlan and Brubaker 1995), Oregon Coast Range (Worona and Whitlock 1995; Grigg and Whitlock 1998), Cascade Range (Sea and Whitlock 1995), and Willamette Valley

(Pearl 1999). During the late-glacial period, when the Cordilleran ice sheet and alpine glaciers were receding, the climate was cooler and wetter than today, but warmer than during full-glacial time. In the northern Puget Trough and Olympic Peninsula, lodgepole pine (*Pinus contorta*) forest, rather than tundra, colonized newly deglaciated substrates, suggesting that the climate was relatively warm by 16,000 years ago. Lodgepole pine was joined by Sitka spruce (*Picea sitchensis*), Douglas fir (*Pseudotsuga menziesii*), and hemlock (*Tsuga*), forming a closed forest by 13,000 years ago. A mixture of high- and low-elevation taxa that has no modern counterpart appeared in the southern Puget Trough during the late-glacial period, replacing earlier subalpine parkland communities. As the climate warmed, montane species were forced to higher elevations, and Douglas fir, red alder (*Alnus rubra*), and oak (*Quercus*) prevailed in the lowlands. In the Oregon Coast Range, Douglas fir and red alder were present as early as 16,000 years ago, supplanting forests of mountain hemlock (*Tsuga mertensiana*) and spruce. The southwestern Columbia Basin supported steppe and areas of spruce parkland as a result of cool dry conditions in both full- and late-glacial time. Farther north in the Okanogan region, steppe or tundra with pine (presumably whitebark pine [*Pinus albicaulis*] and western white pine [*P. monticola*]), fir (*Abies*), and spruce were present.

During the early Holocene (some 11,000–7,800 years ago), drought- and disturbance-adapted species became widespread as a result of summers that were warmer and drier than present. Douglas fir, red alder, and bracken (*Pteridium aquilinum*) were abundant within coastal forests, and these taxa along with prairie species were more extensive in the Puget Trough and Willamette Valley. In the mountains, warmer summers shifted the position of upper treeline above its present position. East of the Cascade Range, cold steppe was replaced by temperate steppe, and the forest/steppe ecotone lay above and north of its present range. In the Great Basin, cool and moist conditions allowed for the expansion of sagebrush (*Artemisia*) and at higher elevations for increased pine and juniper (*Juniperus*) (Mehringer 1985).

In the middle and late Holocene (7,800 years ago to present), lower summer temperatures and greater effective moisture everywhere except in the Great Basin shifted the vegetation toward more mesophytic and fire-sensitive species. Forests became closed, and upper and lower treelines shifted to lower elevations. West of the Cascades, increased moisture in the middle Holocene allowed western red cedar (*Thuja plicata*), Oregon ash (*Fraxinus latifolia*), and big-leaf maple (*Acer macrophyllum*) to expand their ranges. Western hemlock (*Tsuga heterophylla*) and Sitka spruce became more abundant in coastal rain forests in the last 4,400 years. Prairies in the Puget Trough and Willamette Valley shrank in size, and oak and Douglas fir were less abundant than in the early Holocene.

Western hemlock and western red cedar also expanded in the Puget Trough. In the Cascade Range, upper treeline shifted downslope to its present elevation.

In eastern Washington, steppe communities were replaced by ponderosa pine parkland in the early and middle Holocene. This transition occurred quite early in the eastern Cascade Range (9,400 to 7,800 years ago) and somewhat later in the Okanogan region (after 4,400 years ago). In the last 4,000 years, low-elevation pine forests have been invaded by mesophytic conifers, including Douglas fir, fir, hemlock, and spruce, and along the Columbia Gorge by Oregon white oak. In the Great Basin, the driest period occurred between 7,000 and 6,200 years ago, when summer precipitation decreased but temperatures were higher than at present. Between 6,200 and 1,950 years ago, the climate was cool and wet, allowing for the expansion of juniper woodland at low elevations. Generally moist conditions have occurred during the last 1,950 years, with the exception of dry periods between 700 and 500 years ago (Wigand 1987).

This relation between past climate and vegetation in the Pacific Northwest provides a means of assessing the natural variations in fire occurrence on long time scales. West of the Cascade Range, where the climate is mesic, one would expect that periods of drier climate would have higher-than-present fire frequencies, and consequently more fire- and drought-adapted taxa in the vegetation. Regardless of the source of ignition—humans or lightning—a dry climate would promote fires by drying fuels. Conversely, when the climate was wet, the low availability of dry fuel would have reduced the possibility of fire spread no matter what the ignition opportunities. In arid regions east of the Cascade Range, the relation between climate and fire is more complex, because climate variability, in addition to particular climate conditions, would be a factor. Fires would have occurred soon after wet periods or during a short drought within an overall wet period, when grasses produced enough fine fuel to carry fire. Prolonged dry periods would have been relatively fire free, because of the lack of fuel productivity. Of course, the vegetation effects on fire go beyond fuel. For example, some forest ecosystems favor species that have adaptations for maintaining a particular fire regime, such as thick bark or serotinous cones. Anomalous fire regimes, not predicted or explained as a result of prevailing climate or vegetation conditions, would point to human agencies.

Fire, Climate, and Human Activity: Case Studies

The prairie and savanna of the Willamette Valley, the juniper woodland of the Great Basin, and the ponderosa pine forest of the eastern Cascades and Blue Mountains are regions where it has been proposed that indigenous peoples regularly set fires (see Boyd 1999b). Likewise, the changes in vegetation that have occurred in the twentieth century have been ascribed to the elimination of native burning practices and the attendant expansion of forest in the absence of fire. These assertions can be tested to some degree, because paleoecological data are available from these regions to reconstruct the climate, vegetation, and fire history. Archaeologic and ethnographic records and historical journals provide an understanding of indigenous cultures and the use of fire prior to and at the time of Euro-American settlement. However, these materials are often sketchy and subject to different interpretations.

The Willamette Valley of Western Oregon

Changes in the Willamette Valley since Euro-American settlement are widely attributed to the elimination of fire and changes in land use activity in the last 150 years. Comparison of the vegetation in the 1850s with that of the present indicates that the density of tree and shrub cover has increased, and 88 percent of prairie and savanna has been lost (from 688,604 ha to 83,476 ha; Hulse et al. 1998). The vegetation and fire regime at present contrasts greatly with the conditions that existed in the valley in prehistoric times and which were witnessed by early Euro-American visitors. At the time of European contact, the Willamette Valley was occupied by a series of small independent groups within the Kalapuya language group (Zenk 1990). The prehistoric record extends human activities back about 8,000 years (Beckham et al. 1981), and it is thought that prehistoric and historic economies were based on a diverse range of wild foods, including river fish, roots, and seeds, as well as deer (*Odocoileus* spp.), elk (*Cervus*), small mammals, and wildfowl. Societies were highly mobile, ranging seasonally to occupy riparian forest, savanna and woodland, and forest. People occupied open or simple structures in summer and permanent structures that housed several families in winter. Down river of the Willamette Falls, salmon (*Oncorhyncus* spp.) were a large component of the economy, but above the falls and beyond extensive salmon runs, camas was an important food source (Boyd 1986). Hunting sites in the Cascades and Coast Range, attributed to valley groups, attest to seasonal use of the forests (Aikens 1993).

PREHISTORIC RECORDS OF BURNING

Information on prehistoric fires comes from dendrochronological records as well as pollen and charcoal records from the Willamette Valley and adjacent mountains. Many of the oldest trees in the Cascades and Coast Range were established following one or more large fires in the

1500s and early 1600s (Hemstrom and Franklin 1982; Morrison and Swanson 1990; Impara 1997; Weisberg 1998; Berkley 2000). Some fires occurred in the early 1800s, when Kalapuya populations were declining and before Euro-American settlement (Weisberg 1998; Morrison and Swanson 1990); therefore, natural ignitions seem to be the likely source. Data from the foothills of the Cascade Range and Coast Range suggest fires occurred along the valley margin in the middle and late 1700s prior to direct Euro-American influence (Berkley 2000). Fires are also widely registered in the middle and late 1800s and early 1900s, and these burns have been ascribed to logging, mining, and road-building activities of early settlers (Burke 1979; Teensma 1987; Impara 1997; Berkley 2000). Some of the nineteenth-century fires were surprisingly large: the Silverton fire in 1865 affected 400,000 ha in the Cascades and Willamette Valley, and the Yaquina fire of 1853 burned 119,800 ha in the Coast Range. The Tillamook fire of 1933 covered 97,200 ha in the Willamette Valley and Coast Range (Loy et al. 1976). Impara (1997) estimates that 50–70 percent of the old-growth forest of the Coast Range was decimated by Euro-American burning. Settlement activities also led to localized increases in fire frequencies in the mixed-conifer forests of the southern Cascades (Taylor 1993), Klamath Mountain region (Agee 1991), and Sierra Nevada (Skinner and Chang 1996). Fire occurrence has decreased in all these regions during the last 80 years as suppression efforts have become more effective.

A charcoal record of prehistoric fire activity from Little Lake in the Coast Range indicates that the mean fire return interval was 110 years in the early Holocene, when Douglas fir, red alder, and oak were present (Long et al. 1998). By late Holocene time, the mean fire interval had lengthened to 230 years, and fire-sensitive species like Sitka spruce and western hemlock were more common in the forest (Figure 6.2). These long-term trends in fire occurrence in the Coast Range agree with data from the Puget Trough and suggest a widespread response to Holocene climate changes.

Beaver Lake, located in an abandoned meander of the Willamette Valley, is another site where high-resolution charcoal analysis has been undertaken (Pearl 1999). Land surveys in the 1850s show that the lake was surrounded by willow and ash thicket, topographic depressions near the lake supported riparian forest and wet meadows, and nearby upland vegetation was covered by woodland and savanna. The pollen data suggest that wet forest and meadows first appeared ca. 7,000 years ago as a response to cooling and increased moisture. Charcoal levels at Beaver Lake were low until some 4,100 years ago, when they increased dramatically. The interval of highest charcoal occurred between 2,900 and 600 years ago, after which charcoal levels were again low. Two aspects of this

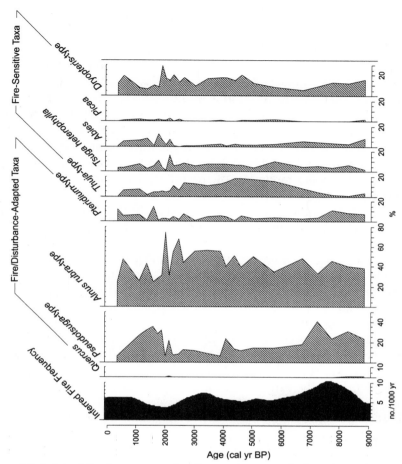

Figure 6.2. Inferred fire frequency and pollen percentages of selected taxa from Little Lake in the Oregon Coast Range (Long et al. 1998). Note the highest fire frequency occurs during periods when fire- and disturbance-adapted species are best represented.

period of abundant charcoal are puzzling. First, the pollen record from Beaver Lake does not indicate any changes in upland vegetation during the period of high charcoal. The fires may have been local and not representative of regional fire frequencies, or they may have occurred in the late summer and fall and thus did not alter the composition of the vegetation. Second, the fire period comes at a time when the climate was shifting to cool, wet conditions in the late Holocene. This juxtaposition of high fire activity during a cool wet period may be evidence of deliberate burning to maintain open vegetation, but it is not obvious why the Kalapuya would have abandoned the effort about 600 years ago, when populations were supposed to have been at their largest (Boyd 1990). The decrease in fires 600 years ago at Beaver Lake may represent (1) an abandonment of the local area for unknown reasons; (2) a decrease in human populations due to disease, starvation, or other factors prior to direct European contact (Ramenofsky 1987; Ubelaker 1988); or (3) the onset of cooler, wetter conditions in the Little Ice Age and a decline in flammability (ca. A.D. 1650–1890; Graumlich and Brubaker 1986; Graumlich 1987). In summary, the Beaver Lake record suggests high fire incidence coincident with Kalapuya occupation, but provides no obvious explanation for decreased burning in the last 600 years. Uncertainties in the timing and interpretation of the record will only be resolved with additional data.

Some have argued that natural ignitions in the valley were not frequent enough in prehistoric time to maintain the fire regime necessary for prairie and savanna (Morris 1936; Johannessen et al. 1971). Lightning strikes are uncommon at present and generally do not occur in summer or early fall when fuels are driest. Moreover, fires in the valley today are actively fought and landscape fragmentation reduces their ability to spread. It is difficult to assess the frequency of natural ignitions in the past, because it would have varied as a component of the climate system. Lightning ignitions were probably more abundant in times of strong convectional activity, such as the early Holocene when monsoonal circulation was enhanced, which is consistent with the charcoal evidence of more fires in the early Holocene at several sites.

EURO-AMERICAN JOURNAL DESCRIPTIONS OF BURNING

Early ethnographers did not gather information on Kalapuya burning practices, and the archaeological record provides few insights. The evidence for burning comes primarily from the accounts of early trappers, explorers, and settlers in the nineteenth century (see Knox 2000 for more detailed discussion of this literature). Contact with the Kalapuya was relatively brief, beginning in 1812 and ending in 1856, when they and other coastal peoples were moved to reservations (Beckham 1990). As early as 1812, Stuart (1995) mentions the decimation of native populations as a result of a smallpox outbreak at the confluence of the Willamette and Columbia Rivers. After 1831, malaria reduced the Kalapuya populations (Boyd 1975, 1986, 1990), and their numbers dropped from some 16,000 at the time of European contact to between 1,175 (Boyd 1990) and 600 (Wilkes 1926) by 1841.

The earliest journals written between 1812 and 1825 (e.g., Douglas 1959; Henry 1992; Seton 1993; Stuart 1995) do not mention native use of fire, either to control or maintain their ecosystem. Most of the accounts were written during June, July, August, and September, and a few were written during winter and spring trips when evidence of fires might have been less obvious. However, as the valley is generally snow-free, burned land would have been visible. Journals from 1826 to 1830 contain some references to fire, but reports of native burning increase after 1840, with expanding Euro-American settlement of the valley. Journals written prior to 1831 (the first year of the malaria outbreak) are probably the most accurate descriptions of Native American burning practices prior to Euro-American settlement. This assertion is based on the fact that hunters and trappers solicited the aid of native peoples, and their relation with the Kalapuya was frequently one of mutual respect and sharing. After 1840, settlers, and missionaries often described indigenous people as ignorant, incompetent, and prone to thievery (e.g., Minto 1900; Riggs 1900; O'Hara 1911). Settlers also altered the ecosystems upon which the Kalapuya depended by farming and by introducing nonnative animals. Pigs, for example, severely damaged camas fields early on (Palmer 1966), and cattle replaced wild game, which had all but disappeared by 1840. Native plant communities were lost as a result of landscape fragmentation, agriculture, intense grazing by cattle and sheep, and the introduction of exotic plants (Hulse et al. 1998).

The most-cited description of the Willamette Valley prior to the 1840s comes from David Douglas, a Scottish botanist who collected plants for the Royal Horticultural Society. He traveled down the Willamette Valley from Fort Vancouver in 1825 and 1826, with members of the Hudson's Bay Company. Douglas's journals are exceptional in their detailed descriptions of the landscape and vegetation, and his perceptions of native peoples seem relatively unprejudiced. Douglas encountered burned areas, some of which were from quite small fires, whereas others were from large conflagrations affecting both his party and the Kalapuya. A careful examination of the Douglas journals, taking his entries in context and chronological sequence, and comparing them with journals written by other members of his expedition, helps to distinguish between prescribed burns set by the Kalapuya and larger, uncontrolled wildfires.

Douglas visited the north end of the valley in 1825, but he undoubtedly spoke with trappers who had traveled farther south. The 1825 journal has no mention of fires, nor does it provide first-person accounts of fires. On an August trip, Douglas was about 25 miles above the falls on the Willamette River in an area of riparian forest and wooded upland (Personal Communication, E. Alverson, 2001). He described a tobacco plantation, which has been cited as one reason for burning by the Kalapuya (Boyd 1986, 1999a). The account suggests the use of fire in wooded areas, but not widespread burning, as Douglas comments on the small acreage that is actually burned:

8/19—Towards afternoon left in a small canoe with one
Canadian and two Indians . . . on a visit to the Multnomah
River. . . . The beaver is now scarce; none alive came under
my notice. I was much gratified in viewing the deserted
lodges and dams. . . . Collected the following plants . . . *Nicotiana pulverulenta.* . . . I have seen only one plant before, in
the Hand of an Indian two months since at the Great Falls of
the Columbia. . . . The natives cultivate it here and although
I made diligent search for it, it never came under my notice
until now. They do not cultivate it near their camps or lodges,
lest it should be taken for use before maturity. An open place
in the wood is chosen where there is dead wood, which they
burn and sow the seed in the ashes. Fortunately I met with
one of the little plantations and supplied myself with seeds
and specimens without delay. (Douglas 1959:140–141)

The 1826 journey of Douglas can be reconstructed with respect to
geography and vegetation with fair confidence (Table 6.2, Figure 6.3).
The vegetation shown in Figure 6.3 is based on 1850 General Land
Office surveys prior to extensive land-use change (Hulse et al. 1998),
and the vegetation distribution was probably similar to that encountered
by Douglas. From September 20 to 26, Douglas described the journey
from Fort Vancouver to meet Alexander McLeod, Chief Trapper for the

TABLE 6.2. Location and distance traveled, vegetation, and fire observations made by David Douglas during the 1826 journey through the
Willamette Valley (see Figure 6.3 for vegetation and geographic location).

Date	Location, Distance traveled	Vegetation circa 1850[1]	Burned ground noted[2]
September 20	Lower valley, 5 miles	Closed forest: upland	No
September 21	Lower valley (at falls)	Closed forest: upland	No
September 22–26	Lower valley, none	Savanna	No
September 27	Lower valley, 5 miles	Woodland and shrubland	Yes
September 28	Lower valley, ~7 miles	Woodland and shrubland	No
September 29	Lower valley, 13 miles	Prairie	No
September 30	Mid-valley, ~10 miles	Savanna	Yes
October 1	Mid-valley, 18 miles	Savanna	Yes
October 2	Mid-valley, 21 miles	Savanna	Yes
October 3	Mid-valley, 9 miles	Prairie	No
October 4	Upper valley, 24 miles	Prairie	Yes
October 5	Upper valley, 19 miles	Savanna	Yes
October 6	Coastal foothills, 16 miles	Woodland and shrubland	Yes
October 7	Coastal foothills, 7 miles	Closed forest: upland	No
October 8	Coastal foothills, 8 miles	Closed forest: upland	Yes

[1]Based on 1850 Land Ordinance Survey (after Hulse et al. 1998).
[2]From David Douglas's 1826 journal entries (Douglas 1959).

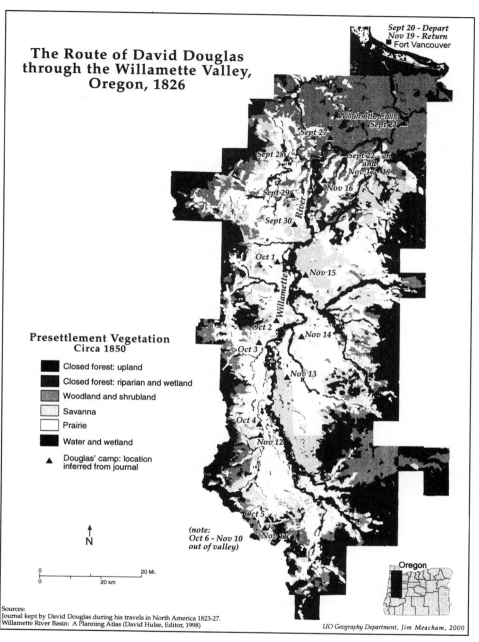

The Route of David Douglas through the Willamette Valley, Oregon, 1826

Sept 20 - Depart
Nov 19 - Return
■ Fort Vancouver

Willamette Falls
Sept 21

Sept 27

Sept 28

Sept 22 - 26
and
Nov 17 - 18

Nov 16

Sept 29

Sept 30

Oct 1

Nov 15

Oct 2

Nov 14

Oct 3

Nov 13

Oct 4

Nov 12

Oct 5

Nov 11

(note:
Oct 6 - Nov 10
out of valley)

Willamette River

Presettlement Vegetation
Circa 1850

- Closed forest: upland
- Closed forest: riparian and wetland
- Woodland and shrubland
- Savanna
- Prairie
- Water and wetland
- ▲ Douglas' camp: location inferred from journal

N

0 ——— 20 Mi.
0 ——— 20 km

Oregon

Sources:
Journal kept by David Douglas during his travels in North America 1823-27.
Willamette River Basin: A Planning Atlas (David Hulse, Editor, 1998)

UO Geography Department, Jim Meacham, 2000

Figure 6.3. The location of David Douglas's camps as he traveled through the Willamette Valley in the fall of 1826. The base map shows the presettlement vegetation ca. 1850, based on surveys of the General Land Office.

Hudson Bay Company and leader of the expedition. McLeod's encampment was near or on the open grassland known as French Prairie. Douglas noted warm weather, heavy dews, and a search for some horses that McLeod had left above the falls on a previous trip; he did not mention fire or burned ground. On September 27, Douglas was west of the Willamette River, between present-day Wilsonville and Newberg, in the same woodland vegetation that had characterized the journey thus far. He detailed landscape conditions, including the effects of a recent fire:

> 9/27—Country undulating: soil rich, light with beautiful solitary oaks and pines interspersed through it and must have a fine effect, but being all burned and not a single blade of grass except on the margins of rivulets to be seen. . . . Marched today five miles. (Douglas 1959:213)

The next day, the group turned south and probably crossed the North Yamhill River. The woodland opened and prairie was possibly evident, but the vegetation did not change significantly. Douglas wrote:

> 9/28—Mr McLeod returned shortly after dusk last night and brought with him one of the Indian guides from the coast south of the country inhabited by the Killimuks. All unfortunate in the chase, and although nine small deer were seen in a group, yet by their keeping in the thickets near the small stream a few miles from our encampment, prevented the hunter from approaching them. Morning pleasant but chilly with heavy dew. Thermometer 41°. Started at eight o'clock, keeping a south-west course. . . . Camped on the south side of the Yamhill River, a small stream about twenty-five yards wide; channel for the greater part mud and sand. Two hundred yards below where we forded are fine cascades 7 feet high. Country much the same as yesterday; fine rich soil; oaks more abundant, and pines scarcer and more diminutive in growth. . . . Picked up a species of *Donia* . . . and . . . *Phlox,* both in rich light dry loam in open woods. . . . Hunters out in search of deer and not yet come home. I expect a fine fall, as seventeen shots were heard in various directions in the woods. (Douglas 1959:213–214)

The September 28 entry notes similar country to that of the previous day, which is probably a reference to the topography and vegetation. The burned area observed on September 27 was apparently small, because the group traveled only 5 miles and made no further mention of it. On September 29, they proceeded southwest, moving between woodland

and savanna. Again, burned vegetation seemed absent and there is no mention of fire, even though the company traveled a fair distance, probably reaching the Eola Hills:

> 9/29—Morning dull and cloudy . . . hunters returned with a very large fine doe. Started at nine and kept a southwest course, and camped not far from the point of a low hill . . . Heavy rain for the remainder of the day and the greater part of the night. Country not different from yesterday. Traveled about thirteen miles. Nothing new came under my notice. (Douglas 1959:214)

On September 30, the company moved into open savanna. The effects of fire reappear in Douglas's comments:

> 9/30—Cloudy until noon, after-part of the day clear and fine with a fanning westerly wind. In the morning dried some of my things which got wet the preceding day. Started at nine and continued our route in a southerly direction, on the opposite side of the hill from where we were yesterday. Most parts of the country burned; only on little patches in the valleys and on the flats near the low hills that verdure to be seen. Some of the Natives tell me it is done for the purpose of urging the deer to frequent certain parts to feed, which they leave unburned and of course are easily killed. Others say that it is done in order that they might better find honey and grasshoppers, which both serve as articles of winter food. (Douglas 1959:214)

Douglas's passages dated September 27, 28, and 30 are widely cited as evidence that the Kalapuya extensively burned the valley (Johannessen et al. 1971; Towle 1982; Boyd 1986, 1999a). However, the full entries for September 28 and September 29, with no mention of fire, are often overlooked. It seems likely that the fires Douglas described on September 27 and 30 were neither contiguous nor part of a single event.

On October 1 the company marched 18 miles and camped on a small stream that entered the Willamette River; the stream could have been Rickreall Creek, Ash Creek, or the Luckiamute River. The distance and description correspond well with the terrain of the Eola Hills. Again, they encountered a burned landscape:

> 10/1—Heavy dew during the night; clear and pleasant during the day, with a refreshing westerly wind . . . continued our route. Had to make a circuitous turn east of south, south, and south-west to avoid two deep ravines that were

impassable for the horses. Walked the greater part of the day, but found nothing new. On my way observed some trees of Arbutus laurifolia, 15 inches to 2 feet in diameter, 30 to 45 feet high, much higher than any I saw last year on the Columbia; fruit nearly ripe; soil deep rich black loam, near springs, and on the gravelly bottom. Passed at noon some Indians digging the roots of Phalangium Quamash in one of the low plains. Bulbs much larger than any I have seen. . . . Camped at four on the banks of a small stream which falls into the Multnomah three miles to the east. . . . In the dusk I walked out with my gun. I had not gone more than half a mile from the camp when I observed a very large waspnest, which had been attached to a tree, lying on the plain where the ground was perfectly bare and the herbage burned, taken there by the bear (Douglas 1959:214–215)

The following day Douglas recorded a possible source of ignition, lightning. Food for the horses was scarce:

10/2—Morning, heavy dew and chilly; clear and fine during the day; sheet lightning in the evening. . . . At noon passed two deep gullies which gave much trouble, the banks being thickly covered with brushwood, willow, dogwood, and low alder. Course nearly due south, inclining to the west. Country same as yesterday, rich, but not a vestige of green herbage; all burned except in the deep ravines. Covered with *Pterius aquilina, Solidago,* and a strong species of *Carduus.* On the elevated grounds where the soil is a deep rich loam, 3 to 7 feet thick on a clay bottom, some of the oaks measure 18 to 24 feet in circumference, but rarely exceeding 30 feet of trunk in height. On the less fertile places, on a gravelly dry bottom, where the trees are scrubby and small, a curious species of *Viscum,* with ovate leaves, is found abundantly. . . . As no place could be found suitable for fodder for the horses, we had to travel till four o'clock, when we camped at a low point of land near a woody rivulet. Marched twenty-one miles. My feet tonight are very painful and my toes cut with the burned stumps of a strong species of *Arundo* and *Spiraea tomentosa.* (Douglas 1959:215)

A recent fire may explain this lack of fodder, but October is generally dry in this region and grass would have been scarce in any event. From

October 4 to 6, the group was in the upper valley and beginning their ascent into the Umpqua Mountains. Douglas noted very warm weather and burned ground:

> 10/4—The morning being cloudy and overcast, we did not start so soon. As it cleared up about ten, the horses were saddled and we proceeded on our route in a southerly direction. Passed in the course of the day three small streams, which all fall into the Multnomah ten miles below this place. As no place could be found fit for camping we were obliged to go until five o'clock, when we put up on the south side of a muddy stream, banks covered with Fraxinus. No deer killed this day, although several were seen. Nothing particular occurred. Marched twenty-four miles; somewhat fatigued. (Douglas 1959:216)

From October 8 to 25, the company was out of the valley. Several references are made to tremendous storms and lightning, and the lack of food in the Umpqua region. The return trip from the upper valley to Fort Vancouver took approximately 8 days. Douglas described the onset of rain and lightning, and the lack of food in camp, but he made no further reference to fire:

> 10/8—Morning cool and pleasant; day clear and warm. Thermometer in the shade 82°; much sheet lightning in the evening, wind westerly. . . . No deer killed and had the last fragments cooked for supper, which gave us all but a scanty meal. . . . We are just living from hand to mouth. All the hunters observe that the animals are very scarce and those shy in consequence of the country being burned. (Douglas 1959:217)

> 10/25—Last night was one of the most dreadful I ever witnessed. The rain, driven by wind, rendered it impossible for me to keep any fire . . . every ten or fifteen minutes immense trees falling producing a crash as if the earth were cleaving asunder, which with the thunder peal on peal before the echo of the former died away, and the lightning in zigzag and forked flashes. . . . My poor horses were unable to endure the violence of the storm without craving of my protection, which they did by hanging their heads over me and neighing. (Douglas 1959:229)

While waiting for Douglas to arrive at French Prairie in September,

Alexander McLeod, the leader of the expedition, made a few references
to fire in his journal:

> 9/18—The country is much overrun by fire, in many
> places we had some difficulty to pass our horses owing to
> their alarm caused by the devouring element. (McLeod
> 1961:175–176)

> 9/19—We had very sultry weather, accompanied by a fresh
> breeze. Continued on our route at 4 P.M. put up at the
> appointed Rendezvous: we had to swim our horses over
> the Willamette to the east shore, the opposite shore being
> burned and destitute of Grass. The report of fire arms
> brought a couple of Indians to us with a canoe which
> proved of service to us to drive our horses over the Chan-
> nel. We are led to understand that some of the freemen are
> in this neighborhood. (McLeod 1961:176)

Traveling south with Douglas, McLeod refers to the occurrence of a
recent fire and its negative impact on available game for themselves and
the Native Americans in the area:

> 9/30—We saw some Indians in quest of game: like our-
> selves they meet with little success in consequence of fire
> having scared the animals. (McLeod 1961:179)

Reading two journals from members on the same expedition allows
for a comparison of events. Douglas was new to the area, whereas
McLeod had traveled through the valley on numerous occasions for the
Hudson Bay Company. Douglas stated the fire was deliberately set by
the natives to attract deer to the area. McLeod noted the difficulty the
Kalapuya encountered because of the recent fire. Using Table 6.2 and
Figure 6.3, the party can be positioned in the savanna vegetation zone,
which may have been maintained by periodic fires. However, the
McLeod entry raises questions as to whether the Kalapuya set this par-
ticular fire, as they seem unprepared for the lack of game in the area. On
October 2, McLeod substantiated Douglas's remark concerning the
storms and lightning:

> 10/2—Fine weather. Met frequent lightning in the course
> of the day suffered much inconvenience from excessive
> heat which tended much to harass our poor horses. Pasture
> is rarely found in the course of this day none has been seen,
> altho' we travelled good twenty miles and had to put up
> along a small river that our horses might have the pickings
> along the margin of the woods, elsewhere the fire
> destroyed all the Grass. (McLeod 1961:179)

From the journals of Douglas and McLeod, two types of fire emerge: small, possibly prescribed burns used in tobacco cultivation, and larger, unexpected conflagrations, possibly ignited by lightning, which depleted hunting resources for both Douglas's party and the Kalapuya.

John Work (1923), an employee of the Hudson Bay Company, traveled from Fort Vancouver to the Umpqua River in 1834. When the company reached present-day Monroe, Work wrote the much-cited entries of July 1 and 2 in his journal describing the native peoples setting fire to the grassland:

> 7/1—Three other Indians passed us but made a very short stay and appeared to be much afraid of something. Parts of the plain gravelly and soil poor, herbage getting dry and the ground has an arid appearance; on the lower spots grass luxuriant. (Work 1923:264)

> 7/2—The Indians set fire to the dry grass on the neighboring hill, but none of them came near us. The plain is also on fire on the opposite side of the Willamet. (Work 1923:264)

However, the next entry suggests that the fires served as a means of protection for the Kalapuya against the Umpqua:

> 7/3—Ten of them visited the camp and traded their beaver. These Indians are much alarmed lest they be attacked by the Umquahs . . . that nation have threatened to come to war upon them. . . . As we were coming on we found a party of 32 men all armed and ready for war, supposing that a party of Umquahs were coming upon them. (Work 1923:264)

And, on July 5 and 6, Work was approximately 40 miles above the falls and still recounted the anticipation of conflict:

> 7/5—These people are preparing to go to war. (Work 1923:266)

> 7/6—They are all armed and prepared for an attack. (Work 1923:266)

Samuel Clarke confirmed the use of fire for protection when he interviewed residents of the Grand Ronde Reservation in the 1880s. Clarke (1905) wrote that burning was used to sight hostile war parties from a distance.

In summary, the reliability of journals as a source of information on indigenous burning practices depends on the time that they were written, the full context of the journal, and the perspectives of the writer and the reader (Knox 2000). Also, by examining single entries from a journal, a biased view of the history for a region may emerge. Only by researching numerous journals, letters, and other papers does the complexity of Kalapuya history at the time of European contact begin to emerge. Early observations must be considered in light of the fact that the Kalapuya were decimated by infectious introduced diseases and their way of life was threatened at the time of even the earliest journals. Only a few of the journals mention the large numbers of Native Americans dying of disease, often by a sentence or single paragraph (e.g., Parker 1840; Wilkes 1926), yet evidence of death must have been pervasive. The early journal accounts that describe fire do not present a picture of broadcast burning to maintain open conditions, although large fires are noted in prairie and savanna areas. Only David Douglas and John Work associate fires with the Kalapuya prior to the 1840s, and the extent of burning from both accounts seems limited.

Juniper Woodland of Eastern Oregon

Western juniper (*Juniper occidentalis*) grows at low and middle elevations (760–1,400 m elevation) in the northern Great Basin and forms the driest forest zone (less than 20 cm annual precipitation) in the Pacific Northwest (Franklin and Dyrness 1973). The fire regime within juniper woodland is determined by the availability of fine fuels in the form of grass, which allows fire to spread. Ground fires remove litter and tree seedlings, enabling grass to resprout, but established juniper trees are fairly fire resistant and can live to be several hundred years old (Burns and Honkala 1990). A fire interval of 30 to 40 years is sufficient to keep juniper from invading sagebrush-grassland communities (Miller and Rose 1995). In the absence of fire, juniper seedlings establish and the woodland becomes more closed. Sagebrush (*Artemisia tridentata*) also replaces perennial bunchgrasses, converting grassland to shrub steppe. Wet periods tend to promote the growth of grass and frequent fires, which in turn limit the ability of juniper and sagebrush to spread. People of the northern Paiute language group occupied the Great Basin at the time of European contact. Current research suggests that prehistoric and historic population densities were never high, and societies were mobile enough to take advantage of the scarce resources (Aikens and Jenkins 1994). Historic accounts highlight the exploitation of mammals, fish, insects, and plants by small family groups during most of the year and the yearly gathering of larger groups at root-processing camps, salmon fisheries, and seed gathering sites (Aikens 1993). Shinn (1980) suggests that fires were regularly set by native groups in historic time for purposes of signaling, hunting, and collecting insects, and Euro-Americans describe burned expanses of prairie that were attributed to Native

Americans. Trapper Peter Skene Ogden, for example, reported in 1826 that the southern Blue Mountains were "overrun by fire" and blamed the fires on native peoples (Langston 1995).

The relationship among fire, grass, and western juniper in prehistoric times is suggested by pollen and charcoal records, particularly those from Diamond Pond in southeastern Oregon, and from plant macrofossils contained in ancient packrat middens (Figure 6.4; Mehringer and Wigand 1990). These data indicate that the period of maximum aridity

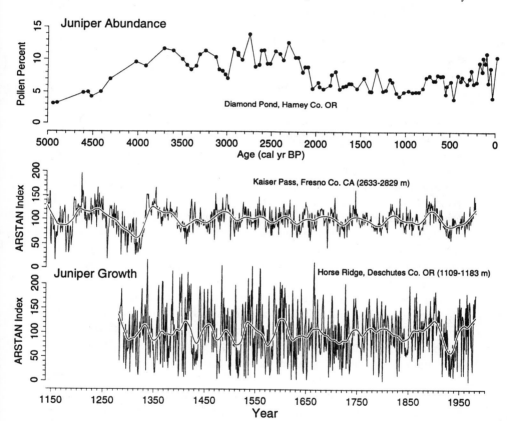

Figure 6.4. Prehistoric and historic juniper expansion. The record of juniper pollen abundance from Diamond Pond (Mehringer and Wigand 1990) shows that juniper pollen was abundant between 4,500 and 2,100 years ago, then present in low amounts from 2,100 to 500 years ago. In the last 500 years, juniper pollen abundance has increased steadily, with the exception of a period of low percentages in the early twentieth century. Growth records of western juniper from the last millennium are available from Kaiser Pass, Calif. (Graumlich 1991), and Horse Ridge, Ore. (Holmes, Adams, and Fritts 1986). The index is high during high growth years. Both records suggest a period of favorable growth since the 1930s, which is consistent with its historic expansion.

occurred between some 7,800 and 4,400 years ago, which is late compared with the rest of the Pacific Northwest (as discussed previously). The archaeological record is sparse during the dry period, probably because populations were focused on wetland and lacustrine resources (Aikens 1983). Wet conditions returned during the Neopluvial period (about 4,400 to 2,000 years ago), and the renewed abundance of upland resources may have allowed populations to become more widely distributed (Aikens 1983).

Pollen and packrat-midden records from Diamond Pond and vicinity describe the vegetation response to a series of climate changes during and since the Neopluvial period (Figure 6.4). With increased moisture after 4,400 years ago, western juniper extended its elevational range downslope by 150 m, and grass was more abundant than sagebrush in the basins (Wigand 1987; Mehringer and Wigand 1990; Miller and Wigand 1994). Between about 2,000 and 1,000–800 years ago, the climate became warmer and drier, and the lower limit of juniper retreated upslope. In the last 1,000 years the climate has become wetter, allowing juniper and grass to expand downslope again (although there was a notable dry period and range contraction from 700 to 500 years ago). The expansion of juniper in the last few centuries has been accompanied by increased sagebrush, not grass, according to the pollen data. The combination of juniper and sagebrush implies greater winter precipitation than before and a reduction in summer precipitation (which would favor sagebrush over grass). Miller and Wigand (1994) note that the "reexpansion of Great Basin woodlands was just getting underway when Europeans first entered the area."

The Diamond Pond record contains little charcoal in sediments dating between 6,200 and 3,700 years ago, which is consistent with a model of few fires when juniper and grass levels were low and sagebrush was abundant. Charcoal values increased in the record about 3,700 years ago and remained generally high until about 1,100 years ago. The increase in fire occurrence coincides with the shift in vegetation towards more juniper and grass in the Neopluvial period. The most recent expansion of juniper woodland, beginning some 1,000 years ago, occurred during a period of few fires.

Dendroclimatological records from eastern Oregon span the last 700 years and indicate several periods of moist conditions that favored juniper growth, including an interval from A.D. 1650 to 1900 that coincides with the Little Ice Age. When the data are filtered to show only interannual and decadal variations, the tree-ring data indicate rapid growth during the 1880s and 1890s, which were some of the wettest years on record, and slow growth during the 1930s, which were among the driest (Figure 6.4) (Garfin and Hughes 1996). Increased precipitation and warm winters must be part of the explanation for the expansion of juniper and decrease in grass in the last 500 years. Decades since 1930 are anomalous compared with other wet periods, however, because of the absence of fires.

Miller and Rose (1995) analyzed the stand ages of western juniper communities and concluded that open stands were present on Steens Mountain from the 1700s to the 1880s. The first increase in tree densities occurred in the late 1800s, and a relatively steady rate of juniper establishment was maintained until the 1950s. Juniper populations increased at a geometric rate after the 1960s. Miller and Rose (1995) speculate that climate change, reduced fire frequencies, and grazing in the late 1800s were the primary factors for juniper expansion. They note that the mild wet winters of the 1880s, following the Little Ice Age, probably promoted vigorous tree growth. The late nineteenth century was also a time of intensive livestock grazing (Burkhart and Tisdale 1976), and the incipient decrease in native bunchgrass eliminated the fuel source that once allowed fire to spread across the landscape. Concurrently the increase in sagebrush provided more safe sites for juniper seedlings. Decreases in Paiute populations during the 1870s may also have been a factor, but their relocation to reservations precedes the greatest expansion of juniper by nearly 90 years. It seems that Euro-American activities and climate change so obvious in this century are more directly responsible for the changes in forest cover.

Ponderosa Pine Forests of the Eastern Cascade Range and Blue Mountains

Ponderosa pine forests form a vegetation zone from 1,450 to 2,000 m elevation in the Oregon Cascades and 900 to 1,500 m elevation in the Blue Mountains (Franklin and Dyrness 1973). The zone lies between mixed communities of Douglas fir, grand fir, pine, and other mesic taxa at higher elevations and juniper woodland and sagebrush steppe at lower elevations. Dendrochronological studies suggest that these forests historically experienced short fire return intervals on the order of decades or less and that fires scarred but often did not kill mature trees (Agee 1993). The extent of individual fires in ponderosa pine forest is not well documented in the Pacific Northwest, but many studies suggest that they were often small and scattered as a result of the discontinuous pattern of fuels (Bork 1985; Agee 1993; Heyerdahl 1997). In areas of frequent fires, the understory was regularly cleared of fuel, and thick-barked, fire-resistant pine trees remained. Where fires were infrequent, the buildup of understory fuels shifted the disturbance regime toward stand-replacement fires, and mesic fire-sensitive species—such as grand fir and Douglas fir and multiple-age stands of ponderosa pine—fill in the understory (Agee 1993). The resiliency of these forests is now of great concern to forest managers, because fire exclusion practices in the late twentieth century have allowed fuels to build up and increase the likelihood of high-intensity burns. Rather than maintaining the forests with low-intensity ground fires, the concern is that the current regime will prove lethal for this forest type.

The open structure of many ponderosa pine forests at the time of Euro-American settlement has been attributed to the effects of frequent fire, and burning by Native Americans may have been one source. The Cascade forests were visited by native peoples from both the Plateau and the Great Basin and also by Inland Valley and Klamath Lake people in historic times (Zucker 1983), and archaeological data extend human occupation to at least early Holocene time (Aikens 1993). Population densities were probably low and consisted of seasonal hunting and gathering groups. Burning may have been used to facilitate travel and hunting and promote the production of grass and berries. Reports of Native American–set fires are mentioned in the journal accounts of early trappers, missionaries, and settlers traveling through and around the Blue Mountains and Northern Rockies (see Gruell 1985; Langston 1995; Barrett and Arno 1999). Whether the observed fires were deliberately set as a means of opening the understory, caused by lightning ignitions, or represent fires escaped from adjacent grassland is not clear from most descriptions.

Tree-ring records confirm that fires in ponderosa pine forests have been controlled by variations in climate on interannual and decadal time scales. Forest ecologists have also described complex linkages between fire, insect outbreaks, and nutrient cycling in these forests (e.g., Mutch et al. 1993). For example, beetle-kill trees increase the likelihood of severe fire, and tree mortality, in turn, introduces nutrients to the soils and allows for seed germination and seedling establishment. Heyerdahl (1997) examined 300 years of tree-ring data from the Blue Mountains and discovered 65 separate fire years at her sites. Xeric forests, dominated by ponderosa pine and juniper, burned more frequently than mesic forests of pine, Douglas fir, fir, and larch, but in extreme drought years both forest types were affected. Xeric forests displayed considerable variation in the size and severity of past fires, depending on local site conditions. The fire-history reconstructions showed strong correlations between drought years and big fire years. The area burned on decadal time scales for the last 300 years also tracked decadal precipitation well. These data are among the strongest and most significant fire-climate relations shown for the Pacific Northwest. A decline in fire occurrence, beginning in the 1880s, was attributed primarily to the effects of grazing but also to variations in climate and insect outbreaks (Heyerdahl 1997). A fire-history study in ponderosa pine forests in the eastern Cascade Range also found a decrease in fire occurrence, which was attributed to grazing and suppression activities in the twentieth century (Bork 1985).

Paleoecological records place the establishment of modern ponderosa pine forest in the middle and late Holocene, following a period of expanded steppe. At Carp Lake near Goldendale, Washington, pollen data suggest that pine forests colonized the region about 7,700 years ago and persisted for the next 3,200 years. The climate became cooler and wetter some 4,400 years ago and allowed Douglas fir, fir, and western hemlock to establish near Carp Lake (Whitlock and Bartlein 1997). Fires were probably more frequent during early Holocene and middle Holocene periods, when the climate was drier than the late Holocene. Unfortunately, charcoal data are not yet available from Carp Lake or other sites in the ponderosa pine forest to allow for reconstruction of the fire history more precisely, but the linkages between vegetation change and climate are well documented. Human impacts on forest composition would have to be discerned on top of those caused by climate.

Native American burning was likely responsible for the open stand structure in ponderosa pine forests in particular localities. Barrett and Arno (1982, 1999) conducted interviews with thirty-one Salish and Kootenai and twenty-seven descendents of early pioneers in northwestern Montana to gather information on human-set fires in ponderosa pine forests during historic times. However, the value of these interviews might be questioned, because no information was provided on the background of the interviewees (were they Salish, Kootenai, or others?), and any account as of 1980 is at least 120 years removed from the critical period. Barrett and Arno (1999) also note that descendants of settlers had more detailed recollections of native burning practices than did native descendants, which raises concerns about possible biases in the data. Twenty-five of the interviewees had some recollection of deliberate burning, and seven could identify the geographic location of such activities. Tree-ring records were analyzed to compare the fire history near historic Native American settlements with that of comparable sites located in remote settings. In nine of ten comparisons the site heavily used by people showed a higher fire frequency than the remote site; in three of the comparisons the difference was statistically significant. The results suggest that Native Americans had an impact on the structure of ponderosa pine forest near densely populated areas, but the impact of burning activities at a larger spatial scale remains unresolved. If the purpose of native-set fires was to influence game, to improve berry gathering and grazing (after the introduction of horses in the 1700s), and to facilitate travel, camping, and communication, such activities would have been geographically limited in scope. The influence of human-set fires on the character of ponderosa pine forest ecosystem at a regional scale has yet to be demonstrated.

Final Comments

Some very large fires have occurred since Euro-American settlement. The worst fire year on record was 1910, when more than 2 million ha of western national forest lands burned in the northern Rocky Mountains and Pacific Northwest (Swetnam and Betancourt 1998). In the last 12 years, these regions have once again experienced a number of large, stand-replacement fires. Fires in 1994 affected more than 11,460 ha of Oregon state forests (Oregon Department of Forestry 1997) and more than 1.2 million ha in eleven western states (Maciliwain 1994). The fires of 2000 consumed more than 7 million acres (National Interagency Fire Center 2000). Many trees were killed by these events, and, as a consequence, forest management practices and fire policy have come under increasing public scrutiny. The size of recent fires has been attributed to changes in vegetation structure, the accumulation of fuel, and climate over the last 100 years. Changes in vegetation and accumulation of fuel have been attributed to the elimination of Native American burning practices (Barrett and Arno 1982; Pyne 1982), effective fire fighting practices since World War II (Pyne 1982), and high tree mortality from recent infestations by mountain pine beetle and western spruce budworm (Mutch et al. 1993). The climate argument is based on the historic occurrence of severe fires in years of intense drought (Balling et al. 1992). It has also been predicted that large fires will continue to occur in the future with global warming as a result of increased greenhouse gases (Franklin et al. 1991; Romme and Turner 1991; Running and Nemani 1991; Bartlein et al. 1997).

Discussions over the degree to which the prehistoric landscape was pristine or humanized filter into the debate of how best to respond to current large fires. If humans altered ecosystems through their use of fire, then a return to presettlement landscapes (i.e., those that existed prior to European contact) is not possible without instigating burning and fuel reduction through forest thinning. It's not surprising that assigning a large role to prehistoric peoples is a popular concept among those who advocate active management of wilderness and commodity lands today. The argument is that some forests are so altered by fire exclusion that fire alone may not restore them. Zyback (1995), for example, suggests that human-set fires, in prehistoric times, altered every acre of the Pacific Northwest, leaving no vegetation unaffected. The

Northwest Forestry Association, which represents commercial timber interests in the region, states that current forests are unnaturally dense and vulnerable to disease in the absence of fires. Restoring forest health, in their opinion as well as that of others, requires immediate thinning and salvage to emulate the effects of native peoples (Bonnicksen 1989; Wagner and Kay 1993). Others note that western forests are spatially variable and have experienced a wide range of fire conditions in the past and at present. A policy of thinning and prescribed burning may be appropriate in low-elevation ponderosa pine forests, but it is less justifiable in areas that historically sustained large stand-replacing events. Given the economic consequences, it is clear that more is at stake in this debate than an academic interest in prehistoric fire regimes.

On the other hand, it is equally incorrect to portray the region as untouched by human action prior to European contact. Historical and ethnographic accounts suggest that Native Americans used fire in the Willamette Valley and at the lower forest-grassland border to open forest and maintain prairie. The frequency and extent of such burning, however, is not clear. Paleoecological data from the Willamette Valley, northern Great Basin, and eastern Cascades and Blue Mountains suggest that climate, vegetation, and fire regimes were closely interlinked in prehistoric times and climate has been a primary determinant of vegetation composition and disturbance regimes. The extent to which fire-regime variability closely tracks independently derived records of climate variability is a convincing measure of the importance of climate relative to other potential causes of fire-regime variability, known or unknown. The principle of Occam's razor suggests that it is not necessary to invoke more complicated arguments or hypotheses than climate variation to explain the temporal patterns we observe in fire regimes.

As climate and climate variability have changed through time, so too have the vegetation and conditions influencing fire occurrence. Wherever we have data, the record shows that fires were generally extensive when prevailing climate and vegetation fostered suitable fuel and weather conditions and an ignition source. Such periods include the early Holocene in most regions, the late Holocene in the northern Great Basin, the late 1500s, the 1850s, the 1930s, and the late 1980s to 1990s. The fire-history record, when viewed on millennial and centennial time scales, indicates no long-term cycle, because the fire regime has continually changed with climate variations.

These climate-vegetation-fire linkages on short and long time scales are the backdrop against which human perturbations must be assessed. Although we have a basic understanding of how fire frequency has changed with climate and vegetation on Holocene time scales, the archaeological and ethnographic records provide little information about the prehistoric use of fire. A relation between human population size and resource utilization seems obvious, but assessing the role of burning requires information on the particular adaptations of the group, their available technologies, and their population size and density, as well as the characteristics of their environment. Without such information, a direct link between fire and humans will never be established.

The case studies described above show a decline in fire occurrence that started between 1,000 and 500 years ago, which coincides with regional cooling and increased moisture at the end of the Medieval Warm period and beginning of the Little Ice Age. Similarly, increases in fire occurred in the Willamette Valley, northern Great Basin, eastern Cascades, and Blue Mountains in the late nineteenth and twentieth centuries following the Little Ice Age. Certainly, the buildup of biomass during the Little Ice Age may have set the stage for more intense fires of recent times, but these environmental changes pale in comparison to the additive effects of Euro-American settlement. Logging, farming, grazing, mining, and fire elimination in the last century have altered vegetation and fire regimes on a regional scale more than any other event of the last 11,000 years. In contrast, prehistoric peoples locally altered the landscape, but there is no strong evidence that their activities created new vegetation types at a regional scale. Even in the Willamette Valley, where early settlers describe the burning activities of the Kalapuya, these activities alone do not explain the presence of prairie, savanna, and oak woodland. Such biomes developed simultaneously in several parts of the Pacific Northwest, as a result of warm dry conditions and frequent fires in the early Holocene, and became restricted in the middle and late Holocene, when conditions were cooler and wetter. Native peoples may have acted as an ignition source for fires, but the ability of vegetation to burn was undoubtedly determined by fuel and weather conditions.

A greater myth than that of the pristine landscape is the assumption that the forests at the time of Euro-American exploration and settlement are representative of all of prehistory. On the contrary, what early Europeans described was only a snapshot of ecosystem change operating on multiple temporal and spatial scales. It would not be possible to re-create the forests that existed 100, 500, or 1,000 years ago, even if we knew past forest conditions perfectly, or the role of Native American activity precisely. A "snapshot" approach to restoration is untenable because the current set of climate conditions is unique on both centennial and millennial time scales. The paleoecological record argues instead that natural ecosystems are dynamic. They should be managed in ways that allow the possibility of changes in species' range and abundance and the occurrence of large, stand-replacing fires in the face of climate change. History suggests that such changes are inevitable in the face of climate change.

Acknowledgments

Helpful reviews were provided by Ed Alverson, Bill Baker, Bob Gresswell, Sarah Shafer, Fred Swanson, and Tom Swetnam. We thank John Christy of the Nature Conservancy and Paula Minear of Oregon State University for allowing us to use the 1850 vegetation data for the Willamette Valley. Jim Meacham of InfoGraphics, University of Oregon, helped us construct Figure 6.3 from these data. The research was supported by the National Science Foundation (SBR–9615961) and USDA Forest Service (Cooperative Agreement PNW 98–5122–1–CA).

Literature Cited

Aikens, C. M. 1983. Environmental archaeology in the western United States. Pp. 239–251 in *Late Quaternary environments of the United States*, vol. 2, ed. H. E. Wright, Jr. Minneapolis: University of Minnesota Press.

———. 1993. *Archaeology of Oregon*. U.S. Department of Interior, Bureau of Land Management. BLM/OR/WA/ST-93/16+8100.

Aikens, C. M., and D. L. Jenkins, ed. 1994. *Archaeological researches in the Northern Great Basin: Fort Rock archaeology since Cressman*. University of Oregon anthropological papers 50. Eugene: University of Oregon, Department of Anthropology and State Museum of Anthropology.

Agee, J. K. 1991. Fire history along an elevation gradient in the Siskiyou Mountains, Oregon. *Northwest Science* 65:188–199.

———. 1993. *Fire ecology of Pacific Northwest forests*. Washington, D.C.: Island Press.

Baker, R. G. 1983. Holocene vegetational history of the western United States. Pp. 109–127 in *Late-Quaternary environments of the United States*, vol. 2, ed. H. E. Wright, Jr. Minneapolis: University of Minnesota Press.

Balling, R. C., Jr., G. A. Meyer, and S. G. Wells. 1992. Climate change in Yellowstone National Park: Is the drought related risk of wildfires increasing? *Climatic Change* 22:34–35.

Barnosky, C. W., P. M. Anderson, and P. J. Bartlein. 1987. The northwestern U.S. during deglaciation: Vegetational history and paleoclimatic implications. Pp. 289–321 in *North America and adjacent oceans during the last deglaciation*, ed. W. F. Ruddiman and H. E. Wright, Jr., *The Geology of North America*, vol. K-3. Boulder: Geological Society of America.

Barrett, S. W., and S. F. Arno. 1982. Indian fires as an ecological influence in the northern Rockies. *Journal of Forestry* 80:647–651.

———. 1999. Indian fires in the Northern Rockies; ethnohistory and ecology. Pp. 50–64 in *Indians, fire, and the land in the Pacific Northwest*, ed. R. Boyd. Corvallis: Oregon State University Press.

Bartlein, P. J., K. H. Anderson, P. M. Anderson, M. E. Edwards, C. J. Mock, R. S. Thompson, R. S. Webb, T. Webb III, and C. Whitlock. 1998. Paleoclimate simulations for North America over the past 21,000 years: Features of the simulated climate and comparisons with paleoenvironmental data. *Quaternary Science Reviews* 17:549–585.

Beckham, S. D. 1990. History of western Oregon since 1846. Pp. 180–188 in *Handbook of North American Indians,* vol. 7: *Northwest coast,* ed. W. Suttles. Washington, D.C.: Smithsonian Institution.

Beckham, S. D., R. Minor, and K. A. Toepel. 1981. *Prehistory and history of BLM lands in west central Oregon: A cultural resources overview.* University of Oregon anthropological papers 25. Eugene, Ore.

Berkley, E. 2000. Temporal and spatial variability of fire occurrence in western Oregon, A.D. 1200 to present. Master's thesis, Department of Geography, University of Oregon, Eugene.

Bonnicksen, T. M. 1989. Fire gods and federal policy. *American Forests* 95:14–16, 66–68.

Bork, J. 1985. Fire history in three vegetation types on the east side of the Oregon Cascades. Ph.D. diss., Oregon State University, Corvallis.

Boyd, R. 1975. Another look at the "fever and ague" of Western Oregon. *Ethnohistory* 22:135–154.

———. 1986. Strategies of Indian burning in the Willamette Valley. *Canadian Journal of Anthropology* 5:67–86.

———. 1999a. Strategies of Indian burning in the Willamette Valley. Pp. 94–138 in *Indians, fire, and the land in the Pacific Northwest,* ed. R. Boyd. Corvallis: Oregon State University Press.

———, ed. 1999b. *Indians, fire, and the land in the Pacific Northwest.* Corvallis: Oregon State University Press.

Boyd, R. T. 1990. Demographic history, 1774–1874. Pp. 135–148 in *Handbook of North American Indians,* vol. 7: *Northwest coast,* ed. W. Suttles. Washington, D.C.: Smithsonian Institution.

Burke, C. J. 1979. Historic fires in the central western Cascades, Oregon. Master's thesis, Department of Forest Science, Oregon State University, Corvallis.

Burkhart, J. W., and E. W. Tisdale. 1976. Causes of juniper invasion in southwestern Idaho. *Ecology* 76:482–484.

Burns, R. M., and B. H. Honkala. 1990. *Silvics of North America,* vol. 1: *Conifers.* USDA Forest Service, agricultural handbook 654.

Butzer, K. W. 1990. The Indian legacy in the American landscape. Pp. 27–50 in *The making of the American landscape,* ed. M. P. Conzen. Boston: Unwin Hyman.

Chase, A. 1987. *Playing God in Yellowstone.* San Diego: Harcourt, Brace, Jovanovich.

Clark, J. S. 1990. Fire and climate change during the last 750 years in northwestern Minnesota. *Ecological Monographs* 60:135–159.

Clark, J. S., and P. D. Royall. 1996. Local and regional sediment charcoal evidence for fire regimes in presettlement northeastern North America. *Journal of Ecology* 84:67–80.

Clark, J. S., J. Lynch, B. Stocks, and J. Goldammer. 1998. Relationships between charcoal particles in air and sediments in west-central Siberia. *The Holocene* 8:19–29.

Clarke, S. 1905. *Pioneer Days of Oregon History* 1:89–90.

Cronon, W. 1995. The trouble with wilderness; or getting back to the wrong nature. Pp. 69–90 in *Uncommon ground: Toward reinventing nature,* ed. W. Cronon. New York: W. W. Norton.

Cwynar, L. C. 1987. Fire and the forest history of the North Cascade Range. *Ecology* 68:791–802.

Denevan, W. 1992. The pristine myth: The landscape of the Americas in 1492. *Annals of the Association of American Geographers* 82:369–385.

Douglas, D. 1959. *Journal kept by David Douglas during his travels in North America 1823–1827.* New York: Antiquarian Press.

Dunwiddie, P. W. 1986. A 6000-year record of forest history on Mount Rainier, Washington. *Ecology* 67:58–68.

Flores, D. 1997. The West that was, and the West that can be. *High Country News* 29:6–7.

Franklin, J. F., and Dyrness, C. T. 1973. *Natural vegetation of Oregon and Washington.* General technical report PNW-8. Portland, Ore.: USDA Forest Service, Pacific Northwest Research Station.

Franklin, J. F., F. J. Swanson, M. E. Harmon, D. A. Perry, T. A. Spies, V. H. Dale, A. McKee, W. K. Ferrell, J. E. Means, S. V. Gregory, J. D. Lattin, T. D. Schowalter, and D. Larson. 1991. Effects of global climate change on forests in northwestern North America. *The Northwest Environmental Journal* 7:233–254.

Fritts, H. C. 1976. *Tree rings and climate.* New York: Academic Press.

Gardner, J. J., and C. Whitlock. In review. Charcoal accumulation following a recent fire in the Cascade Range, northwestern USA, and its relevance for fire-history studies. *The Holocene.*

Garfin, G. M., and M. K. Hughes. 1996. *Eastern Oregon divisional precipitation and Palmer Drought Severity Index from Tree-Rings.* Final Report to USDA Forest Service cooperative agreement PNW 90-174.

Graumlich, L. J. 1987. Precipitation variation in the Pacific Northwest (1675–1975) as reconstructed from tree rings. *Annals of the Association of American Geographers* 77:19–29.

———. 1991. Subalpine tree growth, climate, and increasing CO_2 an assessment of recent growth trends. *Ecology* 72:1–11.

Graumlich, L. J., and L. B. Brubaker. 1986. Reconstruction of annual temperature (1590–1979) for Longmire, Washington, derived from tree rings. *Quaternary Research* 25:223–234.

Grigg, L. D., and C. Whitlock. 1998. Late-glacial climate and vegetation changes in western Oregon. *Quaternary Research* 49:287–298.

Gruell, G. 1985. Fire on the early western landscape: An annotated record of wildland fires, 1776–1900. *Northwest Science* 59:97–107.

Hemstrom, M. A., and J. F. Franklin. 1982. Fire and other disturbances of the forests in Mount Rainier National Park. *Quaternary Research* 18:32–51.

Henry, A. 1992. *The journal of Alexander Henry the Younger 1799–1814,* vol. 2, ed. B. M. Gough. Toronto: The Champlain Society.

———. 1977. Quaternary paleontology of the Pacific slope of Washington. *Quaternary Research* 8:282–306.

Heusser, C. J. 1983. Vegetation history of the northwestern United States, including Alaska. Pp. 239–258 in *Late Quaternary environments of the United States*, ed. S. C. Porter. Minneapolis: University of Minnesota Press.

Heyerdahl, E. K. 1997. Spatial and temporal variation in historical fire regimes of the Blue Mountains, Oregon, and Washington: The influence of climate. Ph.D. diss., University of Washington, Seattle.

Holmes, R. L., R. I. C. Adams, and H. C. Fritts. 1986. *Tree-ring chronologies of western North America: California, eastern Oregon, and northern Great Basin.* Chronology series 6. Tucson: Laboratory of Tree-ring Research.

Hulse, D., A. Branscomb, J. G. Duclos, S. Gregory, S. Payne, D. Richey, H. Dearborn, L. Ashkenas, P. Minear, J. Christy, E. Alverson, D. Diethelm, and M. Richmond. 1998. *Willamette River Basin: A planning atlas*, ver. 1.0. Seattle: University of Washington Press.

Impara, P. C. 1997. Spatial and temporal patterns of fire in the forests of the central Oregon Coast Range. Ph.D. diss., Oregon State University, Corvallis.

Johannessen, C. L., W. A. Davenport, A. Millet, and S. McWilliams. 1971. The vegetation of the Willamette Valley. *Annals of the Association of American Geographers* 61:286–302.

Knox, M. A. 2000. Ecological change in the Willamette Valley at the time of Euro-American Contact, ca. 1800–1850. Master's thesis, Department of Geography, University of Oregon, Eugene.

Kutzbach, J. E., and P. J. Guetter. 1986. The influence of changing orbital patterns and surface boundary conditions on climate simulations for the past 18,000 years. *Journal of Atmospheric Sciences* 43:1726–1759.

Langston, N. 1995. *Forest dreams, forest nightmares: The paradox of old growth in the inland West.* Seattle: University of Washington Press.

Leopold, A. S., S. A. Cain, C. M. Cottam, I. N. Gabrielson, and T. L. Kimball. 1963. Wildlife management in the national parks. *Transactions of the North American Wildlife Natural Resource Conference* 28:28–45.

Long, C. A., C. Whitlock, P. J. Bartlein, and S. H. Millspaugh. 1998. A 9000-year fire history from the Oregon Coast Range based on a high-resolution charcoal study. *Canadian Journal of Forest Research* 28:774–787.

Loy, W. G., S. Allen, and C. P. Patton. 1976. *Atlas of Oregon.* Eugene: University of Oregon Press.

Maciliwain, C. 1994. Western inferno provokes a lot of finger-pointing, but little action. *Science* 370:585.

Martin, P. S. 1984. Prehistoric overkill: The global model. Pp. 345–404 in *Quaternary extinctions: A prehistoric revolution*, ed. P. S. Martin and R. G. Klein. Tucson: University of Arizona Press.

McLachlan, J. S., and L. B. Brubaker. 1995. Local and regional vegetation change on the northeastern Olympic Peninsula during the Holocene. *Canadian Journal of Botany* 73:1618–1627.

McLeod, A. R. 1961. Journal of a trapping expedition along the coast south of the Columbia in charge of A. R. McLeod C. T. Summer 1826. Pp. 141–217 in *Peter Skene Ogden's Snake Country Journal 1826–27*, ed. K. G. Davies. London: The Hudson's Bay Record Society.

Mehringer, P. J., Jr. 1985. Late Quaternary pollen records from the Pacific Northwest and Northern Great Basin of the United States. Pp. 167–189 in

Pollen records of late Quaternary North American sediments, ed. V. M. Bryant, Jr., and R. G. Holloway. Dallas: American Association of Stratigraphic Palynologists Foundation.

Mehringer, P. J., Jr., and P. E. Wigand. 1990. Comparison of late Holocene environments from woodrat middens and pollen: Diamond Craters, Oregon. Pp. 294–325 in *Packrat middens: The last 40,000 years of biotic change*, ed. J. L. Betancourt, T. R. Van Devender, and P. S. Martin. Tucson: University of Arizona Press.

Miller, R. F., and J. A. Rose. 1995. Historic expansion of *Juniperus occidentalis* (western juniper) in southeastern Oregon. *Great Basin Naturalist* 55:37–45.

Miller, R. F., and P. E. Wigand. 1994. Holocene changes in semiarid pinyon-juniper woodlands. *BioScience* 44:465–474.

Millspaugh, S. H., and C. Whitlock. 1995. A 750-year fire history based on lake sediment records in central Yellowstone National Park. *The Holocene* 3:283–292.

Minto, J. 1900. The number and condition of the native race in Oregon when first seen by white men. *Oregon Historical Quarterly* 1:298–315.

Mohr, J. A., C. Whitlock, and C. J. Skinner. 2000. Postglacial vegetation and fire history, eastern Klamath Mountains, California. *The Holocene* 10:587–601.

Morris, W. 1936. Forest fires in western Oregon and Washington. *Oregon Historical Quarterly* 35:313–339.

Morrison, P., and F. J. Swanson. 1990. *Fire history and pattern in a Cascade Range landscape*. USDA Forest Service General technical report PW-254.

Mutch, R. W., S. F. Arno, J. K. Brown, C. E. Carlson, R. D. Ottmar, and J. L. Peterson. 1993. Forest health in the Blue Mountains: A management strategy for fire-adapted ecosystems. In *Forest health in the Blue Mountains: Science perspectives*, ed. T. L. Quigley. USDA Forest Service General technical report PNW-295.

National Interagency Fire Center. 2000. On the Web at *http://www.nifc.gov.*

O'Hara, E. 1911. *Pioneer Catholic History of Oregon*. Portland, Ore.: Glass and Prudhomme.

Ohlson, M., and E. Tryterud. 2000. Interpretation of the charcoal record in forest soils: Forest fires and their production and deposition of macroscopic charcoal. *The Holocene* 10:519–525.

Oregon Department of Forestry. 1970. *Tillamook fires map* [scale: 1:126,720].
———. 1997. On the Web at http://www.odf.state.or.us/atlas/maps/light.gif.

Palmer, J. 1966. *Journal of travels over the Rocky Mountains*. Ann Arbor: University Microfilms.

Parker, S. 1840. *Journal of an exploring tour beyond the Rocky Mountains*. Ithaca, N.Y.: Parker.

Patterson, W. A., III, K. J. Edwards, and D. J. MacGuire. 1987. Microscopic charcoal as a fossil indicator of fire. *Quaternary Science Reviews* 6:3–23.

Pearl, C. A. 1999. Holocene environmental history of the Willamette Valley, Oregon: Insights from an 11,000-year record from Beaver Lake. Master's thesis, Interdisciplinary Studies Program, University of Oregon, Eugene.

Pyne, S. 1982. *Fire in America*. Princeton: Princeton University Press.

————. 2000. Where have all the fires gone? *Fire Management Today* 60:4–6.

Ramenofsky, A. F. 1987. *Vectors of death: The archaeology of European contact.* Albuquerque: University of New Mexico Press.

Riggs, T. 1900. The upper Calapooia. *Oregon Historical Quarterly* 4:74–77.

Romme, W. H., and M. G. Turner. 1991. Implications of global climate change for biogeographic patterns in the Greater Yellowstone Ecosystem. *Conservation Biology* 5:373–386.

Running, S. W., and R. R. Nemani. 1991. Regional hydrologic and carbon balance response of forests resulting from potential climate change. *Climatic Change* 19:349–368.

Sea, D. S., and C. Whitlock. 1995. Postglacial vegetation and climate of the Cascade Range, central Oregon. *Quaternary Research* 43:370–381.

Seton, A. 1993. *Astorian adventure: The journal of Alfred Seton 1811–1815,* ed. R. F. Jones. New York: Fordham University Press.

Shinn, D. A. 1980. Historical perspectives on range burning in the inland Pacific Northwest. *Journal of Range Management* 33:415–423.

Skinner, C. N., and C. Chang. 1996. Fire regimes, past and present. Pp. 1041–1069 in *Sierra Nevada Ecosystem Project: Final report to Congress,* vol. 2: *Assessments and scientific basis for management options.* Davis: University of California, Davis, Centers for Water and Wildland Resources.

Stuart, R. 1995. *The discovery of the Oregon Trail,* ed. P. Rollins. Lincoln: University of Nebraska Press.

Stuiver, M., and P. J. Reimer. 1993. Extended ^{14}C data base and revised CALIB 3.0 ^{14}C age calibration program. *Radiocarbon* 35:215–230.

Stuiver, M., P. J. Reimer, E. Bard, J. W. Beck, G. S. Burr, K. A. Hughen, B. Kromer, G. McCormac, J. Van der Plicht, and M. Spurk. 1998. INTCAL89 radiocarbon age calibration, 24,000-0 cal BP. *Radiocarbon* 40:1041–1083.

Sugita, S., and M. Tsukada. 1982. The vegetation history in western North America I. Mineral and Hall Lakes. *Japanese Journal of Ecology* 32:499–515.

Suttles, W., and Ames, K. 1997. Pre-European History. Pp. 255–274 in *The rainforests of home: Profile of a North American bioregion,* ed. P. K. Schoonmaker, B. von Hagen, and E. C. Wolf. Washington, D.C.: Island Press.

Swetnam, T. W., and J. L. Betancourt. 1998. Mesoscale disturbance and ecological response to decadal climatic variability in the American Southwest. *Journal of Climate* 11:3128–3147.

Taylor, A. H. 1993. Fire history and structure of red fir (*Abies magnifica*) forests, Swain Mountain Experimental Forest, Cascade Range, northeastern California. *Canadian Journal of Forest Research* 23:1672–1678.

Teensma, P. D. A. 1987. Fire history and fire regimes of the central western Cascades of Oregon. Ph.D. diss., University of Oregon, Eugene.

Thompson, R. S., C. Whitlock, P. J. Bartlein, S. Harrison, and W. G. Spaulding. 1993. Climatic changes in the western United States since 18,000 yr B.P. Pp. 468–513 in *Global climates since the last glacial maximum,* ed. H. E. Wright, Jr., J. E. Kutzbach, T. Webb III, W. F. Ruddiman, F. A. Street-Perrott, and P. J. Bartlein. Minneapolis: University of Minnesota Press.

Towle, J. C. 1982. Changing geography of the Willamette Valley woodlands. *Oregon Historical Quarterly* 83:66–87.

Ubelaker, D. 1988. North American population size, A.D. 1500–1985. *American Journal of Physical Anthropology* 77:289–294.

Wagner, F. H., and Kay, C. E. 1993. "Natural" or "healthy" ecosystems: Are U.S. national parks providing them? Pp. 257–270 in *Humans as components of ecosystems*, ed. M. J. McDonnell and S. T. A. Pickett. New York: Springer-Verlag.

Weisberg, P. J. 1998. Fire history, fire regimes, and development of forest structure in the central western Oregon Cascades. Ph.D. diss., Department of Forest Science, Oregon State University, Corvallis.

Whitlock, C. 1992. Vegetational and climatic history of the Pacific Northwest during the last 20,000 years: Implications for understanding present-day biodiversity. *The Northwest Environmental Journal* 8:5–28.

Whitlock, C., and Bartlein, P. J. 1997. Vegetation and climate change in northwest America during the past 125 kyr. *Nature* 388:57–61.

Whitlock, C., and C. P. S. Larsen. 2000. Charcoal as a Fire Proxy. In *Tracking environmental change using lake sediments*, vol. 2: *Biological techniques and indicators*, ed. J. P. Smol, H. J. B. Birks, and W. M. Last. Dordrecht, Netherlands: Kluwer Academic.

Whitlock, C., and S. H. Millspaugh, 1996. Testing assumptions of fire history studies: An examination of modern charcoal accumulation in Yellowstone National Park. *The Holocene* 6:7–15.

Wigand, P. E. 1987. Diamond Pond, Harney County, Oregon. *Great Basin Naturalist* 47:427–458.

Wilkes, C. 1926. *Diary of Wilkes in the Northwest*, ed. E. S. Meany. Seattle: University of Washington Press.

Williams, G. W. 2000. Early fire use in Oregon. *Fire Management Today* 60:13–20.

Work, J. 1923. John Work's journey from Fort Vancouver to Umpqua River, and return, in 1834. *Oregon Historical Quarterly* 24:238–268.

Worona, M. A., and Whitlock, C. 1995. Late-Quaternary vegetation and climate history near Little Lake, Central Coast Range, Oregon. *Geological Society of America Bulletin* 107:867–876.

Zenk, H. B. 1990. Kalapuyans. Pp. 547–553 in *Handbook of North American Indians*, vol. 7: *Northwest coast*, ed. W. Suttles. Washington, D.C.: Smithsonian Institution.

Zucker, J. 1983. *Oregon Indians, culture, history and current affairs: An atlas and introduction*. Portland: Western Imprints, The Press of the Oregon Historical Society.

Zyback, R. 1995. Interview. *Forests Today and Forever* 9:6.

FIRE IN SIERRA NEVADA FORESTS: EVALUATING THE ECOLOGICAL IMPACT OF BURNING BY NATIVE AMERICANS

Albert J. Parker

Fire is universally recognized as a crucial agent that shapes vegetation patterns, regulates biomass accumulation and nutrient cycling, and mediates landscape dynamics in the Sierra Nevada (Chang 1996; Figures 7.1 and 7.2). McKelvey et al. (1996) concluded their overview of fire in the Sierra Nevada by noting that under the prevailing climate, fire has served as a frequent, potent influence on Sierran ecosystems for millennia. The focus of this chapter is to contemplate the role of aboriginal human agency as a significant shaper and modifier of vegetation in the Sierra Nevada through the use of fire. On this issue, controversy remains. The range of views that frame this controversy in California may be exemplified by two quotes:

> The recent stability of vegetation across diverse ecological gradients in the San Bernardino Mountains before fire control indicates that plant cover had equilibrated to fire regimes that extend far into the past, and man's burning activities had little impact on the ecology and biogeography of the chaparral and forest ecosystems. (Minnich 1988:74)

233

Our rich natural heritage is also linked with the historical use and stewardship of vegetation by Native Americans. Through the introduction of time-tested horticultural techniques such as burning, tilling, weeding, and selective harvesting practices of different tribes, California's ecosystems were profoundly shaped by human influence over thousands of years. (M. K. Anderson 1997:9)

The assertion that the landscape of the Sierra Nevada has been domesticated or thoroughly remade by human action is a recent one, but its scholarly roots extend back to the 1950s and the works of Reynolds (1959) and Lewis (1973, republished in 1993). These authors

Figure 7.1. Map of California and surrounding region, emphasizing the Sierra Nevada and locating places mentioned in the text.

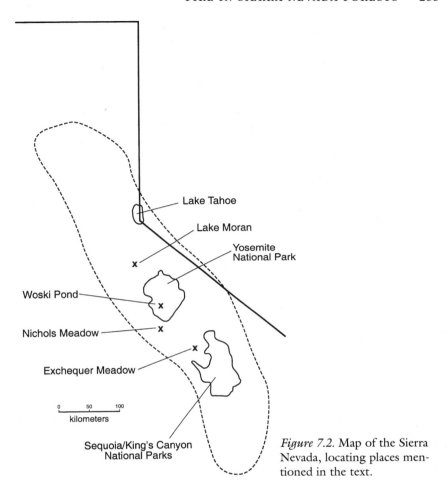

Figure 7.2. Map of the Sierra Nevada, locating places mentioned in the text.

Lake Tahoe

Lake Moran

Yosemite National Park

Woski Pond

Nichols Meadow

Exchequer Meadow

0   50   100
kilometers

Sequoia/King's Canyon National Parks

attempted to construct ecological arguments that blended the relatively meager contemporary physical and ethnographic evidence for aboriginal burning in the Sierra with then-emerging principles of fire ecology. Each concluded that indigenous humans have had an important influence, at least locally, on lower- and middle-elevation forests on the western flank of the Sierra Nevada, although Lewis is careful not to overstate his point. He concludes a review chapter on Indian burning in California with a qualified observation:

> It is undoubtedly the case that Indians did not set all or even most of California to the torch in any given set of years. Despite a precontact population that is estimated to be among the highest in North America, they probably

> lacked sufficient numbers to burn all or even most of the
> vegetation on any regular and consistent basis, even had
> they so wanted. (Lewis 1993:114)

In evaluating the ecological impact of burning by aboriginal humans on Sierra Nevada landscapes, I will adopt the premise of Vale (1998:232): "A landscape may be labeled pristine, or natural . . . if the fundamental characteristics of vegetation, wildlife, soil, hydrology, and climate are those that result from natural nonhuman processes, and *if these conditions would exist whether or not humans were present*" (my italics for emphasis). The central issue is not whether humans were present in the Sierra Nevada, or whether they used fire as a powerful tool in their technologies of economic production. Both points are undoubtedly correct. The key ecological issue is whether aboriginal burning produced novel vegetation compositions, forest structures, or physical environments—whether it pushed the Sierra Nevada landscape outside the bounds of variability imposed by nonhuman forces (Landres et al. 1999).

In musing on the role of indigenous peoples as shapers of Sierran vegetation through the use of fire, the following sets of questions merit consideration:

- How does physical setting influence vegetation patterns and fire in the Sierra Nevada? How have linkages among climate, vegetation, and fire regime varied during the late Quaternary in the Sierra?
- What is the history of human occupancy of the Sierra Nevada? How large and stable were indigenous populations in the Sierra? What were the principal cultural uses of fire?
- How well documented are precontact fire regimes and forest structures in the Sierra Nevada? Were Sierran forests uniform expanses of open woodlands, or were they characterized by considerable spatial heterogeneity? Do spatial and temporal patterns of fire in the Sierra match expectations if they are constrained by physical setting? Are there modern analogs that might provide clues to pre-European fire regimes in the Sierra?
- Is lightning sufficiently common to account for the geography and return interval of fires in Sierran vegetation types, or is augmentation by human ignition sources necessary to account for observed patterns of fire behavior? Does ignition source matter in explaining the geography of fire?
- Have favored plant species or communities become more abundant (perhaps even been created) after human entry into the Sierra?
- Who are the principal voices in this debate? What are their scholarly roots, intellectual affinities, or sociopolitical agendas?

As I review the evidence bearing on these questions, I shall emphasize several key points that summarize my findings. The preponderance of physical evidence of climatic variation and vegetation response in the Sierra Nevada over the past 20,000 years suggests strong and consistent climatic controls on both vegetation cover and fire regimes throughout this period. Although the exact details of vegetation structure are difficult to reconstruct with certainty over large areas, it is likely that Sierran landscapes embraced a high degree of spatial heterogeneity associated with complex topography and microclimate, related variation in vegetation types and fuel loading patterns, and spatial variation in the physical intensity of and biological response to disturbance events. Humans may have locally augmented this natural spatial heterogeneity, but it is not necessary to invoke human agency to explain this feature of the Sierran landscape. Tree-ring reconstructions from fire scars portray a fire regime in lower-elevation mixed-conifer forests dominated by frequent surface fires, with occasional, more intense burns serving as an important ecological influence in the landscape. Lightning strike densities in the Sierra Nevada are sparse compared with much of the rest of the United States, but twentieth-century records of lightning-caused fires suggest a concentration of natural ignitions in lower-elevation mixed-conifer forests, especially those dominated by ponderosa pine. Lightning incidence appears to be sufficient in the Sierra Nevada to account for pre-European fire frequencies, although aboriginal humans may have locally increased fire incidence in settings with high concentrations of herbaceous fuels. I conclude that aboriginal humans may have had significant influences on vegetation cover in some places (especially around permanent settlements or frequently used camp sites), but there is little evidence to suggest that they moved the vegetation mosaic of the Sierra Nevada to a condition outside of the natural realm of historical variability.

The Environmental Setting

The climate of the Sierra Nevada reflects the seasonal rhythms characteristic of Mediterranean-type environments. Precipitation is concentrated in the cool winter season in association with frequent passage of Pacific cyclones along the polar front jet stream. This precipitation falls primarily as snow above 1,500–1,800 m. Summers are warm and dry under the influence of the persistent Pacific subtropical anticyclone. At higher elevations, summer drought is occasionally mitigated by orographically reinforced thundershowers. Strong precipitation seasonality imposes an annual pattern of fuel production in spring and early summer that is followed by chronic, late-summer drought stress that predisposes vegetation to elevated fire risk in most years.

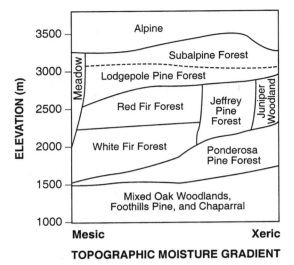

Figure 7.3. A generalized mosaic diagram of vegetation patterns in California uplands (adapted from Vankat 1982 and Barbour 1988).

The vegetation that cloaks the Sierra Nevada varies in response to both macroclimatic and microclimatic gradients. Vertical zonation ensues from a gradient of decreased temperature and enhanced effective moisture with increasing elevation. Strong contrasts in moisture regime between the moister western and drier eastern slope are generated by rainshadow effects. Locally, the effects of topography, soils, and hydrology add complexity to this vegetation mosaic (Figure 7.3; see Barbour 1988; Parker 1989).

At lower elevations on the western slope, foothills pine (*Pinus sabiniana*) and blue oak (*Quercus douglasii*) savannas intermix with foothills chaparral. These assemblages grade into mixed-conifer forests in the lower montane zone, dominated by ponderosa pine (*Pinus ponderosa*) on drier sites and white fir (*Abies concolor*) on mesic sites. Giant sequoia (*Sequoiadendron giganteum*) occurs locally in mixed-conifer forests of the central and southern Sierra. Upper montane forests are dominated by red fir (*Abies magnifica*) on mesic settings and Jeffrey pine (*Pinus jeffreyi*) on drier sites. Subalpine forests are dominated by lodgepole pine (*Pinus contorta* var. *murrayana*) alone or mixed with mountain hemlock (*Tsuga mertensiana*) and various five-needled pines. Much of the Sierran crest is above tree line, especially farther south where elevations are highest.

The eastern flank of the Sierra supports a mixed woodland of subalpine species, including lodgepole pine, Jeffrey pine, and Sierra juniper (*Juniperus occidentalis*). At lower elevations are montane woodlands of single-needle pinyon (*Pinus monophylla*) and Utah juniper (*Juniperus osteosperma*), and finally, at the eastern base of the Sierra, sagebrush-dominated (*Artemisia tridentata*) Great Basin desert.

Paleoenvironmental reconstructions of conditions during the late Quaternary in the Sierra Nevada portray a vegetation-environment mosaic that is sensitive to climatic forcing. (For a thorough review of Sierran paleoenvironments, see Kinney [1996] and Woolfenden [1996].) Anderson and Smith (1994) summarized late Quaternary dynamics of pollen, charcoal, and meadow sediment stratigraphy in the central and southern Sierra Nevada. They emphasized strong vegetation/climate/fire linkages throughout the Holocene.

From about 20,000 to 13,500 B.P., a mix of xerophytic sagebrush and pine pollen dominated lake sediments at midelevations on the western slope in the central Sierra (Smith and Anderson 1992; see Table 7.1). This pollen assemblage resembles modern conditions on the east slope of the Sierra, at elevations 500–1,000 m higher. Smith and Anderson inferred cooler and drier climates than the present during this late glacial period.

From 13,500 to 10,000 B.P., warming fostered development of mixed forests of conifers that today span a broad elevational range (Table 7.1).

TABLE 7.1. Timeline of climatic change and aboriginal human occupancy in the Sierra Nevada (adapted from Moratto 1984; Kinney 1996; and Woolfenden 1996).

Yr. (B.P.)	Paleoclimatic Record	Cultural Record
200		Spanish settlement of California (1770s)
	Little Ice Age (A.D. 1450–1850)	Postcontact disease spread reduced aboriginal population
400		European contact in California (1550s)
		Miwok cultural expansion into central Sierra (A.D. 1300–1400)
800	Medieval Warm Period (A.D. 1000–1300)	Depopulation of Sierra, violence, restricted carrying capacity (A.D. 700–1300)
1,600	Cool wet period (A.D. 500–800)	
	Neo-glacial episode	First permanent settlements, acorn
3,200	(3,500–1,500 B.P.)	processing technologies elaborated (3500–1300 B.P.)
	Resembled modern con-	
6,400	ditions (6,500–3,500 B.P.)	
	Very warm, dry (Altithermal)	First evidence of humans, temporary
	(10,000–6,500 B.P.)	camps (ca. 10,000 B.P.)
12,800	Wet, varied temperatures (13,700–10,400 B.P.)	
	Cool, dry period (16,000–13,700 B.P.)	
25,600		

These forests lack a modern analog, but were relatively mesophytic compared with both antecedent and subsequent periods. From 10,000 to 6,500 B.P., warmer and drier conditions predominated in the Sierra, as evidenced by Holocene maxima in both charcoal production and oak pollen, as well as a dearth of pollen from mesic tree species such as fir, hemlock, and sequoia in mid-elevation lake cores. This timing matches the Altithermal episode described for other locales in North America. Koehler and Anderson (1994) documented increased sediment delivery to subalpine meadows during this period, which they attributed to increased denudation rates with more open vegetation cover.

After ca. 6,000 B.P., forests closed and vegetation patterns began to resemble those characteristic of today (Table 7.1). Giant sequoia pollen concentrations rise to modern levels only in the last 4,500 years (Anderson and Smith 1994), suggesting that the modern distribution of sequoia groves has emerged in that time. Anderson (1990) and Anderson and Smith (1997) related these mid-Holocene vegetation changes to continental-scale adjustments in synoptic climatology. Prior to 6,000 B.P., they suggested that the Sierra was drier due to a weaker Pacific polar front jet stream, whereas after 6,000 B.P., Pacific cyclonic activity strengthened. At about this same time, they suggested that El Niño/Southern Oscillation cycles began to play a stronger role in shaping interannual wet/dry cycles in the Sierra Nevada.

By 4,000–3,500 B.P., the cooler and wetter Neoglacial period began in the Sierra. The alpine tree line descended in response to these cooler, wetter conditions (Lloyd and Graumlich 1997). Wet meadow stratigraphy shifted from mineral sediments to peat-rich biogenic soils (Anderson and Smith 1994), an indicator of wetter conditions and elevated water tables during this period.

For the last millennium, tree-ring records from foxtail pine (*Pinus balfouriana*) near the tree line in the southern Sierra Nevada suggest an episode somewhat warmer than the present from A.D. 1100–1375 (corresponding to the Medieval Warm period) and a cooler interval from A.D. 1450–1850 (associated with the Little Ice Age) (Graumlich 1993). Since 1850, Sierran climates have been warm and anomalously wet relative to most of the last millennium.

In summary, several points of significance to the ecological impact of aboriginal burning on Sierra Nevada vegetation are relevant. Climate has been the preeminent force shaping vegetation distributional adjustments and fire regimes throughout the late Quaternary. Variation in climate has been substantial in the late Quaternary, with relatively few periods of multimillennial stasis in the configuration of vegetation and fire regimes. What appear to be long intervals of stable climate (the mid-Holocene Altithermal) most likely experienced the same smaller fluctuations evi-

dent during the past millennium; the precision of environmental reconstructions declines as detailed lines of evidence, such as tree-ring
chronologies, are lost with time. Against this backdrop of changing
physical environments and resources, charcoal stratigraphy (the best
remaining evidence of fire over this time period) reflects strong climatic
controls on fire ecology in the Sierra. More detailed consideration of evidence regarding fire regimes in the Sierra Nevada follows after a summary of human activities in the range.

Human Presence in the Sierra Nevada

At the time of Euro-American contact, indigenous peoples of the Sierra
Nevada were organized into tribal bands that generally occupied elevational transects of land, from the foothills to the High Sierra. This permitted access to a broad seasonal range of biotic resources. There were
thirty to thirty-five small tribes, collectively representing nine language
groups from three stocks (Moratto 1984). Prominent tribes in late Sierran prehistory included the Washoe (northern Sierra Nevada), Western
Mono (southern Sierra Nevada), and Paiute (eastern slopes of the south-
ern/central Sierra Nevada) with Great Basin affinities, and the Maidu
(northern Sierra), Miwok (central Sierra), and Foothills Yokut (southern
Sierra) with California lowland affinities (Figure 7.4).

Technologies of food procurement were those of hunter/gatherers,
augmented by protection, encouragement, and cultivation of wild plants
(Anderson et al. 1997; see Vale, chapter 1 of this volume). In general,
indigenous people were sustained by an abundance of harvested plants
and animals, including acorns, pine nuts, other plant foods, native
wildlife, and fish. Moratto (1984) describes the typical settlement pattern as one of permanent villages of dozens to hundreds of people, with
homes scattered in surrounding hinterlands as well. Permanent settlements were largely confined to lower elevations on the western slope
(1,000–1,250 m), and larger villages were located along major streams.
With rare exceptions, higher-elevation sites were only seasonally occupied. Population densities were substantially higher on the western slope
of the Sierra than on the more arid eastern slope.

Indigenous peoples of the Sierra Nevada used fire to enhance plant
food production (especially acorns), to maintain selected grasses and
shrubs as a source for basket-making materials, to improve forage for
game animals, to aid in hunting game, and to reduce the hazard of severe
fire (Anderson and Moratto 1996; Chang 1996). Anderson (1993;
Anderson 1997) cites interviews with living tribal elders in which they
consistently observe that fuel reduction to help prevent severe fire was a
strong rationale for burning, at least in the immediate vicinity of village

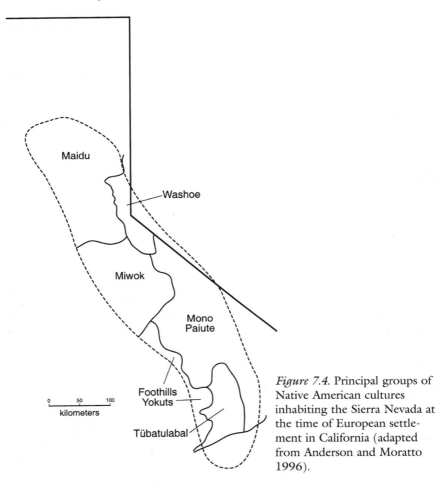

Figure 7.4. Principal groups of Native American cultures inhabiting the Sierra Nevada at the time of European settlement in California (adapted from Anderson and Moratto 1996).

sites. Peri and Patterson (1993) provide strong ethnographic evidence of the importance of basket-making to material culture among Sierran Indians, the fiber and other raw materials for which were often from shrub complexes likely maintained by fires. Clearly, fire was a significant tool used by indigenous cultures to promote their material well-being (Barbour et al. 1993). Nevertheless, direct physical evidence of burning by aboriginal people is scanty, so that the spatial extent and ecological impacts of such burning remains unclear (Skinner and Chang 1996).

The first archeological evidence of human presence in the Sierra Nevada comes from the northern Sierra and dates to ca. 9,500 B.P. (Moratto 1984; see Table 7.1). The earliest archeological sites appear to be campsites of transient hunter/gatherers. Of course, it is plausible that humans could have been present in the Sierra prior to this (perhaps as early as 11,000–12,000 B.P.), despite a lack of physical evidence to date. Archeological evidence of entry of humans into the central and southern Sierra is delayed until ca. 6,000 to 5,000 B.P. Population levels apparently fluctuated throughout the Holocene, primarily in response to environmental constraints and adoption/development of technological innovations. Anderson and Moratto (1996:194) identify three periods of "notably intense cultural activity": 7500–6000 B.C., 1000 B.C.–A.D. 700, and A.D. 1300–1800. Supporting material evidence from the first period is scanty, most of it coming from the northern Sierra in the form of temporary camps. Permanent settlements in the Sierra appear in the archeological record between 1500 B.C. and A.D. 1. This wave of occupation of the Sierra was apparently triggered by environmental changes at the inception of the Neoglacial (cooler/wetter conditions) and may have corresponded with widespread adoption of the acorn as a principal food source (Moratto 1984).

The period from A.D. 800 to 1400 was one of substantially reduced human populations in the Sierra (Table 7.1) and, indeed, throughout much of California (Moratto et al. 1978; Raab and Larson 1997). This period includes the Medieval Warm Period, which appears to be among the warmest, driest periods in the last 6,000 years. Moratto (1984) links general population decline, abandoned villages, and a high degree of violence (based on forensic evidence) with the climatically rigorous conditions during this period.

With the entry of the Miwok and Mono cultures into the central/southern Sierra Nevada around A.D. 1400 came intensive use of the mortar and pestle for processing acorns and other foods. Moratto (1984) suggests that this period of population growth and cultural elaboration in the Sierra also coincided with the onset of improved environmental conditions, in association with the shift to cooler/wetter conditions following the Medieval Warm period and leading into the Little Ice Age. Hence the Sierran landscape at the time of Spanish occupation of California (around the mid-1700s) had been influenced by relatively large numbers of technologically advanced indigenous peoples for approximately 350 years. It is reasonable to assert (despite "the lack of" direct physical evidence in all but a few locales) that indigenous people in this period may have produced substantial modification of environmental settings in areas near settlements or seasonal camps. But, as Parsons et al. (1986) have observed, it is an exaggeration to suggest that the human population of the Sierra Nevada has been sustained at a high level for thousands of years. Rather, the human population seems to have fluctuated in response to climatically induced changes in available food and water supplies since the early to middle Holocene. This contradicts the popular image of aboriginal humans that modified the landscape in order to live in "a world of balance and plenty" (Anderson et al. 1997).

Native American population levels in the Sierra Nevada around 1830 have been estimated at ca. 55,000 (Cook 1955; Moratto 1984), although this is probably conservative because these estimates rely on records and observations made following initial contact and following the epidemic wave of Eurasian diseases that killed a substantial percentage of indigenous people. Anderson and Moratto (1996) suggested that these figures should be nearly doubled to 90,000–100,000, based on the ecological assumption that the range permits a much higher carrying capacity. Of course, carrying capacity fluctuates with environmental change, as evidenced by the substantial depopulation evident for the period from A.D. 800 to 1400.

In the latter half of the nineteenth century, the Sierra Nevada was altered in dramatic ways by European settlers. The Gold Rush of 1849 raised the stakes for land access in the Sierra Nevada, and indigenous groups were soon displaced from native lands and the lifeways that sustained them. Miners and prospectors were soon followed by large herds of sheep foraging in the summer range of the High Sierra. Sheep grazing played a major role in altering the Sierran vegetation structure (McKelvey and Johnston 1992). Between the 1860s and early 1900s, large numbers of sheep (estimates run into the millions in some years) were seasonally present in Sierran subalpine meadows and forests. Direct removal of biomass by foraging was significant; purposeful burning by sheepherders to improve meadow forage and open the understory of surrounding forests for better herd movement also shaped forest structure. This may have contributed to the prevalence of early descriptions of Sierran forests as open, parklike stands of trees. Overgrazing may also have facilitated range invasion by Eurasian exotics.

Logging was localized in the Sierra Nevada prior to 1900, occurring around mines and towns as a source for lumber and fuelwood. With the opening of regional economic markets and development of the timber industry in the twentieth century, logging activities have grown substantially (McKelvey and Johnston 1992). Today, local economies in the Sierra Nevada are driven by logging interests on national forest lands and heavy recreational use in park lands. Except in designated wilderness and larger national parks since about 1970, fires have been intentionally suppressed throughout the twentieth century in the Sierra. (Even in national parks, only certain fires in prescribed zones are permitted to burn naturally, and most of these are at higher elevations.) The result has been a thickening of stand densities, an increase in understory fuel loads, and a conversion in species composition to more fire intolerant (and shade tolerant) taxa (Vankat and Major 1978) in fire-prone settings. Assigning causation to a single agent for these vegetation changes is difficult, because reductions in indigenous population size and associated lifeways, changes in grazing pressure and other Euro-American land uses, and changes in fire regimes are all overlain on substantial climate warming since 1850 and increased precipitation during the past century (Graumlich 1993; Millar and Woolfenden 1999).

Sierran Fire Regimes: Past and Present

Fire plays a crucial role in structuring the Sierran vegetation mosaic as it responds to the effects of biological and physical constraints. Kilgore (1973) observed that fire is inevitable in the Sierra Nevada, given the climatically dictated imbalance between biomass production (which can be high in most spring and early-summer months) and decomposition (which is arrested by dry conditions during summer).

Tree-Ring and Fire-Scar Evidence of Fire History

Traditionally, most fire ecologists have recognized surface fires as the predominant mode of Sierran wildfires, at least in the well-studied, lower-montane, mixed-conifer forests (Kilgore 1973). These burns were typified by relatively low heat release and flame intensity. They consumed surface herbaceous and small woody fuels, but generally did not kill thick-barked adult trees, except perhaps in localized hot spots fed by inordinate fuel accumulations (Bonnicksen and Stone 1985). Fire-scar records indicate that fires recurred frequently, with a mean fire return interval of about 8–15 years in mixed-conifer forests (Skinner and Chang 1996). Generally, individual surface fires were assumed to remain small in size (Kilgore and Taylor 1979).

Skinner and Chang (1996) summarized published fire histories from throughout the Sierra Nevada (Table 7.2; see their Table 38.1 for more detail). Their findings generally reinforce the traditional wisdom of frequent, localized, surface fires, but they also emphasize that there is con-

TABLE 7.2. Summary of fire return intervals in montane forests of California uplands (adapted from Table 38.1 in Skinner and Chang 1996).

Vegetation type	Median fire return interval (yr)	Range of fire return interval (yr)
Ponderosa pine/California black oak	6–9	2–23
Ponderosa pine/mixed conifer	5–11	3–50
Giant sequoia/mixed conifer	5–18	1–30
White fir/mixed conifer	10–18	3–40
Douglas fir/mixed conifer	14–16	3–60
Red fir	11–20	5–70
Jeffrey pine	13–29	4–150

Note: Data are based on various published sources from throughout the Sierra Nevada or ecologically similar California uplands. Fire intervals were generally reconstructed with tree-ring counts from fire-scar collections in a small sampling area. Periods of record for studies range from < 100 to 1,350 years, but are generally from 100 to 400 years.

siderable spatial and temporal heterogeneity in fire return intervals throughout Sierran forests.

In recent decades, alternative views have emerged that emphasize the importance of occasional larger, more intense fires in mixed-conifer forests of California uplands. The executive summary of the Sierra Nevada Ecosystem Project (SNEP Science Team and Special Consultants 1996) provided a box in its chapter on fire that acknowledged this simmering debate. Cast as observations by those who question the accuracy of the traditional fire regime, it noted that there is considerable spatial heterogeneity in fire-return intervals within mixed-conifer forests, so that some areas might have remained open and parklike while others were closed forest.

Caprio and Swetnam (1995) addressed the issue of larger fires in the Sierra by noting that early fire-scar reconstructions in the Sierra were based on tree-ring counts without the benefit of cross-dating. As a consequence, the same fire, though recorded on several adjacent trees, was often attributed to a different year. They argued that this methodological shortcoming produced biased estimates of fire return intervals (shorter than actual values) and area burned by individual fires (smaller than actual values). With accurately cross-dated fire scars, Caprio and Swetnam reported greater synchroneity in the historical record of fire from mixed-conifer forests in Sequoia National Park, so that occasional fires burned larger areas and fire return intervals were longer than traditionally reported. Caprio and Swetnam linked larger, more intense fires with distinct drought periods, and they found evidence that within a single drainage basin, large fires occasionally burned across the elevational gradient from lower montane to subalpine settings.

The significance of occasionally intense, large fires in mixed-conifer forests was addressed by Stephenson et al. (1991), who discussed the regeneration and growth response of giant sequoia after intense fires. A high percentage of giant sequoia cones are serotinous; seeds remain in closed cones until the cones are exposed to sufficiently high temperatures to induce opening and allow seed dispersal. Stephenson et al. observed profuse sequoia regeneration in "hot spots," areas of intense surface burning sustained by localized concentrations of high fuel loads. Moreover, adult sequoia that survived these hot fires typically exhibited a growth release triggered by reduced competition due to the thinning of surrounding stems. They concluded that maintenance of sequoia populations may require occasional fires of greater intensity. They, along with Swetnam (1993), identified several decades in the late thirteenth century (near the end of the Medieval Warm period) that exhibited a higher frequency of intense fires throughout sequoia groves (and doubtless the surrounding mixed-conifer forests of the central/southern Sierra

Nevada) than before or after. As Stephenson et al. (1991:323) note, the occurrence of fire may track closely the temporal variability in climate: "On the timescale of centuries, the fire regime itself may change in response to climatic change, making it difficult to pinpoint one particular fire regime as 'natural' for a region."

Swetnam (1993) reinforced this theme in a 1,500–2,000 year record of fires dendrochronologically reconstructed from five giant sequoia groves spanning a distance of ca. 200 km on the western slope in the central and southern Sierra. Over the long period of record, fire intervals varied from less than 5 to 30 years. Mean fire frequencies were lower (13–29 fires per century in a grove) during wetter/cooler periods (A.D. 500–800) and higher (27–46 fires per century in a grove) during drier/warmer periods (A.D. 1000–1300). Swetnam found that fire years co-occurred among sequoia groves more often than would be expected by chance. He linked fire behavior to interannual variability in precipitation (more widespread, synchronous fires in drought years) and to multidecadal variability in temperature (which he attributed to alteration of the fuel mosaic). Swetnam's work provides persuasive evidence of climatic control of fire behavior in Sierran mixed-conifer forests and emphasizes that fire regimes are nonstationary—they change in response to secular climatic change. These findings provide significant historical context for interpreting the role of humans in shaping fire regimes in California uplands. Over the last 1,500–2,000 years, the time period when human populations would have most significantly altered Sierran fire regimes, the spatial and temporal patterns of burning appear to be strongly responsive to climatic control. If fuel accumulations and meteorological conditions were conducive, fires burned with little apparent alteration by human agency.

As might be expected, the nature of fire varies in scope and intensity among Sierran vegetation types. In the foothills chaparral, more intense crown fires that recurred at intervals of 20 to 30 years were typical, at least prior to fire suppression efforts. In higher-elevation Sierran forests, estimates of fire return intervals prior to the twentieth century lengthen to several decades (Skinner and Chang 1996; Potter 1998). In general, although fire regimes in subalpine forests are less well documented, it has been assumed that fire intensities remained low, with surface fires being predominant. Fire return intervals were longer, presumably in response to reduced production of fuels, increased effective precipitation that limits periods of critically low fuel moisture, and a higher incidence of rock outcrops and riparian settings in the High Sierra that interrupt the connectivity of the fuel mosaic (Skinner and Chang 1996). Work by Taylor and Halpern (1991) and Chappell and Agee (1996) in red fir forests of the Cascade Range in northern California and southern Oregon suggests that fires in compositionally similar Sierran upper montane forests were of variable intensity, with light surface burns intermixed with areas of more severe crown fires. Fire history is poorly documented for subalpine forests in the Sierra Nevada, as well as throughout the vegetation types found on the eastern slope. It is generally assumed that subalpine forests rarely burned and that pinyon-juniper woodlands on the eastern slope experienced surface fires when herbaceous fuels reached unusually dense accumulations.

Charcoal Evidence of Holocene Fire History

Reconstructions of charcoal profiles from meadow and lake sediments reveal a long history of fire that has been characterized by substantial temporal variability. Edlund and Byrne (1991) reported on a 15,000-year record of fossil charcoal accumulation from Lake Moran in the central Sierra (Figure 7.5). Their stratigraphy showed minimal charcoal

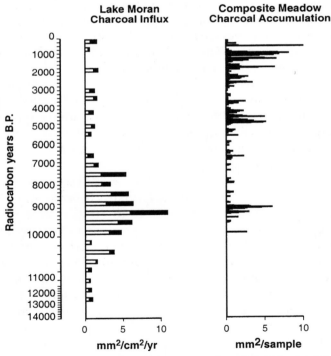

Figure 7.5. Charcoal accumulation/influx curves from Lake Moran sediments (Edlund and Byrne 1991) and a composite of eight meadow stratigraphies (Anderson and Smith 1997). Units on horizontal axes are not comparable, but temporal variation in the relative magnitude of charcoal accumulation/influx is evident.

accumulations during the early Holocene (12,500–10,000 B.P.), which they related to: moist climate; dense, closed forests; and possibly deeper, more persistent snowpacks. The ensuing mid-Holocene thermal maximum (10,000–7,000 B.P.) was characterized by Edlund and Byrne as possessing the Holocene peak in sedimentary charcoal influx. They provided macrofossil evidence of forest conversion from more mesic five-needled pines and lodgepole pines to more xeric ponderosa pine at this time. They reported a decline in charcoal accumulation to modern levels between 7,000 and 3,000 B.P., by which time modern mixed-conifer forests were established in the surrounding drainage.

Anderson and Smith (1997), like Edlund and Byrne, reported sedimentary charcoal records, although they drew their sample from meadow sediments (rather than lake cores) and they restricted their attention to charcoal particles larger than 100 micrometers in maximum diameter (as opposed to particles larger than 10 micrometers for Edlund and Byrne). Like Edlund and Byrne, they argued for climatic control of the Sierran charcoal record throughout the Holocene. There are, however, substantial differences in the temporal patterns reported and the associated environmental interpretation. In keeping with Edlund and Byrne, Anderson and Smith report a mid-Holocene peak in charcoal accumulation, around 9,200–8,700 B.P. However, they suggested that this fairly brief interval of peak charcoal deposition was embedded within a longer period of relatively low charcoal production. Indeed, they suggested that the drier, more open vegetation cover of the early to middle Holocene produced lower woody biomass, so that fewer fuels were available to burn and produce macroscopic charcoal. Anderson and Smith also reported charcoal accumulation patterns opposite to that of Edlund and Byrne for the last 4,500 years. They found greater rates of charcoal accumulation in Sierran meadow sediments during this period and suggested that the wetter climatic conditions promoted greater woody fuel production, which was converted to charcoal when fires burned through the landscape. Resolving these two contradictory reconstructions of charcoal stratigraphy in the Holocene may involve accounting for contrasts in depositional environments and sizes of charcoal particles sampled (which affects the size of the source region for airborne charcoal). In any event, it is clear that fire was prominent in Sierran landscapes throughout the late Quaternary, that charcoal production may predate human occupancy of the region, and that charcoal production varies in concert with climatic fluctuations, although the details of this variation may be debated.

The most striking paleoenvironmental evidence that supports the role of humans in altering fire regimes, at least in areas of high settlement density, comes from Woski Pond in Yosemite Valley (Anderson and Carpenter 1991). Yosemite Valley was heavily populated by aboriginal people, at least after entry of the Miwok culture into the region around A.D. 1300–1400. Anderson and Carpenter recovered a 1,550-year record of pollen, macrofossils, and charcoal from Woski Pond. They observed a substantial spike in charcoal accumulation around A.D. 1300. Although they link this event with the arrival of Miwok culture in Yosemite Valley, Anderson and Carpenter do not directly assign the ignition source to humans. Indeed, the fires reported by Stephenson et al. (1991) and Swetnam in sequoia groves throughout the southern half of the Sierra Nevada in the late 1200s could have been caused by a climatic episode that also resulted in the large pulse of charcoal observed in the sediments of Woski Pond. Rather than indigenous populations opening Yosemite Valley vegetation with fire, it may well be that large, intense fires, followed by climatic amelioration over the next century, shifted the pathway of vegetation recovery to support meadows and savannas in the valley. This change in fire/vegetation/climate linkages might have provided the pulse of oak and herbaceous regeneration necessary to permit expansion of Miwok cultures into the central Sierra. After the charcoal peak around A.D. 1300, Anderson and Carpenter reported little charcoal accumulation to the present. They attributed this reduction in charcoal to the maintenance of more open, herbaceous-dominated vegetation by cultural burning. (Herbs generate little macroscopic charcoal compared with woody plants.) They convincingly argued that human intervention was necessary to maintain open vegetation in Yosemite Valley, because the ensuing Little Ice Age would have favored denser woody vegetation and higher production of macroscopic charcoal, if the vegetation mosaic in the Valley were responding to climatic stimuli alone.

Reflections on Sierran Fire Regimes and Forest Structure

Stephenson (1999), in a review of the application of natural variability concepts to vegetation management in the Sierra Nevada, observed that we have reasonably good evidence for fire regime reconstruction (at least in lower-elevation forests on the western slope of the Sierra), but poor evidence for the reconstruction of specific vegetation structures. Most work that documents forest spatial pattern or demographic structure in the Sierra is either restricted to small plots or is qualitative in nature (see Stephenson 1999 for a review of work that characterizes forest structure in sequoia groves).

Historically, the prevailing image of lower montane Sierran forests is that of open parkland, as captured in the evocative prose of John Muir:

> The inviting openness of the Sierra woods is one of their
> most distinguishing characteristics. The trees of all the

species stand more or less apart in groves, or in small irregular groups, enabling one to find a way nearly everywhere, along sunny colonnades and through openings that have a smooth, park-like surface. (Muir 1894:140–142)

Biswell (1967:60) reinforced this image of widespread open woodlands maintained by frequent surface fires, suggesting that forest cover and surface fires reflected "nature's balance," that repetitive surface fires kept the forest "almost immune from extensive crown fires."

The executive summary of the Sierra Nevada Ecosystem Project (SNEP Science Team and Special Consultants 1996) coupled its discussion of the ecological importance of larger, more intense fires with observations that challenged traditional views among ecologists regarding the prevalence of widespread open woodlands in the lower montane zone of the pre-European Sierran landscape. They cited the journal of J. Goldsborough Bruff—an 1850 immigrant who recorded in his journal the relative occurrence of open, parklike stands versus dense, mixed-conifer forests on the western slope. He reported dense forests six times more often than open stands. It seems reasonable to conclude that spatial heterogeneity of both fire regimes and forest structures in the pre-European Sierra Nevada was pronounced, although the details, particularly of forest structure, remain elusive. This fits well with the topographic, microclimatic, edaphic, and geomorphic heterogeneity of the terrain. Such environmental heterogeneity would foster dramatic local contrasts in fuel characteristics (such as biomass production, fuel moisture content, or the ratio of dead-to-living fuels) that would perpetuate a heterogeneous spatial pattern by its influence on fire behavior, irrespective of ignition source (Miller and Urban 1999a). Indeed, the spatial heterogeneity that develops in association with localized variation in the physical intensity of and biological response to a single disturbance event (such as a large fire or windstorm) is an emerging theme from recent work on large natural disturbances (White and Pickett 1985; Turner et al. 1997).

Lewis (1993 [1973]) and Anderson (1997) have argued that the structural heterogeneity of Sierran forests is a product of human-induced clearing and tending—that there is too much localized complexity to be derived from natural agents. Although it is plausible that indigenous humans may have locally altered forest structures and fostered increased spatial heterogeneity in vegetation cover, it is hardly necessary to invoke human agency through the use of fire as the creator and manager of that heterogeneity. Lightning fires, coupled with windstorms, disease and pest infestations, occasional drought and large floods, and tectonically triggered mass movements, would maintain a structurally heterogeneous landscape and vegetation cover, with or without human agency. By this argument, I am not denying the possibility of locally important human influences; but I am suggesting that the natural variability imposed by climate change, the operation of disturbance regimes, and the landscape-scale complexity of physical gradients in the Sierra Nevada would be sufficiently broad to incorporate most indigenous human influence within the embrace of natural patterns.

The Sierra San Pedro Martir: A Possible Modern Analog?

Because fire suppression has altered mixed-conifer forests in the Sierra Nevada, twentieth-century fire regimes are not reliable indicators of pre-European conditions. Minnich et al. (1993) and Minnich and Vizcaíno (1998) have argued that the extant mixed-conifer forests in the Sierra San Pedro Mártir of Baja California may provide a modern analog for the Sierra Nevada, although this assertion is subject to debate. The mixed-conifer forests of the Sierra San Pedro Mártir are drier than those in the Sierra Nevada. Moreover, although Minnich and his collaborators argue that fire suppression is minimal in the uplands, there is a history of grazing and related land use changes in the latter half of the twentieth century concentrated in the lowlands surrounding the Sierra San Pedro Mártir that may have altered patterns of fire occurrence in recent decades. Nevertheless, observations from the Sierra San Pedro Mártir provide a useful perspective on the general nature of fire regimes in the Sierra Nevada and emphasize the potential ecological importance of larger fires in the landscape. Minnich et al. (2000) reconstructed fire history for the period from the early 1920s to the late 1980s with a historical sequence of air photos from the Sierra San Pedro Mártir. They reported that the majority of fires in this period were less than 5 ha in area. (Remotely sensed imagery is subject to spatial resolution limits in discerning small areal events, so small fires may be even more common, but undetected in this work.) They emphasized the ecological significance of larger fires in their data set, with 10 percent of detected fires consuming more than 90 percent of the burned area. The three largest fires each burned more than 6,400 ha. Their reconstructions of burn geometry produced an estimated fire return interval of 52 years, with a range from 38 to 85 years, depending on vegetation type. This is substantially longer than estimates derived from fire-scar reconstructions in pre-European mixed-conifer forests of the Sierra Nevada, although comparisons are complicated by the differential spatial sensitivities of the techniques used to record individual events. Minnich and his collaborators noted considerable heterogeneity of burn patterns within fire perimeters in mixed-conifer forests of the Sierra San Pedro Mártir, with estimates of 23–31 percent of burned areas experiencing intense surface fires, and about 16 percent of the area within burn perimeters experiencing greater than 90 percent canopy-tree mortality. Although some caution in making a direct analogy between the modern Sierra San Pedro Mártir and the pre-European Sierra Nevada is warranted, these results lend additional support to the importance of larger, more intense fires in shaping mixed-conifer forest dynamics in California uplands, and they underscore the spatial heterogeneity of burn intensity produced by individual fires.

Ignition Sources and Fire in the Sierra Nevada

One of the earliest arguments favoring the importance of burning by indigenous peoples was Reynolds's (1959) assertion that lightning incidence was inadequate to account for the high frequency of fires evident from fire-history reconstructions in lower-elevation Sierran forests. This assertion was not based on direct evidence, but rather the relative uncommonness of thunderstorms in lowland California. Vankat (1977) has occasionally been cited to support this claim, but that is a clear misrepresentation of his position. Although he quotes Reynolds's thesis as a suggestion that lightning was an inadequate ignition source to account for fires at lower elevations in the Sierra, he prefaces this citation by observing that "the ecological significance of this [aboriginal] burning is unclear, since lightning fires have always been frequent in the dry summer environment of the Sierra Nevada" (Vankat 1977:19). Biswell (1989), in a chapter on lightning and human ignition sources for California wildfires, noted that lightning has been historically underestimated as an ignition source in California lowlands. He described direct ignition of grassy surface fuels by lightning and summarized a small data set from the 1940s and 1950s that suggested relatively high lightning-fire incidence in California lowlands.

Within the past two decades, several works have illuminated the geography of lightning and lightning-caused fires in California uplands. Vankat (1983) and van Wagtendonk (1986) produced spatial summaries of lightning-caused fires that occurred during the twentieth century. The observation period corresponds with an era of aggressive fire suppression, so that numbers of fires and especially area burned may not be indicative of pre-European conditions in all vegetation types. Nevertheless, the spatial patterns of ignitions identified are probably accurate. Vankat reported 848 lightning-caused fires from 1921 to 1982 in Sequoia National Park (0.84 fires per 100 square km per year); van Wagtendonk reported 2,023 such fires from 1930 to 1983 in Yosemite National Park (1.22 fires per 100 square km per year). In both parks, lightning-caused fires were predominantly located in the western half of the park, at lower to middle elevations. Both authors found spatial relationships between fire and topography, with more fires on westerly exposures and ridge tops. Both identified the highest lightning-fire incidence in lower- to midelevation mixed-conifer forests, despite the fact that lightning strikes are more common at higher elevations in the eastern half of each park. In both cases, lightning fires were more frequent than would have been expected by chance in ponderosa pine–dominated mixed-conifer forests. The twentieth-century record of lightning fires from these parks reveals that lightning-caused fires are potentially abundant. Some 80 to 85 percent of lightning-caused fires in both Sequoia and Yosemite National Parks occurred from July to September. The high incidence of dry thunderstorms in this period corresponds with the most pronounced seasonal soil-moisture deficits.

McKelvey and Busse (1996) provided a similar environmental analysis of patterns of lightning fires on national forest lands of the Sierra Nevada during the twentieth century. They found a strong and stable elevational gradient in the incidence of lightning fires, with fires far more common at lower elevations (peaking at 500–1000 m). Large fires were common in hot, dry years, although such conditions alone did not ensure widespread lightning fire in the Sierra. They reported results of a logistic regression analysis that discriminates between burned and unburned terrain; lower elevation, steeper slopes, and drier settings were associated with lightning fires in Sierran national forests. Like Vankat and van Wagtendonk, they found a high occurrence of fires in ponderosa pine forests, with actual burned area exceeding expectations based on a random areal standard.

With the development of lightning detection networks, van Wagtendonk (1991) reported that lightning struck in the region of Yosemite National Park approximately 2,000 times per year in the 6-year period from 1985 to 1990 (65 strikes per 100 square km per year), although interannual variability in lightning-strike frequencies was apparent. Lightning frequency was greatest along the Sierran crest in the eastern portion of the park and least at lower elevations on the western margin of the park. Van Wagtendonk commented that despite the low lightning frequency recorded at lower elevations, occasional lightning-caused fires have burned substantial acreage; an August 1990 fire ignited at 1,200 m burned more than 8,000 ha.

Summaries of lightning-flash measurements from the National Lightning Detection Network for the period from 1992 to 1998 (Orville and Silver 1997; Orville and Huffines 1999) confirm van Wagtendonk's lightning-strike density estimates of less than 100 strikes per 100 square km per year and substantiate the relatively low lightning-strike density over California, compared with much of the rest of the contiguous United States. Maps of median peak current for positive polarity lightning strikes indicate high values over California, with amperage measures among the highest in the contiguous United States (at least for the 3-year period reported in Orville and Huffines [1999]). Whereas lightning-strike density is low over California, the current carried by individual strikes is high. Although I know of no direct evidence demonstrating that peak-current delivery is correlated with ignition probability, this relationship is plausible and, if valid, suggests that lightning strikes may be effective ignition agents over California. Clearly, this relationship merits testing.

Minnich et al. (1993) reported on lightning-strike densities and related them to lightning-caused fires in the Sierra Juarez and Sierra San Pedro Mártir of northern Baja California. In the Sierra Juarez, a lower-elevation range where convective thunderstorms are uncommon, they reported about seventeen times more lightning strikes than lightning fires. In the higher Sierra San Pedro Mártir, lightning strikes occurred forty six times more often than lightning fires. Minnich et al. concluded that both ranges were supersaturated with lightning strikes and that fire incidence was related more to fuel accumulation than to ignition source.

Minnich (1987) and Caprio and Swetnam (1995) both emphasized the importance of long-burning fires in California uplands. After an ignition event, fires may alternate between flaming combustion and glowing combustion, depending on meteorological conditions. Fires banked in large-diameter fuels, such as logs, often smolder for weeks, only to reignite when meteorological conditions become favorable. Thus, a single lightning strike may account for an extended period of burning over a fairly large area. Minnich noted that, prior to the twentieth century, such fires were often not fully extinguished until the following winter wet season began. As a consequence of this banking behavior, Parsons (1981) observed that few ignitions are needed to burn large areas of chaparral and oak woodland in the foothills of the Sierra Nevada.

Based on the geography of lightning fires and patterns of burning, there appears to be ample, although not abundant, lightning incidence to account for the frequency and scale of fires (determined from fire scars) throughout the mountainous uplands of California (Vale 1998). Claims regarding the inadequacy of lightning strikes to account for historical patterns of burning appear to be exaggerated, particularly in lower-elevation mixed-conifer forests dominated by ponderosa pine (where advocates of human agency have focused their claims).

This leaves open for debate a fundamental question regarding the role of cultural burning in modifying a landscape: To what extent does ignition source influence the geography of fire? The preponderance of evidence from fire-prone ecosystems—such as the lodgepole pine forests of the Yellowstone Plateau (Romme and Despain 1989), the chaparral of the coastal hills of California and Baja California (Minnich 1983), and the mixed-conifer forests of the Sierra San Pedro Mártir (Minnich et al. 2000)—suggests that fuel accumulation patterns are far more influential than ignition source in governing the timing and spatial extent of fires. Crown fires in the Yellowstone Plateau recur after protracted intervals of forest growth (perhaps 200–300 years), prior to which the fuel mosaic does not readily carry fire. Similarly, chaparral will reburn only after a sufficient refractory period of 20–30 years, and mixed-conifer forests exhibit a similar delay in fire recurrence related to development of the requisite fuel loading (ca. 50 years, according to Minnich et al. 2000). Once sufficient fuels exist, meteorological conditions often determine when fires occur, since the fuel's moisture content must be relatively low. Assuming adequate concentration of dried fuels, fire is highly likely, regardless of ignition source.

Minnich et al. (1993) developed a conceptual model that contrasts fire regimes between vegetation types dominated by herbaceous versus woody fuels. According to these authors, herbaceous fuels exhibit a short refractory period—fuels return to preburn levels rapidly, so that fires may recur frequently. In drier environments of the West, herbaceous fuel accumulation and fire risk are maximized following wet years. Fires in settings with an herbaceous fuel matrix burn in a spatially random manner, without regard to past burn patterns. Miller and Urban (1999b), in a spatially explicit climate/vegetation/fire model of surface fire regimes in the Sierra Nevada, derived similar outcomes in simulations for herbaceous fuel settings. They observed considerable spatial heterogeneity in patterns of fire effects in their simulations of herbaceous-fuel-dominated systems. In contrast to herbaceous fuels, Minnich et al. (1993) characterized woody fuels as possessing long refractory periods; buildup of fuel accumulations capable of carrying a fire is delayed. In woody-fuel-dominated systems, fire perimeters are often nonoverlapping. Older patches with sufficient fuel burn to the edges of surrounding younger patches that lack adequate fuel to sustain a fire. Both chaparral and mixed-conifer forests conform to this spatially and temporally self-limiting behavior, according to Minnich and Vizcaíno (1998). Christensen (1993:237) invoked similar logic in his review of fire regimes and ecosystem dynamics when he observed: "On many landscapes, fire frequency is less determined by ignition events [than] by fuel and landscape conditions that determine fire spread."

Applying these contrasts in fire-regime properties between herbaceous- and woody-fuel-dominated settings, ignition source is probably only a potential influence on fire frequency where herbaceous fuels recharge rapidly. In the Sierra Nevada, vegetation in parts of the lower montane zone, including oak savanna and foothills or ponderosa pine woodland, possess sufficient herbaceous fuels to allow the possibility of human-caused fires to increase the frequency of lightning ignitions. Even here, however, interannual climatic variability and topographic complexity would impose limits on patterns of accumulation, continuity, and flammability of herbaceous fuels.

Fire as a Landscape Element or Cultural Artifact?

Parsons et al. (1986:22), in a review of fire management practices in the Sierra Nevada, observed that Sierran plant communities "have evolved with periodic fire for tens of thousands of years." Although some have suggested that humans have promoted oak and grass species through planting and burning practices (Anderson 1997), Adam et al. (1989) documented fairly continuous and abundant concentrations of oak and grass pollen in a 3-million-year-long core recovered from Tule Lake in northeastern California. Moreover, Adam and West (1983) used a ratio of oak and pine pollen abundance from Clear Lake (in the northern coastal range) to provide a crude temperature index for northern California over the last 130,000 years. This link between oak abundance and temperature characteristics underscores the responsiveness of oak species to climatic controls; oak pollen abundance was greater at the peak of the previous interglacial than at any time during the Holocene, including the Altithermal. If humans have deliberately augmented the abundance of oak species, it has been too recent or too localized to have been recorded in such reconstructions.

Anderson (1997:23) asserted a cultural origin for several vegetation types: "Ecosystem diversity was also enhanced through the maintenance of ecosystems that would disappear in the absence of human influence, including coastal prairies, dry montane meadows, and mixed conifer forests where black oak and ponderosa pine predominate." The evidence on which this claim is based, however, is tenuous, at best. For ponderosa-pine/black oak–dominated mixed-conifer forests, the proof of her strong assertion rests on Kilgore and Taylor's (1979) assumption that lightning was inadequate to account for fire frequencies in mixed-conifer forests (an assumption that appears to be unfounded) and that black oaks have been overtopped by more shade-tolerant conifers in the last 100 years. The latter observation is virtually assured, given the modern fire suppression policy. Allowing fires to burn in this zone would return frequent small and occasional large fires to the vegetation mosaic. California black oaks would probably respond favorably to occasional intense fires, because they would benefit for several decades after burning by their habit of resprouting from root collars. Fire suppression is the culprit here, regardless of the ignition source. The logic behind Anderson's inclusion of ponderosa pine as an artifact of aboriginal management activities is unclear, given its long record in the regional flora (Edlund and Byrne 1991) and its propensity to experience lightning fires in the historical record (Vankat 1983; van Wagtendonk 1986).

Anderson's assertion that dry montane meadows in the Sierra Nevada are an artifact of cultural burning is equally dubious. Koehler and Anderson (1994) noted that several authors uncritically proclaim that dry meadows first appeared in the Sierra around 3,000 B.P. They suggested that this is a misimpression promoted by the lack of radiometrically datable materials from meadow sediments prior to this time. These authors identified older dry meadow sediments in Nichols Meadow (11,500 to 8,700 B.P.), based on pedogenesis in paleosols. They observed that many modern dry meadows in the Sierra contain these old paleosols and hence extend back at least to the early Holocene. Indeed, Davis and Moratto (1988) observed the presence of dung spores in the basal Graminae zone of Exchequer Meadow, dated at 13,500–10,700 B.P. They linked this evidence of excrement with the presence of large grazing mammals in Sierran dry meadows of that period. The origin of dry montane meadows more likely lies in a long history of pest infestations that defoliate trees and create open treeless patches where grasses can gain a foothold in the vegetation mosaic. In the case of both ponderosa pine/black oak mixed-conifer forests and dry montane meadows, there is little if any evidence to support the contention that they (or any other vegetation type in the Sierra Nevada) are a human artifact dependent on cultural burning for their very existence.

Nature, Culture, Evidence, and Academic Roots

Discord over the role of indigenous humans in shaping the landscape is fueled by contrasts in the academic roots and ideological affinities of the principal voices in this debate (see Vale, chapter 1 of this volume). Evidence that argues against a pervasive role for aboriginal humans in shaping the Sierra Nevada landscape comes primarily from physical and biological scientists, foresters, and fire ecologists, who have addressed issues of late Quaternary paleoenvironments, precontact fire regimes, and the geography of lightning and lightning-caused fires. Their evidence is principally physical, and taken in aggregate, it provides a logically consistent history of climate/vegetation/fire linkages that have operated to structure the Sierran landscape over the last 20,000 years, primarily without significant human alteration.

Evidence favoring the view that humans have domesticated the Sierran landscape comes primarily from human geographers and cultural anthropologists. After the early work of Reynolds and Lewis, M. Kat Anderson has championed the role of indigenous humans as agents of landscape change in the Sierra Nevada. Most of the evidence presented to support this position is ethnographic, based on interviews of past and present living elders descended from Sierran tribal communities. These individuals presumably retain an oral tradition of past lifeways; some still practice traditional arts, such as basket-weaving. Beyond these interviews, there is virtually no physical evidence available to evaluate the assertion of pervasive human modification of the Sierran landscape prior to European contact. That indigenous peoples used fire as a tool to improve their material economy is undeniable. It is the spatial extent and ecological importance of that influence on which the debate hinges. We are left to weigh the words of those with memories of a former time against the incomplete physical evidence of past environments. Logical inference is all that may be available to resolve this debate, and that logic will always be subject to challenge.

Much of the work of Anderson and others who champion the image of a Sierra domesticated by aboriginal humans is reasoned, cautious, and scholarly. Work on the ethnobotany of culturally significant taxa, such as deergrass (*Muhlenbergia rigens*), is well designed, carefully executed, and convincing in detail (Anderson 1996). Even in more strident voice, some of Anderson's claims are tempered with appropriate caution, as when Anderson and Moratto (1996) observe that human influence in the Sierra Nevada varied in space and time, with some areas maintained solely by lightning fires, some areas reflecting a mix of lightning and human-caused fires, and some areas largely shaped by anthropogenic forces.

Blackburn and Anderson (1993) observe that many ecologists and physical scientists are slow to embrace the anecdotal nature of ethnographic data and bemoan the lack of quantitative or experimental evidence that would address this shortcoming. This does not dissuade them from making a number of sweeping assertions that approach hyperbole. To what extent is Blackburn and Anderson's belief in the broad scope of aboriginal human influence in pre-European California rooted in a desire to preserve cultural diversity? Anderson (1997) pursues this line vigorously when she attempts to entangle cultural and biological diversity. She assumes that environmental well-being is linked to maintenance of biological diversity, which, in turn, she assumes, is a product of cultural diversity. By losing indigenous culture, we lose environmental health. But there is little empirical evidence to support either of these assumptions in the Sierra Nevada, just a strong urge to atone for past sins of aggression and transgression, both cultural and environmental. Anderson's words are charged with a political agenda: put the Sierra back in the hands of native peoples, who, in the image of the Noble Savage, were excellent stewards of the land. This resurrection of the Noble Savage image is keenly expressed by Heizer and Elsasser (1980:59–60), whom Anderson quotes to introduce her chapter (Anderson 1993) on native Californians as ancient and contemporary cultivators:

> The California Indians were highly accomplished practical botanists, perhaps as knowledgeable about subtle differences in form, color, and behavior as some university professors who have spent their adult lives reading and making field observations. But they were also knowledgeable in a different way—a way directed at understanding nature in such a manner as to use it without destroying it.

Anderson claims that we can learn much about sustainability by emulating the ways of Sierran indigenous cultures. By making such claims, she attempts to seize a moral high ground that unites a common sympathy for environmental well-being and displaced indigenous cultures. Nostalgia is a strong force in this politically charged linkage, but nostalgia should not serve as the basis of a land management policy, nor should it be used to advocate exacting restoration of a specific vegetation cover, when the heterogeneity, in both space and time, of vegetation and fire regimes in the Sierra Nevada is substantial and shows strong linkages to the operation of broader natural forces, such as climatic change (Vale 1987; Sprugel 1991). In short, nostalgia and political agendas are no substitute for valid evidence.

Concluding Remarks

What were the relative roles of aboriginal humans and the physical environment in shaping Sierra Nevada vegetation? The majority of the evidence favors a strong role for physical environmental controls. In specific places and times, such as areas of intense human settlement in the centuries preceding European contact, humans most likely opened forests and maintained preferred plants by judicious use of fire. Undoubtedly, there were localized tracts of land that were significantly altered by human settlement and cultural burning, such as Yosemite and Hetch Hetchy Valley. One might readily envision a geographic gradient of influence: from intensive alternations in the immediate vicinity of larger settlements in the lowlands; to less intense but still significant sporadic influences in adjacent foothills and lower montane vegetation types, as well as around frequently used summer camps in the High Sierra; to decreasing cultural influence on vegetation mosaics in higher-elevation forests, tundra, and east-slope environments. Despite these cultural effects, pollen, charcoal, macrofossil, and tree-ring records converge to portray an extended environmental history of climatic control of fire and vegetation dynamics across the breadth of the Sierra Nevada. Fire is a virtual certainty in the Sierran environment, given its climatic rhythms of fuel accumulation and drying. Postglacial climates have fluctuated substantially, forcing concomitant changes in vegetation patterns and fire regimes at timescales ranging from decades to millennia. Against this backdrop, the effect of aboriginal human populations appears to have been limited by relatively small population sizes and by geographic constraints on the distribution of larger settlements (primarily at lower elevations in the Sierra along major drainages).

Formerly, lightning was underestimated by some as an agent of ignition in lower-elevation Sierran environments. Direct evidence of lightning fires in the past century indicates that lower-elevation mixed-conifer forests, especially those dominated by ponderosa pine, burned often. Traditional characterizations of frequent, light-burning, localized fires may understate the importance of more ecologically significant larger fires, which occasionally burned with great intensity in Sierran mixed-conifer forests. The habit of fire, which may alternately rage for days and then smolder for weeks in larger fuels, allows few ignition events to induce complex patterns of burning. Ultimately, ignition source is probably of less ecological importance to the operation of fire regimes of the Sierra than are fuel-accumulation patterns and architecture, meteorological circumstances, topography, and spatial heterogeneity of vegetation cover. Within some parts of this naturally maintained matrix, areas of higher settlement density and repeated human use may have been modified in significant ways by the actions of aboriginal people, especially through their use of fire. But there is little physical evidence to suggest that they moved the vegetation mosaic outside of the bounds of naturally occurring variability or that they manipulated vegetation cover over large areas of the Sierra Nevada.

What additional research would illuminate or embellish our understanding of aboriginal human agents of change in the Sierran landscape? Reconstructions of opal phytolith concentrations in Sierran soils during the late Quaternary might provide insights into the prominence of grasses as important herbaceous fuels in selected Sierran ecosystems, such as mixed-conifer forests. Widespread and persistent presence of herbaceous fuels would admit the possibility of an increase in fire frequencies over that likely from lightning-caused fires alone, although widespread herbaceous fuel would facilitate the spread of all fires, regardless of ignition source. To date, I know of no published work on opal phytoliths in the Sierra Nevada. Careful examination of fire scars to establish the seasonality of fires and how that seasonality might have changed over time could provide some evidence for aboriginal human influence, at least in settings where humans ignited brush prior to the peak of the lightning-fire season to control the intensity of fires. To date, investigations of fire seasonality reveal a strong concentration of fires in the late summer, when lightning-caused burns are most common (Swetnam et al. 1992, 1998). With the development of an increasingly sophisticated lightning-detection network, the broad outlines of the geography of lightning strikes should fill in. Reconstructions of fire regimes that explore the contribution of larger, more intense fires in mixed-conifer forests would be most useful. This understanding, coupled with reconstruction of fire regimes in settings other than mixed-conifer forests, would greatly increase understanding and management of Sierran vegetation resources. The gap-based simulation models of Sierran surface fire regimes developed by Miller and Urban (1999a, 1999b) promise another fruitful avenue of exploration of the natural heterogeneity of postfire landscapes and may help identify the range of historical variability of vegetation structures in mixed-conifer forests of the Sierra Nevada. Finally, as Anderson (1997) observes, there is more need for interdisciplinary communication and joint study of Sierran environments, so that a comprehensive image of the environmental history of the Sierra Nevada may be forged by persuasive evidence, rather than strident opinion.

Literature Cited

Adam, D. P., and G. J. West. 1983. Temperature and precipitation estimates through the last glacial cycle from Clear Lake, California, pollen data. *Science* 219:168–170.

Adam, D. P., A. M. Sarna-Wojcicki, H. J. Rieck, J. P. Bradbury, W. E. Dean, and R. M. Forester. 1989. Tulelake, California: The last 3 million years. *Palaeogeography, Palaeoclimatology, Palaeoecology* 72:89–103.

Anderson, K. 1993. Native Californians as ancient and contemporary cultivators. Pp. 55–116 in *Before the wilderness: Environmental management by native Californians*, ed. T. C. Blackburn and K. Anderson. Menlo Park, Calif.: Ballena.

Anderson, M. K. 1996. The ethnobotany of deergrass, *Muhlenbergia rigens* (Poaceae): Its uses and fire management by California Indian tribes. *Economic Botany* 50:409–422.

———. 1997. California's endangered peoples and endangered ecosystems. *American Indian Culture and Research Journal* 21:7–31.

Anderson, M. K., and M. J. Moratto. 1996. Native American land-use practices and ecological impacts. Pp. 187–206 in *Sierra Nevada Ecosystem Project: Final report to Congress*, vol. 2: *Assessments and scientific basis for management options*. Davis: University of California, Davis, Centers for Water and Wildland Resources.

Anderson, M. K., M. G. Barbour, and V. Whitworth. 1997. A world of balance and plenty: Land, plants, animals, and humans in a pre-European California. *California History* 76:12–47.

Anderson, R. S. 1990. Holocene forest development and paleoclimates within the central Sierra Nevada, California. *Journal of Ecology* 78:470–489.

Anderson, R. S., and S. L. Carpenter. 1991. Vegetation change in Yosemite Valley, Yosemite National Park, California, during the protohistoric period. *Madroño* 38:1–13.

Anderson, R. S., and S. J. Smith. 1994. Paleoclimatic interpretations of meadow sediment and pollen stratigraphies from California. *Geology* 22:723–726.

———. 1997. The sedimentary record of fire in montane meadows, Sierra Nevada, California, USA: A preliminary analysis. Pp. 313–327 in *Sediment records of biomass burning and global change*, ed. J. S. Clark, C. Cachier, J. G. Goldammer, and B. Stocks. Berlin: Springer-Verlag.

Barbour, M. G. 1988. California upland forests and woodlands. Pp. 131–164 in *North American terrestrial vegetation*, ed. M. G. Barbour and W. D. Billings. Cambridge: Cambridge University Press.

Barbour, M., B. Pavlik, F. Drysdale, and S. Lindstrom. 1993. *California's changing landscapes: Diversity and conservation of California vegetation.* Sacramento: California Native Plant Society.

Biswell, H. H. 1967. Forest fire in perspective. *Proceedings of the Tall Timbers Ecology Conference* 7:43–63.

———. 1989. *Prescribed burning in California wildlands vegetation management.* Berkeley: University of California Press.

Blackburn, T., and K. Anderson. 1993. Introduction: Managing the domesticated environment. Pp. 15–25 in *Before the wilderness: Environmental management by native Californians*, ed. T. C. Blackburn and K. Anderson. Menlo Park, Calif.: Ballena.

Bonnicksen, T. M., and E. C. Stone. 1985. Restoring naturalness to national parks. *Environmental Management* 9:479–486.

Caprio, A. C., and T. W. Swetnam. 1995. Historic fire regimes along an elevational gradient on the west slope of the Sierra Nevada, California. Pp. 173–179 in *Proceedings: Symposium on fire in wilderness and park management, March 30–April 1, 1993, Missoula, Montana*, ed. J. K. Brown, R. W. Mutch, C. W. Spoon, and R. H. Wakimoto. General technical report INT-320. Ogden, Utah: USDA Forest Service, Intermountain Research Station.

Chang, C. 1996. Ecosystem responses to fire and variations in fire regimes. Pp. 1071–1099 in *Sierra Nevada Ecosystem Project: Final report to Congress*, vol. 2: *Assessments and scientific basis for management options*. Davis: University of California, Davis, Centers for Water and Wildland Resources.

Chappell, C. B., and J. K. Agee. 1996. Fire severity and tree seedling establishment in *Abies magnifica* forests, southern Cascades, Oregon. *Ecological Applications* 6:628–640.

Christensen, N. L. 1993. Fire regimes and ecosystem dynamics. Pp. 233–244 in *Fire in the environment: The ecological, atmospheric, and climatic importance of vegetation fires*, ed. P. J. Crutzen and J. G. Goldammer. New York: John Wiley.

Cook, S. F. 1955. The aboriginal population of the San Joaquin Valley, California. *University of California Anthropological Records* 16:31–80.

Davis, O. K., and M. J. Moratto. 1988. Evidence for a warm dry early Holocene in the western Sierra Nevada of California: Pollen and plant macrofossil analysis of Dinkey and Exchequer Meadows. *Madroño* 35:132–149.

Edlund, E. G., and R. Byrne. 1991. Climate, fire, and late Quaternary vegetation change in the central Sierra Nevada. Pp. 390–396 in *Fire and the environment: Ecological and cultural perspectives*, ed. S. S. Nodvin and T. A. Waldrop. Asheville, N.C.: USDA Forest Service, Southeastern Forest Experiment Station.

Graumlich, L. J. 1993. A 1000-year record of temperature and precipitation in the Sierra Nevada. *Quaternary Research* 39:249–255.

Heizer, R. F., and A. B. Elsasser. 1980. *The natural world of the California Indians*. California natural history guides no. 46. Berkeley: University of California Press.

Kilgore, B. M. 1973. The ecological role of fire in Sierran conifer forests. *Quaternary Research* 3:496–513.

Kilgore, B. M., and D. Taylor. 1979. Fire history of a sequoia–mixed conifer forest. *Ecology* 60:129–142.

Kinney, W. C. 1996. Conditions of rangelands before 1905. Pp. 31–45 in *Sierra Nevada Ecosystem Project: Final report to Congress*, vol. 2: *Assessments and scientific basis for management options*. Davis: University California, Davis, Centers for Water and Wildland Resources.

Koehler, P. A., and R. S. Anderson. 1994. The paleoecology and stratigraphy of Nichols Meadow, Sierra National Forest, California, USA. *Palaeogeography, Palaeoclimatology, Palaeoecology* 112:1–17.

Landres, P. B., P. Morgan, and F. J. Swanson. 1999. Overview of the use of natural variability concepts in managing ecological systems. *Ecological Applications* 9:1179–1188.

Lewis, H. T. 1993. (Orig. pub. 1973.) Patterns of Indian burning in California: Ecology and ethnohistory. Pages 55–116 in *Before the wilderness: Environmental management by native Californians*, ed. T. C. Blackburn and K. Anderson. Menlo Park, Calif.: Ballena.

Lloyd, A. H., and L. J. Graumlich. 1997. Holocene dynamics of treeline forests in the Sierra Nevada. *Ecology* 78:1199–1210.

McKelvey, K. S., and K. K. Busse. 1996. Twentieth-century fire patterns on forest service lands. Pp. 1119–1153 in *Sierra Nevada Ecosystem Project: Final report to Congress*, vol. 2: *Assessments and scientific basis for management options*. Davis: University of California, Davis, Centers for Water and Wildland Resources.

McKelvey, K. S., and J. D. Johnston. 1992. Historical perspectives on forests of the Sierra Nevada and the Transverse Ranges of southern California: Forest conditions at the turn of the century. Pp. 225–246 in *The California spotted owl: A technical assessment of its current status*, ed. J. Verner, K. S. McKelvey, B. R. Noon, R. J. Gutierrez, G. I. Gould, Jr., and T. W. Beck. General technical report PSW-133. Albany, Calif.: USDA Forest Service, Pacific Southwest Research Station.

McKelvey, K. S., C. N. Skinner, C. Chang, D. C. Erman, S. J. Husari, D. J. Parsons, J. W. van Wagtendonk, and C. P. Weatherspoon. 1996. An overview of fire in the Sierra Nevada. Pp. 1033–1040 in *Sierra Nevada Ecosystem Project: Final report to Congress*, vol. 2: *Assessments and scientific basis for management options*. Davis: University of California, Davis, Centers for Water and Wildland Resources.

Millar, C. I., and W. B. Woolfenden. 1999. The role of climate change in interpreting historical variability. *Ecological Applications* 9:1207–1216.

Miller, C., and D. L. Urban. 1999a. A model of surface fire, climate, and forest pattern in the Sierra Nevada, California. *Ecological Modelling* 114:113–135.

———. 1999b. Interactions between forest heterogeneity and surface fire regimes in the southern Sierra Nevada. *Canadian Journal of Forest Research* 29:202–212.

Minnich, R. A. 1983. Fire mosaics in southern California and northern Baja California. *Science* 219:1287–1294.

———. 1987. Fire behavior in southern California chaparral before fire control: The Mount Wilson burns at the turn of the century. *Annals of the Association of American Geographers* 77:599–618.

———. 1988. *The biogeography of fire in the San Bernadino Mountains of California*. Berkeley: University of California Press.

Minnich, R. A., M. G. Barbour, J. H. Burk, and J. Sosa-Ramírez. 2000. California mixed-conifer forests under unmanaged fire regimes in the Sierra San Pedro Mártir, Baja California, Mexico. *Journal of Biogeography* 27:105–129.

Minnich, R. A., and E. F. Vizcaíno. 1998. *Land of chamise and pines: Historical accounts and current status of northern Baja California's vegetation*. University of California Publications in Botany No. 80. Berkeley: University of California Press.

Minnich, R. A., E. F. Vizcaíno, J. Sosa-Ramírez, and Y.-E. Chou. 1993. Lightning detection rates and wildland fires in the mountains of northern Baja California, Mexico. *Atmósfera* 6:235–253.

Moratto, M. J. 1984. The Sierra Nevada. Pp. 285–338 in *California archeology*, ed. M. J. Moratto. Orlando: Academic Press.

Moratto, M. J., T. F. King, and W. B. Woolfenden. 1978. Archeology and California climate. *Journal of California Anthropology* 5:147–161.

Muir, J. 1894. *The mountains of California*. Berkeley, Calif.: Ten Speed Press.

Orville, R. E., and G. R. Huffines. 1999. Lightning ground flash measurements over the contiguous United States: 1995–1997. *Monthly Weather Review* 127:2693–2703.

Orville, R. E., and A. C. Silver. 1997. Lightning ground flash density in the contiguous United States: 1992–1995. *Monthly Weather Review* 125:631–638.

Parker, A. J. 1989. Forest/environment relationships in Yosemite National Park, California. *Vegetatio* 82:41–54.

Parsons, D. J. 1981. The historic role of fire in the foothill communities of Sequoia National Park. *Madroño* 28:111–120.

Parsons, D. J., D. M. Graber, J. K. Agee, and J. W. Van Wagtendonk. 1986. Natural fire management in national parks. *Environmental Management* 10:21–24.

Peri, D. W., and S. M. Patterson. 1993. (Orig. pub. 1976.) "The basket is in the roots, that's where it begins." Pp. 175–193 in *Before the wilderness: Environmental management by native Californians*, ed. T. C. Blackburn and K. Anderson. Menlo Park, Calif.: Ballena.

Potter, D. A. 1998. *Forested communities of the upper montane in the central and southern Sierra Nevada*. General technical report PSW-169. Albany, Calif.: USDA Forest Service, Pacific Southwest Research Station.

Raab, L. M., and D. O. Larson. 1997. Medieval climatic anomaly and punctuated cultural evolution in coastal southern California. *American Antiquity* 62:319–336.

Reynolds, R. D. 1959. The effect upon the forest of natural fire and aboriginal burning in the Sierra Nevada. Master's thesis, University of California, Berkeley.

Romme, W. H., and D. G. Despain. 1989. Historical perspectives on the Yellowstone fires of 1988. *BioScience* 39:695–699.

Skinner, C. N., and C. Chang. 1996. Fire regimes, past and present. Pp. 1041–1069 in *Sierra Nevada Ecosystem Project: Final report to Congress*, vol. 2: *Assessments and scientific basis for management options*. Davis: University of California, Davis, Centers for Water and Wildland Resources.

Smith, S. J., and R. S. Anderson. 1992. Late Wisconsin paleoecologic record from Swamp Lake, Yosemite National Park, California. *Quaternary Research* 38:91–102.

SNEP Science Team and Special Consultants. 1996. *Sierra Nevada Ecosystem Project: Final report to Congress*, vol. 1: *Assessment summaries and management strategies*. Davis: University of California, Davis, Centers for Water and Wildland Resources.

Sprugel, D. G. 1991. Disturbance, equilibrium, and environmental variability: What is "natural" vegetation in a changing environment? *Biological Conservation* 58:1–18.

Stephenson, N. L. 1999. Reference conditions for giant sequoia forest restoration: Structure, process, and precision. *Ecological Applications* 9:1253–1265.

Stephenson, N. L., D. J. Parsons, and T. W. Swetnam. 1991. Restoring natural fire to the sequoia–mixed conifer forest: Should intense fire play a role? *Proceedings of the Tall Timbers Fire Ecology Conference* 17:321–337.

Swetnam, T. W. 1993. Fire history and climate change in giant sequoia groves. *Science* 262:885–889.

Swetnam, T. W., C. H. Baisan, A. C. Caprio, R. R. Touchan, and P. M. Brown. 1992. *Tree-ring reconstruction of giant sequoia fire regimes*. Final report to Sequoia and Kings Canyon National Parks. Tucson: Laboratory of Tree-Ring Research, University of Arizona.

Swetnam, T. W., C. H. Baisan, K. Morino, and A. C. Caprio. 1998. *Fire history along elevational transects in the Sierra Nevada, California*. Final report to Sierra Nevada Global Change Research Program, United States Geological Survey, Biological Resources Division, Sequoia, Kings Canyon, and Yosemite National Parks. Tucson: Laboratory of Tree-Ring Research, University of Arizona.

Taylor, A. H., and C. B. Halpern. 1991. The structure and dynamics of *Abies magnifica* forests in the southern Cascade Range, USA. *Journal of Vegetation Science* 2:189–200.

Turner, M. G., V. H. Dale, and E. H. Everham. 1997. Fires, hurricanes, and volcanoes: Comparing large disturbances. *BioScience* 47:758–768.

Vale, T. R. 1987. Vegetation change and park purposes in the high elevations of Yosemite National Park, California. *Annals of the Association of American Geographers* 77:1–18.

———. 1998. The myth of the humanized landscape: An example from Yosemite National Park. *Natural Areas Journal* 18:231–236.

Vankat, J. L. 1977. Fire and man in Sequoia National Park. *Annals of the Association of American Geographers* 67:17–27.

———. 1982. A gradient perspective on the vegetation of Sequoia National Park, California. *Madroño* 29:200–214.

———. 1983. General patterns of lightning ignitions in Sequoia National Park, California. Pp. 408–411 in *Proceedings of the symposium and workshop on wilderness fire*, ed. J. E. Lotan, B. M. Kilgore, W. C. Fischer, and R. W. Mutch. General technical report INT-182. Ogden, Utah: USDA Forest Service, Intermountain Research Station.

Vankat, J. L., and J. Major. 1978. Vegetation changes in Sequoia National Park, California. *Journal of Biogeography* 5:377–402.

van Wagtendonk, J. W. 1986. The role of fire in the Yosemite wilderness. Pp. 2–9 in *Proceedings of the national wilderness research conference: Current research*, ed. R. C. Lucas. General technical report INT-212. Ogden, Utah: USDA Forest Service, Intermountain Research Station.

———. 1991. Spatial analysis of lightning strikes in Yosemite National Park. Pp. 605–611 in *Proceedings of the eleventh conference on fire and forest meteorology*, ed. P. Andrews and D. F. Potts. Bethesda, Md.: Society of American Foresters.

White, P. S., and S. T. A. Pickett. 1985. Natural disturbance and patch dynamics: An introduction. Pp. 3–13 in *The ecology of natural disturbance and patch dynamics*, ed. S. T. A. Pickett and P. S. White. Orlando: Academic Press.

Woolfenden, W. B. 1996. Quaternary vegetation history. Pp. 47–70 in *Sierra Nevada Ecosystem Project: Final report to Congress*, vol. 2: *Assessments and scientific basis for management options*. Davis: University of California, Davis, Centers for Water and Wildland Resources.

PRE-EUROPEAN FIRE IN CALIFORNIA CHAPARRAL

Jacob Bendix

The vegetation of California offers richness in both structure and composition, but no type is more intimately tied to fire than chaparral. This relationship lends import to assertions that the burning activities of native peoples influenced the chaparral. However, several lines of evidence suggest that human impacts were marginal: ethnographic records are ambiguous; natural factors of lightning and vegetation flammability seem adequate to account for the known fire record; stratigraphic data suggest no change in fire history through the time period of initial European contact; and the richness of species composition implies spatial differences in fire return times, a pattern more consistent with varying environmental conditions that influence natural burning than regular human controls on ignitions. After a brief introduction, each of these four major points will be discussed in detail.

Fire and Chaparral

California's chaparral is notable both for its flammability and for the adaptations of its component species to recurring fire. As with other sclerophyllous shrublands found in the Mediterranean-climate regions of the world, both the composition of the vegetation community and the characteristics of the individual species are known to be intimately related to fire (Keeley 1987, 1991; Keeley and Keeley 1988; Moreno and Oechel 1991).

Given the linkages between chaparral and fire, any suggestion that the pre-European fire regime was controlled by people implies by extension that the chaparral was (and is) actually something of a human artifact. Such an argument has been made explicitly by anthropologist Henry Lewis:

> The strategy of fall and spring burnings involved a quite different kind of "management" of the chaparral areas by both the intensification and a dramatic shift from the seasonality of natural fires. This idea implies, of course, that the Indians played a fundamental role, not only in the maintenance of the chaparral belt, but that they were probably active in the very evolution of California's chaparral. (1973:59)

Others have responded with skepticism, asserting that the fire adaptations of chaparral are better explained by a natural fire regime:

> There is no compelling evidence that the use of fire by Indians or any other primitive man had any effect in developing the adaptations to fire exhibited by the vegetation in California. . . . [F]ires due to natural causes—chiefly lightning—which have occurred since remote geologic time, have been a significant force in determining the characteristics and adaptations of our California chaparral. (Burcham 1974:117–118)

This chapter explores the possibility that native Californians actively altered the chaparral, managing it through their use of fire. Such exploration requires consideration of several interlocking questions: How common was anthropogenic ignition? How did anthropogenic ignition differ from natural ignition (i.e., lightning)? To what degree was the frequency and extent of fire determined by ignition, as opposed to fuel load and weather conditions? How important was fire in determining species composition and characteristics? And for each of these aspects, how much spatial variability was there within the overall area dominated by chaparral?

These questions are complicated somewhat by variance among scholars regarding the delineation of the area involved. California chaparral grows on steep terrain between sea level and 2,000 meters. It is common in the Coast and Transverse Ranges and in the western foothills of the Sierra Nevada. Chaparral's common occurrence in a mosaic with other vegetation types (Keeley and Keeley 1988) complicates the already complex task of delineating vegetation boundaries (Küchler 1973). The distribution shown in Figure 8.1 is conservative; it is based on Küchler

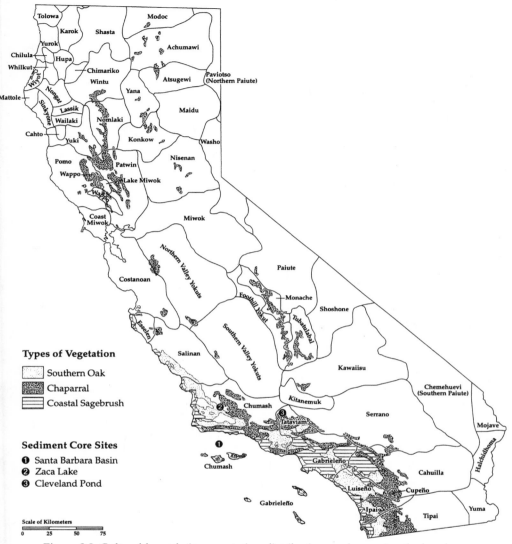

Figure 8.1. Cultural boundaries, vegetation distribution, and core sites (cultural and vegetation boundaries are from Donley et al. 1979:8, 147; sediment core locations are from Mensing 1993:31).

(1977), but covers a lesser area than the map illustrating Hanes's (1977) chapter on chaparral within that same volume. Lewis (1973) showed chaparral covering a still more expansive area, broadening the fringe around the Sacramento Valley and encompassing much of Southern California, including virtually all what Küchler (1977) mapped as coastal sagebrush and southern oak forest. Because these maps simply reflect varying degrees of cartographic generalization, none is inherently more "correct" than the others; therefore, Figure 8.1 is presented as a general guide rather than an definitive source.

Burning by Native Californians

The idea that Native Californians altered the chaparral through their use of fire is scarcely a new one. A half century ago, anthropologist Omer Stewart (1951) declared that the cessation of such burning had led to the substantial expansion of chaparral and cited Storer (1932) in support of this claim. Storer had, in fact, written about reduced burning, but in reference to fire suppression, with no mention of native burning. Because much of Stewart's article generalized about North America, it is unclear which purposes he felt were served by fire in the chaparral, although he did make reference to fire used as a tool of warfare in California and to fire as a protection from snakes for "barefoot California Indians" (Stewart 1951:320). Geographer Homer Aschmann (1959) also saw anthropogenic fire as a land-management tool with significant ecological impacts: "Above all, the Indians would burn the landscape to promote the growth of desired grasses and herbs. . . . Did it cause the degradation of a complex chaparral to the less useful chamise or coastal sage association or did it expand the oak-grassland parks?" (1959:48).

Henry Lewis and the Case for Anthropogenic Fire in Northern California

Whereas Stewart and Aschmann had made largely undocumented assertions, Lewis (1973) provided a coherent compilation of ethnohistorical evidence for native Californian burning in the northern and central parts of the state. This evidence was drawn from published records of interviews with native informants in the early twentieth century. The informants were discussing ancestral practices presumed to have been common before European and Euro-American contact. It is worth reviewing Lewis's contribution in some detail, because he provided the first data-based argument for extensive anthropogenic fire, because he inspired much of the interest and research on the topic (Blackburn and Anderson 1993), and because in the ensuing decades his work has been cited as authoritative on the topic (e.g., Aschmann 1977; Baumhoff 1978; Shipek 1989; Pyne et al. 1996).

Lewis (1973) began his description of the evidence for anthropogenic fire in the chaparral with extensive quotes from Harrington's (1932) Karok informant, who said her people used to "burn up the brush at various places, so that some good things will grow up" (Harrington

1932:63). She went on to make contradictory statements (as Lewis noted) about the timing of the fires:

> It is summer when they set fire to the brush, at the time when everything is dry, that is the time that is good to set fire, in the fall before it starts to rain. . . . they burn it any time in the summer. (Harrington 1932:64–65)

Was this informant actually discussing chaparral? Although Lewis's (1973) own map shows a substantial area of chaparral within the Karok territory, Küchler mapped no chaparral there (Figure 8.1); Baumhoff (1963), whom Lewis cites elsewhere as a source for similar information, lists less than 1.5 percent (15.1 square miles) of Karok area as chaparral. As Lewis himself noted, the "good things" growing after fire were more characteristic of coniferous forests than chaparral; they were "huckleberry bushes . . . hazel bushes . . . and the bear lilies" (Lewis 1973:51). None of the huckleberry species listed in Hickman (1993) is described as growing in chaparral. Hazel, presumably *Corylus cornuta*, used by the Karok for basket-making (Bright 1978; Anderson 1999) grows in many habitats (Hickman 1993), although in treatments of California vegetation it appears in descriptions of evergreen forest understory (Griffin 1977a; Franklin 1988) and is absent from those of chaparral (Hanes 1977; Keeley and Keeley 1988). Lewis took "bear lily" to be a reference to *Xerophyllum tenax*, another species that he noted was associated with coniferous forests. This same informant also mentioned tanbark oak and manzanita. Lewis described the former (*Lithocarpus densiflorus*) as being "effectively on the border" (1973:53) between chaparral and Douglas fir/redwood forests, but again it is generally described as occurring in various forest types (Barbour 1988; Franklin 1988), and not in chaparral (Keeley and Keeley, 1988). Many manzanita species, on the other hand, are indisputably characteristic of chaparral. Given the limited extent of chaparral in Karok territory and that most of the plants mentioned were actually atypical of chaparral, it is puzzling that Lewis used these quotes to establish chaparral burning.

The next native group discussed by Lewis were the Pomo, for whose customs he referenced Stewart (1943) and Kniffen (1939). According to Lewis, "In discussing both redwood forest and chaparral areas of the northern Pomo, Stewart notes that 'the brush was burned at intervals, making hunting much easier than at present'" (Lewis 1973:53–54). But if one reads Stewart's statement in its entirety, one gets a different impression:

> The plants in the redwood forests yielded tan-oak acorns, iris fiber, and berries; the forest was also hunting territory.

> The brush was burned at intervals, making hunting much
> easier that [sic] at present. Redwood bark was used for
> houses. (Stewart 1943:34)

The entire paragraph seems to refer to redwood forest, and the clearing
of brush within that forest. Nor is there mention of chaparral in the preceding or following paragraphs, suggesting that the reference to burning
was more far-reaching. This pattern holds true for the remaining references to Pomo fire in Stewart's (1943) monograph: "In Latcupda the
clearings in the forests were kept free of brush by annual burning" (48)
and "The usual openings in the trees, kept free from brush by burning,
furnished them bulbs and grass seeds" (51). These statements all seem
more consistent with firing of forest understory than of chaparral.

The applicability of Kniffen's statements about Pomo burning to the
chaparral is also equivocal. In his statements (which Lewis quoted extensively) about Redwood Valley in the Russian River watershed, he
described chaparral as occupying middle to high elevations:

> An association of live oak, black oak, and Oregon oak
> graded with altitude into a chaparral composed mainly of
> scrub oak, manzanita, buckbrush, and chamise, with fre-
> quent additions of madroña, Christmas berry, and the like.
> (Kniffen 1939:373)

But his reference to burning seems to describe lower elevation:

> Acorn gathering lasted until late November. That the gath-
> ering might be easier, all the dry weeds and brush were
> annually burned after the seed gathering was over, so that
> there remained no underbrush in the *valley or on the lower
> hillsides.* (Kniffen 1939:378; italics added)

Although Lewis concluded that "the pattern of autumn burning in the
chaparral areas was clearly stated" (1973:57), comparison of these statements suggests that fires were set in the oaks, below the chaparral.
Indeed, the chaparral of the hillside was valued as well, making it unlikely
that the Pomo would deliberately extend fire up to elevations where it
would destroy a significant food resource: "The first of the important
crops was the manzanita berry. . . . [T]he manzanitas of the hillsides, so
conspicuous in the chaparral, were communal property" (Kniffen
1939:378).

Similar questions arise for the Yurok and Tolowa, who, like the
Karok, had equivocal contact with chaparral. Baumhoff (1963) classified
more than 6 percent of the territory for each group (45.4 and 60.5

square miles, respectively) as chaparral, but Küchler (1977) mapped the same area as a mosaic of forest types, with no chaparral. Lewis (1973) quoted sources to the effect that both groups set fires to facilitate hunting and that the Tolowa specifically burned brush to keep clearings open in which grass would thrive, attracting deer. Lewis acknowledged that it was unclear whether either instance referred to chaparral, but thought it a reasonable assumption, since clearings in chaparral were known to be primary game areas. There appears to be no means of either proving or disproving these assumptions.

In the Sierran foothills, the Nisenan did clearly occupy an area inclusive of chaparral. Beals (1933) emphasized the importance of fall fire drives through brush in deer hunting, and Lewis's assumption that this was chaparral is not unreasonable. Beals also described fire use in preparation for tobacco planting: "Burn ground clear in winter, scatter seeds in ashes in spring" (1933:356). Lewis assumed that for burning to have been done in winter it must have been "Below the snowline and probably within the chaparral belt" (1973:56). But the existence of such a "belt" is questionable: most of this area is actually ponderosa pine forest and blue oak foothill pine forest, albeit with an understory inclusive of chaparral species and areas of interspersed chaparral (Küchler 1977). Of course, in any given locale the regime of anthropogenic fire may have helped to determine whether chaparral components like ceanothus and manzanita were dominant species or understory shrubs, or were entirely absent. Similarly, Lewis cited a source indicating that the Miwok planted tobacco in the spring on burnt ground; Lewis assumed this to be spring burning in chaparral, but the informant he cites does not specify the vegetation type, whether the burns were new or old, or whether the Miwok set the fires or exploited areas that had naturally burned.

Lewis also included grasshopper burning by the Wintu in his enumeration of chaparral fires, based on Du Bois's (1935) description. But the latter is quite specifically a reference to grassland, not chaparral:

> The grassy area was encircled by people who sang and danced as they whipped the grass and drove the grasshoppers into a center ring. The grass within the narrowed circle was then fired. (Du Bois 1935:14)

The Shasta used fire in hunting deer, but again Lewis's application of the available information to chaparral was purely speculative. He quotes Holt:

> . . . on the more open hills on the north side of the river, where the white oaks grew. When the oak leaves began to fall fires were set . . . in the late fall . . . they had the big

drive, encircling the deer with fire. (Holt, quoted in Lewis 1973:55)

Lewis asserted that "'the open hills on the north side of the river' would also be the areas of concentrated chaparral cover" (1973:55), but without any explanation as to why. He speculated that "white oak" was actually a reference to Oregon oak (*Quercus garryana*), which does indeed sometimes occur in stands of chaparral although commonly in other vegetation types (Griffin, 1977b). It is unclear why Holt's informants would have specified oaks if they were part of a dense scrubby mix; it seems at least as likely that the vegetation referred to was oak woodland or savanna (which would also have been an easier environment in which to control fire behavior).

In the valley of the Pit River, Lewis cited Kniffen's description of the Madesi subgroup of the Achumawi:

> The heavy precipitation results in a dense and varied vegetational cover. With the pine and fir of the hills are the manzanita, dogwood, yew, ash, maple and oak of the valley. What would have been a dense undergrowth was prevented by annual spring burnings following the retreating snow. (Kniffen 1929:314)

This is a difficult statement to interpret, as it refers to dense growth in one sentence and its absence in the next. But the reference to manzanita suggests that some chaparral components were reduced by deliberate burning in a setting where they might otherwise have had at least some prominence.

In his summation regarding native Californian burning of the chaparral, Lewis (1973) emphasized the seasonality he perceived in anthropogenic fire:

> The patterns of fall, and, secondarily, spring burning involve, not simply an intensification of the natural pattern of fires, since lightning fires occur during the summer and early fall, but, rather, a pronounced departure from the seasonal distribution of natural fires. (Lewis 1973:58)

He went on to conclude that the overall pattern of anthropogenic fire in the chaparral represented a "carefully managed environment of plants and animals" (Lewis 1973:59).

This detailed review of Lewis's argument is not intended to denigrate his work. In fact, he provided a compelling argument that native Californians did indeed set frequent fires in the northern part of the (future) state. The concern here is whether those fires were set in the chaparral.

BOX 8.1. Breakdown of chaparral burning patterns ascribed to native Californians by Lewis (1973). Groups are included if published works have identified them as burning chaparral; the final column gives this author's assessment of the likelihood that the fires were actually in chaparral, based on the evidence discussed in the text.

Tribe	Purpose for burning	Burning season	Applicability to chaparral
Karok	Promote favorable growth	Summer or fall	Uncertain
Pomo	Facilitate hunting and acorn gathering	Fall	Unlikely
Yurok	Facilitate hunting	Unstated	Unlikely
Tolowa	Facilitate hunting	Unstated	Unlikely
Nisenan	Deer hunting drives and tobacco cultivation	Fall and winter	Uncertain
Miwok	Tobacco cultivation	Unstated	Uncertain
Wintu	Grasshopper hunting	Unstated	Very unlikely
Shasta	Dear hunting	Fall	Uncertain
Achumawi	Unstated	Spring	Likely

In this regard, the foregoing discussion of his data suggests that he fell short of proving his theory that the chaparral had been substantially managed through the deliberate use of fire (Box 8.1).

Evidence for Anthropogenic Fire in Southern California

Timbrook et al. (1982) have collected extensive historical evidence of fires in the coastal region near Santa Barbara; they argue that these were deliberately set by the Chumash so as to increase and maintain the extent of grassland at the expense of chaparral and coastal sage. Several herbaceous species (most notably chia, *Salvia columbariae*) served as sources of edible seeds; hence, maximizing grassland would presumably have been a means to guarantee food supplies (Timbrook 1986).

The evidence is drawn from the written accounts of early Spanish explorers. Among the accounts most cited by Timbrook et al. and others (e.g., Stewart 1951; Aschmann 1959; Shipek 1989) are those of Fr. Juan Crespi, who accompanied the Portolá expeditions along the southern and central California coast in 1769 and 1770. Fr. Crespi's diary is available in a published translation (Bolton [1927] 1971), but Timbrook et al. (1982) rely on an unpublished translation which they consider more reliable; I use their version where possible.

Several of Crespi's journal entries from 1769 mention fire, and some specifically attribute it to the native population:

> [Northwest of San Juan Capistrano, July 24] After traveling a short distance in it we came to two good villages, whose people were all very friendly. We greeted them in passing, and they made us their speech, of which we understood nothing. We traveled through this valley for about two leagues; it is of good land, but they had burned all the grass. (Bolton [1927] 1971:137)

> [West of Santa Barbara, August 20] We went over land that was all of it level, dark and friable, well covered with fine grasses, and very large clumps of very tall, broad grass, burnt in some spots and not in others. (Timbrook et al. 1982:166)

> [West of Goleta, August 21] . . . some low-rolling tablelands with very good dark friable soil and fine dry grasses; in many places it had all been burnt off. (Timbrook et al. 1982:166)

> [East of Gaviota, August 24] . . . tablelands that end in high bold cliffs near the sea, but are all very good dark friable soil, well covered with very fine grasses that nearly everywhere had been burnt off by the heathens. (Timbrook et al. 1982:166)

> [Between the Santa Ynez and Santa Maria rivers, August 29] . . . fine soil and dry grass almost all of which had been burned by the heathens. (Timbrook et al. 1982:167)

Timbrook et al. take these descriptions as evidence that areas now covered by chaparral (e.g., near Gaviota) were maintained as a grassy, parklike landscape by frequent fire. Furthermore,

> It is also clear that what Crespí saw was the result of fires which were set deliberately in grasslands by the Indians, rather than escaped campfires or lightning-caused fires, since he speaks of grass being "burnt off by the heathens." (Timbrook et al. 1982:167)

This assertion sounds reasonable, but the evidence is not as definitive as the statement makes it out to be. None of the Crespi journal entries actually describes seeing natives set fires or even gives the source of his belief that they set the fires. In at least one instance (the July 24 entry), the "information" cannot have come from the native people themselves, since he specifically notes his group's inability to understand the native language. Because there are enough instances in American history of Whites erroneously ascribing "negative" practices to Native Americans, one wishes that Crespi, or any of the other eighteenth-century diarists, had specified why they assumed "heathens" were responsible for the fires.

Other, similar, late-eighteenth-century diarists also provide evidence for Timbrook et al. The journals of Fernándo Rivera y Moncada and José Longinos Martínez refer to burning by heathens (or "gentiles") in much the same terms used by Crespi. They also cite proclamations from the 1790s that prohibited "the burning of the fields, customary up to now among both Christian and gentile Indians" (Timbrook et al. 1982:171). It is unclear, however, to what extent the latter reflect "native" practices, given that there was by then extensive European contact.

Taken together, these historical sources leave little doubt that the Spanish found a landscape in which grass fires were common in the coastal region near and north of Santa Barbara. Two corollary possibilities have been inferred but not proven: that the fires were set and "managed" by the Chumash and that they prevented the growth of chaparral—chaparral that has subsequently expanded during two centuries of fire exclusion (Aschmann 1976; Timbrook et al. 1982).

Historical evidence for burning in southern California is not limited to the Santa Barbara region (Bean and Lawton 1973). An early, oft-cited example is a diary (of uncertain authorship) from the expedition headed by Juan Rodríguez Cabrillo and Bartolomé Ferrelo in 1542. In October of that year, they described Santa Monica Bay:

> On the following Sunday, the 8th of said month, they drew near to the mainland in a large bay which they called Bay of Los Fumos, (Bay of Smokes), because of the many smokes which they saw on [around] it. (Bolton 1916:24–25)

Sixty years later, another diary of unknown authorship, from the expedition lead by Sebastián Vizcaino, attributed fires near San Diego to the native Californians:

> The Indians made so many columns of smoke on the mainland that at night it looked like a procession and in the daytime the sky was overcast. (Bolton 1916:79–80)

More than two centuries later, Crespi also noted burns in the San Diego area:

> We ascended a little hill and entered upon some mesas cov-
> ered with dry grass, in parts burned by the heathen for the
> purpose of hunting hares and rabbits which live there in
> abundance. (Bolton [1927] 1971:132)

The problem remains, however, that none of these journals provides a
source for the assumption that native Californians set the fires, let alone
for assumptions regarding their motives.

The emphasis on historical evidence in southern California has
derived in large part from the unavailability of the type of ethnographic
sources used by Lewis in the north (Timbrook et al. 1982). In his 1973
monograph, Lewis had said that he omitted the southern part of the
state because ethnographic evidence was lacking for "the major tribal
groups within the woodland-grass and chaparral belts of the central and
southern coastal range—mainly the Costanoan, Salinan, and Chumash"
(1973:14).

Ethnographic evidence, however, is not entirely absent. In a paper
based on interviews with an elderly Tipai informant, Spier (1923)
reported:

> A hot day is chosen for a rabbit hunt (inyaigEaRX). A group
> from one locality, of indiscriminate gentile affiliation, sur-
> round and set fire to a patch of brush to drive the animals
> out, hallooing the while.
>
> Nets are set over the runways with cords which, passing
> through the meshes as draw strings, are entined in the
> bushes. When many are hunting together they drive the
> rabbits into these purse nets; but when there are only few,
> they set fire to the brush to drive the rabbits. (Spier
> 1923:337)

Nor is the evidence limited to a single source. Shipek (1989) described
details of deliberate burning by Kumeyaay [Tipai-Ipai] peoples, based on
interviews with multiple informants. Interestingly, the emphasis was on
vegetation manipulation, rather than hunting. Shipek discussed two
types of burning. One was burning of grasses in summer prior to broad-
casting seeds of desired "grain-grasses." She concluded that chaparral
had expanded into extensive areas of former grassland after Europeans
forced a halt to such burning. The other was burning of chaparral as part
of a detailed pattern of planting, maintaining, and harvesting edible
species:

> Many shrubs, such as manzanita (*Arctostaphylos* sp.) and
> ceanothus (*Ceanothus* sp.), provided food and were
> planted in numerous eco-niches, including steep slopes, as

were wild grapes (*Vitis* sp.) and various berries. Seeds of agave (*Agave* sp.) and yucca (*Yucca* sp.), plants which provided both food and fibre, were saved and tried in many locations. The seed was planted immediately before burning a slope, and germination was induced by the heat of the fire. . . . Regular burning of chaparral also improved browse for deer, thus doing double duty by providing food for meat animals. (Shipek 1989:164)

Of all the available evidence, Shipek's seems the most supportive of the notion of active, sophisticated environmental management espoused by Lewis. Not surprisingly, given its intensity, Shipek describes this kind of management as having been concentrated around homes and villages.

Overall, the ethnographic and historical evidence regarding native Californian burning of chaparral is mixed. In northern California, fire was apparently a much-used tool and was applied to facilitate both hunting and gathering activities. There is some uncertainty over the relevant vegetation types, perhaps because large stands of chaparral are not common as they are in southern California, and chaparral elements often intergrade with forest and woodland. Where chaparral occurs as a definitive unit, however, there is virtually no evidence that fire was applied to it (Box 8.1). In southern California, fires were apparently common in grasslands on the coastal terraces; given the available evidence, conclusions that they were set by native Californians (primarily Chumash) and that they reduced the extent of chaparral are purely inferential. Finally, there is specific ethnographic evidence that in southernmost California the Tipai-Ipai did burn chaparral, but these fires were apparently limited spatially to sites proximate to their homes.

Natural Ignition

For Native Californian burning to have had a significant ecological impact, two requirements need to have been met. The first, clearly, is that they set fires. The second is that the fires be different from those that would have burned absent human action. The role of natural ignition is therefore as critical to the question as the role of humans. Realistically, the only widespread natural ignition source is lightning (Pyne 1982; Pyne et al. 1996), so our attention turns to the availability of lightning ignition in the chaparral.

As a starting point, we know that cloud-to-ground lightning is rare on the West Coast—indeed, rarer than anywhere else in the contiguous United States (Orville 1991; Orville and Silver 1997). Of the lightning that does occur, however, an unusually high proportion of it is positively charged (Orville and Silver 1997); this is the type of lightning that some consider most effective as an agent of ignition (Pyne et al. 1996).

Within California, lightning frequency generally increases with elevation (e.g., Wells and McKinsey 1995), making it a relative rarity at the moderate elevations within which chaparral dominates. But in his northeastern California analysis, Court (1960) has demonstrated that the occurrence of lightning does not correlate well with the occurrence of lightning-caused fire. His analysis was focused on temporal distribution (lightning fires were not clustered in the months with the most lightning), but the logic presumably applies to spatial variation as well: ignition in a given place within a given season depends not so much on the quantity of lightning strikes as on the polarity of the strikes and on the fuel conditions where the strikes occur. And although lightning may be rare in the low to middle elevations where chaparral is found, it does still occur with some regularity (e.g., Wells and McKinsey 1995). As Burcham has noted:

> Within those general areas where lightning does occur, it is highly sporadic. It varies greatly in frequency and intensity from one year to another; in the time of year when it does occur; and in its distribution over an area. (1974:104)

Minnich (1987) provided a detailed argument that prior to Euro-American fire suppression chaparral fires also resulted from lightning strikes at higher elevations: lightning ignited fires in higher-elevation forests, where they smoldered until weather and fuel conditions allowed them to spread downslope into chaparral.

If lightning frequency does not provide a reliable guide to the occurrence of lightning fires, we must turn to actual fire records. Keeley (1982) analyzed the distribution of California wildfires in records from the U.S. Forest Service (USFS) for the decade of the 1970s. He cited 19 percent of the lightning fires in that decade as having occurred in chaparral. Many of California's wildfires are not included in Keeley's USFS data, because they occur within lands under the jurisdiction of the California Department of Forestry and Fire Protection (CDF, formerly California Division of Forestry). Table 8.1 shows records for those lands. The CDF records unfortunately do not specify the same detail of fuel type, so Table 8.1 shows the frequency of lightning fire in "brush" for the 1990s. Not all the fires in that category were in chaparral (some were likely in sagebrush and coastal sage), but it can be safely assumed that a large proportion were.

It is clear from these data that while the majority of California's lightning fires are at higher elevations, a substantial number do occur in the chaparral. Certainly the raw numbers, if not the percentages, would be

TABLE 8.1. Occurrence of lightning fire in brush within CDF jurisdictions (data from California Department of Forestry and Fire Protection records).

Year	Number of lightning fires in brush	Percent of total lightning fires
1990	73	12.8
1991	30	9.4
1992	95	13.9
1993	13	8.6
1994	40	8.9
1995	25	16.2
1996	53	15.9
1997	41	16.3
1998	36	15.2
1999	77	16.9
TOTAL	483	13.4

higher if it were not for the role of humans. The majority of California wildfires are started by humans; indeed, in data for CDF fires in the 1970s (Keeley 1982) and 1990s (unpublished CDF data), scarcely 5 percent of total fires were ignited by lightning. This is largely because human ignition (accidental or deliberate) is ubiquitous in the modern California landscape, and many fuel accumulations that might otherwise have been ignited by lightning are consumed by human-caused fires.

The role of fuel accumulation is of critical importance here. Most vegetation types become more flammable with time: a stand that has gone longer without burning becomes easier to ignite. In the case of chaparral, this trend is particularly important, although with an exception. The exception is that in the immediate postfire period woody chaparral shrubs are replaced by herbaceous species and subshrubs that may be easily ignited (Zedler et al., 1983; but note that this phenomenon may be dependent on exotic herbaceous annuals that were absent from the pre-European landscape). Within a few years, however, these more flammable species are crowded out by the reestablishment of chaparral shrubs, which are themselves relatively nonflammable for as much as two decades, after which they become significantly more fire-prone with age (Figure 8.2; Philpot 1977; Minnich and Dezzani 1991).

The importance of chaparral stand age to flammability has spurred some debate over the impact of fire suppression on fire magnitudes. Minnich and colleagues have argued that frequent fires in the pre-Euro-

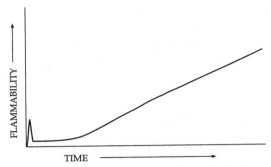

Figure 8.2. Change in flammability of a chaparral stand with time since previous fire.

pean era maintained a mosaic in which many patches were immature (hence nonflammable) chaparral that acted as natural firebreaks and limited fire size; they assert that fire suppression has allowed the expansion of mature (highly flammable) stands and resulted in larger fires (Minnich 1983, 1998; Minnich and Dezzani 1991; Minnich and Chou 1997). Keeley et al. (1999) have challenged that view, noting that the largest chaparral fires in California occur when desiccating downslope foehn winds blow. They argue that under the influence of such winds, any vegetation will burn, and the age of stands becomes irrelevant to fire spread. Of note, both these views stress factors other than ignition as being key. Minnich emphasized that fuel load was key, with lightning a sufficient combustion source:

> Over the several decades necessary for chaparral to mature, thunderstorms are sufficiently numerous for lightning to be a ubiquitous source of combustion. Although native Americans and early European settlers also set fires deliberately or accidentally, human acceleration of burning in chaparral is unlikely given its nonflammability during the first decades of succession. (1983:1292)

Keeley et al., while emphasizing weather rather than fuel load, agreed on the adequacy of lightning:

> Large catastrophic wildfires in brush-covered regions of California are often driven by high winds. . . . Today, people ignite most of these fires; however, in their absence, lightning storms that typically occur just weeks before the autumn foëhn winds would have provided a natural source of ignition. (1999:1831)

In sum, specific studies of fire ecology, fire history, and fire behavior in California chaparral suggest that this vegetation would burn periodically, even in the absence of a human role. There are disagreements on the relative impacts of stand age and fire weather on the size of the fires, but both theory and data suggest that some scale of fire would burn a given stand on timescales of decades to centuries.

Stratigraphic Evidence

If native Californians were responsible for the fires that burned chaparral in the past, then the frequency of fire should have decreased with the arrival of Europeans, who forbad such burning (and in many instances decimated the native populations). Thus any record allowing a comparison of fire frequency before and after European arrival should help to clarify the importance of anthropogenic fire. The best (perhaps only) way to reconstruct fire frequency over centennial to millennial timescales is by the analysis of charcoal preserved in radiocarbon-dated sediment cores (Millspaugh et al. 2000). Similarly, if vegetation has changed in response to altered fire regimes, the changes should be apparent in pollen preserved within the same or similar sediments (Clark and Royall 1996).

Unfortunately, there are few sedimentary records available that shed light on the California chaparral. The best available information of this type is from the Santa Barbara region. One site in that area (Santa Barbara Basin; see Figure 8.1) provides a charcoal record of nearby fires (Byrne et al. 1977; Mensing 1993; Mensing et al. 1999) and along with two other sites (Zaca Lake and Cleveland Pond) has also yielded pollen data reflecting vegetation change (Mensing 1993, 1998).

Mensing et al. (1999) analyzed charcoal in a core from Santa Barbara Basin, representing 560 years of deposition from the coastal plain and western Transverse Ranges (which have extensive chaparral cover). They reported that large fires had occurred in all centuries of their record, with small fires also common. There was no significant change in the occurrence of large fires between the pre-European period (when presumably native Californian—locally Chumash—burning was prevalent) and the (Spanish) Mission and subsequent periods. Mensing et al. concluded that what variation they did see in charcoal concentrations and inferred fire frequency was better correlated with climatic variability (large fires coming just after transitions from fuel-growing wet periods to fuel-drying droughts) than with human history.

The pollen record also seems to suggest that the ecological impacts of Chumash fires were limited in scale. Mensing (1998) reported on pollen trends in the Santa Barbara Basin core and in a core from Zaca Lake that he calculated conservatively to extend at least two centuries before Spanish settlement. His pollen record does not show the increase of chaparral taxa (*Rhamnaceae/Rosaceae*) that should appear if the cessation of Native burning allowed chaparral expansion at the expense of grassland (cf. Dodge 1975; Timbrook et al. 1982). Indeed, at Santa Barbara Basin, chaparral pollen declined slightly in the last century. Similarly, a core farther east at Cleveland Pond reveals no increase of chaparral at or following the transition from unhindered native burning to the Mission period (Mensing 1993). With regard to the pollen record from all three sites, Mensing concluded:

> In the case of Santa Barbara [i.e., the region], fires in the coastal grassland were probably more frequent in the immediate pre-European period as a result of burning by Indians. . . . However, there is no evidence that frequently set Indian fires substantially altered the boundary of chaparral vegetation. Even if fires escaped into the chaparral, as they must have sometimes, this caused no expansion of coastal sage scrub and grassland into chaparral areas. (1993:116)

Fire Regimes and Chaparral Fire Ecology

Ultimately, our concern is for the ecological impacts of anthropogenic fire, rather than with proving or disproving its occurrence. So the final question is whether the characteristics of California chaparral can be adequately explained by a natural fire regime or instead depend on factors that would have been unique to anthropogenic fire.

A natural regime of lightning-caused fires would presumably have been characterized by a high degree of spatial and temporal variation in the distribution of burns. Given the relative rarity of lightning in the California chaparral, the ignition variable alone would have favored more frequent fires near topographic prominences that would be likely lightning targets, with longer fire intervals in the declivities less likely to be struck. That picture is complicated by the impacts of fuel maturation (Minnich and Dezzani 1991), meteorological conditions (Keeley et al. 1999), and climatic variation (Mensing et al. 1999) upon the occurrence and size of fires. The net result would have been a heterogeneous, uneven-grained mosaic characterized by varied stand ages and sizes. All stands would presumably burn eventually, but the length of time between fires would be variable, as would the size of the burns. Fires would have been seasonally concentrated in the summer and autumn, when fuels were dry and thunderstorms likely; and large fires would have been limited to the latter season, when foehn winds were common.

By contrast, a landscape in which anthropogenic fire dominated would presumably have burned more consistently and frequently. Aschmann (1977) estimated a doubling of fire frequency, Shipek described "regular burning of chaparral" (1989:164), and Timbrook et al. (1982) suggested that fires were set at the grassland/chaparral ecotone at 1- to 3-year intervals. If, as most authors suggest, fires were used with great care to control their impacts, they were probably set in conditions that favored low-intensity fire to prevent their spreading beyond control. The size of the fires is less clear. Lewis (1973) suggested that anthropogenic fires would generally be small in area, a view implicitly supported by Shipek's (1989) descriptions of careful and precise fire usage. On the other hand, the fires must have been reasonably large to have the significant ecological impacts claimed by many authors (e.g., Stewart 1951; Lewis 1973; Dodge 1975). Descriptions of seasonality are inconstant for anthropogenic fires; every season has been mentioned in one account or another. Even within Lewis's (1973) paper emphasizing spring and fall fires, his sources mention burning at every season of the year (Box 8.1).

Fire ecology research over the past 25 years has revealed an enormous variety of fire-related adaptations in California chaparral species. Woody taxa range in reproductive strategy from "obligate-sprouters" (e.g., *Cercocarpus betuloides*) that only regenerate vegetatively to "obligate-seeders" (e.g., *Arctostaphylos glauca*) that reproduce only from seed; there are also species capable of producing both resprouts and seedlings (e.g., *Adenostoma fasciculatum*). Beyond this, some species' seeds will germinate only when exposed to a fire-related stimulus (heat for some, charred wood for others), whereas others are unresponsive to fire cues but require the moist conditions following winter rains (Keeley 1991, 1992). There is also variation among both seeds and sprouts in the degree of fire intensity through which they can retain their viability (Odion and Davis 2000).

This diversity of adaptations is, apparently, best explained by an environment in which fire is inevitable but unpredictable—that is, in the kind of landscape described above for a natural fire regime. Keeley (1977) and Keeley and Zedler (1978) have suggested that obligate-seeders in the chaparral evolved because occasional fire intervals greater than 100 years bestowed a competitive advantage as stands aged and individual shrubs died. Under this scenario, seeds would remain to germinate when the stand eventually did burn, but there would be few live shrubs remaining to serve as a source of competing sprouts. Keeley and Zedler concluded "chaparral is adapted to both short and long fire-free periods. *This is undoubtedly a reflection of the unpredictability of fire* in the environment" (1978:159, italics added).

Zedler (1977) also argued that some chaparral species cannot survive indefinitely in stands that burn at short intervals. He observed that *Cupressus forbesii* required 40 years to mature sufficiently to provide enough seed to ensure its representation in the postfire seed pool. Thus its continued presence (and occasional prominence) in the chaparral indicates that at least some chaparral stands must go several decades between fires, and that it is not a newcomer to the chaparral indicates that this fire cycle must have been prevalent in the pre-European period. And although reproduction of sprouters has traditionally been thought to be favored by fire (e.g., Hanes and Jones 1967), Keeley (1992) has more recently suggested that some obligate sprouters may also require long fire-free intervals for successful reproduction.

The low intensity of "controlled" fires would also have militated against the success of some chaparral species. Riggan et al. (1988) reported that low-intensity fire fails to trigger successful germination by obligate-seeding *Ceanothus* species and noted that because of resultant changes in fuel composition repeated low-intensity fire could become self-perpetuating, permanently "degrading" the chaparral composition. The widespread occurrence of *Ceanothus*-dominated chaparral thus suggests an environment in which low-intensity anthropogenic fire, at least those consciously set, has been rare.

All these studies lend support to the notion of a multifaceted chaparral landscape that owes its diversity of species and species' adaptations to a fire regime in which burns are quite irregular, temporally and spatially. Although virtually all species require fire, many of them actually need long intervals between fires for conditions to develop that will allow for successful postfire regeneration. As noted earlier, this accords most closely with the characteristics of a lightning-dependent fire regime.

Conclusions

What, then, can we conclude from the disparate types of evidence, and the disparate conclusions, that have been published regarding native Californian fire in the chaparral?

There is little doubt that native Californians did make extensive use of fire. There is, however, considerable doubt as to the extent of its use and impacts in the chaparral. In northern California, anthropogenic fire appears to have been far more common in other vegetation types; most of the descriptions that have been cited as evidence of chaparral burning do not hold up under scrutiny. In southern California, it seems equally apparent that at least the margins of chaparral *were* affected by anthropogenic fire. Repeated (arguably anthropogenic) burning of grasslands must have meant at least some fire along the grassland/chaparral ecotone, and the Tipai-Ipai apparently did deliberately burn within the chaparral, albeit on a limited spatial scale. But again, there is no evidence that the bulk of the chaparral landscape was subject to a human-modified fire regime. There is no ethnographic evidence to support such a regime, the characteristics of the vegetation are better explained by a lightning-dependent fire regime, and the limited stratigraphic evidence available indicates that both fire frequency and the chaparral vegetation itself remained unchanged through the transition from the pre-European to the colonial periods.

It would be reasonable to summarize the impact of native Californian fire in the following terms: a variety of Native cultures made sophisticated use of fire, both to favor edible species and to facilitate (directly or indirectly) hunting. The scale of fire use was so limited, however, that the bulk of the chaparral as we know it evolved under a natural, lightning-dependent fire regime. Undoubtedly, anthropogenic fire did have some ecological impacts, but those impacts were spatially limited to the immediate surroundings of population centers and to the preexisting (i.e., quasinatural) ecotones. Because of the limited spatial extent of anthropogenic burning, the overall chaparral environment was unchanged by the cessation of native burning, as evidenced by the static nature of the stratigraphic record.

This conclusion should not be seen as derogatory of the environmental management skills of native Californians. Rather, it recognizes the sophistication of the pre-European population: they saw advantages in manipulating their environment and had the skills to do so, but they chose to do it where it would be to their specific advantage, rather than indiscriminately burning an entire landscape.

Acknowledgments

I thank Becky Carlson of the Syracuse University Cartographic Laboratory for preparation of Figure 8.1, Bonnie VonHoffmann for providing CDF fire records, and Tom Vale for numerous stimulating conversations about the issues discussed here.

Literature Cited

Anderson, M. K. 1999. The fire, pruning, and coppice management of temperate ecosystems for basketry material by California Indian tribes. *Human Ecology* 27(1):79–113.

Aschmann, H. 1959. The evolution of a wild landscape and its persistence in southern California. *Annals of the Association of American Geographers* 49(3):34–56.

———. 1976. Man's impact on the Southern California flora. Pp. 40–48 in

Symposium proceedings: Plant communities of southern California, ed. J. Latting. Berkeley, California, Native Plant Society special publication no. 2.

————. 1977. Aboriginal use of fire. Pp. 132–141 in *Proceedings of the symposium on the environmental consequences of fire and fuel management in Mediterranean ecosystems*, ed. H. A. Mooney and C. E. Conrad. General technical report WO-3. Washington, D.C.: USDA Forest Service.

Barbour, M. G. 1988. California upland forests and woodlands. Pp. 132–164 in *North American terrestrial vegetation*, ed. M. G. Barbour and W. D. Billings. New York: Cambridge University Press.

Barbour, M. G., and J. Major. 1977. *Terrestrial vegetation of California*. New York: John Wiley.

Baumhoff, M. A. 1963. Ecological determinants of aboriginal California populations. *University of California Publications in American Archaeology and Ethnology* 49(2):155–236.

————. 1978. Environmental background. Pp. 16–24 in *Handbook of North American Indians*, vol. 8: *California*, ed. R. F. Heizer. Washington, D.C.: Smithsonian Institution.

Beals, R. L. 1933. Ethnology of the Nisenan. *University of California Publications in American Archaeology and Ethnology* 31:335–414.

Bean, J. L., and H. W. Lawton. 1973. Some explanations for the rise of cultural complexity in native California with comments on proto-agriculture and agriculture. Pp. v–xlvii in *Patterns of Indian burning in California: Ecology and ethnohistory*. Ramona, Calif.: Ballena.

Blackburn, T. C., and K. Anderson. 1993. Introduction: Managing the domesticated environment. Pp. 15–25 in *Before the wilderness: Environmental management by native Californians*, ed. T. C. Blackburn and K. Anderson. Menlo Park, Calif.: Ballena.

Bolton, H. E. 1916. *Spanish exploration in the Southwest, 1542–1706*. New York: Scribner's.

————. [1927] 1971. *Fray Juan Crespi, missionary explorer on the Pacific Coast, 1769–1774*. Reprint. New York: AMS Press.

Bright, W. 1978. Karok. Pp. 180–189 in *Handbook of North American Indians*, Vol. 8: *California*, ed. R. F. Heizer. Washington, D.C.: Smithsonian Institution.

Burcham, L. T. 1974. Fire and chaparral before European settlement. Pp. 101–120 in *Symposium on living with the chaparral proceedings*, ed. M. Rosenthal. San Francisco: Sierra Club.

Byrne, R., J. Michaelsen, and A. Soutar. 1977. Fossil charcoal as a measure of wildfire frequency in southern California: A preliminary analysis. Pp. 361–367 in *Proceedings of the symposium on the environmental consequences of fire and fuel management in Mediterranean ecosystems*, ed. H. A. Mooney and C. E. Conrad. General technical report WO-3. Washington, D.C.: USDA Forest Service.

Clark, J. S., and P. D. Royall. 1996. Local and regional sediment charcoal evidence for fire regimes in presettlement northeastern North America. *Journal of Ecology* 84(3):365–382.

Court, A. 1960. *Lightning fire incidence in northeastern California*. Technical paper No. 17. USDA Forest Service, Pacific Southwest Forest and Range Experiment Station.

Dodge, J. M. 1975. Vegetation changes associated with land use and fire history in San Diego County. Ph.D. thesis, University of California, Riverside.

Donley, M. W., S. Allan, P. Caro, and C. P. Patton. 1979. *Atlas of California.* Culver City, Calif.: Pacific Book Center.

Du Bois, C. 1935. Wintu ethnography. *University of California Publications in American Archaeology and Ethnology* 36(1):1–148.

Franklin, J. F. 1988. Pacific Northwest forests. Pp. 104–130 in *North American terrestrial vegetation,* ed. M. G. Barbour and W. D. Billings. New York: Cambridge University Press.

Griffin, J. R. 1977a. Mixed evergreen forest. Pp. 359–381 in *Terrestrial vegetation of California,* ed. M. G. Barbour and J. Major. New York: John Wiley.

———. 1977b. Oak woodland. Pp. 383–415 in *Terrestrial vegetation of California,* ed. M. G. Barbour and J. Major. New York: John Wiley.

Hanes, T. L. 1977. Chaparral. Pp. 417–469 in *Terrestrial vegetation of California,* ed. M. G. Barbour and J. Major. New York: John Wiley.

Hanes, T. L., and H. W. Jones. 1967. Postfire chaparral succession in southern California. *Ecology* 48(2):259–264.

Harrington, J. P. 1932. *Tobacco among the Karuk Indians of California.* Smithsonian Institution Bureau of American Ethnology bulletin 94. Washington, D.C.: U.S. Government Printing Office.

Hickman, J. C. 1993. *The Jepson manual: Higher plants of California.* Berkeley: University of California Press.

Keeley, J. E. 1977. Fire-dependent reproductive strategies in *Arctostaphylos* and *Ceonothus.* Pp. 391–396 in *Proceedings of the symposium on the environmental consequences of fire and fuel management in Mediterranean ecosystems,* ed. H. A. Mooney and C. E. Conrad. General technical report WO-3. Washington, D.C.: USDA Forest Service.

———. 1982. Distribution of lightning- and man-caused wildfires in California. Pp. 431–437 in *Proceedings of the symposium on dynamics and management of Mediterranean-type ecosystems,* ed. C. E. Conrad and W. C. Oechel. General technical report PSW-58. Berkeley, Calif.: USDA Forest Service, Pacific Southwest Range and Experiment Station.

———. 1987. Role of fire in seed germination of woody taxa in California Chaparral. *Ecology* 68(2):434–443.

———. 1991. Seed germination and life history syndromes in the California chaparral. *Botanical Review* 57(2):81–116.

———. 1992. Recruitment of seedlings and vegetative sprouts in unburned chaparral: *Ecology* 73(4):1194–1208.

Keeley, J. E., C. J. Fotheringham, and M. Morais. 1999. Reexamining fire suppression impacts on brushland fire regimes: *Science* 284:1829–1832.

Keeley, J. E., and S. C. Keeley. 1988. Chaparral. Pp. 165–207 in *North American terrestrial vegetation,* ed. M. G. Barbour and W. D. Billings. New York: Cambridge University Press.

Keeley, J. E., and P. H. Zedler. 1978. Reproduction of chaparral shrubs after fire: a comparison of sprouting and seeding strategies. *The American Midland Naturalist* 99(1):142–161.

Kniffen, F. B. 1929. Achomawi geography. *University of California Publications in American Archaeology and Ethnology* 23(5):297–332.

———. 1939. Pomo geography. *University of California Publications in American Archaeology and Ethnology* 36(6):353–400.

Küchler, A. W. 1973. Problems in classifying and mapping vegetation for ecological regionalization. *Ecology* 54(3):512–523.

———. 1977. The map of the natural vegetation of California. Pp. 909–938 in *Terrestrial vegetation of California*, ed. M. G. Barbour and J. Major. New York: John Wiley.

Lewis, H. T. 1973. *Patterns of Indian burning in California: Ecology and ethnohistory*. Ramona, Calif.: Ballena.

Mensing, S. A. 1993. The impact of European settlement on oak woodlands and fire: Pollen and charcoal evidence from the transverse range, California. Ph.D. diss., University of California, Berkeley.

———. 1998. 560 years of vegetation change in the region of Santa Barbara, California. *Madroño* 45(1):1–11.

Mensing, S. A., J. Michaelsen, and R. Byrne. 1999. A 560-year record of Santa Ana fires reconstructed from charcoal deposited in the Santa Barbara Basin, California. *Quaternary Research* 51(3):295–305.

Millspaugh, S. H., C. Whitlock, and P. J. Bartlein. 2000. Variations in fire frequency and climate over the past 17,000 years in central Yellowstone National Park. *Geology* 28:211–214.

Minnich, R. A. 1983. Fire mosaics in southern California and northern Baja California. *Science* 219:1287–1294.

———. 1987. Fire behavior in southern California chaparral before fire control: The Mount Wilson burns at the turn of the century. *Annals of the Association of American Geographers* 77(4):599–618.

———. 1998. Landscapes, land-use and fire policy: Where do large fires come from? Pp. 133–158 in *Large forest fires*, ed. J. M. Moreno. Leiden, Netherlands: Backhuys.

Minnich, R. A., and Y. H. Chou. 1997. Wildland fire patch dynamics in the chaparral of southern California and northern Baja California. *International Journal of Wildland Fire* 7(3):221–248.

Minnich, R. A., and R. J. Dezzani. 1991. Suppression, fire behavior, and fire magnitudes in California chaparral at the urban/wildland interface. Pp. 67–83 in *California watersheds at the urban interface: Proceedings of the third biennial watershed conference*, ed. J. J. DeVries and S. G. Conard. Riverside: University of California Water Resources Center report no. 75.

Moreno, J. M., and W. C. Oechel. 1991. Fire intensity effects on germination of shrubs and herbs in southern California chaparral. *Ecology* 72:1993–2004.

Odion, D. C., and F. W. Davis. 2000. Fire, soil heating, and the formation of vegetation patterns in chaparral. *Ecological Monographs* 70(1):149–169.

Orville, R. E. 1991. Lightning ground flash density in the contiguous United States—1989. *Monthly Weather Review* 119:573–577.

Orville, R. E., and A. C. Silver. 1997. Lightning ground flash density in the contiguous United States: 1992–95. *Monthly Weather Review* 125:631–638.

Philpot, C. W. 1977. Vegetative features as determinants of fire frequency and intensity. Pp. 12–16 in *Proceedings of the symposium on the environmental consequences of fire and fuel management in Mediterranean ecosystems*, ed. H. A. Mooney and C. E. Conrad. General technical report WO-3. Washington, D.C.: USDA Forest Service.

Pyne, S. J. 1982. *Fire in America: A cultural history of wildland and rural fire*. Princeton: Princeton University Press.

Pyne, S. J., P. L. Andrews, and R. D. Laven. 1996. *Introduction to wildland fire*. New York: John Wiley.

Riggan, P. J., S. Goode, P. M. Jacks, and R. N. Lockwood. 1988. Interaction of fire and community development in chaparral of Southern California. *Ecological Monographs* 58(3):155–176.

Shipek, F. C. 1989. An example of intensive plant husbandry: The Kumeyaay of southern California. Pp. 159–170 in *Foraging and farming: The evolution of plant exploitation*, ed. D. R. Harris. London: Unwin Hyman.

Spier, L. 1923. Southern Diegueño customs. *University of California Publications in American Archaeology and Ethnology* 20:297–358.

Stewart, O. C. 1943. Notes on Pomo ethnogeography. *University of California Publications in American Archaeology and Ethnology* 40(2):29–62.

———. 1951. Burning and natural vegetation in the United States. *Geographical Review* 41:317–320.

Storer, T. I. 1932. Factors influencing wildlife in California, past and present. *Ecology* 13(4):315–327.

Timbrook, J. 1986. Chia and the Chumash: A reconsideration of sage seeds in southern California. *Journal of California and Great Basin Anthropology* 8(1):50–64.

Timbrook, J., J. R. Johnson, and D. D. Earle. 1982. Vegetation burning by the Chumash. *Journal of California and Great Basin Anthropology* 4(2):163–186.

Wells, M. L., and D. E. McKinsey. 1995. Lightning strikes and natural fire regimes in San Diego County, California. Pp. 193–194 in *The Biswell symposium: Fire issues and solutions in urban interface and wildland ecosystems*, ed. D. R. Weise and R. E. Martin. General technical report PSW-158. Albany, Calif.: USDA Forest Service, Pacific Southwest Range and Experiment Station.

Zedler, P. H. 1977. Life history attributes of plants and the fire cycle: A case study in chaparral dominated by *Cupressus forbesii*. Pp. 451–458 in *Proceedings of the symposium on the environmental consequences of fire and fuel management in Mediterranean ecosystems*, ed. H. A. Mooney and C. E. Conrad. General Technical Report WO-3. Washington, D.C.: USDA Forest Service.

Zedler, P. H., C. R. Gautier, and G. S. McMaster. 1983. Vegetation change in response to extreme events: The effect of a short interval between fires in California chaparral and coastal shrub. *Ecology* 64(4):809–818.

REFLECTIONS

Thomas R. Vale

Truth can be elusive, sometimes even receding when it is approached. The question addressed by the contributors to this book—Did burning by Native Americans in pre-European times alter the fundamental character of vegetation in the American West?—might seem, even after reading their essays, to defy a categorical answer. Qualifications, contextualizations, hesitations—the authors analyzed their regions with caution, an open honesty that could trouble those who seek absolute and definitive truths. But even if the diogenean lamp fails to chase away all shadows of doubt, it does brighten the scene and enlighten our minds. The authors in this book provide more than equivocation.

Both environmental and cultural variability in space and time render difficult many, but not all, generalizations about pre-European fire regimes or burning habits of Native Americans. All the authors recognize the importance of differences in fire histories among vegetation types and human groups in the American West. More specifically and as examples, Baker postulates that the incidence of lightning could more easily limit the occurrence of natural fires in the northern Rocky Mountains than in the lightning-richer southern Rockies, where fuel may be more limiting; Whitlock and Knox argue that fire history in the Pacific Northwest closely tracks climate history, with temporal variations in fire frequencies tied to distinctive climate episodes; Griffin suggests that Indian ignitions may have augmented lightning ignitions in the shrublands of the northern intermountain West, although the postfire recovery of shrubs might have made the humanizing influence temporally short-lived; A. Parker reports the importance of temporally occasional large fires in the ecology of mixed-conifer forests of the Sierra Nevada, where the conventional wisdom has stressed frequent ground fires; Bendix interprets the variability in the ecological response of chaparral species to fire as suggesting that the temporal persistence of the plants has been made possible by a spatially varying pattern of burning; K. Parker concludes that human use of fire cannot be divorced from the temporally and spatially varying cultural groups—each with different burning behaviors—inhabiting the lowlands of the Southwest; and Allen notes the role of warfare between Apache and European peoples as a stimulus to Indian-ignited fires in southwestern mountain forests, a change in Indian-burning that distinguishes historic time from that of prehistory.

Collectively, then, the authors identify a confounding array of fire factors: spatially varying lightning incidence and temporally varying climate conditions, temporal recovery of burned vegetation and spatial variability of fire characteristics, temporally varying cultural groups and spatially distinctive responses to European invaders. All these elements contribute to the richness of pre-European fire regimes and to the difficulty of identifying single or simple patterns in those regimes. This complexity confuses the meaning of "snapshot" views of the past, constraining not only those who seek a simple pre-European wilderness condition—a state of nature—but also those who hope for simple Native American behaviors and impacts—a universally humanized landscape.

Good evidence for pre-European fire histories is spatially uneven in the American West, but in regions where documentation is strongest, the importance of Indian burning as a vegetation factor at the landscape scale seems weakest. Consider the types of evidence invoked and assessed by the authors in this book: archival and anecdotal sources, reasoning based on the fire ecology of vegetation types, reasoning based on Indian subsistence patterns, fire history data from the past several centuries, and fire history data from deeper time. Both Griffin and K. Parker treat vegetation types with a paucity of fire history data (i.e., the lack of fire-scarred trees renders difficult the reconstruction of fire history in the regions of their studies), and thus they depend, by necessity, upon more informal or less rigorous evidence. Griffin argues the possibility of an Indian impact on the fire regime of the shrubland of the northern inter-mountain West, where fire was moderately frequent but likely important as a vegetation factor. K. Parker, on the other hand, deals with vegetation in the southern intermountain West with such contrasting characteristics that even the informal evidence of fire behavior does not point to an importance for Indian ignitions; the highly flammable desert grassland burned frequently but occurs in a region with a documented high incidence of lightning ignitions, and the highly unburnable Sonoran desert shrubland lacks fuels to carry fires even with an abundance of "dry" lightning. Bendix, who seems to accept Indian ignitions as a possible influence on parts of the vegetation of lowland California, nonetheless concludes from both archival and inferential ecological data that the pattern of chaparral in the general landscape was, and is, a likely consequence of nonhuman factors. In western forests, where fire scars and other ecological data permit the construction of more complete and precise fire histories, the various authors argue—even while accepting the limitations of data and thus of understanding an uncertain past—that lightning incidence and fuel characteristics seem to explain burning regimes. Both Baker on a timescale of centuries and Whitlock and Knox on a timescale of millennia analyze, in part, forests burned by infrequent crown fires, which strongly relate to both long-term climate and short-term weather episodes of drought (rather than revealing the greater regularity generated by human ignitions in forests that are frequently flammable). Moreover, these authors find interpretive problems with archival and anecdotal sources (which are usually employed at timescales of decades or a century or two); Baker, in particular, makes the insightful and intriguing point that early human observers seemed ignorant of lightning as an ignition source for fire. A. Parker and Allen discuss forests with frequent ground fires—regimes that create particularly rich ecological data (fire-scarred trees)—and with a high incidence of lightning ignitions. Both authors find little evidence that Indian burning altered vegetation at the landscape scale; this indication of a natural fire regime seems particularly pervasive in the pine forests of the Southwest, where, arguably, fire history data are more detailed than anywhere else on the continent.

In vegetation regions not explicitly treated in this book, the same linkage—good data and unlikely Indian impact, few data and possible Indian impact—occasionally emerges. The Great Plains region, for example, is sometimes grouped with other grasslands in North America as "manufactured . . . by the Indians" (Budiansky 1995:111) or "of anthropogenic rather than climatic origin" (Denevan 1992:372), although the data from a variety of paleoecological studies clearly indicate otherwise: long before humans invaded the continent, "the glacial-age vegetation of the southern Great Plains was a grassland" (Hall and Valastro 1995:237); "the Southern High Plains has been primarily a grassland . . . throughout most of the Quaternary" (Holliday 1987:242); "widespread grass-dominated ecosystems . . . occur[red in North America in] the early to middle Miocene" (Jacobs et al. 1999:590). In the forests of the Northeast, where appropriate ecological data are ambiguous, Budiansky (1995:108) asserts categorically that

" 'Old Growth' was a rarity," and Denevan (1992:371) suggests that "much of the forest [was] successional (fallow) growth and . . . grassy openings," but Whitney (1994:76) argues that it is equally misleading to envision the pre-European forest as either an unbroken old-growth forest or "an amalgamation of pioneer species recovering from one form of disturbance or another." Finally, in lowland California outside of chaparral stands, with its particularly dense native population, fire in pre-European times was probably widespread, but it is difficult to document or assess the role of humans as initiators of burns. Most generally, better data will not necessarily lead arguments away from an important role for Indian burning, but they will likely guide us toward nuanced appreciation of the spatial and temporal variability in that role.

The pre-European landscape in the American West was a mosaic: some areas were altered by the activities of native peoples, including increased burning, and some areas were molded by natural processes. With an expansion of Baker's classification of humanized landscape perceptions (and simplifying the names of the types), a resulting seven-part scheme spans the range of possible landscape conditions in the otherwise dichotomous distinction between "humanized" and "pristine" (Figure 9.1; compare with the four-part classification by Russell [1993]). At one extreme, the *intensely humanized landscape* sees the modification by people as both ubiquitous and major. Located away from this humanization pole but still involving human modifications are the visions of the *unevenly humanized landscape*, with a universal human imprint but a

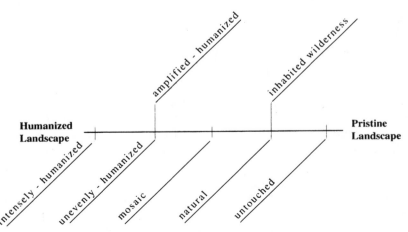

Figure 9.1. Landscape characteristics on a continuum between the extreme conditions of universally humanized and universally pristine. The five below the continuum line represent major categories, with the two above the line depicting modifications of the major category with which each is paired.

spatial variability in the degree to which nature is so altered, and an *amplified humanized landscape*, in which a human role accentuates the characteristics of landscape driven by natural factors. The *mosaic landscape* occupies a middle ground, with spatial variability in the human modification of nature; different areas reveal widely ranging degrees of humanization and at least some areas lack any such modifications. The *natural landscape* sees the fundamental structural and functional characteristics of vegetation specifically and landscapes generally as determined by natural processes, even if human activity might modify some of the specific features of that natural world. A modified natural landscape perspective might concede the preeminence of natural process but elevate the importance of human presence as the essential humanization characteristic of the *inhabited wilderness landscape*. Finally, at the other polar extreme, the *untouched landscape* finds neither a human function nor a human presence in a scene utterly devoid of people—this landscape is unambiguously pristine.

For the authors in this book, the *mosaic landscape* is clearly favored; only Griffin, for the sagebrush vegetation in the northern intermountain West, seems partial toward a different perspective, the *unevenly humanized landscape*. Moreover, the authors hardly argue for a sort of balance between humanized and nonhumanized components within the landscape mosaic: at least for the effects of anthropogenic burning, the *intensely humanized landscape* seems localized amid a dominating *natural landscape*. Does this conclusion imply that the perspective now branded as archaic, the romantic view of a pre-European pristine continent, may be closer to the truth than its more fashionable antithesis?

The presence of native people, rather than their nature-modifying impacts, seems a more universal "humanization" of pre-European North America. In the absence of a ubiquitous human-modification of the natural world, pre-Columbian North America might be nonetheless characterized as "humanized" because the continent was "home" to millions of Indians. In this sense, "humanization" recognizes that the landscape of home embraces not only the places of everyday living and of resource production but also the larger contextual places that may include locales of symbolic meaning—whether or not the natural characteristics of these places are modified by human action. (A parallel to contemporary times sees the protected landscapes of nature preserves across the country as rooms in our modern "home.") If both the *intensely humanized landscape* and the *untouched landscape* seem naively inaccurate as models of past North American environments, and if the *mosaic landscape* captures the essential character of the physical landscape, the *inhabited wilderness landscape* may describe the cultural meaning of that pre-Columbian landscape of home.

Natural wildernesses, pristine landscapes, existed at the time of European contact. The excesses of past convictions should not yield simply to excesses of a newer faith: landscapes in a state of nature sprawled across large parts of North America when Columbus made his fateful landfall. Not occurring everywhere, surely, they did exist in places; they did exist *somewhere*. This conclusion will not strike many people as novel, but it will be resisted by those for whom "wilderness" seems a politically incorrect challenge to social justice or a strategically unwise ideal for conservation goals, or by those who argue that "nature" is merely a socially constructed category, an artifact of the human mind and human language. For people involved in the policies that guide protected landscapes—national parks, statutory wilderness, and other areas intended for nature preservation—the conclusion may offer some reassurance that their efforts have legitimacy, that "nature" does in fact exist. But even this recognition will not eliminate decision dilemmas. Perplexing questions remain: Was the landscape of some particular locale at the time of European contact humanized, pristine, or some hybrid of both? If a hybrid, do the characteristics of nature or those of human impact loom as more important to contemporary sensibilities? If in a state of nature, was the landscape condition at that moment in time any more to be valued than those that preceded it in deep time or that might have occurred with a different history of developmental events? Does hands-off preservation or hands-on restoration capture what society wants in its protected landscapes? The reality of a Western wilderness does not, or at least should not, mean that the 1492 state of nature is unambiguously and unquestionably to be desired as a sort of privileged condition. But such considerations more reflect human value and human purpose than landscape realities: a western wilderness, an American wilderness—a natural landscape—greeted the first Europeans.

Literature Cited

Budiansky, S. 1995. *Nature's keepers: The new science of nature management*. New York: Free Press.

Denevan, W. 1992. The pristine myth: The landscape of the Americas in 1492. *Annals of the Association of American Geographers* 82:369–385.

Hall, S. A., and S. Valastro, Jr. 1995. Grassland vegetation in the southern Great Plains during the last glacial maximum. *Quaternary Research* 44:237–245.

Holliday, V. T. 1987. A reexamination of late-Pleistocene boreal forest reconstructions for the southern high plains. *Quaternary Research* 28:238–244.

Jacobs, B., J. Kingston, and L. Jacobs. 1999. The origin of grass-dominated ecosystems. *Annals of the Missouri Botanical Garden* 86:590–643.

Russell, E. W. B. 1993. Discovery of the subtle. Pp. 81–90 in *Humans as com-*

ponents of ecosystems, ed. M. McDonnell and S. Pickett. New York: Springer-Verlag.

Whitney, G. 1994. *From coastal wilderness to fruited plain: A history of environmental change in temperate North America from 1500 to the present.* Cambridge: Cambridge University Press.

Contributors

CRAIG D. ALLEN is a research scientist with the U. S. Geological Survey at Bandelier National Monument in New Mexico. He studies extensively the fire histories of upland forests of the American Southwest, with special attention to both spatial and temporal variations in those histories.

WILLIAM L. BAKER is a professor of geography at the University of Wyoming in Laramie. His research evaluates the ecological dynamics of Rocky Mountain forests and their responses to human-induced environmental change, particularly in the context of landscape ecology.

JACOB BENDIX is an associate professor of geography at Syracuse University in New York. His research spans biogeography and geomorphology, with a focus on the dynamics of riparian vegetation, in part in the mountains of southern California.

DUANE GRIFFIN is an assistant professor of geography at Bucknell University in Lewisburg, Pennsylvania. His work, bridging the natural and social sciences, explains patterns of ecological diversity and explores human interactions with that diversity, notably in the intermountain West.

MARGARET A. KNOX is a graduate student in the Department of Geography at the University of Oregon in Eugene, Oregon. She works on the ecological history of forests in the Pacific Northwest and the northern Rocky Mountains, with particular focus on the use of pollen sequences.

ALBERT J. PARKER is a professor of geography at the University of Georgia in Athens, Georgia. He studies coniferous forests, including those in the Sierra Nevada, with an eye to both species-environment relationships and disturbance ecologies.

KATHLEEN C. PARKER is a professor of geography at the University of Georgia in Athens, Georgia. Her ecological research evaluates the dynamics and environmental patterns of both vegetation, including columnar cactus, and birds in the southern intermountain West.

THOMAS R. VALE is a professor of geography at the University of Wisconsin in Madison, Wisconsin. He focuses on human-related vegetation change, national parks, and human assessment of landscapes, especially in the American West.

CATHY WHITLOCK is a professor of geography at the University of Oregon in Eugene, Oregon. Her research on the ecological history of forest vegetation spans a broad area of the Pacific Northwest and the Rocky Mountains, from Yellowstone country to the southern Cascades.

Index

Abolt, R. A. P., 152
Adam, D. P., 257
Adams, R. I. C., 217
Adrade, E. R., 104
Agee, J. K., 88, 170, 177, 196, 197,
    199, 204, 208, 219, 220, 247
Agriculture in pre-European American
    West, xiv, 14–18
    in upland Southwest, 159, 160, 162,
    182
Ahlstrand, G. M., 111
Aikens, C. M., 195, 196, 200, 203,
    216, 218, 220
Allen, Craig D., 143–83, 296, 297
Alverson, E., 207
Ames, K., 200
Amplified humanized landscape, 299
Anasazi, 115, 122, 159, 161, 182
Anderson, K., 9, 21, 257
Anderson, M. K., 160, 162, 234, 241,
    244, 251, 259, 260, 262, 273
Anderson, R. S., 145, 239, 240, 248,
    249–50, 258
Anschuetz, K. F., 159
Apaches, 48, 124, 126–27, 158, 161,
    163, 165, 168–69, 178, 179,
    296
Arapahos, 48
Archer, S., 109, 154
Arkush, B. S., 86
Arno, S. F., 43, 49, 52, 60, 61, 62, 63,
    64, 65, 66, 68, 160, 220, 221,
    222
Aschmann, Homer, 272, 277, 287
Axelrod, D. I., 80

Babbitt, Bruce, 6
Bahre, C., 24, 101, 107, 108,
    109, 124, 126, 129, 154, 160,
    161
Bailey, A. W., 80, 86, 87, 88, 89, 109,
    164
Bailey, Vernon, 175, 178
Baisan, C., 28, 45, 46, 110, 128, 129,
    130, 143, 144, 146, 149, 150,
    152, 153, 165, 168, 180
Bakeless, J., 2
Baker, William L., 41–71, 85, 170,
    197, 295, 297, 298
Bandelier National Monument, 159
Bannock tribe, 48
Barbour, M., 9, 238, 242, 273
Barnosky, C. W., 197
Barrett, S. W., 43, 47, 49, 51, 52, 53,
    57, 58, 59, 60, 61, 62, 63, 65,
    66, 67, 68, 69, 70, 160, 220,
    221, 222
Barrows, J. S., 46, 54, 56, 146, 147,
    150, 174, 177
Bartlein, P. J., 221, 222
Basket-making, 241, 242
Baumhoff, M. A., 272, 273, 274

305

Baxter, J. O., 171, 178
Beals, R. L., 274
Bean, J. L., 279
Bean, L., 12, 21
Beckham, S. D., 203, 206
Bell, W. H., 124, 125
Bendix, Jacob, 269–89, 296, 297
Bennett, S. P., 108, 129
Berkley, E., 204
Bessie, W. C., 45
Betancourt, J., 21, 23, 24, 104, 113,
　　115, 122, 130, 145, 146, 148,
　　151, 153, 159, 160, 179, 222
Bettinger, R. L., 82
Billings, W. D., 52, 61, 78, 80
Biswell, H. H., 251
Blackburn, T., 9, 259
Blackfeet tribe, 47–48
Blue Mountains, vegetation and fire
　　regime in prehistoric ponderosa
　　pine forests of the eastern
　　Cascade region and, 219–22
Bock, C. E., 131
Bock, J. H., 131
Bogan, M. A., 143, 149, 150, 179
Bohning, J. W., 131
Bohrer, V. L., 119, 127, 128
Bolton, H. E., 277, 278, 279–80
Bonnicksen, T. M., 160, 165, 181,
　　223, 245
Borher, V. L., 21
Bork, J., 219, 221
Botkin, D., 6
Bowers, J. E., 110
Boyd, R. T., 50, 57, 196, 203, 206,
　　207, 211
Bracker, S. D., 159
Bradfield, M., 15
Bright, W., 273
Britton, C. M., 86, 87
Brown, D. E., 104, 105, 106, 107,
　　149
Brown, P. M., 149
Brubaker, L. B., 200, 206
Bruff, J. Goldsborough, 251
Bruner, A. D., 88
Brunner-Jass, R., 145, 146
Brunton, B. B., 48, 49, 50
Buck, C. C., 107
Budiansky, S., 28, 297–98
Buffington, L. C., 109

Bunting, S. C., 86, 87
Burcham, L. T., 270, 282
Burgess, T. L., 102, 107
Burke, C. J., 204
Burkhardt, J. W., 87, 89, 219
Burns, R. M., 216
Burwell, T., 22, 88
Busse, K. K., 254
Butzer, K. W., 159, 195
Byrne, R., 248, 249, 258, 285

Cabeza de Vaca, Alvar Nuñez, 126,
　　162, 167
Cable, D. R., 129, 131
Cabrillo, Juan Rodríguez, 279
California chaparral, pre-European fire
　　in, 269–89, 296, 297
　chaparral and fire, relationship of,
　　269–72
　conclusions, 288–89
　distribution of chaparral, 270–72
　fire regimes and chaparral fire
　　ecology, 286–88
　Henry Lewis's evidence of, 272–77
　natural ignition, 281–85
　in Northern California, 272–77
　opposing views about, 270
　overview, 269
　in Southern California, 277–81
　stratigraphic evidence of, 285–86
California Department of Forestry and
　　Fire Protection (CDF), 282, 283
Callaway, D., 12
Callicott, B., 2
Cappannari, S., 12
Caprio, A. C., 110, 246, 255
Carpenter, S. L., 249–50
Cartledge, T., 25
Cascade Forest Reserve, 172
Cassells, E. S., 48
Casterrer, E. F., 124, 125
Cave, G. H., 111
Chaddle, S., 25
Chang, C., 204, 233, 241, 242, 245,
　　247
Chappell, C. B., 247
Chase, A., 2, 195
Chavez, F. A., 85, 86
Cheyenne, 48
Choquette, 53
Chou, Y. H., 284

Christensen, E., 80, 256
Chumash people, 277, 279, 281, 285
Churchill, M., 14
Clark, J. C., 160
Clark, J. S., 199, 285
Clark, R. G., 86, 87
Clarke, Samuel, 215
Clements, F. E., 174
Cole, K. L., 94
Cook, S. F., 78, 243
Cooper, C. F., 149, 154, 160, 161,
    162, 165, 179
Cordell, L., 14, 17, 111, 112n, 113,
    115, 116, 122, 124, 126, 157
Coronado, Francisco Vasquez de, 126,
    167
Cottam, W. P., 80, 85
Court, A., 282
Covey, C., 162
Coville, F., 172, 176
Covington, W. W., 149, 150, 151, 152,
    154, 179
Cox, J. R., 109
Crandall, C. S., 55
Crespi, Juan, 277–80
Cronon, W., 9, 195
Cronquist, A., 78
Crosswhite, F. S., 124, 125
Crown, P., 15, 18, 119
Crow tribe, 48
Crum, S., 48
Cwynar, L. C., 199
Czech, B., 27

D'Antonio, C. M., 95
Davis, D. H., 61
Davis, F. W., 287
Davis, O. K., 113, 258
Day, G. M., 160
D'Azevedo, W., 12, 47, 78
Dean, J., 23, 116, 117n, 121, 122,
    123, 132
Dean, J. S., 115, 148
deBuys, W., 167, 170
deLaguna, F., 12
Delcourt, H. R., 160
Delcourt, P., 28, 160
Deloria, V., Jr., 43, 58
Denevan, W., 2, 10, 28, 42, 43, 49,
    69, 78, 159, 171, 195, 196, 297,
    298

Despain, D., 26, 28, 63, 66, 256
Dezzani, R. J., 283, 284, 286
Dick-Peddie, W. A., 107, 109, 129
Dieterich, J. H., 110
Doak, D., 25
Dobyns, A. F., 101, 110, 124, 125,
    126, 127, 131
Dobyns, H. E., 144, 160, 162
Dodge, J. M., 59, 286, 287
Doelle, W. H., 111, 116
Donley, M. W., 271
Doolittle, W., 14, 18, 19, 159
Douglas, David, 206–13, 216
Downs, J. F., 83, 84, 85
Doyel, D. E., 119, 122
Du Bois, C., 274
Dunwiddie, P. W., 199
Dyrness, C. T., 216, 219

Edlund, E. G., 248, 248n, 249,
    258
Elliott, M. L., 159, 165
El Niño-Southern Oscillation (ENSO),
    46, 104, 148
Elsasser, A. B., 260
Equilibrium models, 6
Espejo, 167
Euler, R. C., 115, 158, 159
Ewers, J. C., 48, 50

Fall, P. L., 67
Felger, R. S., 124
Fenneman, N. M., 78
Ffolliott, P., 24
Fires in the American West
    in California chaparral, see California
        chaparral, pre-European fire in
    lightning as ignition source, see
        Lightning as ignition source of
        fires
    in northern intermountain region,
        see Northern intermountain
        West, prehistoric human impacts
        of fire regimes and vegetation in
        the
    Pacific Northwest, see Pacific
        Northwest, prehistoric burning
        in the
    as preeminent human impact, xiv, 31
    pristine vs. humanized landscape,
        27–30

Fires in the American West (*continued*)
  in the Rocky Mountains, *see* Rocky
    Mountains, Indians and fire in
  in Sierra Nevada forests, *see* Sierra
    Nevada, ecological impact of
    burning by Native Americans in
  in Southwest lowlands, *see* Southwest
    lowlands, fire in the pre-
    European
  in upland Southwest, *see* Upland
    Southwest, ecological history of
    fire in the
Fish, P., 14, 15, 16, 19, 20, 114, 115,
    116, 119, 120, 122, 123
Fish, S., 14, 15, 16, 19, 20, 114, 115,
    116, 119, 120, 122, 125, 126,
    127, 128, 129, 131, 158, 159,
    160, 162, 163, 164
Fisher, R. F., 47, 48, 49, 52, 64, 66,
    68
Flatheads, 48
Flores, D., 2, 195
Floyd, M., 22
Fontana, B. L., 124, 125, 126
Foothills Yokut, 241
Ford, R. I., 114
Forest Service, *see* U.S. Department of
    Agriculture (USDA), Forest
    Service
Forman, R. T. T., 160
Fowler, C., 12, 82, 83, 84
Foxx, T. S., 152
Francis, J. E., 47
Franklin, J. F., 204, 216, 219, 222,
    273
Frederickson, E., 179
Fritts, H. C., 217
Fritz, S. C., 56
Fulé, P. Z., 149, 152, 154
Funkhouse, G. S., 148

Gardner, J. J., 199
Garfin, G. M., 218
Gartner, F. R., 52, 59
Gasser, R. E., 119, 128
Gold Rush of 1849, 244
Gomez-Pompa, A., 27
Gosz, J. R., 108, 128–29
Gottesfeld, L. M. J., 160
Gottfried, G., 24
Graumlich, L. J., 114, 129, 206, 217,

240, 244
Grayson, A. W., 79, 81, 86
Grayson, D. K., 78, 82, 83
Griffin, Duane, 77–95, 295, 296, 299
Griffin, J. R., 273, 275
Griffiths, D., 109
Grigg, L. D., 200
Grissino-Mayer, H. D., 66, 68, 110,
    115, 121, 122, 125, 148, 153,
    154, 165, 168, 177, 179
Gross, F. A., 109
Grover, H. D., 109
Gruell, G. E., 51, 52, 53, 54, 56, 58,
    60, 61, 65, 69, 85, 220
Guetter, P. J., 200

Haase, W., 15
Habeck, J. R., 54
Hackenberg, R., 12, 125
Haines, F., 48
Hajda, Y., 12
Hales, J. E., Jr., 104
Hall, S. A., 297
Halpern, C. B., 247
Hammett, J., 12
Hanes, T. L., 271, 273, 288
Harniss, R. O., 87
Harper, K. T., 78, 79, 80, 89
Harrington, J. P., 163, 167, 272,
    273
Harris, A. H., 160
Hasse, W., 16
Hastings, J. R., 109, 126
Haury, E. W., 116
Heizer, R. F., 260
Hemphill, M. L., 67
Hemstrom, M. A., 204
Henderson, J., 163, 167
Hennessey, J. T., 109
Henry, A., 206
Herbel, C. H., 109
Hess, K., 26
Heusser, C. J., 197
Heyerdahl, E. K., 86, 219, 220, 221
Hickman, J. C., 273
Hidy, G. M., 78, 80
Higgins, K. F., 56, 62, 66
Hogan, P., 19, 21
Hohokam culture, 115–16, 119–23,
    128, 131
Holle, R. L., 108, 129

Holmes, R. L., 217
Holmgren, N. H., 78, 79
Holsinger, S. J., 160–61, 162
Honaker, J. J., 52
Honkala, B. H., 216
Hopi Indians, 178
Hough, F. B., 55, 169
Hough, W., 160, 163
Houghton, J. T., 56
Houston, D. B., 26, 52, 65, 87
Huber, E. K., 159
Huckell, B. B., 114
Huffines, G. R., 254, 255
Hughes, M. K., 218
Hull, A. C., Jr., 80
Hull, M. K., 80
Hulse, D., 203, 207, 208
Humanized pre-European landscape,
    see Pre-European landscape
Humphrey, R. R., 107, 109, 110, 154
Hungry Wolf, A., 48
Hungry Wolf, B., 48
Hunting, fire as strategy for, 162–63,
    216, 241
Hunting in pre-European American
    West, 25–27
Huyll, H., 23

Idso, S. B., 109
Impara, P. C., 204
Intensely humanized landscape, 298,
    299
Irwin-Williams, C. C., 84

Jackson, J. G., 173
Jackson, S. T., 145
Jacobs, B., 297
Janetski, J., 12, 48
Jemez Mountains, northern New
    Mexico, 182
    fire history of, 144, 145–46, 147n,
    148n, 151–52, 154–56, 163,
    165, 179
    prehistoric populations, 159
    Spanish settlements in, 167
Jenkins, D. L., 216
Jenkins, M. J., 89, 200
Jennings, J., 21
Johannessen, C. L., 206, 211
Johnson, E. A., 45
Johnson, H., 80

Johnston, J. D., 244
Jones, H. W., 288
Juniper woodland of eastern Oregon,
    vegetation and fire regime of
    prehistoric, 216–19

Kaib, M., 108, 109, 110, 124, 126,
    130, 152, 160, 163, 167, 168,
    169
Kalapuya populations, 203, 204, 206,
    207, 215
Karok people, 272–73, 277
Kaufmann, M. R., 152, 154
Kaus, A., 27
Kay, C., 2, 25, 26, 27
Kay, C. E., 160, 170, 223
Kaye, M. W., 126, 130, 168
Keeley, J. E., 269, 270, 273, 282, 283,
    284, 286, 287, 288
Keeley, S. C., 269, 270, 273
Kilgore, B. M., 245, 257
Kinney, W. C., 239
Kipfmueler, K. F., 45
Klebenow, D. A., 88
Klein, R. G., 157
Klieforth, H. E., 78, 80
Kloor, K., 6
Klopatek, J., 24
Knapp, P. A., 25, 80, 86, 89, 90, 91,
    95
Kniffen, F. B., 273, 274, 275, 276
Knox, Margaret A., 89, 195–224, 215,
    295, 297
Koehler, P. A., 240, 258
Kohler, T., 16, 22, 23, 158, 159
Komarek, E. V., Sr., 45, 56, 107
Komme, W. H., 222
Kootenai tribe, 48
Krech, S., 181
Krider, E. P., 146
Küchler, A. W., 79, 80, 87, 270, 271,
    273, 274
Kumeyaay peoples, 280, 289
Kutzbach, J. E., 200
Kwiatkowsi, S. M., 119, 128

Lahren, S., 12
Landres, P. B., 236
Lane, B., 12
Lang, R. W., 160
Langston, N., 217, 220

Larsen, S. H., 199
Larson, D. O., 243
Larson, M. L., 47
Lawton, H., 22, 279
Lawton, H. W., 84
Leenhouts, B., 87
Leiberg, J. B., 54, 173
Leland, J., 81, 85
Leopold, Aldo, 109, 149, 162, 177,
    178
Levine, F., 163, 167
Lewis, H. T., 45, 51, 58, 69, 160, 165,
    234, 235–36, 251, 270–77, 280,
    287
Lightning as ignition source of fires,
    297
  in California chaparral, 281–85, 286
  in northern intermountain region,
    85, 93–94
  in Pacific Northwest, 196–97, 206,
    214, 215
  in Rocky Mountains, 41, 45, 53–57,
    60, 64, 66
  in Sierra Nevada forests, 237, 251,
    253–57, 261, 262
  in Southwest lowlands, 102, 107–10,
    128–29
  in upland Southwest, 143–57, 177,
    180–81, 182
Liljeblad, S., 12
Lipe, W., 15, 16
Lloyd, A. H., 240
Logging, 244
Long, C. A., 199, 204, 205
Loope, L. L., 52, 60, 61, 65, 69
Lorenz, D. C., 170
Lowe, C. H., 104, 105
Loy, W. G., 204

McAuliffe, J. R., 107
McCarthy, H., 21, 22
McClaran, M. P., 107
McCoy, E. D., 42
McCune, B., 63, 69
McDonnell, M., 6
McGuire, R. H., 111
Maciliwain, C., 222
McKelvey, K. S., 233, 244, 254
McKinsey, D. E., 282
McLachlan, J. S., 200
McLaughlin, S. P., 110

McLeod, Alexander, 208, 210, 214
McPherson, G. R., 109
Madany, M. H., 179
Madesi subgroup of the Achumawi,
    276, 277
Madsen, J., 19, 20n
Major, J., 244
Malinowski, S., 12, 17
Malouf, C. I., 48, 49
Martin, P. S., 157, 195
Martin, R. E., 87, 107, 128, 131
Martínez, José Longinos, 279
Masse, W., 15
Mast, J. N., 152
Maston, R., 15
Mathews, M. A., 158
Matson, R., 16
Matthews, M., 16, 159
Meagher, M., 26
Mehringer, P. J., Jr., 67, 70, 87, 89,
    128, 197, 201, 217, 218
Meinig, D. W., 167
Meisner, B. N., 45
Meko, D. M., 148
Mensing, S. A., 271, 285–86
Merlan, T., 163, 167
Merriam, C. H., 149, 175
Meyer, G. A., 93
Miksicek, C., 19, 119, 125, 127, 128,
    132
Millar, C. I., 244
Miller, C., 251, 256, 262
Miller, R. F., 87, 89, 216, 218, 219
Miller, R. G., 87
Mills, L., 25
Millspaugh, S. H., 67, 68, 70, 199,
    285
Mimbres, 115, 116–19, 122
Minnich, R. A., 44, 129, 233, 252,
    255, 256, 282, 283, 284, 286
Minnis, P., 12, 15, 24, 116, 121,
    128
Minto, J., 207
Miwok people, 275, 277
Miwok tribe, 241, 243, 250
Mohr, J. A., 199
Mono tribe, 241, 243
Mooney, J., 50
Moore, C. T., 51, 53, 56, 57, 58, 68,
    154, 179
Moore, M. M., 151

Moratto, M. J., 241, 242, 243, 244, 258, 259
Moreno, J. M., 269
Morino, K. A., 126, 130, 152, 154, 155, 168
Morris, W., 206
Morrison, P., 204
Mosaic landscape, 299
Motsinger, T., 14
Muir, John, 2, 171, 250–51
Murray, R. B., 87
Musick, H. B., 109
Mutch, R. W., 220, 222

Nabhan, G. P., 115, 124, 127
National Academy of Sciences, 172
National Fire Occurrence Database, 89, 90
National Forests Fire Reports, 30
Navajo, 48, 124, 167, 178
NCDC Global Historical Climatology Network, 102
Neilson, R. P., 109, 114, 130
Nelson, J. G., 65
Nelson, M., 2
Nemani, R. R., 222
Neumann, T., 26, 27
Newman, D. E., 84
Nez Perce, 48
Nials, F. L., 116, 122
Nichols, R., 21
Nisenan people, 275, 277
Nonequilibrium models, 6
Northern intermountain West, prehistoric human impacts on fire regimes and vegetation in the, 77–95, 295–96
  aboriginal inhabitants, 81–86
  description of the region, 78–80
  environmental manipulation, 84–86
  fire and succession, 86–88
  historic subsistence patterns, 82–83
  resource use, 83–84
Northwest Forestry Association, 223
Nydegger, N. C., 88

Odion, D. C., 287
Oechel, W. C., 269
Ogden, Peter Skene, 217
O'Hara, E., 207
Ohlson, M., 199

O'odham, 124–26
Orcutt, J. D., 15, 159, 163
Oregon Department of Forestry, 196, 197, 222
Ortiz, B., 22
Orville, R. E., 45, 46, 90, 107, 146, 254, 255, 281, 282
Osborn, A. J., 160

Pacific Northwest, prehistoric burning in the, 195–224, 295
  case studies, 202–22
  climate and vegetation changes since the last Ice Age, 199–202
  Euro-American journal descriptions of burning, 206–16
  final comments, 222–24
  juniper woodland of eastern Oregon, 216–19
  overview, 195–99
  Ponderosa pine forests of the eastern Cascade region and Blue Mountains, 219–22
  populations at time of Spanish exploration, 196
  prehistoric records of burning, 203–6
  sources of evidence, 197–99
  Willamette Valley of western Oregon, 203–16
Paiutes, 158, 216, 219, 241
Paleoindians, 113–14, 157
Palmer, J., 207
Parker, Albert J., 233–62, 296, 297
Parker, Kathleen C., 101–32
Parker, S., 216
Parsons, D. J., 243, 255, 257
Patayan, 115
Patencio, F., 21
Patten, D. T., 110, 111
Patterson, S., 21, 242
Patterson, W. A., 199
Pearl, C. A., 199, 201, 204
Peirce, E. S., 45
Pend d'Oreille tribe, 48
Pendleton, L., 12
Peri, D. W., 21, 242
Periman, R. D., 159
Petersen, K. L., 56, 67, 162
Philpot, C. W., 283
Picker, S. T. A., 251

Pickett, S. T. A., 6
Pilling, A., 12, 13n
Pinchot, Gifford, 171
Plains Indians, 47, 48, 50
Plog, F., 143, 158
Plummer, F. G., 54, 55, 174, 177
Pollan, M., 2
Pomo people, 273, 274, 277
Ponderosa pine forests of the eastern
    Cascade region and Blue
    Mountains, vegetation and fire
    regime in prehistoric, 219–22
Population size of native people living
    in pre-European American West,
    10–11, 49
  in Rocky Mountains, 49–51
Potter, D. A., 247
Potter, J., 14
Potter, L. D., 152
Powell, John Wesley, 162, 171, 178,
    179
Power, M., 6, 25
Powers, R. P., 159, 163
Pre-European landscape
  agriculture, 14–18
  ambiguities behind the arguments,
    2–5
  amplified humanized landscape, 299
  characteristic affecting individual
    observers, 6–9
  as humanized or pristine, xiii, 1–31,
    236, see also individual
    geographic areas of the American
    West
  hunting of wild animals, 25–27
  intensely humanized landscape, 298,
    299
  middle ground between pristine and
    humanized camps, xiii–xiv, 299
  mosaic landscape, 299
  population size, 10–11
  protective activities, 22
  regional differences and pristine
    landscapes in the American West,
    9–31
  settlements, 11–14
  summary, 30–31, 295–300
  tree cutting, 23–25
  unevenly humanized landscape,
    298–99
  vegetation modifications, 18–23

  wild fire, 27–30
Price, C., 56
Pristine pre-European landscape, see
    Pre-European landscape
Propper, J., 25
Puebloan peoples, 158, 159, 163, 165,
    167, 178
Pyne, Stephen, 2, 42, 101, 127, 143,
    144, 145, 157, 160, 161,
    162–63, 164, 166, 169, 176,
    177, 179, 180, 181, 195, 222,
    272, 281, 282

Raab, L. M., 243
Ramenofsky, A. F., 206
Ravesloot, J. C., 101, 159
Rea, A. M., 125
Reap, R. M., 88
Reid, J., 15
Reimer, P. J., 198
Reynolds, H. G., 131
Reynolds, R. D., 234, 253
Rhode, David, 78, 89, 94
Riggan, P. J., 288
Riggs, T., 207
Rind, D., 56
Rivera y Moncada, Fernándo, 279
Robbins, W. W., 163, 167
Rocky Mountains, Indians and fire in
    the, 41–71, 295
  climate and, 44–47
  early historical accounts by Euro-
    Americans, 51–58
  ecological fire history evidence,
    60–66
  evidence of burnings by Indians,
    51–68
  generalizing from the evidence and
    the wilderness hypothesis, 68–70
  Indian oral history, 58–60
  overview, 41–44
  plausibility and alternative
    hypotheses, 68
  pollen/charcoal evidence, 66–68
  recent history, 47–51
Rogers, G. F., 94, 109, 110, 111, 129
Rollins, M. G., 146, 150
Romme, W. H., 59, 61, 62, 63, 66,
    154, 170, 256
Roosevelt, Theodore, 2
Rose, J. A., 87, 216, 219

Royall, P. D., 160, 199, 285
Running, S. W., 222
Russell, E. W. B., 44, 49, 66–67, 69, 160, 298

Salazar, Leandro, 176, 177
Salish tribe, 48, 58
Samuels, M., 24, 159
Saubel, S., 21, 23
Sauer, C., 21, 23, 28, 129, 160, 180
Savage, M., 178
Schlesinger, W. H., 109
Schmid, M. K., 109, 110, 111, 129
Schmidt, K. M., 89, 90
Schrader-Frechette, K., 42
Schroeder, A. H., 107, 158
Scurlock, D., 167
Sea, D. S., 200
Secklecki, M. T., 124, 126, 127, 153, 168
Sellers, W. R., 104
Service, E. R., 85
Seton, A., 206
Settlements in pre-European American West, 11–14
Shafer, D. S., 113
Shasta people, 275, 277
Shaw, J., 26
Sheep grazing, 171, 176–77, 178, 244
Shimkin, D. B., 48
Shinn, D. A., 216
Shinn, D. E., 85, 89
Shipek, F. C., 9, 272, 277, 280–81, 287
Shoshone tribe, 48
Shreve, F., 78, 104
Sierra Nevada, ecological impact of burning by Native Americans in, 233–62, 296
  academic roots of participants in debate over, 258–60
  charcoal evidence of Holocene fire history, 248–50
  climate and vegetation, 237–41
  conclusions, 237, 260–61
  fire as landscape element or cultural artifact, 257–58
  fire regimes, past and present, 245–53
  forest structure and, 250–52

ignition sources, 253–57
indigenous peoples, 241–44
questions to be considered, 236
Sierra San Pedro Martír as possible modern analog, 252–53
tree-ring and fire scar evidence, 245–48
Sierra Nevada Ecosystem Project, 246, 251
Sierra San Pedro Martír, 252–53
Silver, A. C., 45, 90, 107, 146, 254, 281, 282
Silver, S., 12
Sioux, 48, 64
Skinner, C. N., 204, 242, 245, 247
Smith, D., 21
Smith, G. W., 88
Smith, S. J., 239, 240, 248n, 249
Snow, D., 10
Snyder, G., 42
Snyderman, D., 146, 151, 152, 154
Soulé, M., 25
Southwest lowlands, fire in the pre-European, 101–32, 296, 298
  agricultural zenith, 115–22
  Archaic period, 114–15
  conclusion, 131–32
  discussion, 126–31
  key points emerging from data on, 102
  maps, 112
  Paleoindians, 113–14
  physical environment in historic times, 102–11
  post-abandonment/pre-European contact, 122–26
  pre-Columbian cultures, 111–26
Southwest uplands, see Upland Southwest, ecological history of fire in the
Spaulding, W. G., 114, 129, 145
Spier, L., 280
Spier, R., 12
Spoerl, P. M., 101, 159
Sponholz, B. R., 93
Sprague, R., 47
Sprugel, D. G., 260
Statistical Abstract of the United States, 11n, 13, 15
Steele, J., 110, 111
Stellar, T., 23

Stephenson, N. L., 246, 247, 250
Stevens, W., 2
Stevenson, J. J., 165
Steward, Julian, 82, 84, 88
Stewart, J., 22, 31
Stewart, K., 12
Stewart, O. C., 12, 42, 69, 70, 101,
    127, 160, 162, 174, 180, 272,
    273–74, 277, 287
Stiger, M., 14, 16
Stone, E. C., 245
Storer, T. I., 272
Stuart, R., 206
Stuiver, M., 198
Sturtevant, W. C., 49, 50
Sugita, S., 199
Sullivan, A. P., 162
Suttles, W., 12, 200
Swanson, F. J., 43, 204
Swetnam, T., 28, 45, 46, 104, 108, 110,
    122, 126, 128, 129, 130, 143,
    144, 145, 146, 148, 149, 150,
    151, 152, 153, 154, 155, 164,
    165, 168, 169, 177, 178, 179,
    180, 222, 246, 247, 255, 262
Szuter, C. R., 119, 121

Taylor, A. H., 204, 247
Taylor, D., 245, 257
Taylor, D. L., 65
Teensma, P. D. A., 204
Theodoratus, D., 12
Thomas, D., 12, 82
Thomas, P. A., 111
Thompson, R. S., 113, 114, 129
Thompson, R. S., 197, 200
Thompson, W. W., 52, 59
Thornton, R., 49, 50
Timbrook, J., 277–78, 279, 280, 286,
    287
Tipai-Ipai peoples, 280, 289
Tipton, F., 87
Tisdale, E. W., 87, 89, 219
Tolowa people, 274, 277
Touchan, R., 110, 152, 154, 155, 164,
    165, 175, 178
Towle, J. C., 211
Towne, A., 12
Towner, R. H., 158
Tree cutting in pre-European American
    West, 23–25

Trierweiler, W. N., 159
Trimble, S., 78, 79
Trombold, C., 14
Tryterud, E., 199
Tsukada, M., 199
Tuggle, H., 15
Turner, M. G., 95, 106, 222, 251
Turner, R. M., 109, 126, 132

Ubelaker, D., 10, 11n, 15, 49, 50,
    196, 206
Unevenly humanized landscape,
    298–99
U.S. Bureau of Biological Survey, 175
U.S. Department of Agriculture
    (USDA), 179
    Forest Service, 24, 177, 282
U.S. Department of Energy, 146
U.S. Department of the Interior, 179
Upland Southwest, ecological history
    of fire in the, 143–83
    climate, 146–49, 153
    conclusions, 180–82
    cultural history, 157–79
    fire scar chronologies, 152–54
    fuel conditions, 149–50
    high levels of lightning activity, 146
    historic Euro-Americans and fire,
        170–79
    historic human effects on Southwest
        fire regimes (since A.D. 1600),
        166–69
    lines of evidence, 144–46
    natural history of fire in the region,
        145–57
    overview, 143–44
    prehistoric human effects, 157–66
    the region, 144
    twentieth-century records of fire
        suppression, 150–52
Urban, D. L., 251, 256, 262
Utes, 48, 59, 61, 158, 178

Valastro, S., Jr., 297
Vale, Thomas, 1–31, 42, 78, 81, 84,
    87, 88, 94, 128, 196, 234, 241,
    255, 258, 260, 295–300
Van Devender, T., 24, 113, 114, 115,
    129, 145
Vankat, J., 9, 238, 244, 253, 258
van Wagtendonk, J. W., 253, 254, 258

Veblen, T. T., 46, 67, 170
Vint, M. K., 110
Vitousek, P. M., 95
Vivian, R., 15
Vizcaíno, E. F., 252, 256
Vizcaino, Sebastían, 279
Vogl, R., 28

Wadleigh, L., 89
Wagner, F., 25, 223
Waldman, C., 47
Walker, D. E., Jr., 47
Wallace, H. D., 111, 116
Warner, T. J., 85, 86
Washoe tribe, 241
Waters, M. R., 116, 118n, 122, 123,
    132
Weaver, H., 154, 177, 179
Weisberg, P. J., 204
Wellner, C. A., 46
Wells, M. L., 282
Wells, P. V., 80
Wells, S. G., 93
Weng, C., 145
West, E., 26
West, G. J., 257
West, N. E., 78, 79, 80, 86, 88, 89
West, N. W., 179
Western Mono tribe, 241
Whisenant, S. J., 86, 87
White, P. S., 251
Whitlock, Cathy, 67, 89, 195–224,
    295, 297
Whitney, G., 9, 23, 69, 298
Wigand, P. E., 87, 89, 202, 217, 218
Wilde, J. D., 84
Wilkes, C., 206, 216

Willamette Valley of western Oregon,
    vegetation and fire regime in
    prehistoric times, 203–16
Euro-American journal descriptions
    of burning, 206–16
prehistoric records of burning,
    203–6
Williams, G. W., 160, 181, 195
Williams, M., 15, 17
Wills, W. H., 114
Wilshusen, R., 14
Wilson, N., 12
Wilson, R. C., 111
Winter, J., 19, 21
Wintu people, 275, 277
Winward, A. H., 86, 87
Wolf, J. J., 152
Woodbury, R., 15, 18
Woolfenden, W. B., 239, 244
Wooton, E. O., 108, 176, 179
Work, John, 215, 216
Worona, M. A., 200
Wright, H. A., 80, 86, 87, 88, 89, 109,
    111, 129
Wyckoff, D., 14, 159, 162

York, J. C., 109
Young, J. A., 87
Yurok people, 274, 277

Zedler, P. H., 283, 287, 288
Zenk, H. B., 203
Zimmerer, K., 6, 21
Zucker, J., 220
Zwolinski, M. J., 110
Zyback, R., 222